Tolerance and Coercion in Islam
Interfaith Relations in the Muslim Tradition

Since the beginning of its history, Islam has encountered other religious communities both in Arabia and in the territories conquered during its expansion. The most distinctive characteristic of these encounters was that Muslims faced other religions from the position of a ruling power. They were, therefore, able to determine the nature of that relationship in accordance with their world-view and beliefs. Yohanan Friedmann's original and erudite study examines questions of religious tolerance and coercion as they appear in the Qur'ān and in the prophetic tradition, and analyses the principle that Islam is exalted above all religions, discussing the ways in which this principle was reflected in various legal pronouncements. The book also considers the various interpretations of the Qur'ānic verse according to which 'No compulsion is there in religion …', noting that, despite the apparent meaning of this verse, Islamic law allowed religious coercion to be practiced against Manichaeans and Arab idolaters, as well as against women and children in certain circumstances.

YOHANAN FRIEDMANN is Max Schloessinger Professor of Islamic Studies at the Hebrew University of Jerusalem, and Member, The Israel Academy of Sciences and Humanities. His publications include *Shaykh Aḥmad Sirhindī: An Outline of His Thought and a Study of His Image in the Eyes of Posterity* (1971, 2000), and *Prophecy Continuous: Aspects of Aḥmadī Religious Thought and its Medieval Background* (1989, 2002).

CAMBRIDGE STUDIES IN ISLAMIC CIVILIZATION

Published titles in the series are listed at the back of the book

In memory of my parents
Moshe and Jolana Friedmann

יהי זכרם ברוך

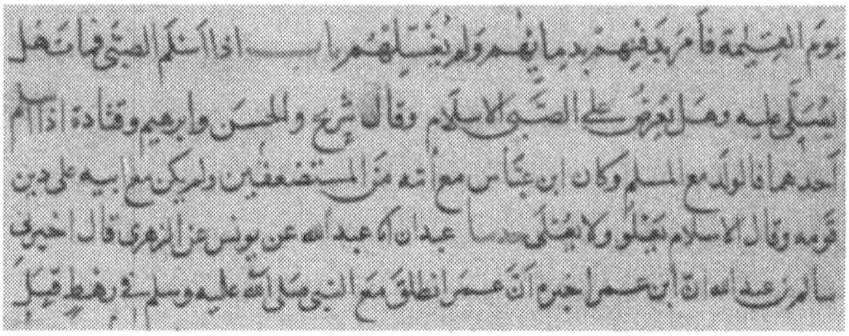

يوم القيامة فأمر بدفنهم بدمائهم ولم يغسلهم باب اذا اسلم الصبي فمات هل
يصلى عليه وهل يعرض على الصبي الاسلام وقال شريح والحسن وابرهيم وقتادة اذا اسلم
احدهما فالولد مع المسلم وكان ابن عباس مع امه من المستضعفين ولم يكن مع ابيه على دين
قومه وقال الاسلام يعلو ولا يعلى حدثنا عبدان انا عبد الله عن يونس عن الزهري قال اخبرني
سالم بن عبد الله ان ابن عمر اخبره ان عمر انطلق مع النبي صلى الله عليه وسلم في رهط قبل

Passage from a manuscript of al-Bukhārī's *Ṣaḥīḥ*, Hebrew University Manuscript Yahuda Ar. 301, calligraphed by Aḥmad b. ᶜAbd al-Raḥmān, also known as al-Shihāb, in 854 A.H. / 1450 A.D.

"If a boy embraces Islam and dies, is the funeral prayer performed for him? Is Islam offered to the boy? Shurayḥ, al-Ḥasan, Ibrāhīm and Qatāda said: 'If one of his parents embraces Islam, the boy is (from the point of view of religious affiliation) with his Muslim parent. Ibn ᶜAbbās was with his (Muslim) mother who was of weak social standing, and not with his father who belonged to the (non-Muslim) religion of his tribe. Islam is exalted and nothing is exalted above it.'"

Tolerance and Coercion in Islam

Interfaith Relations in the Muslim Tradition

YOHANAN FRIEDMANN
The Hebrew University of Jerusalem

CAMBRIDGE
UNIVERSITY PRESS

CAMBRIDGE UNIVERSITY PRESS
Cambridge, New York, Melbourne, Madrid, Cape Town, Singapore, São Paulo

Cambridge University Press
The Edinburgh Building, Cambridge CB2 2RU, UK

Published in the United States of America by Cambridge University Press, New York

www.cambridge.org
Information on this title: www.cambridge.org/9780521827034

First published 2003
Hardback version transferred to digital printing 2006
Digitally printed first paperback version 2006

A catalogue record for this publication is available from the British Library

National Library of Australia Cataloguing in Publication data

Friedmann, Yohanan.
Tolerance and coercion in Islam: interfaith relationships
in the Muslim tradition.
Bibliography.
Includes index.
ISBN 0 521 82703 5.
1. Religious tolerance – Islam. I. Title.
297.5699

ISBN-13 978-0-521-82703-4 hardback
ISBN-10 0-521-82703-5 hardback

ISBN-13 978-0-521-02699-4 paperback
ISBN-10 0-521-02699-7 paperback

Table of Contents

Preface

The purpose of the present study is to survey and analyze a substantial body of Sunnī Muslim tradition relevant to the notions of religious tolerance and coercion, religious diversity, hierarchy of religions, the boundaries of the Muslim community and the ramifications of all these on several topics in classical Islamic thought and law. I have made wide us of the *ḥadīth* collections and of exegesis on the relevant Qurʾānic verses. An attempt has been made to cover the views of the four *madhāhib* and, at times, of Ibn Ḥazm. I have tried to make wide use of the most representative works of each *madhhab*. It was not possible to refer to all relevant passages in the various sources: this would cause the footnotes to reach unmanageable proportions. It has been my primary goal to represent faithfully the views attributed to the classical traditionists and jurisprudents, and to evoke the atmosphere prevalent in the primary sources. To achieve this objective, I have frequently allowed the sources speak for themselves and have translated the more significant passages in their entirety. Some of the topics that were treated only briefly deserve independent monographs, but attempting this was not possible in the framework of this study. Wherever necessary because of dense print or large page format, I have indicated line numbers to enable the interested readers to locate the references as easily as possible. Qurʾānic translations generally follow Arthur J. Arberry's *The Koran Interpreted*, though in some cases modifications of his wording were deemed necessary.

I am indebted to the Rockfeller Foundation for granting me a month of undisturbed writing in the serene atmosphere of their Study and Conference Center, Villa Serbelloni, Bellagio, Italy. Most of Chapter Four was written during my residency there in September and October 1997. Most of Chapter Three was written during my residency at the Institute for Advanced Studies of the Hebrew University in the fall of 1999. I wish to express my gratitude to the authorities of the Institute for granting me this opportunity. Some of the material was collected in the Firestone Library of Princeton University. Most of the book was written in the Asian and African Studies Reading Room of the Jewish National and University Library at the Hebrew University of Jerusalem. The staff of the Reading Room, headed by Ms. Gail Levin (and including Ms. Shoshana Adelstein, Ms. Naʿama Israeli-David, Ms. Esther Shapira, Ms. Michal Zadok, Ms. Shoshana Zur and

Ms. Hilla Zemer) deserve my gratitude for their untiring efforts to supply me with the necessary books from the stacks.

A slightly shorter version of Chapter Two was published in *Jerusalem Studies in Arabic and Islam* 22(1998), pp. 163–195. Parts of Chapter Three were presented to the research group on "Law and the State in Classical Islam", which was active at the Institute of Advanced Studies of the Hebrew University during the fall term of 1999–2000. Chapter One, section VI, was presented on December 7, 1999 (in Hebrew) to the Israel Academy of Sciences and Humanities under the title "Equality and inequality in the *sharīʿa*: the law of retaliation as a case-study."

It is finally my pleasant duty to thank friends and colleagues who assisted me in various ways. Frank Stewart, Aharon Layish and David Wasserstein read various chapters of the draft and offered most useful comments. I am also indebted to Ella Almagor, Albert Arazi, Etan Kohlberg, Ella Landau-Tasseron, Milka Levy-Rubin and Nurit Tsafrir for sharing with me their insights. My numerous discussions with Professor M.J. Kister, my life-long mentor and the real dean of *ḥadīth* studies, were as invaluable as always. My wife Zafrira was sympathetic and supportive all along. The two anonymous readers of Cambridge University Press also deserve my gratitude for their comments. I also thank Marigold Acland for seeing the book expeditiously through the review process and to Dr. Valina Rainer for her professional copy-editing. It goes without saying that all imperfections and infelicities of style are mine alone.

Yohanan Friedmann
Institute of Asian and African Studies
The Hebrew University of Jerusalem

Introduction

Since the very beginning of its long and chequered history, Islam has encountered various religious communities both in the area in which it emerged, and in the vast territories which it conquered during the period of its phenomenal expansion. The most distinctive characteristic of these encounters was the fact that Muslims faced the other religions from the position of a ruling power, and enjoyed in relation to them a position of unmistakable superiority. They were therefore able to determine the nature of their relationship with the others in conformity with their world-view and in accordance with their beliefs. Barring the earliest years of nascent Islam in Mecca, the first two or three years in Medina, the period of the Crusades in certain regions and a few other minor exceptions, this characterization holds true for the pre-modern period of Islamic history in its entirety. Islam formulated toward each community that it faced a particular attitude, which was shaped by the historical circumstances in which the encounter took place, and was influenced to a certain extent by the nature of the respective non-Muslim religious tradition.

These attitudes were intimately related to the matter of religious tolerance or intolerance and interfaith relations between Muslims and others. This was a prominent theme in the Muslim tradition since the early period of Islam. It was extensively discussed in Qurʾānic exegesis, in the various collections of *ḥadīth* and in the literature of jurisprudence throughout the medieval period. A survey and analysis of a portion of these sources will form the mainstay of the present work.

The Qurʾān does not have a specific term to express the idea of tolerance, but several verses explicitly state that religious coercion (*ikrāh*) is either unfeasible or forbidden; other verses may be interpreted as expressing the same notion.[1] Modern Muslim writers find the idea of tolerance mentioned in the prophetic tradition as well. A favourite proof-text adduced in support of the idea of religious tolerance is the *ḥadīth* which reads: "Let (the) Jews know that in our religion there is latitude; I was sent with (the) kindly *ḥanīfiyya*" (*li-taʿlama yahūd anna fī dīninā fusḥatan innī ursiltu bi-ḥanīfiyya samḥa*).[2] Another *ḥadīth* says in a similar vein: "The religion most beloved to Allah is the kindly *ḥanīfiyya*" (*aḥabbu al-dīn ilā Allāh*

[1] See Chapter Three, sections II–VI.

[2] Ibn Ḥanbal, *Musnad*, vol. 6, pp. 116 infra, 233.

al-ḥanīfiyya al-samḥa).[3] Because of the linguistic affinity of *samḥa* with *tasāmuḥ* or *samāḥa*, the modern Arabic terms for tolerance, these *aḥādīth* are sometimes understood as supportive of the idea of Islamic tolerance toward other religions.[4] In their original context, however, the traditions in question carry a substantially different meaning. In Bukhārī's *Ṣaḥīḥ*, the latter tradition is included in a section entitled "The religion (of Islam) is lenient" *(al-dīnu yusrun)* and is pertinent to the Qur'ānic idea according to which Islam is a religion which is considerate to its believers and does not impose on them excessively arduous duties.[5] Several details in Muslim ritual are perceived as examples of such leniency. Muslims are allowed to postpone the obligatory fast of Ramaḍān to the following month of Shawwāl in case of sickness or travel. They may shorten their prayers when they are in danger of attack and may use sand for ritual purification when water is not available.[6] This was also the commentators' understanding of *ḥanīfiyya samḥa*: Islam is a "lenient religion which does not impose hardship or constraints on the people" (*wa al-milla al-samḥa allatī lā ḥaraja fīhā wa lā taḍyīqa fīhā ʿalā al-nās*).[7] Thus, this *ḥadīth* speaks of the lenient nature of Islam for its own adherents rather than about its relationship with members of other faiths.

With the beginning of modern European scholarship on Islam, the subject received a fresh impetus. Responding to criticism directed at the alleged intolerance of Islam as reflected in the idea of *jihād*, both Muslim and non-Muslim thinkers and scholars wrote a substantial number of rebuttals, marshalling arguments in support of the tolerant nature of Islam and of its civilization.[8] Many asserted that

[3] Bukhārī, *Ṣaḥīḥ, Kitāb al-īmān* 29 (ed. Krehl, vol. 1, p. 17). For further references to these two traditions, see S. Bashear, "Ḥanīfiyya and the *ḥajj*", in his *Studies in the early Islamic tradition*, Collected Studies in Arabic and Islam II, The Max Schloessinger Memorial Series, Jerusalem, 2003, XIV, p. 2, note 6.

[4] See, e.g., Shawqī Abū Khalīl, *al-Tasāmuḥ fī al-islām*, Beirut: Dār al-fikr al-muʿāṣir, 1993, pp. 41–42.

[5] In contradistinction to the leniency of Islam, some Muslim traditions perceive the Jewish religion as being excessively harsh. Al-Qasṭallānī (*Irshād al-sārī*, vol. 1, p. 123, ll. 11–10 from bottom) explains *al-ḥanīfiyya al-samḥa* as "the *ḥanīfiyya* which is opposed to the religions of Banū Isrā'īl and the arduous duties (*shadā'id*) which their religious leaders imposed upon themselves." For an analysis of traditional Muslim views on this matter, see M. J. Kister, "On 'concessions' and conduct: a study in early *ḥadīth*", in G. H. A. Juynboll, ed., *Studies on the first century of Islamic society*, Carbondale and Edwardsville 1982, pp. 89–107, at p. 91 (= *Society and religion from Jāhiliyya to Islam* (Variorum Collected Studies reprints, Aldershot 1990, XIII, pp. 6–7)).

[6] See Qur'ān 4:42, 100–101, 5:7, 22:78,

[7] See Aynī, *ʿUmdat al-qāri'*, vol. 1, p. 235, l. 4 from bottom; cf. ʿAsqalānī, *Fatḥ al-bārī*, vol. 1, p. 101 infra. See also Azharī, *Tahdhīb al-lugha*, Cairo: al-Dār al-miṣriyya li-'l-ta'līf wa al-tarjama, 1966, vol. 4, p. 346 (*al-ḥanīfiyya al-samḥa: laysa fīhā ḍīqun wa lā shidda*). Cf. Ibn Taymiyya, *Majmūʿ fatāwā*, vol. 20, p. 114.

[8] Such books are a legion. One of the first works belonging to this genre is Cherágh Ali, *A critical exposition of the popular "jihád," showing that all the wars of Mohammad were defensive; and that aggressive war, or compulsory conversion, is not allowed in the Koran*. The book was first published in Calcutta in 1883 and has seen numerous editions since. Among the non-Muslim scholars, one should mention T. W. Arnold, whose *The preaching of Islam* was first published 1896. More important in this group is I. Goldziher whose works abound in critical empathy with Islam. See J. Waardenburg, *L'Islam dans le miroir de l'Occident*, Paris and The Hague: Mouton, 1963, pp. 267–270. For an example of Goldziher's defense of Islam, see his *Introduction to Islamic theology and law*, Princeton: Princeton University Press, 1981, pp. 16–19, where he strongly rejects another scholar's view that "Islam lacks the critical concept we call 'conscience'". For his exposition of

Islam was misrepresented in Western scholarship and public opinion as an intolerant religion and aggressive civilization. As a result of this argument and in view of the generally heightened interest in the significance of religious diversity in the twentieth century, the tolerance theme acquired major importance in modern Muslim apologetics and in some modern descriptions of Islam. The whole issue has frequently aroused heated controversy.

Recent decades have seen a dramatic increase in the activities of radical religious groups, and, consequently, in the amount of public and academic debate on questions of interfaith relations. Academic serials dedicated to this field, such as *Islamochristiana*, *Islam and Christian–Muslim relations* and *Studies in Muslim–Jewish relations*, have come into being. Conferences on various aspects of it are repeatedly organized and a substantial number of pertinent collective volumes have seen the light of day.[9] The debates have often been conducted within the framework of interfaith dialogue – or polemics – between Judaism, Christianity and Islam. Frequently they have been sparked by political events, and the protagonists tended to use their perception of the subject in order to influence public opinion in favor of their particular religious group. In this context, it is easy to find simplistic and naive comparisons between the lofty ideals of one's own civilization and the unsavory practices of the opponents. Such comparisons are standard tools of the trade for any polemicist.[10] At other times, the participants strive to achieve a different objective: by stressing the more appealing features of Islam and minimizing the importance of the less appealing ones, they attempt to increase the chances of improving the relationship between their own community and the Muslims. One gains the distinct impression that in such debates the Christian participants are far more receptive to the point of view of their interlocutors than are their Muslim counterparts. It should come as no surprise that in these circumstances only facts and issues supporting the objectives of the participating

Muslim tolerance, see ibid., pp. 32–36. See also B. Lewis, "The pro-Islamic Jews", in his *Islam in history: ideas, people and events in the Middle East*, Chicago and La Salle: Open Court, 1993, pp. 137–151.

[9] As prominent examples of this genre, we may mention L. Swidler, ed., *Muslims in dialogue*; G. Speelman et alii, eds., *Muslims and Christians in Europe: Breaking new ground. Essays in honor of Jan Slomp*, Kampen (The Netherlands), 1993; Y. Y. Haddad and W. Z. Haddad, eds., *Christian-Muslim encounters*, Gainsville: University Press of Florida, 1995; H. Lazarus-Yafeh, ed., *Muslim authors on Jews and Judaism: The Jews among their Muslim neighbours*, Jerusalem: The Zalman Shazar Center for Jewish History, 1996 (in Hebrew); J. Nasri Haddad, ed., *Déclarations communes islamo-chrétiennes*, Beirut: Dār al-mashriq, 1997; J. Waardenburg, ed., *Muslim perceptions of other religions: a historical survey*, New York and Oxford: Oxford University Press, 1999; idem, *Muslim-Christian perceptions of dialogue today. Experiences and expectations*, Leuven: Peeters, 2000 (with extensive bibliography).

[10] An excellent example of this is S. Zwemer, *The law of apostasy in Islam*. The author castigates Islam for punishing apostasy with death, and bemoans the consequent paucity of Muslim converts to Christianity. The book is written as if the Christian church has always been an embodiment of the principles of religious freedom and tolerance. On the other hand, Syed Barakat Ahmad (in his "Conversion from Islam") disregards the whole corpus of *ḥadīth* and *fiqh* literature in order to argue that the capital punishment for apostasy is not really sanctioned in Islam. For the development of Muslim attitudes to apostasy in the Qurʾān, *ḥadīth* and *fiqh*, see Chapter Four, below. There is also extensive modern Muslim literature on the question of apostasy; this deserves separate treatment.

protagonists are brought up; others are suppressed or explained away. No clarification of the real issues involved can be expected to emerge from these debates, though some of them have served as significant venues in which adherents of diverse faiths became more conscious of each other's sensibilities and points of view.

Many travelers along this path have commendable goals at heart: they endeavor to increase the chances of achieving interreligious amity and peace. Some are able to contribute to the advancement of these goals while preserving at the same time their scholarly integrity.[11] In other cases, this approach makes inroads into scholarship and tends to obscure certain issues while preventing the discussion of others. This seems to be caused by the unwarranted but pervasive notion that scholarly research that surveys and analyzes intolerant elements in a medieval religious tradition is derogatory toward its modern adherents and will hinder efforts at religious reconciliation. This notion should be resisted. Rather than denying the existence of certain intolerant elements in medieval Islamic thought, modern Muslims might instead admit that such elements exist, while at the same time exercising their power to reject these and embrace the more liberal and tolerant principles of their tradition. Some modern Christian institutions have already taken this way: they grapple with their historical guilt for acts such as the massacres perpetrated by the Crusaders or for the excesses of the Spanish inquisition by decrying, in Vatican II, "the hatreds, persecutions and manifestations of anti-Semitism directed against the Jews at any time and by anyone",[12] rather than embarking on futile attempts to deny their historicity. Muslims can take comfort in the commonly held view that the living conditions of non-Muslims under medieval Muslim rulers were significantly better than those imposed on Jews and other religious minorities by their Christian counterparts.[13] Undisputed facts speak loudly in favor of this proposition, and it need not be substantiated by the patently false claim that medieval Islam was tolerant in the modern sense of the word. Modern interfaith dialogue and understanding should not depend on glowing – but questionable – descriptions of religious tolerance in the Middle Ages; they should emerge from autonomous decisions of contemporary believers. These believers have the freedom to choose from their tradition elements that are compatible with

[11] See, for instance, the judicious article by Christian W. Troll ("Der Blick des Koran auf andere Religionen", in Kerber, ed., *Wie tolerant ist der Islam?*, pp. 47–69). The article bears the subtitle "Gründe für eine gemeinsame Zukunft."

[12] *The declaration on the relation of the Church to non-Christian religions. Vatican II Documents*, Glen Rock: Paulist Press, 1966, p. 14.

[13] For a recent statement by a prominent scholar, see B. Lewis, *The multiple identities of the Middle East*, New York: Schocken Books, 1998, p. 129: "... there is nothing in Islamic history to compare with the massacres and expulsions, the inquisitions and persecutions that Christians habitually inflicted on non-Christians and still more on each other. In the lands of Islam, persecution was the exception; in Christendom, sadly, it was often the norm." See also idem, *The Jews of Islam*, Princeton: Princeton University Press, 1984, p. 62 and B. Z. Kedar, "Expulsion as an issue of world history", *Journal of World History* 7 (1996), pp. 165–180. Expulsions of non-Muslims from Muslim lands were few and far between; for medieval and early modern rulers of Europe expulsions of Jews and "deviant" Christians was routine. See also below, Chapter Three, end of section II.

their values and to disregard those that contradict them.[14] A contemporary Muslim may stress the tolerant elements in Islam, present them as reflecting his own faith and urge his coreligionists to adopt his liberal convictions. For instance, he could adopt the broadest interpretation of Qurʾān 2:256 ("No compulsion is there in religion …") or the strikingly humanistic approach attributed to Ibrāhīm al-Nakhaᶜī according to whom a Zoroastrian – and, by extension, any other unbeliever – "is a free and inviolable human being, akin to a Muslim."[15] The adoption of al-Nakhaᶜī's approach does not make it necessary to deny the existence of other ideas which also existed in the medieval Islamic tradition, but which are less appealing to a modern person with liberal convictions. And if the historical context of these less appealing ideas is taken into account, even the Muslim law of apostasy – to the denial of whose existence some modern Muslims have devoted so much attention[16] – will not appear so uniquely odious: civilizations comparable with the Islamic one, such as the Sassanids and the Byzantines, also punished apostasy with death.[17] Similarly, neither Judaism nor Christianity treated apostasy and apostates with any particular kindness.[18] The real predicament facing modern Muslims with liberal convictions is not the existence of stern laws against apostasy in medieval Muslim books of law, but rather the fact that accusations of apostasy and demands to punish it are heard time and again from radical elements in the contemporary Islamic world.[19]

Creating a personal system of values by choosing appropriate elements from one's religious tradition is legitimate for a believer and desirable for all, especially in view of the fact that the building blocks for a tolerant version of Islam are indeed available in the Muslim tradition if interpreted with this purpose in mind.[20]

[14] For an excellent example of such an approach among modern Muslim intellectuals, see Abdullahi Ahmad an-Naᶜim, *Toward an Islamic reformation: civil liberties, human rights, and international law*, Syracuse: Syracuse University Press, 1990, pp. 86–91, 170–181 and passim.

[15] See Chapter One, the end of section VI and Chapter Three, section V.

[16] S. A. Rahman, *Punishment of apostasy in Islam*, Lahore: Institute of Islamic Culture, 1978; Muhammad Zafrullah Khan, *Punishment of apostacy in Islam*, London: The London Mosque, n.d.; Muḥammad Munīr Idlibī, *Qatl al-murtadd – al-jarīma allatī ḥarramahā al-islām*, Damascus: M. M. Idlibī, 1991. But see Ṣaᶜīdī, *Ḥurriyyat al-fikr fī al-islām*, pp. 83–87, who surveys the traditions concerning the punishment of apostates and lends his support to the view of Ibrāhīm al-Nakhaᶜī and other scholars who were willing to wait for the apostate's repentance indefinitely, thereby avoiding the infliction of capital punishment. See Chapter Four, at notes 44–48.

[17] A. Christensen, *L'empire des Sassanides: le peuple, l'état, la cour*, København: Bianco Lunos Bogtrykkeri, 1907, p. 69; idem, *L'Iran sous les Sassanides*, Copenhague: Ejnar Munksgaard, 1944, pp. 488, 490; G. Harmenopoulos, *A manual of Byzantine law*, vol. 6 (English translation by E. H. Freshfield), Cambridge: Cambridge University Press, 1930, p. 40; A. Linder, *The Jews in the legal sources of the early Middle Ages*, p. 136 and index, s.v. "Proselytism." See also below, Chapter Five, notes 53–54.

[18] See "Apostasy (Jewish and Christian), in *Encyclopaedia of Religion and Ethics*, s.v. (F. J. Foakes-Jackson), and "Apostasy", in *The Encyclopaedia of Religion*, s.v. (H. G. Kippenberg).

[19] See below, Chapter Five, note 53.

[20] A remarkable recent example utilizing this approach is Ṣaᶜīdī's *al-Ḥurriyya al-dīniyya fī al-islām*. The author surveys much of the material which we analyze in Chapter Four, below, and endorses the view that an apostate should enjoy the same religious freedom as any non-Muslim. He must not, in any way, be coerced into reverting to Islam. For the controversy related to the publication of this book, see Muḥammad al-Ṭaḥlāwī, "Raʾy jadīd aqarrahu Majmaᶜ al-buḥūth al-islāmiyya: al-murtadd ᶜan al-islām lā yuqtal." *October*, April 15, 2001, pp. 62–63. I am indebted to Ms. Aluma Solnick of the Hebrew University for this reference.

It is a quite different matter when a scholar presents one aspect of Islam, or one passage from a Muslim text, disregards all others, arrives at sweeping conclusions and bestows upon them the aura of scholarly truth.[21]

The understanding of these distinctions is essential especially in view of the fact that discussions of religious tolerance or intolerance in the books of Muslim tradition and law are conducted against the background of a Muslim government being in charge of a religiously heterogeneous population. These discussions are therefore irrelevant to modern situations which involve relationships between autonomous political units belonging to different religious traditions, rather than situations in which a community not in power seeks governmental tolerance for its religious beliefs and practices. For example: religious tolerance or intolerance, as defined in Muslim books of *ḥadīth* and in the *sharīʿa*, may be relevant to the treatment of the non-Muslim population in southern Sudan, of the Bahāʾīs in Iran, or of the Coptic minority in Egypt, but is irrelevant to the solution of the Arab–Israeli conflict, which does not revolve around the rights and obligations of Jews living under Muslim rule.

Modern discussions of our theme have typically focused on the question of whether classical Islam allowed Jews and Christians who lived under Muslim rule to retain their ancestral religion and, additionally, whether it allowed them to practice it freely. These are two distinct questions; yet too often it is assumed that an affirmative answer to the former necessarily implies the same answer to the latter. It is not self-evident that if Jews and Christians were allowed to adhere to their respective creeds, they were also permitted unrestricted freedom of religious observance, particularly in the public sphere. The restrictions imposed by Muslim law on the construction, maintenance and repair of non-Muslim places of worship and on the public manifestations of non-Muslim ritual are cases in point. The total ban on non-Muslim presence in a substantial part of the Arabian peninsula is also a significant part of the over-all picture.[22] Moreover, if the question of religious

[21] Examples of this kind of work are numerous and only a few representative samples need be mentioned here. Issa J. Boullata ("Fa-stabiqū al-khayrāt: A Qurʾānic principle of interfaith relations", in Yvonne Y. Haddad and Wadi Z. Haddad, eds., *Christian–Muslim encounters*, pp. 43–53) states, on the basis of several Qurʾānic verses, that "one of the doctrinal principles enunciated in the Qurʾān is that of religious pluralism" (ibid., p. 43). An uninformed reader of the article may gain from it the impression that the Qurʾān never spoke about Islam as the only true religion, that it never said anything harsh about the non-Muslims, that classical Islamic tradition never imposed restrictions on non-Muslim observance in *dār al-islām* and never designated the Arabian peninsula as a region where Islam was the only faith to be tolerated. The article certainly does not take account of the development of the Prophet's views of these matters throughout his career. For another example in which Islam is described as an absolutely tolerant religion, in total disregard of any evidence to the contrary, see Farooq Hasan, *The concept of state and law in Islam*, Lanham (MD, USA): University Press of America, 1981, pp. 225–247. See also al-Ḥūfī, *Samāḥat al-islām*, p. 77 infra, where Muslims and *dhimmīs* are said to be equal in matters concerning retaliation (*qiṣāṣ*) and blood-money (*diya*), in total disregard of the pertinent controversy in the books of law (see below, Chapter One, section VI). On the other hand, the issue of pluralism is treated in a profound manner, taking into account the complexities of the sources and of the changing historical situations, by Sachedina, *The Islamic roots of democratic pluralism*, pp. 63–97.

[22] See below, Chapter Three, section II, at notes 13–30.

freedom is to be discussed in its modern sense, its scope becomes much wider than that defined by the two considerations mentioned above. It would include, in that case, not only the freedom to practice one's religion but also to preach it; it would involve the same rights with regard to religions other than Judaism and Christianity; the freedom to change one's religious affiliation at will, or to practice no religion at all. Thus, the ruthless attitudes of early Muslims to Arab idolatry are evidently relevant to the subject of this inquiry. The ᶜAbbāsī persecutions of the Manichaeans and of other groups and individuals subsumed under the term *zanādiqa*,[23] as well as the more tolerant stance of Muslim jurisprudents vis-à-vis the Iranian tradition of Zoroastrianism, are also part of the overall picture of Muslim attitudes to other faiths. Nevertheless, they are only infrequently treated in modern descriptions of Islam, written for the benefit of the western reading public. With regard to idolatry, the reason is obvious: Jews and Christians had been as harsh on idolatry as Muslims, and their modern coreligionists are hardly in a position to take the Muslims to task because they would brook no compromise with ancient Arab idol worship. The Muslim stance on idolatry certainly does not evoke the emotional overtones often associated with the treatment extended by Islam to Judaism or Christianity. Like other non-monotheists, Arab idolaters do not have a contemporary "lobby" in the West and there is hardly anyone in the modern world who is willing to take up their forlorn cause; yet the suppression of idolatry in the Arabian peninsula is, in principle, comparable to the suppression of any other religion and deserves the same scholarly attention. The case of the Manichaeans is similar: the Manichaean community hardly exists in modern times, but its erstwhile treatment by the Muslims and their refusal to grant the Manichaeans *dhimmī* status[24] should receive appropriate attention when an evaluation of Muslim tolerance or intolerance is made.

Questions of religious change have also a place in the framework of this inquiry. It stands to reason that few people converted to Christianity, Judaism or Zoroastrianism under Islamic rule in the Middle Ages, even if abandonment of Islam was not involved. Nevertheless, Muslim traditionists and jurists deal with this rather theoretical issue. As we shall see in the forthcoming chapters, they often make a distinction between non-Muslims who had adhered to a religion

[23] G. Vajda, "Les zindīqs en pays d'Islam au début de la période abbaside", *Rivista degli studi orientali* 17 (1938), pp. 173–229; S. and G. G. Stroumsa, "Aspects of anti-Manichaean polemics...", pp. 38–39; Ḥusayn ᶜAṭwān, *al-Zandaqa wa al-shuᶜūbiyya fī al-ᶜaṣr al-ᶜAbbāsī al-awwal*. Beirut: Dār al-jīl, 1984, pp. 25–26. See also Mahmood Ibrahim, "Religious inquisition as social policy: the persecution of the *zanādiqa* in the early Abbasid caliphate," *Arab Studies Quarterly* 16/2 (1994), pp. 53–72. Ibrahim maintains that the persecution of the Manichaeans should not be seen as mainly religious, but as "an attack on an undesirable political culture inimical to aristocratic and absolutist rule." (p. 68) In a similar vein, D. Gutas (*Greek thought, Arabic culture*, London and New York: Routledge, 1998, p. 67) maintains that "al-Mahdī took them (i.e. the Manichaeans) very seriously because of the Persian revivalist trends they represented and their ideological appeal to many in the ᶜAbbāsid administration with Persian background ..." I am indebted to Professor S. Stroumsa for the last reference. The most recent comprehensive treatment of the *zanādiqa* is Melhem Chokr's *Zandaqa et zindīqs en Islam.*

[24] See, for instance, al-Khallāl, *Ahl al-milal*, pp. 527–528 (nos. 1340–1341).

before the emergence of Islam, and those who embraced such a religion at a later time. Belonging to the Jewish, Christian or Zoroastrian community while Islam was not yet in existence is considered within the natural order of things and thus acceptable. Continuing to belong to these faiths after the emergence of Islam is regrettable but tolerated. Embracing one of them during the Muslim period (even if no apostasy from Islam is involved) is controversial and according to some views such converts are not to be tolerated by Muslims and should be expelled from the land of Islam.[25] The present writer is not aware of any expulsions carried out by Muslim governments in accordance with this ruling, but it does reflect a pervasive notion that adherents of non-Muslim religions should not increase in number after the emergence of Islam.

Wholly different is the case of religions which came into being after the revelation of the Qur³ān. For them the harshest treatment is reserved, especially if they are derived from Islam. Few people tried to establish a new religion in the lands ruled by Muslims in the medieval period and no toleration was accorded to those who did. In view of the dogma asserting the finality of Muḥammad's prophethood, any prophetic claim in the Muslim period was nipped in the bud.[26] Modern times, on the other hand, saw several significant attempts to launch new religions or religious groups. Again, none of them was tolerated. The emergence of the Bābīs and Bahā³īs in Iran and of the Aḥmadiyya in British India are two cases in point. The two groups are similar in the sense that their first adherents had been Muslims, but they are different from each other in numerous other respects. The Bahā³īs eventually ceased to be Muslims by their own admission; the Aḥmadīs, on the other hand, have always insisted that they were Muslims in the fullest sense of the word. The Bābīs and Bahā³īs emerged in a country ruled by Muslims, while the Aḥmadīs came into being in British India. The Bābīs and Bahā³īs were ruthlessly persecuted by successive Muslim governments;[27] the Aḥmadīs aroused vehement opposition of the Muslim mainstream, but as long as the British were the sovereign power in India, they were allowed to preach and practice their beliefs freely. At that stage, the dispute concerning the Aḥmadīs was

[25] See Chapter Four, section VII.

[26] See Friedmann, "Finality of prophethood in Sunnī Islam", pp. 193–197 (= *Prophecy continuous*, pp. 64–68).

[27] The literature on the Bābīs and Bahā³īs is constantly growing. For a survey of Bābī religion, see A. Amanat, *Resurrection and renewal*; P. Smith, *The Bābī and Bahā³ī religions: from messianic Shī^c ism to a world religion*, Cambridge: Cambridge University Press, 1987; Juan R. I. Cole, *Modernity and the Millennium: the genesis of the Bahā³ī faith in the nineteenth century Middle East*, New York: Columbia University Press, 1998 (especially pp. 26–29). For a Bahā³ī survey of the persecution of their community after the revolution of 1979, see *Die Bahā³ī im Iran. Dokumentation der Verfolgung einer religiösen Minderheit*, Hofheim-Langenhain: Baha'i-Verlag, 1985. It is noteworthy that Khumaynī explicitly refused to accord protection to the Bahā³īs as a religious minority, arguing that "they are a political faction; they are harmful; they will not be accepted." See Denis MacEoin, *A people apart. The Bahā³ī community of Iran in the twentieth century*, London: School of Oriental and African Studies, 1989, p. 5. Denying the religious nature of the Bahā³ī movement is intended to obviate the glaring contradiction between the treatment of the Iranian Bahā³īs and the principle of religious tolerance. For rulings of some Egyptian courts on the Bahā³ī question, see Aḥmad Rashād Ṭāḥūn, *Ḥurriyyat al-^c aqīda fī al-sharī^c a al-islāmiyya*, Cairo, 1998, pp. 339–349.

between voluntary religious organizations, none of which had a state machinery or powers of coercion at its disposal. Only when the Aḥmadiyya moved its headquarters to the state of Pakistan after its establishment in 1947, did it come into conflict with the power of a professedly Islamic state. The religious establishment of Pakistan immediately tried to use the state machinery for the attainment of its anti-Aḥmadī goals. The Pakistani government resisted these attempts in its early years, but has succumbed to them more and more since 1974. In that year, the Aḥmadīs were declared non-Muslims in a constitutional amendment passed by the parliament of Pakistan; in 1984, a decree issued by President Źiyā al-Ḥaqq transformed practically any religious activity of the Aḥmadīs into a criminal offense. Anti-Aḥmadī riots and persecutions followed the promulgation of the 1974 amendment and of the 1984 decree.[28] Thus, neither the Bābīs and the Bahā'īs, nor the Aḥmadīs were treated with any toleration by the Muslim mainstream or by the Muslim states in which they were active.

Furthermore, questions of religious freedom are pertinent not only to non-Muslims who live in a Muslim state, but also to Muslims who deviate from beliefs considered orthodox by the religious establishment of their time and place. With regard to the Muslims, we should ask whether they are allowed to abandon Islam, to question its basic tenets, or to refrain from religious observance or from some of its aspects. Keeping these considerations in mind, our discussion will include the laws concerning apostasy.[29] The attitude to Muslims who fail to fulfill such religious obligations as participation in the Friday prayer or observance of the fast of Ramaḍān, are also relevant to the subject of this inquiry. One should also consider the stance taken towards Muslims who deviate from a doctrine held by the religious establishment of their times; the *miḥna* during the period of the ᶜAbbāsī caliph al-Ma'mūn is a case in point.[30] The martyrs of Cordova who were done to death in the mid-ninth century for provocatively disparaging Islam and the Prophet[31] and the execution of al-Ḥallāj in 922 A.D. may be mentioned as well. These and similar matters are pertinent to the question of Islamic tolerance, though they do not constitute part of the present study.

It goes without saying that the purpose of the present writer is not to measure medieval Muslim attitudes by the yardstick of an absolute ideal of religious freedom that has not been implemented even at the present time in most areas of the world. The period in which classical Islamic thought came into being was not

[28] See Friedmann, *Prophecy continuous*, pp. 45–46, 192–194; Antonio R. Gualtieri, *Conscience and coercion: Aḥmadī Muslims and orthodoxy in Pakistan*, Montreal: Guernica, 1989; B. A. Rafiq, ed., *From the world press: persecutions and atrocities against the Ahmadiyya movement in Pakistan as seen through the world press*, London: The London Mosque, 197?; Ṭāhir Aḥmad, *Madhhab kē nām par khūn* ("Blood in the name of religion"), Rabwa, n.d.

[29] See Chapter Four, below.

[30] The most recent treatment of this topic seems to be J. A. Nawas, *Al-Ma'mūn: miḥna and caliphate*, Nijmegen, 1992.

[31] See Kenneth B. Wolf, *Christian martyrs in Muslim Spain*, Cambridge: Cambridge University Press, 1988; Jessica A. Coope, *The martyrs of Córdoba. Community and family conflict in an age of mass conversion*, Lincoln and London: University of Nebraska Press, 1995.

one in which religious tolerance, religious freedom, or equality of religions in the modern sense were considered as positive notions or desirable goals; and Islam should not be blamed for its failure to transcend the mood of the times. Bernard Lewis has written in one of his recent works that "for Christians and Muslims alike, tolerance is a new virtue and intolerance a new crime";[32] and we should keep this apt observation in mind as we proceed. We should also keep in mind that classical Muslim traditionists and jurisprudents had no hesitation about unabashedly proclaiming the exaltedness of their religion and way of life. For them it was only natural that this exaltedness be expressed in a concrete manner wherever possible. More than a few details in Muslim law and world-view in general were explained by classical jurists as being based on this premise.[33] In this respect, Muslims were clearly not different from their non-Muslim contemporaries: the positive self-image of the Byzantines was apparently as ingrained as their own.[34] Comparable feelings were the norm in medieval civilizations. When the Muslims reached China in the eighth century A.D., "they found a Confucian élite with a heightened sense of its own superiority. Chinese civilization was, to the officials, scholars and landlords ... more advanced than any other culture."[35] In his classic description of Indian civilization in the eleventh century A.D., al-Bīrūnī reports that the Hindūs rarely engage in religious disputes among themselves and certainly do not put their life or limb in harm's way because of conflicting views; however, as far as foreigners are concerned, they consider them impure (*mlechha*) and refuse to have any association with them.[36] They believe that

> there is no other country on earth but theirs, no other race but theirs, no kings other than their leaders and no religion except theirs. (They believe) that science is (only) what is in their possession. They are haughty, self-conceited and ignorant ... (*yataraffaʿūn wa yatabaẓramūn wa yuʿjabūn bi-anfusihim fa-yajhalūn*). They do not think that ... anyone except them has any knowledge. Thus, when they are told about a science or a scholar in Khurāsān or Persia, they consider the one who told them about it as ignorant ...[37]

32 B. Lewis, *The Jews of Islam*, p. 3; idem, *The multiple identities of the Middle East*, pp. 128–130. See also the judicious remarks of R. Peters, "Islamic law and human rights: a contribution to an ongoing debate", in *Islam and Christian-Muslim relations* 10 (1999), pp. 5–13 and C. Troll, "Der Blick des Koran auf andere Religionen", in W. Kerber, ed., *Wie tolerant is der Islam?*, p. 56.

33 See Chapter One, section V.

34 See Chapter One, at note 109.

35 Morris Rossabi, "China and the Islamic World", in B. Lewis et alii, eds., *As others see us. Mutual perceptions, East and West.* New York: International Society for the Comparative Study of Civilizations, 1985, p. 270. For a more general exposition of "Sinocentrism" and of the assumption of Chinese superiority, see J. K. Fairbank, "A preliminary framework", in idem, ed., *The Chinese world order*, Cambridge: Harvard University Press, 1968, pp. 1–4; W. Gungwu, "Early Ming relations with Southeast Asia: a background essay", in ibid., pp. 34–47. I am indebted to my colleague Dr. Michal Biran for the last two references.

36 Bīrūnī, Abū Rayḥān Muḥammad b. Aḥmad, *Taḥqīq mā li-'l-Hind min maqūla maqbūla fī al-ʿaql aw mardhūla*, Ḥaydarābād (Deccan): Dāʾirat al-Maʿārif al-ʿUthmāniyya, 1958, pp. 14–15; for a critical analysis of al-Bīrūnī's view of the Hindus, see Arvind Sharma, "Albīrūnī on Hindu xenophobia", in *Studies in "al-Beruni's India"*, Wiesbaden: Otto Harrasowitz 1983, pp. 117–122.

37 Bīrūnī, *Taḥqīq mā li-'l-Hind*, p. 17. See also Sachau's translation in *Al-Beruni's India*, London: Kegan Paul 1910, pp. 22–23.

And medieval Europeans viewed as "barbarians" not only the Mongols, the Muslims and later the Turks; they frequently used the term also for European ethnic groups other than their own.[38]

The purpose of this book is to survey and analyze the material relevant to our topic in the Qur'ān and its classical exegesis, in the *ḥadīth* and in the early works of *fiqh*. Our analysis will show the great variety of views which permeated early Muslim tradition. We shall see that some traditionists viewed the non-Muslim world as monolithic, while others perceived is as manifold.[39] Some viewed all prophets as equals, while others considered the Prophet Muḥammad to be superior to all others.[40] Some propagated the idea of strict equality before the law and maintained that the punishment for premeditated murder should invariably be death, while others held that no death penalty should apply when the victim was not a Muslim.[41] The Ḥanafī and Mālikī schools argued that non-Arab polytheists can be included in the *dhimmī* category, while the Shāfiʿīs and some Ḥanbalīs rejected this outright.[42] Most noticeable is the variety of rulings concerning the apostate: these include immediate execution on the one hand, and various ways of providing the apostate with an opportunity to repent on the other; some jurists extend the repentance option for ever, thereby making the capital punishment for apostasy effectively abolished. Another controversy concerns the ruling on female apostates and on persons who convert from one non-Muslim religion to another.[43]

It is our hope that the variety and abundance of our sources will enable us to make a substantial contribution to the clarification of the issues at hand; this seems to be an important desideratum in view of the fact that some of the more substantial works on our topic are based exclusively on the few relevant Qur'ānic verses and, surprisingly enough, have no recourse to the enormous amount of material in *ḥadīth*, *tafsīr* and *fiqh*.[44]

The present work is not a book of political or social history and does not try to compare the treatment of religious minorities in various civilizations. Nor does it deal with the history of non-Muslims in the Muslim world, with the treatment meted out to them by Muslim rulers, or with the question to what extent Muslim laws regarding religious freedom or religious coercion were implemented in the various periods. It rather deals with the laws themselves and with the various ways in which they were explained, interpreted and related to the Qur'ān and *ḥadīth*, the

38 A. Borst, "Barbarians: The history of a European catchword", in idem, *Medieval Worlds. Barbarians, heretics and artists in the Middle Ages.* Translated by E. Hansen. Chicago: Chicago University Press, 1992, pp. 3–15 (with bibliography on pp. 251–252).

39 See Chapter One, section II.

40 See Chapter Six, at notes 7–11.

41 See Chapter One, section VI.

42 See Chapter Two, section V.

43 See Chapter Four.

44 See R. Paret, "Toleranz und Intoleranz im Islam"; Kerber, ed., *Wie tolerant ist der Islam?* In the latter work (p. 103) we find a curious statement about the enormous numbers of *aḥādīth* attributed to the Prophet ("Von diesen *aḥādīth* gibt es fast eine Million, mindestens 800,000, einige sagen auch nur 300,000"), but no reference to any specific *ḥadīth* pertinent to the subject of Muslim religious tolerance.

two textual sources of the *sharīʿa*. It is a book concerned with Muslim ethos rather than with Muslim history. The book does not deal with the extensive modern discussions of these issues by Muslim thinkers and scholars. There is a wide ranging and constantly growing pertinent literature which deserves separate treatment;[45] we have referred to contemporary Muslim views only sporadically. The focus is on classical Islamic tradition and law; we shall therefore restrict ourselves to the survey and analysis of material which has explicit doctrinal or legal significance. Finally, it is hoped that our work will serve as a useful corrective to the facile generalizations which tend to plague research in those facets of Islamic civilization which have become subjects of interreligious or intercultural controversy and polemics.

[45] For a survey of modern Muslim views on religious liberty, with some attention to the classical material as a background and an extensive bibliography, see Muhammad Hashim Kamali, *Freedom of expression in Islam*, Cambridge: Islamic Texts Society, 1997, pp. 87–116. For a broader philosophical approach, see Richard K. Khuri, *Freedom, modernity and Islam. Toward a creative synthesis*, Syracuse: Syracuse University Press, 1998. For a judicious discussion of both classical and modern material, see Abdulaziz Sachedina, *The Islamic roots of democratic pluralism.* Sachedina formulates a methodology which allows him to arrive at a pluralistic interpretation of Islam's attitude to the religious "other". For an example, see ibid., pp. 38–39.

CHAPTER ONE

Religious diversity and hierarchy of religions

I

Since the earliest period of their history, Muslims have been conscious of the religious diversity of the human race and considered it a problem of importance. In an illuminating discussion, W. C. Smith has shown the unique attitude of Islam to the multiplicity of religions.[1] Muslim tradition debated the nature of religious diversity since its inception and invested considerable effort in trying to understand its significance and the background for its development. Furthermore, classical Muslim literature reflects intense curiosity concerning the religious history of mankind, from the creation onward. Numerous verses of the Qur'ān express the idea that humanity had been united in faith during the primeval stages of its existence. For various reasons discussed in the tradition, dissension set in afterward, the primordial faith became corrupt and distinct religious communities came into being. Several verses of the Qur'ān are devoted to descriptions and appraisals of religions other than Islam. Qur'ānic exegesis, *ḥadīth* and jurisprudence have expanded the treatment of this topic and contain wide-ranging discussions of the religious traditions encountered by Muslims in the nascent stage of their history: idolatry, Judaism, Christianity, Zoroastrianism and Sabianism. A whole literary genre, known in Arabic as *al-milal wa al-niḥal*, developed since the eleventh century onward and include detailed treatment of Jewish, Christian and Muslim sects, as well as extensive descriptions of the religions and philosophies of Iran, India and Greece.[2]

At the outset, let us describe the development of mankind's religious diversity as seen by the Muslim tradition. Muslim traditionists maintain that the phenomenon of religion started contemporaneously with creation. Since the very beginning, Allah gave divine guidance to all. Adam was His first prophet, followed by a long succession of prophets and messengers who were entrusted time and again with

[1] W. C. Smith, *The meaning and end of religion*. New York: MacMillan, 1963, pp. 80ff.

[2] See "Al-milal wa 'l-niḥal", in *EI²*, s.v. (D. Gimaret); G. Monnot, *Islam et religions*. A major work belonging to this genre, al-Shahrastānī's *Kitāb al-milal wa al-niḥal*, is now available in a new French translation by D. Gimaret, G. Monnot and J. Jolivet, *Livre des religions et des sects*, 2 volumes, Peeters/Unesco 1986. This literary genre will not be included in our analysis.

communicating Allah's message to all created beings, both men and *jinn*. Though the message was identical in its essentials because all prophets preached absolute monotheism, it varied in particulars and the detailed laws imposed on the various communities were not identical. Barring idolatry, which was never considered as possessing divine origin, all the prophetic religions that had existed prior to the mission of Muḥammad were initially true and reflected the divine will. At a certain stage of their development, however, Judaism and Christianity deviated from their pristine condition and became hopelessly corrupt. A prophetic mission would have been required to ameliorate this situation. However, no prophets were sent to accomplish this task between the missions of Jesus and Muḥammad[3] and, consequently, true religion ceased to exist. Only with the emergence of Islam in the seventh century, the situation was transformed. The final and immutable expression of divine will, designed for all humanity, appeared on the scene. Muslim traditionists frequently express the idea that the coming of Islam abrogated Judaism and Christianity; following these two religions after their abrogation is therefore tantamount to straying from the straight path.[4] Because of the stubborn refusal of their believers to see the truth of Islam and embrace it, Judaism, Christianity and other religions continue to exist during the Islamic period and religious diversity is still in evidence; yet much of its erstwhile legitimacy has been lost. Islam superseded its predecessors in the realm of religion and is now the only true faith, clearly exalted above all others. The idea of Muslim superiority is central to the Islamic world-view, and figures prominently in numerous chapters of Islamic law and tradition. Some of this material will be discussed later in this chapter.

II

Muslim tradition maintains that diversity of religions has been the hallmark of human society for a very long time, but it had not been its primordial condition. According to the prevalent interpretation of two Qurʾānic verses, mankind started its existence on earth as one religious community. The verses in question are Qurʾān 2:213 and 10:19: both of them include the sentence asserting that "the people were one community" (*kāna al-nāsu ummatan wāḥida*). The nature of that community's religious faith is not specified in this phrase and the commentators have, therefore, ample opportunity to discuss the question and offer solutions nourished by their exegetical ingenuity and theological predilections. According to one view, this primordial community consisted mainly of infidels and included only a limited number of believers. Kohlberg demonstrated that this view had been prevalent especially among the Shīʿīs who saw an analogy between the believing minority in the earliest period of human history and the situation of the Shīʿīs in

3 A "prophetless" period is known as a *fatra* in the Muslim tradition. See *EI*², s.v. (Ch. Pellat) and below, at note 21.

4 See, for instance, Jaṣṣās, *Aḥkām al-Qurʾān*, vol. 3, p. 112.

Islam.[5] This interpretation finds support in Qur'ān 2:213 which says that "the people were one community and Allah sent (to them) prophets, preaching and warning ...". These words are taken to imply that the early *umma* was predominantly infidel: had it consisted of believers, these prophetic missions would have been superfluous.[6]

While the idea that the ancient *umma* was an infidel one is sometimes attributed also to traditionists such as Ibn ᶜAbbās,[7] al-Ḥasan (al-Baṣrī) and ᶜAṭā' (b. Abī Rabāḥ) (d. 114 or 115 A.H. / 732 or 733 A.D.),[8] the Sunnī commentaries normally reject this interpretation in favor of the opposite one: they maintain that the early *umma* was united in true faith. They find support for this understanding in Ibn Masᶜūd's *qirā'a* of Qur'ān 2:213: "The people were one community, then they dissented, and Allah sent (to them) prophets, preaching and warning ..." (*kāna al-nāsu ummatan wāḥida fa-'khtalafū fa-baᶜatha Allāh al-nabiyyīn mubashshirīn wa mundhirīn* ..., and in Qur'ān 10:19 which reads: "The people were one community, then they dissented" (*wa mā kāna al-nāsu illā ummatan wāḥida fa-'khtalafū*).[9] These formulations are understood to mean that the early *umma* consisted in the very beginning of believers; later religious dissension set in and the situation which ensued had to be rectified by prophets sent by God to preach and warn. The primordial believing *umma* is frequently defined as the ten generations presumed to have existed between Adam and Nūḥ, though some early traditionists maintain that the religious unity lasted for a minimal period of time, and existed only on the day when all people expected to be born in future generations were extracted from Adam's loins and testified that Allah was their Lord.[10] Others maintain that since *umma* can refer to a single individual,[11] Adam alone is meant;[12] alternatively, it

5 Kohlberg, "Some Shīᶜī views of the antediluvian world", pp. 47–48.

6 Rāzī, *Mafātīḥ al-ghayb*, vol. 6, p. 12. Rāzī also adduces a *ḥadīth* quoted by supporters of this view according to which "God set His eyes on the people of earth and hated them, the Arabs and the non-Arabs, except the remnants of the People of the Book." It has to be said, however, that this *ḥadīth* starts in other sources in a way which does not support the argument: "I created My servants *ḥunafā'*, all of them, then the devils came to them and caused them to go astray from their religion ... then God set His eyes ..." (*wa innī khalaqtu ᶜibādī ḥunafā'a kullahum wa innahum atathum al-shayāṭīn fa-aḍallathum* (or *ijtālathum*) *ᶜan dīnihim ... wa inna Allāh naẓara ilā ahl al-arḍ fa-maqatahum ᶜarabahum wa ᶜajamahum illā baqāyā ahl al-kitāb* ...). See Ibn Ḥanbal, *Musnad*, vol. 4, p. 162; Muslim, *Ṣaḥīḥ*, *kitāb al-janna* ... 63 (vol. 4, p. 2197). Rāzī (vol. 6, p. 12, l. 22) has *baᶜathahum* instead of *maqatahum*; for the correct version see vol. 17, p. 50, ll. 19–20.

7 Ibn ᶜAbbās is also credited with expressing the opposite view, for which see below.

8 Rāzī, *Mafātīḥ al-ghayb*, vol. 6, p. 12; Ṭabrisī, *Majmaᶜ al-bayān*, vol. 2, p. 186; vol. 11, pp. 27–28; Qurṭubī, *al-Jāmiᶜ li-aḥkām al-Qur'ān*, vol. 3, p. 31; Ibn Qayyim al-Jawziyya, *Ighāthat al-lahfān*, vol. 2, p. 249; Suyūṭī, *al-Durr al-manthūr*, vol. 1, p. 242. For the Meccan jurist ᶜAṭā' b. Abī Rabāḥ, see *EI*², s.v. (J. Schacht), H. Motzki, *Anfänge*, pp. 70–157 and Khuḍayrī, *Tafsīr al-tābiᶜīn*, vol. 1, pp. 184–199.

9 Ṭabarī, *Jāmiᶜ al-bayān*, vol. 2, p. 334; Muqātil, *Tafsīr*, vol. 2, p. 232; Rāzī, *Mafātīḥ al-ghayb*, vol. 6, pp. 11–12; cf. Majlisī, *Biḥār al-anwār*, Tehran, 1343 A.H., vol. 11, p. 10.

10 Qur'ān 7:172; Ṭabarī, *Jāmiᶜ al-bayān*, vol. 2, p. 335; idem, *Ta'rīkh al-rusul wa al-mulūk*, series I, pp. 183–184. Bayḍāwī, *Anwār al-tanzīl*, vol. 1, p. 112; Zamakhsharī, *al-Kashshāf*, vol. 1, p. 355.

11 This interpretation is based on Qur'ān 16:120: *inna Ibrāhīm kāna ummatan* ... For a similar usage in the *ḥadīth*, see Qurṭubī, *al-Jāmiᶜ li-aḥkām al-Qur'ān*, vol. 3, p. 31: *yuḥsharu yawm al-qiyāma ummatan waḥdahu* (on Quss b. Sāᶜida).

12 Ṭabarī, *Jāmiᶜ al-bayān*, vol. 2, p. 335; Ṭabrisī, *Majmaᶜ al-bayān*, vol. 2, p. 186; Qurṭubī, *al-Jāmiᶜ li-aḥkām al-Qur'ān*, vol. 3, p. 30; Majlisī, *Biḥār al-anwār*, vol. 11, p. 24 (attributed to Mujāhid).

could mean the people who accompanied Nūḥ in the ark.[13] The religion of these people was the religion of truth;[14] in most cases it is not more precisely defined, but in some traditions it is explicitly equated with Islam.[15] We can learn from this that according to the Islamic tradition Islam is not only the historical religion and institutional framework, which was brought into existence by the Prophet Muḥammad in the seventh century, but also the primordial religion of mankind, revealed to Adam at the time of his creation. This is intimately related to the conception that Adam was a prophet,[16] and to the notion that Ibrāhīm was a Muslim in this metahistorical sense.[17]

The idea that Islam had been the primordial religion of mankind, preached by the prophets of old, created an affinity between the Prophet Muḥammad and his predecessors in the prophetic office. Muslim tradition frequently presents the Prophet as a brother, or a spiritual heir, of ancient prophets. Numerous episodes in his traditional *sīra* reflect this perception. During his visit to the city of Ṭā᾿if, the Prophet met a young man from the city of Nīnawā (= Nineveh) and described himself as brother of Yūnus b. Mattā (= Jonah) who hailed from the same city (*dhāka akhī kāna nabiyyan wa anā nabī*).[18] When he reached Medina and was told that the Jews were fasting on the tenth day of the first month (*ᶜāshūrā᾿*, corresponding to the Day of Atonement, *yom ha-kippurim*), because on that day Allah saved the sons of Israel from their enemies and Moses fasted on that day, Muḥammad said: "I am more deserving of Moses than you are" (*anā aḥaqqu bi-Mūsā minkum*) and fasted on that day.[19] He is also reported to have said that he was "the person worthiest of Jesus" (*anā awlā al-nās bi-ᶜĪsā b. Maryam*).[20] The intimate relationship between Jesus and Muḥammad is sometimes explained by the belief that no prophet was

[13] Muqātil, *Tafsīr*, vol. 1, p. 181; Ṭabrisī, *Majmaᶜ al-bayān*, vol. 2, p. 186 (view attributed to al-Wāqidī and al-Kalbī); Qurṭubī, *al-Jāmiᶜ li-aḥkām al-Qur᾿ān*, vol. 3, p. 30. These restrictive interpretations of *umma* can be seen as close to the Shīᶜī attempts to draw a comparison between Nūḥ and ᶜAlī b. Abī Ṭālib: both are said to have been supported only by a minority of their people. See Kohlberg, "Some Shīᶜī views of the antediluvian world", pp. 49ff.

[14] The terms used are: *sharīᶜa min al-ḥaqq* (Ṭabarī, *Jāmiᶜ al-bayān*, vol. 2, p. 334); (*kānū*) *ummatan wāḥida ᶜalā al-īmān wa dīn al-ḥaqq, dūna 'l-kufr bi-'llāh wa al-shirk bihi* (Ṭabarī, *Jāmiᶜ al-bayān*, vol. 2, pp. 336–337); *ᶜalā al-fiṭra wa dīn al-ḥaqq* (Ibn al-ᶜArabī, *Tafsīr*, vol. 1, pp. 128–130); Rāzī, *Mafātīḥ al-ghayb*, vol. 6, pp. 11–12; Bayḍāwī, *Anwār al-tanzīl*, vol. 1, p. 112.

[15] "They were one community when they were presented to Ādam. Allah created them on that day as Muslims, and they consented to be (Allah's) servants. They were one community, all of them Muslims" (*kānū ummatan wāḥida ḥaythu ᶜuriḍū ᶜalā Ādam fa-faṭarahum yawma᾿idhin ᶜalā al-islām, wa aqarrū bi-'l-ᶜubūdiyya wa kānū ummatan wāḥida muslimīna kullahum*). See Ṭabarī, *Jāmiᶜ al-bayān*, vol. 2, p. 335; Zamakhsharī, *al-Kashshāf*, vol. 1, p. 355; Rāzī, *Mafātīḥ al-ghayb*, vol. 6, pp. 11–12. One of the traditionists credited with this view is Ibn ᶜAbbās; see, e.g., al-Suyūṭī, *al-Durr al-manthūr*, vol. 1, pp. 242. See also Ibn Qayyim al-Jawziyya, *Aḥkām ahl al-dhimma*, vol. 2, p. 536: *inna Allāh khalaqa Ādam wa banīhi ḥunafā᾿a muslimīn.*

[16] See, for instance, Ibn Saᶜd, *Ṭabaqāt*, vol. 1/i, p. 10; Kister, "Ādam ...", pp. 117–118.

[17] See Qur᾿ān 3:65–67 and the standard commentaries on these verses.

[18] Ibn Hishām, *al-Sīra al-nabawiyya*, ed. Muṣṭafā al-Saqqā, Ibrāhīm al-Abyārī and ᶜAbd al-Ḥafīẓ Shalabī, Beirut: Dār al-Khayr, 1990, vol. 2, p. 47–48; Tabarī, *Ta᾿rīkh al-rusul wa al-mulūk*, series I, p. 1202.

[19] Bukhārī, *Ṣaḥīḥ, Kitāb al-Ṣawm*, 69 (ed. Krehl, vol. 1, p. 498).

[20] Bukhārī, *Ṣaḥīḥ, Kitāb al-anbiyā᾿* 48 (ed. Krehl, vol. 2, p. 369, ll. 8–9).

sent by Allah between them.[21] All these traditions can be subsumed under the general statement according to which "the prophets are half-brothers: their mothers are different, but their religion is one" (... *al-anbiyā᾽ ikhwatun li-ᶜallāt ummahātuhum shattā wa dīnuhum wāḥid*).[22] This is understood to mean that the prophets' belief in the unity of God and in the principles of their respective religions (*uṣūl al-dīn*) is one, but they differ with regard to the particular laws (*furūᶜ*, *ᶜamaliyyāt, fiqhiyyāt*).[23] This is comparable with certain changes which occurred in the religion of Islam itself: at one time the Muslims were commanded to face Jerusalem in prayer; later their *qibla* was changed to Mecca. Nevertheless, Islam remained the same religion. Similar developments can be discerned in the development of the prophetic religions in general. For instance, the Children of Israel had been commanded to keep the Sabbath; when Islam emerged, the observance of the Sabbath was forbidden and replaced by Friday. Thus, though particular laws have been changed by Allah in the course of time, the religion of all the prophets is still the same.

Religious thinkers with a more philosophical bent of mind tend to describe the primordial religion as being based on human understanding rather than on revelation: according to the Mālikī *qāḍī* ᶜIyāḍ (476 A.H. / 1088 A.D. – 544 A.H. / 1149 A.D.)[24] and the Muᶜtazilī Abū Muslim (al-Iṣfahānī),[25] the early generations were clinging to "laws based on reason, such as the acknowledgment of the Creator and His attributes ... and the avoidance of acts repugnant to reason, such as iniquity, deceit, ignorance, worthless, foolish behavior and the like" (*sharā᾽iᶜ ᶜaqliyya wa hiya al-iᶜtirāf bi-wujūd al-ṣāniᶜ wa ṣifātihi ... wa al-ijtināb ᶜan al-qabā᾽iḥ al-ᶜaqliyya ka-al-ẓulm wa al-kadhib wa al-jahl wa al-ᶜabath wa amthālihā*).[26]

All these interpretations view the relevant Qur᾽ānic verses as describing the religious development of mankind as a whole. There is, however, another exegetical trend which maintains that these verses treat the religious history of the Arabs

[21] Bukhārī, *Ṣaḥīḥ, Kitāb al-anbiyā᾽* 48 (ed. Krehl, vol. 2, p. 369, l. 6); Ibn Taymiyya, *Iqtiḍā᾽ al-ṣirāṭ al-mustaqīm*, vol. 2, p. 848. This belief is not compatible with the traditions about pre-Islamic prophets such as Khālid b. Sinān and Ḥanẓala b. Ṣafwān.

[22] Bukhārī, *Ṣaḥīḥ, kitāb al-anbiyā᾽* 48 (vol. 2, p. 369); Abū Dāwūd, *Sunan, kitāb al-sunna 13* (vol. 4, p. 302). *ᶜAllāt* are wives of the same husband, known also as *ḍarā᾽ir.* See al-ᶜAynī, *ᶜUmdat al-qāri᾽*, vol. 16, p. 36, for the etymology of the term, and Sachedina, *The Islamic roots*, p. 68.

[23] Ibn Ḥazm, *al-Iḥkām*, vol. 2, p. 959; Nawawī, *Sharḥ Ṣaḥīḥ Muslim*, vol. 15, pp. 128–129; ᶜAsqalānī, *Fatḥ al-bārī*, vol. 7, p. 299; ᶜAynī, *ᶜUmdat al-qāri᾽*, vol. 16, p. 36; Qasṭallānī, *Irshād al-sārī*, vol. 5, p. 416; Sahāranpūrī, *Badhl al-majhūd*, vol. 18, p. 199.

[24] See for him *EI*², s.v. "ᶜIyāḍ b. Mūsā" (M. Talbi).

[25] See for him W. Madelung, "Abū Moslem Moḥammad b. Baḥr al-Eṣfahānī", *Encyclopaedia Iranica*, s.v.; Sezgin, *GAS*, vol. 1, pp. 42–43; Suyūṭī, *Bughyat al-wuᶜāt*, Cairo 1964, vol, 1, p. 59 (no. 107). According to these sources, Abū Muslim lived between 254 A.H. / 868 A.D. and 322 A.H. / 934 A.D.). In another work, Suyūṭī has an entry on Muḥammad b. ᶜAlī b. Muḥammad b. al-Ḥusayn b. Mihrīzad Abū Muslim al-Iṣbahānī, describes him him as a zealous Muᶜtazilī exegete, *adīb* and grammarian (*kāna ᶜārifan bi-'l-tafsīr wa al-naḥw wa al-adab ghāliyan fī madhhab al-iᶜtizāl*), and gives his dates as 366 A.H. – 459 A.H. See Suyūṭī, *Ṭabaqāt al-mufassirīn*, ed. Meursinge, Leiden: S. and J. Luchtmans 1839 (reprint Tehran, 1960), p. 32 (no. 95).

[26] Rāzī, *Mafātīḥ al-ghayb*, vol. 6, pp. 12–13; vol. 17, pp. 50–51.

in particular. According to al-Zajjāj,[27] the verse refers to the Arabs who were polytheists before the coming of the Prophet. As a result of Muḥammad's mission they split: some of them became believers while others remained infidels.[28] More interesting is the interpretation offered by Fakhr al-Dīn al-Rāzī. According to his understanding, the original religion of the Arabs was Islam. They adopted it as a result of Ibrāhīm's activities in the Arabian peninsula, and remained faithful to it until ᶜAmr b. Luḥayy corrupted their religion and established idolatry in Arabia.[29] Fakhr al-Dīn al-Rāzī contends that this view is highly significant: it shows that idolatry was not the original religion of the Arabs; on the contrary, they had initially been Muslims. He maintains that if the Arabs become aware of the notion that idolatry had not been their ancient religion, they will withdraw their support from it, will not be hurt if it is declared false and will not be averse to its abolition (*wa al-gharaḍ minhu anna al-ᶜarab idhā ᶜalimū anna hādha al-madhhab mā kāna aṣliyyan fīhim wa annahu innamā ḥadatha baᶜda an lam yakun lam yataᶜaṣṣabū li-nuṣratihi wa lam yataʾadhdhaw min tazyīf hādhā al-madhhab wa lam tanfur ṭibāᶜuhum min ibṭālihi*).[30] It is fascinating to observe that the desire to weaken the devotion of Arabs to idolatry was an issue for al-Rāzī who died in 606 A.H. / 1209 A.D., while the jurists usually contend that all Arabs embraced Islam by the time of the Prophet's death.[31]

We have started this discussion with the religious history of mankind, and moved later to the same facet in the history of the Arabs. We have seen that according to the preponderant trend in Muslim tradition, humanity was initially united in true faith, frequently identified with Islam. The same idea is sometimes held also with regard to the Arabs, though in their case it does not seem to have been the prevalent one. And if we constrict our viewing angle even further and focus on the individual, we shall find a similar perception. Like humanity as a whole, the individual is also created a believer in the true and natural faith, the *fiṭra*. If he is fortunate enough to be born into a Muslim family, the faith in which he was born is reinforced by parental guidance. If, however, he happens to be born outside the Muslim community, his parents uproot him from his natural faith and transform him into a Jew, a Christian or a Zoroastrian.[32]

Whatever the primordial faith of mankind may have been, there was, according to all traditional views, a great deal of religious unity in the early stages of human history. This unity, however, was not destined to last. There is no unanimity regarding the question when it was first disrupted. According to some, the first

[27] Probably the philologist and exegete Ibrāhīm b. al-Sarī … al-Zajjāj who died in around 311 A.H. / 923 A.D. See Brockelmann, *GAL*, vol. 1, p. 109.

[28] Samarqandī, *Tafsīr*, vol. 2, p. 92.

[29] See "ᶜAmr b. Luḥayy", *EI²*, s.v. (J. W. Fück); Muḥammad b. Ḥabīb, *Kitāb al-muḥabbar*, Beirut: al-Maktab al-tijārī li-'l-ṭibāᶜa wa al-nashr wa al-tawzīᶜ, n.d., pp. 99–100; further references on the establishment of idolatry in Arabia can be found in Friedmann, "Medieval Muslim views of Indian religions", *Journal of the American Oriental Society* 95(1975), p. 214.

[30] Rāzī, *Mafātīḥ al-ghayb*, vol. 17, pp. 50–51. See also Ṭabrisī, *Majmaᶜ al-bayān*, vol. 11, p. 27.

[31] See below, Chapter Two, end of section VII.

[32] Ibn Qayyim al-Jawziyya, *Aḥkām ahl al-dhimma*, vol. 2, p. 490. See also Chapter Three, section VIII.

split (*ikhtilāf*) occurred after Adam or, possibly, as a result of Abel's murder at Cain's hands.[33] Sometimes, Qur'ān 71:21–24 (where the idols Wadd, Suwā', Yaghūth, Ya'ūq and Nasr are mentioned) is understood as a reference to the occurrence of polytheism on earth during the times of Nūḥ.[34] According to others, the initial split occurred among the Children of Israel who fought each other for the sake of attaining mundane power.[35] Naturally enough, the Shī'ī traditionists who contend that humanity consisted in the beginning primarily of infidels tend to interpret the split with reference to the righteous minority, which embraced Islam (as a result of the successive prophetic missions) and dissociated itself from the unbelieving multitude.[36]

When the traditionists leave the discussion of pre-historic times behind and move chronologically forward, the religious split which they describe is between the Muslims on the one hand, and the Jews, the Christians and the Zoroastrians on the other.[37] The polytheists of various ethnic affiliations also figure prominently in the books of law, though some Qur'ānic commentators have devoted to them less attention in their exegesis. The treatment of all these groups in Muslim tradition and law will constitute the main part of the present book. But before we can move to the heart of our subject, we must expound one additional theme: the diversity of religious laws followed by the various communities and the reasons for its emergence, as seen by the early Muslim traditionists and exegetes.

III

It is a matter of common knowledge that Islam incorporated abundant material from the Judaeo-Christian tradition. It is not necessary to dwell here on this issue in general; this has been repeatedly done in academic studies of Islam. There is, however, one issue in this wide-ranging field which is relevant to our inquiry: the nature and the provenance of the differences between the religions of Judaism, Christianity and Islam. It is well known that Moses and Jesus figure prominently in the Muslim tradition which maintains that they were prophets, were favored with divine revelation and each one of them was entrusted with transmitting a revealed book of God to his community. Muslim tradition has no doubt that their two books, the Tawrāt and the Injīl, were initially divinely revealed books, to be implemented by the Jews and the Christians. Furthermore, some Qur'ānic verses can be easily understood as implying that the religion revealed to the Prophet

33 Ṭabarī, *Jāmi' al-bayān*, vol. 2, p. 337; vol. 11, p. 98; Zamakhsharī, *al-Kashshāf*, vol. 2, 230; Rāzī, *Mafātīḥ al-ghayb*, vol. 6, pp. 11–12; Bayḍāwī, *Anwār al-tanzīl*, vol. 1, p. 411.

34 Ṭabarī, *Jāmi' al-bayān*, vol. 29, pp. 97–100; Ibn Qayyim al-Jawziyya, *Ighāthat al-lahfān*, vol. 1, p. 267.

35 al-Suyūṭī, *al-Durr al-manthūr*, vol. 1, p. 242;

36 Majlisī, *Biḥār al-anwār*, vol. 11, p. 31; cf. Kohlberg, "Some Shī'ī views of the antediluvian world", pp. 47–48.

37 Ṭabarī, *Jāmi' al-bayān*, vol. 12, pp. 141–142; Samarqandī, *Tafsīr*, vol. 2, p. 147; Suyūṭī, *al-Durr al-manthūr*, vol. 3, p. 356.

Muḥammad was the same as that which had been revealed to former prophets, such as Nūḥ, Mūsā, ᶜĪsā and especially Ibrāhīm.[38] Other verses appear to instruct the Prophet to follow the guidance of his predecessors in the prophetic office.[39] Nevertheless, the two religions associated with Moses and Jesus are not identical with Islam, and this discrepancy requires an explanation. At this point of our exposition, many students of Islam will almost instinctively think of the famous notion of *taḥrīf*: though the founding prophets of Judaism and Christianity received a genuine book of God, their adherents – especially the Jews – corrupted the text to such an extent that the books in their possession no longer reflect the divine will when they differ from the Qurʾān.[40] This being the case, all humanity, inclusive of Jews and Christians, was called upon to embrace Islam. It is considered one of the special characteristics of Muḥammad that his mission was intended for all people, while each former prophet had been sent only to his particular community.[41]

For all its importance, the theory of *taḥrīf* is neither the entire nor the sole explanation provided by the Muslim tradition for the disparity between Islam and the two former religions. This disparity is also explained by the perception that God did not reveal to the various prophets absolutely identical material. Certain parts of the three revelations were, indeed, the same. Not surprisingly, these were the belief in the absolute unity of God, frequently referred to as *dīn* or *īmān*, and the obligation to observe divine commandments and prohibitions.[42] In other elements, however, the revelations differed from each other. The *locus classicus* for this idea is Qur'ān 5:48: "… To every one of you We have appointed a right way and an open road. If God had willed, He would have made you one community …" (*… li-kullin jaᶜalnā minkum shirᶜatan wa minhājan wa law shāʾa Allāhu la-jaᶜalakum ummatan wāḥida …*).[43] Most commentators maintain that this verse was

[38] See Qurʾān 4:125 ("And who is there that has a fairer religion than he who … follows the creed of Ibrāhīm, a man of pure faith?"), and 42:13 ("He has laid down for you as religion that He charged Noah with, and that We have revealed to you, and that We have charged Abraham with, Moses and Jesus: …")

[39] See Qurʾān 6:90 ("Those whom God has guided – follow their guidance"), 16:123 ("Follow the creed of Abraham, a man of pure faith and no idolater"), 5:47 ("Surely, We sent down the Torah, wherein is guidance and light; thereby the prophets who had surrendered themselves (*alladhīna aslamū*) gave guidance for those of Jewry …")

[40] See H. Lazarus-Yafeh, *Intertwined Worlds*, Princeton: Princeton University Press, 1992, pp. 19–35; "Taḥrīf", *EI*², s.v. (H. Lazarus-Yafeh); B. Lewis, *The Jews of Islam*, pp. 69–70.

[41] Tirmidhī, *Ṣaḥīḥ*, vol. 7, pp. 41–42.

[42] Ṭabarī, *Jāmiᶜ al-bayān*, vol. 6, p. 270; Qurṭubī, *al-Jāmiᶜ li-aḥkām al-Qurʾān*, vol. 6, p. 153. An extensive list of elements common to the three religions can be found in Walī Allāh Dihlawī, *Ḥujjat Allāh al-bāligha*, Cairo: Dār al-kutub al-ḥadītha, n.d., vol. 1, p. 183. The question of the sources which inspired this eighteenth-century Indian Muslim scholar remains to be investigated.

[43] This verse is important also in the context of interreligious polemics: though it does not explicitly deal with the question whether Muslims are obliged to observe the laws of the Tawrāt and the Injīl, it is perceived as a decisive answer to those who criticized Islam for deviating from the laws revealed to the Jews and the Christians. Islam is not bound by the laws of these: God bestowed upon the Muslims a law of their own. See Zamakhsharī, *al-Kashshāf*, vol. 1, p. 618; Qurṭubī, *al-Jāmiᶜ li-aḥkām al-Qurʾān*, vol. 6, p. 153; Bayḍāwī, *Anwār al-tanzīl*, vol. 1, p. 260. See also Qur'ān 22:34 and 22:67.

revealed regarding the books of law given to Moses, Jesus and Muḥammad. They assert that certain laws (*sharāʾiʿ*) imposed on the Jews, the Christians and the Muslims were diverse. The diversity stemmed from the fact that God in His wisdom knew what was best for each community, and some of the laws that He had revealed varied accordingly. Some commentators state only the principle of *sharʿī* variety without expounding its details, while others do list the particular laws in which the divergence between the three communities exists in their perception. A few examples may be useful. The Tawrāt stipulates only retaliation (*qiṣāṣ*) for intentional murder, while the Injīl requires pardon, and the Muslim *sharīʿa* allows for retaliation, blood-money or pardon. The punishment for fornication is also different in the three religions: the Tawrāt knew only stoning, and the Injīl only flogging;[44] in Islam stoning is imposed on the non-virgins (of both sexes) and flogging on the virgins.[45] Other differences include the ways of fasting, the weekly day of communal worship, the manner of prayer, its direction, and similar matters.[46]

In view of this diversity, how should one view the contents of the Tawrāt and the Injīl? Have they been corrupted to such an extent that they lost their validity for all? Are the laws included in them still valid, or have they been superseded by Islam? Are they valid for Jews and Christians only, or, being of divine origin, have they some relevance for Muslims as well?[47]

All these questions have been extensively discussed in the literature of *uṣūl al-fiqh* which includes a considerable variety of pertinent views. According to one conception, once a *sharīʿa* was revealed to a prophet, it remains valid until there is proof of its abrogation. Hence a subsequent prophet must follow that *sharīʿa* as long as its abrogation was not made manifest to him. Other traditionists maintain that the situation is the opposite: the validity of a *sharīʿa* brought by a certain prophet is terminated by the mission of his successor in the prophetic office, unless the latter announces its continuity.

The Ḥanafī scholar al-Sarakhsī (d. circa 483 A.H. / 1090 A.D.) devotes to this issue a substantial chapter in his *Uṣūl*. At the beginning of his discussion, he surveys the pertinent views current among Muslim jurists. Some of them maintain

44 For the punishment of fornication and adultery in the Christian canon law, see W. M. Foley, "Adultery (Christian)", in *Encyclopaedia of religion and ethics*, Edinburgh: T. and T. Clark, 1908, s.v. Foley mentions penance as the usual punishment for these offences in church law. See also James A. Brundage, *Law, sex and Christian society in medieval Europe*, Chicago: Chicago University Press, 1987, p. 388, where flogging of adulterous women is mentioned, but the punishment is inflicted by the civil rather than the ecclesiastical authorities.

45 Muqātil, *Tafsīr*, vol. 1, pp. 481–482. Cf. J. Burton's introduction to Abū ʿUbayd, *al-Nāsikh wa al-mansūkh*, pp. 24–27.

46 Suyūṭī, *al-Durr al-manthūr*, vol. 1, p. 243.

47 This issue has been referred to in a different context by Wael B. Hallaq, *Islamic legal theories*, pp. 115–117. A short summary, taking into account modern Muslim views, can be found in Kamali, *Principles of Islamic jurisprudence*, pp. 229–234. The notion of abrogation of Mosaic law in Judaeo-Muslim polemics is discussed by C. Adang, *Muslim writers on Judaism and the Hebrew Bible*, Leiden: E. J. Brill, 1996, pp. 192–255. For a modern analysis of this issue and its social and political relevance to contemporary conditions, see A. Sachedina, "Political implications ...".

that the laws revealed to the pre-Islamic communities are binding on the Muslims exactly like the *sharīʿa* of the Prophet Muḥammad, unless there is proof of their abrogation. For them it is immaterial whether these laws were communicated to the Muslims by the People of the Book, transmitted by Muslims on the basis of a Book (i.e., the Tawrāt or the Injīl) in their possession, or confirmed in the Qurʾān or the prophetic *ḥadīth*.[48] This idea is supported by the general principle that if an idea is phrased in absolute terms, it is valid for all times if its content allows for such an understanding. A time limit for its validity is a modification of the idea, and, as such, may not be introduced without proof. Furthermore, a prophet who had been sent with a *sharīʿa* does not cease to be a prophet because another prophet was sent after him; his *sharīʿa* remains in force as long as there is no proof of its abrogation. This can be supported by Qurʾānic verses in which the believers are said to have faith in God, in His angels, in His books and in His messengers without making any distinctions between them.[49] Whatever was agreeable to God when he sent a certain prophet does not cease to be so because of the mission of a subsequent one. The presumption (*al-aṣl*) is compatibility (*muwāfaqa*) of the laws revealed to the various prophets. All remain valid unless changed or replaced by abrogation.[50]

The idea of continuous validity of former revelations can also be supported by the argument that these revelations became part of the Muslim *sharīʿa* through their inclusion in the Qurʾān. Such a perception can be based on Qurʾānic verses which enjoin the Prophet to follow his predecessors in the prophetic office, especially Ibrāhīm.[51] This way of presenting the issue has the advantage of avoiding reliance on material which might have been corrupted by the People of the Book, in view of the *taḥrīf* problem.[52] This advantage is evident in al-Āmidī's (d. 631 A.H. / 1233 A.D.)[53] presentation: the Prophet "observed the authentic laws of those who preceded him by way of (direct) revelation to him rather than by (basing himself on) their corrupted books and on their transmission (... *anna al-nabī ... kāna mutaʿabbidan bi-mā ṣaḥḥa min sharāʾiʿ man qablahu bi-ṭarīq al-waḥyi ilayhi lā min jihati kutubihim al-mubaddala wa naqli arbābihā*).[54] These verses also preclude the idea that the *sharīʿa* of a prophet lapses with the missions of his successors: the Qurʾān would not have instructed Muḥammad to follow the *sharīʿa* of Ibrāhīm if it had been superseded.

The opposite view, according to which each prophet abrogates the laws of his predecessor, can also find support in Qurʾānic material. Qurʾān 5:48 can easily be

48 Sarakhsī, *Uṣūl*, vol. 2, p. 99.
49 Qurʾān 2:136, 2:285, 3:84.
50 Sarakhsī, *Uṣūl*, vol. 2, pp. 100–101.
51 Sarakhsī quotes Qurʾān 2:135, 3:95 (*qul: ṣadaqa Allāh fa-'ttabiʿū millata Ibrāhīma ḥanīfan wa mā kāna min al-mushrikīn*; "Say: God has spoken the truth; therefore follow the creed of Abraham, a man of pure faith and no idolater."), and 4:124.
52 Sarakhsī, *Uṣūl*, vol. 2, pp. 102–105.
53 See, for him, *EI*², s.v. al-Āmidī, ʿAlī b. Abī ʿAlī ... (D. Sourdel).
54 Āmidī, *al-Iḥkām fī uṣūl al-aḥkām*, vol. 4, p. 123.

understood as reflecting the diversity of revelations given to various communities, and some verses explicitly state that the Tawrāt was given as guidance to the Children of Israel (only).[55] This is understood as restricting the validity of the Tawrāt to one community and as implying that the Muslims are under no obligation to follow its laws. It is also argued that laws promulgated by one prophet lapse with the coming of the next one; if this was not the case, there would be no need for the latter prophet's mission. Each *sharīʿa* is abrogated by the promulgation of the subsequent one. It goes without saying that the abrogation of the former laws does not apply to the basic principles of religion, such as the belief in one God, which are common to all prophets.[56]

In accordance with this general principle, the proponents of the latter view assert that the coming of Islam abrogated the laws of the People of the Book. There is some divergence of opinion whether it was Islam that abrogated both Judaism and Christianity, or first Christianity abrogated Judaism and then Islam abrogated Christianity. Their abrogation notwithstanding, a measure of sacredness (*ḥurma*) continues to pertain to the Tawrāt and the Injīl, and in the eyes of some jurists this is the reason why Jews and Christians are allowed to retain their faith upon payment of the *jizya*. The situation is similar to the abrogated verses of the Qurʾān, which retain their sacred nature despite the abrogation of the ruling included in them.[57] In any case, the Prophet called upon all people to follow the Islamic *sharīʿa* and to discard the laws of the Jews and of the Christians. In a tradition repeatedly quoted in support of this perception, ʿUmar b. al-Khaṭṭāb is seen by the Prophet while holding a Torah fragment in his hands. The Prophet is infuriated to such an extent that his cheeks blush and he says: "Are you perplexed like the Jews and the Christians were?! By God, were Moses alive, he would have no alternative except following me" (*a mutahawwikūna kamā tahawwakat al-yahūd wa al-naṣārā?! wa-'llāhi law kāna Mūsā ḥayyan mā wasiʿahu illā 'ttibaʿī*)![58] Here we have the rather surprising notion that the former prophets, whose laws were superseded by Islam, ought to be considered as followers of the Prophet Muḥammad despite the fact that they had been sent by God long before him.

In his discussion of *uṣūl al-fiqh*, Abū Ḥāmid al-Ghazālī (d. 505 A.H. / 1111 A.D.) joins those who reject the validity of pre-Islamic laws for Muslims. The idea that "the law of the prophets who had been before us (is law for us) in matters that were not explicitly abrogated by our law" (*sharʿu man qablanā min al-anbiyāʾ fīmā lam yuṣarriḥ sharʿunā bi-naskhihi*) is considered by him the first of four "fictitious sources" (*al-uṣūl al-mawhūma*) of law.[59] Al-Ghazālī is, however, also aware of the

[55] Qurʾān 17:2, 32:23. But see Qurʾān 3:3–4, 6:91 where the Tawrāt and the Injīl are described as "guidance to mankind" (*hudan li-'l-nās*).

[56] Sarakhsī, *Uṣūl*, vol. 2, p. 101.

[57] Māwardī, *al-Ḥāwī*, vol. 9, pp. 220; 221, ll. 1–2; 222, ll. 16–18.

[58] Sarakhsī, *Uṣūl*, vol. 2, p. 102. Cf. Ṣanʿānī, *Muṣannaf*, vol. 10, pp. 313–314 (no. 19213); Ibn Ḥanbal, *Musnad*, vol. 3, p. 387; Ibn Qudāma, *Rawḍat al-nāẓir*, vol. 2, pp. 519 supra, 524.

[59] Ghazālī, *al-Mustaṣfā min ʿilm al-uṣūl*, vol. 1, p. 245. Other *uṣūlīs*, expressing themselves in a less categorical manner, call them "Sources of law subject to disagreement" (*uṣūlun mukhtalafun fīhā*); see Hallaq, *Islamic legal theories*, p. 115.

controversy on this matter among Muslim jurisprudents. The controversy came into being, in his view, because in particular cases the Prophet was obliged to follow the former religions unless he received a revelation different from theirs (*fa-idhā nazalat wāqiᶜatun lazimahu ittibāᶜu dīnihim illā idhā nazala ᶜalayhi waḥyun mukhālifun li-mā sabaqa*). Nevertheless, al-Ghazālī asserts that this does not amount to the Prophet being bound by former laws (*wa al-mukhtār annahu … lam yataᶜabbad bi-sharīᶜati man qablahu*). Had he been bound by these laws, he would have been only a transmitter of information about them (*mukhbir*) rather than a legislator (*shāriᶜ*). Such a perception is flatly contradicted by the consensus of the entire Muslim community, which maintained that the *sharīᶜa* is of the Prophet and abrogated former *sharāʾiᶜ*.[60] In order to substantiate this position, al-Ghazālī needs to interpret several Qurʾānic verses that may be understood as implying the opposite. The basic assumption of his interpretation is the idea that Islam has not abrogated the basic principles of the former religions, such as the belief in one God and a few other commandments, such as the prohibition of fornication, theft and unjustified killing. Therefore, whenever the Qurʾān enjoins the Muslims to follow the former religions, it should be understood as instructing them to follow their basic principles rather than their particular laws. The terms *hudan*, *milla* and *dīn* which appear in this context in Qurʾān 5:47, 6:90, 16:123 and 42:13 are explained along these lines.[61] Identical conclusions are drawn from the Prophet's behavior in certain instances. When he was asked a question of legal import, he used to wait for a relevant revelation to descend rather than act upon the laws of the Tawrāt and the Injīl, though Jewish converts such as ᶜAbd Allāh b. Salām, Kaᶜb al-Aḥbār and Wahb b. Munabbih were on hand to supply the required information. The Companions were not required to study the Tawrāt and the Injīl and they did not resort to them in legal questions that were disputed among them. The only case in which the Prophet did refer to the Tawrāt – the stoning of the two Jewish fornicators – is not to be used to prove the opposite: in this case the Prophet referred to the Tawrāt only in order to convince the culprits that the punishment inflicted on them is not contrary to their own religion. When Muᶜādh b. Jabal was sent to the Yemen, he said that he would judge on the basis of the Qurʾān, the *sunna* and *ijtihād*. The Prophet agreed. Muᶜādh did not mention the Tawrāt, the Injīl or, in general, the laws of the former religions. If the laws of the Tawrāt and the Injīl had been a source of law (*law kāna dhālika min madārik al-aḥkām*), it would not have been permissible to resort to *ijtihād* without looking into them first.[62]

[60] Ghazālī, *al-Mustaṣfā min ᶜilm al-uṣūl*, vol. 1, pp. 250–251, 255. Cf. Āmidī, *al-Iḥkām fī uṣūl al-aḥkām*, vol. 4, pp. 124, 127.

[61] Ghazālī, *al-Mustaṣfā min ᶜilm al-uṣūl*, vol. 1, p. 255. Cf. Āmidī, *al-Iḥkām fī uṣūl al-aḥkām*, vol. 4, p. 128. Al-Āmidī has an additional way to substantiate this position: the term *milla* never means the particular laws and, therefore, one never says *millat al-Shāfiᶜī* or *millat Abī Ḥanīfa* when referring to the *furūᶜ* characteristic of their respective *madhāhib*.

[62] Ghazālī, *al-Mustaṣfā min ᶜilm al-uṣūl*, vol. 1, pp. 251–260. Cf. Ibn Qudāma, *Rawḍat al-nāẓir*, vol. 2, p. 519; Āmidī, *al-Iḥkām fī uṣūl al-aḥkām*, vol. 4, pp. 123–124.

The Ḥanbalī *qāḍī* Abū Yaᶜlā Ibn al-Farrāᵓ (d. 458 A.H. / 1066 A.D.)[63] maintained that laws revealed to former prophets that had not been abrogated became part and parcel of Islamic law. This is the reason because of which it is incumbent upon the Muslims to follow these laws; solely their inclusion in the books of the former prophets would not have brought about their validity for Muslims. Therefore, the question whether a law had indeed been imposed on the former communities must be ascertained by a Qurᵓānic verse or a *ḥadīth*, not by reference to the former books themselves.[64]

The later Ḥanbalī scholar Ibn Taymiyya (d. 728 A.H. / 1328 A.D.) included in his *Iqtiḍāᵓ al-ṣirāṭ al-mustaqīm li-mukhālafat aṣḥāb al-jaḥīm* a lengthy and intricate discussion of the validity of Jewish and Christian laws for the Muslims and reached conclusions similar to those of Abū Yaᶜlā. He gives a highly restrictive interpretation to the idea that "the law of those who were before us is law for us as long as our law does not contradict it" (*sharᶜu man qablanā sharᶜun lanā mā lam yarid sharᶜunā bi-khilāfihi*). First, it must be proven that the law in question was, indeed, imposed on the People of the Book. The proof must be incontrovertible: a Qurᵓānic verse, a reliable prophetic statement or a tradition related by multiple transmitters (*mutawātir*). The mere inclusion of such a law in the Jewish or Christian scriptures, or a scriptuary report about its existence are not sufficient: neither the books nor the reports of the scriptuaries are to be trusted. Second, one must be sure that the *sharīᶜa* really does not include any directive concerning the matter at hand. But even if all these conditions are fulfilled and the imposition of a certain law on the People of the Book is reliably established, the Prophet still commanded the Muslims to differentiate themselves from the Jews and the Christians. Identity exists only in a few accidental laws (such as circumcision or ransoming a child with a sacrificial animal), not in the essentials of religion (*wa innamā tajīᵓu al-muwāfaqa fī baᶜḍ al-aḥkām al-ᶜāriḍa lā fī al-hady al-rātib wa al-shiᶜār al-dāᵓim*).[65] In order to make this principle compatible with the *ᶜāshūrāᵓ* tradition,[66] which seems to indicate – in some of its versions – that the Prophet instructed the Muslims to embrace a Jewish ritual, Ibn Taymiyya asserts that the Prophet fasted on the day of *ᶜāshūrā* before he had asked the Jews about it, and the tribe of Quraysh also used to fast on it in the Jāhiliyya. Thus, the Prophet's fasting on the day of *ᶜāshūrāᵓ* was not in emulation of the Jews; both the Jews and the Muslims emulate Moses, and the Muslims are more deserving to do this than the Jews. Furthermore, according to some traditions, the Prophet instructed his followers to fast on the ninth or the eleventh (rather than the tenth) of Muḥarram in order to differ from the Jews.[67] As for his desire to emulate the People of the Book in matters concerning which he did not receive any specific commands, this

[63] See "Ibn al-Farrāᵓ", in *EI*², s.v. (H. Laoust).
[64] Ibn al-Farrāᵓ, *al-ᶜUdda*, vol. 3, pp. 753ff.
[65] Ibn Taymiyya, *Iqtiḍāᵓ al-ṣirāṭ al-mustaqīm*, vol. 1, pp. 412–414.
[66] See above, section II.
[67] Ibn Taymiyya, *Iqtiḍāᵓ al-ṣirāṭ al-mustaqīm*, vol. 1, pp. 414–420.

had been true only in the early days of Islam when the Muslims were weak. Later – when Islam became strong by means of *jihād* and humiliation was inflicted on the People of the Book – God put an end to this emulation and ordered the Prophet to differ from the Jews (*inna hādhā kāna mutaqaddiman thumma nasakha Allāh dhālika wa sharaʿa lahu mukhālafat ahl al-kitāb wa amarahu bi-dhālika*). Two examples of such development are given. According to a tradition recorded by Bukhārī and Muslim,[68] in the pre-Islamic period the polytheists used to part their hair while the People of the Book used to let it fall freely on their shoulders. In the beginning, the Prophet desired to follow the example of the People of the Book in their hairstyle and let his hair hang loosely; later he changed this and parted his hair with a comb. Eventually, the parting of hair became a symbol of the Muslims and the People of the Book were forbidden to adhere to this custom.[69] The other, and more famous example of this process, is the change of the *qibla* from Jerusalem to Mecca.[70]

Ibn Taymiyya's conclusion is that Muslims are forbidden to follow non-Muslim laws and customs when they are the dominant community. Only Muslims dwelling in the "abode of war" (*dār al-ḥarb*), or in the "abode of infidelity which is not in a state of war" (*dār kufr ghayr ḥarb*) with the Muslims, may act differently. For them it is at times desirable or even obligatory to act in emulation of their infidel rulers: such behavior may save them from harm, give them the opportunity to summon the unbelievers to Islam and enable them to acquire information beneficial to the Muslims.[71]

In abrogating the laws of the People of the Book, Islam is a link in the universal scheme of successive revelations which supplant each other. From another – and crucial – point of view it is, however, unique. In contradistinction to his predecessors in the prophetic office, Muḥammad was sent to all humanity rather than to one ethnic group; furthermore, he is the last prophet and there will be no prophet after him. This means that Islam supersedes the laws which preceded it, but no one will supersede the Muslim *sharīʿa* which is destined to be valid for all people and for all times. Islam's immunity from abrogation is an essential component of its superiority in comparison with all other religions.[72]

The preceding survey clearly shows that early Muslim scholars were not of one mind concerning the relationship between the *sharīʿa* and the laws revealed to the pre-Islamic prophets. In order to grasp better the significance of this controversy,

[68] Bukhārī, *Ṣaḥīḥ, Kitāb al-libās* 70 (ed. Krehl, vol. 4, p. 98); Muslim, *Ṣaḥīḥ, Kitāb al-faḍāʾil*, vol. 4, p. 1816 (no. 2336).

[69] Ibn Taymiyya, *Iqtiḍāʾ al-ṣirāṭ al-mustaqīm*, vol. 1, pp. 413, 416, 420–421.

[70] Ibn Taymiyya, *Iqtiḍāʾ al-ṣirāṭ al-mustaqīm*, vol. 1, p. 416. The Muslim obligation to avoid customs similar to those of non-Muslims has been exhaustively discussed and analyzed in M. J. Kister, "Do not assimilate yourselves...*Lā tashabbahū*", *Jerusalem Studies in Arabic and Islam* 12 (1989), pp. 322–353. The issue of hairstyle is referred to on pp. 324, 329 (note 30), 351.

[71] Ibn Taymiyya, *Iqtiḍāʾ al-ṣirāṭ al-mustaqīm*, vol. 1, pp. 420–422.

[72] Sarakhsī, *Uṣūl*, vol. 2, pp. 101–102. For a more extensive treatment of the finality of Muḥammad's prophethood, see my "Finality of prophethood in Sunnī Islam", in *Jerusalem Studies in Arabic and Islam* 7 (1986), pp. 177–215 (= *Prophecy continuous*, pp. 49–82).

it would be helpful if the various views on the issue could be related to their proponents. Some sources indicate that the support for the ongoing validity of former laws came from the Ḥanafī school,[73] though al-Sarakhsī does not identify them as such. Al-Sarakhsī himself supports this view in principle, but with a caveat: only those parts of former laws are acceptable which were confirmed in the Qur᾽ān or in a prophetic *ḥadīth*. Material transmitted by the People of the Book is suspect as corrupted and cannot be accepted without corroboration by a trustworthy Muslim source. Al-Sarakhsī provides three examples for the adoption of pre-Islamic laws into the *sharīᶜa*: the first – and a rather curious one – deals with the rules by which drinking water ought to be distributed and is based on the Qur᾽ānic story of the she-camel belonging to the pre-Islamic Arab prophet Ṣāliḥ;[74] the adoption into Islam of the "life for life" rule revealed in the Tawrāt and confirmed in Qur᾽ān 5:45;[75] and the stoning of the two Jewish fornicators by the Prophet, in conformity with the law of Moses. In all these cases it can be argued that the laws in question had been revealed to Ṣāliḥ and Moses respectively, but also became part of the revelation to the Prophet. This perception of the relationship between Islam and the former revelations is, for al-Sarakhsī, easier to support than the indiscriminate acceptance of pre-Islamic laws into Islam.[76]

Al-Sarakhsī's survey of these divergent views seems to be the most comprehensive treatment of the subject among the early *uṣūlī*s. He also seems to be the only jurist who mentions the possibility of accepting laws revealed to pre-Islamic prophets even if the information about these laws reached the Muslims from fragments of previous scriptures, or by transmission of the People of the Book. Though al-Sarakhsī himself does not accept such a wholesale adoption of these laws into Islam, he clearly knows of Muslim groups who were willing to do this. Other *uṣūlī*s are also aware of such views, but they reject them much more vehemently.

The preponderant view according to which each *sharīᶜa* abrogates the one that had been revealed before it is the *uṣūlī*s' way to define the process by which Islam disengaged itself from the two former religions. The following section will discuss the Muslim traditions which describe how Islam determined its own direction of prayer and dispensed with that of Jerusalem, how it abandoned the fast of *ᶜāshūrā᾽* in favor of Ramaḍān and how it adopted the call to prayer by human voice in preference to the Jewish usage of the horn and the Christian use of the *nāqūs*. The development of the tradition on these matters settled the controversy on the continued validity of pre-Islamic laws after the revelation of the Qur᾽ān: even those who supported such a possibility in principle conceded that such laws may be considered valid only if included in a trustworthy Muslim source. The suspect scriptures of the Jews and the Christians could not serve as a proof of their validity.

73 Ibn Qudāma, *Rawḍat al-nāẓir*, vol. 2, p. 517.
74 Qur᾽ān 54:28; 26:155.
75 For the controversy among the *madhāhib* concerning the application of this verse by the Muslims, see section VI below.
76 Sarakhsī, *Uṣūl*, vol. 2, pp. 99–100.

IV

The preceding sections dealt with the way in which Muslim tradition perceived religious unity and diversity before the emergence of Islam in the seventh century A.D. They also dealt with the question how the events of the seventh century and, more specifically, the revelation of the Qurʾān and the crystallization of Islamic law altered the nature of the religious situation. The Muslim perception of the relationship between the various religions after the appearance of the Prophet Muḥammad is substantially different from that of the previous period. The successes of Muslim arms created conditions in which Muslims could govern themselves and their non-Muslim subjects in accordance with their world-view. Islam gradually developed the conviction that it was the final and superior religion. The military and civilizational achievements of Islam nourished this conviction for the whole pre-modern period, excluding only the twelve years of Muḥammad's prophetic activity in Mecca, the first two or three years after his *hijra* to Medina and the period of the Crusades.[77] From this vantage point, the fifteen years between 610 and 625 A.D. are a unique period in the history of Islam and it seems appropriate to devote some attention to the way in which the tradition describes this embryonic stage of its development.

According to Muslim sources, the only religion encountered by the Prophet in Mecca before the *hijra* was *shirk*, the belief in numerous deities who were deemed "associates" (*shurakāʾ*) of Allah, the supreme God.[78] In its crystallized form, Islam would brook no compromise with polytheism of any kind. In the canonical text of the Qurʾān we find only total rejection of any belief in deities other than Allah. Yet Muslim tradition does refer to a pre-*hijrī* episode which indicates that nascent Islam did not exclude the possibility of forging a compromise with Meccan idolatry. This is the now notorious episode of the "Satanic verses", which were – according to the traditional account – interpolated by Satan into the divine revelation of the Qurʾān and accorded recognition to al-Lāt, al-ʿUzzā and Manāt, the three goddesses of the Jāhiliyya believed to have been daughters of Allah. Significantly enough, the "Satanic verse" in question is almost identical with a pre-Islamic ritual cry (*talbiya*) of Quraysh.[79] In the scholarly literature, the historicity

[77] For a survey of Muslim life under the Crusaders, see B. Z. Kedar, "The subjected Muslims of the Frankish Levant", in J. Powell, ed., *Muslims under Latin rule*, Princeton: Princeton University Press, 1990, pp. 135–174 (with extensive bibliography).

[78] Muḥammad b. Ḥabīb included in his *Kitāb al-Muḥabbar* (p. 161) a tradition about the existence of *zanādiqa* in pre-Islamic Mecca. Chokr reached the conclusion that this tradition is part of anti-Umayyad polemics and, in this context, *zandaqa* is synonymous with pre-Islamic idolatry. See Chokr, *Zandaqa et zindīqs*, pp. 310–315.

[79] See Ibn al-Kalbī, *Kitāb al-aṣnām*, ed. Aḥmad Zakī Bāshā, Cairo: Maṭbaʿat dār al-kutub al-miṣriyya, 1924, p. 19: "Quraysh used to circumambulate the Kaʿba, saying: 'By al-Lāt and al-ʿUzzā, and Manāt, the third, the other! These are the exalted cranes whose intercession is hoped for'" (*wa kānat Quraysh taṭūfu bi-'l-Kaʿba wa taqūlu: wa-'l-Lāt wa 'l-ʿUzzā wa Manāt al-thālitha al-ukhrā! fa-innahunna al-gharānīq al-ʿulā wa inna shafāʿatahunna la-turtajā*). For an exhaustive analysis of the connection between the Jāhilī *talbiyāt* and emerging Islam, as well as for additional references, see M. J. Kister, "Labbayka, Allahumma, Labbayka. On a monotheistic aspect of a Jāhiliyya practice." *Jerusalem Studies in Arabic and Islam* 2 (1980), pp. 33–57, especially pp. 47–49.

of the episode has been called into question and it has been interpreted in a variety of ways. It is not necessary to dwell upon these interpretations here.[80] But even if the pertinent historical details, like many other matters related to early Islam, are ultimately unverifiable, the episode is significant, and we would like to highlight here one of its aspects. In a version included in al-Ṭabarī's *Ta᾿rīkh*, the "Satanic verses" episode is related to the Prophet's fervent desire to improve his relationship with Quraysh. The tradition gives a cogent and revealing account of Muḥammad's frame of mind at the time. He is depicted as deeply troubled by the rejection of his monotheistic faith by the Quraysh, by their animosity toward him and by their boycott. Social boycott is a severe sanction in any society, and its severity is greatly intensified in a community where the individual heavily depends on his social unit. The Prophet's desire to mend his relationship with Quraysh is therefore easily understandable. It is also understandable that from the vantage point of crystallized Islam, it would not be possible to describe the Prophet as attempting a compromise with Meccan idolatry on the basis of his own initiative. The tradition therefore depicts him as longing for a divine message that would, in some fashion, effect a reconciliation. Muḥammad's intense expectation of such a message provided Satan with a unique opportunity. Making devious use of the Prophet's desire to attenuate the hostility of Quraysh, Satan resolved to undermine Muḥammad's monotheistic message, and caused him to utter a verse in which he mentioned the three goddesses favorably and recognized them as exalted beings, able to intercede with God. This recognition had an immediate and dramatic impact on the people of Mecca. They were thrilled by the apparent change in the attitude of the Prophet towards their polytheistic religion, worshipped together with the Muslims and there was the clear impression that an accommodation was reached between Islam and the polytheistic beliefs of the Arabs. However, this accommodation was not destined to last. After an unspecified period of time, the angel Gabriel appeared before the Prophet, explained to him that the verse in question was Satanic rather than divine, and replaced it with a new verse that reaffirmed the total renunciation of idolatry and the total break with the polytheistic faith of ancient Arabia.[81]

In view of the later development of Islam as an independent and fiercely monotheistic faith, the "Satanic verses" incident is one of the more embarrassing episodes in early Islam. In the first two centuries of Islamic history, it constituted "a standard and widespread element in the historical memory of the early Muslim community", but in later periods the decisive majority of scholars, with the remarkable exception of Ibn Taymiyya, rejected the historicity of the incident as incompatible with the belief in the Prophet's immunity from error (*ᶜiṣma*).[82]

80 The most recent analysis of some relevant texts and references to previous research can be found in U. Rubin, *The eye of the beholder*, Princeton: The Darwin Press, Inc., 1995, pp. 156–166, and in G. Hawting, *The idea of idolatry*, pp. 130–149. Hawting's work includes a full translation of Ṭabarī's version of the story.

81 Ṭabarī, *Ta᾿rīkh al-rusul wa al-mulūk*, series 1, pp. 1192–1193.

82 See the seminal article of Ahmed, "Ibn Taymiyya and the Satanic verses", p. 122 and *passim*.

If we subject the episode to an analysis which eliminates Satan from the story, we are shown a vivid picture of the Prophet facing a painful dilemma. On the one hand, he was sincerely convinced that he had a divine mission to perform and to bring the message of monotheism to his people. On the other hand, his insistence on performing faithfully his religious task caused him to be ridiculed, rejected and ostracized. The animosity which he encountered caused the Prophet a great deal of anguish and engendered in him a fleeting willingness to reach a compromise with the religious beliefs of pre-Islamic Arabia.

Mutatis mutandis, the Satanic verses episode in Mecca has significant parallels during the first part of the Prophet's activity in Medina. Here also the Prophet initially sought religious accommodation with the non-Muslim segment of the local population. However, the religions with which a compromise might have been reached in Medina were monotheistic, and the conditions in Medina were different. Therefore none of the Prophet's overtures to the non-Muslims in Medina acquired the controversial nature and pungency of the Satanic verses. Yet in Medina also significant approaches were made toward the non-Muslims, in this case the People of the Book. The Qur'ān promised them salvation in the hereafter, saying that "their wage await them with their Lord, and no fear shall be on them, neither shall they sorrow."[83] They were only required to believe in God, in the Last Day and do good works; no requirement of conversion to Islam is mentioned. Furthermore, the Prophet is shown as disposed to adopt certain rituals associated with the Jewish (or Christian) tradition. In some cases, a reason for this willingness is given; in others these rituals are introduced without an explanation.

Pride of place in the first category belongs to the famous issue of praying in the direction of Jerusalem after the *hijra*. *Ḥadīth* and *tafsīr* literatures have preserved a great variety of traditions concerning the *qibla* and its eventual change from Jerusalem to Mecca. This significant event in the dissociation process of nascent Islam from Judaism deserves separate treatment and it is not possible to do this adequately in the framework of this inquiry.[84] Suffice it to say here that Muslim tradition is not unanimous in describing the development of this ritual detail in early Islam. We have three traditions concerning the situation in Mecca before the *hijra*: according to one, the Prophet prayed in the direction of the Kaᶜba; according to a second, he prayed in in the direction of Jerusalem; according to a third, he prayed in the direction of Jerusalem, but saw to it that the Kaᶜba be on the straight line between himself and Jerusalem.[85] Regarding the situation in Medina after the *hijra*, which is more important for the question at hand, the tradition is unanimous.

[83] Qur'ān 2:62, 5:69. In his attempt to formulate a "theology for the twenty-first century", Sachedina accords central importance to these verses. See his *The Islamic roots of democratic pluralism*, passim.

[84] U. Rubin has now made a substantial contribution toward this goal in his "Kivvun ha-tfilla be–islam – le-toldotav shel ma'avaq beyn-pulḥanī" ("The direction of prayer in Islam: a contribution to the history of a struggle between rituals"), *Hisṭoriya* 6 (5460 / 2000), pp. 5–29.

[85] See "Ḳibla", *EI*², s.v. (A. J. Wensinck); Ṭabarī, *Ta'rīkh al-rusul wa al-mulūk*, series I, p. 1280; Ibn al-Murajjā, *Faḍā'il Bayt al-Maqdis*, pp. 99–101.

The Prophet prayed in the direction of Jerusalem for sixteen, seventeen or eighteen months. At the end of this period, Qur'ān 2:144[86] was revealed and established Mecca as the *qibla* of the Muslims. Similarly to the Satanic verses episode, this development is also described in the tradition as a result of the Prophet's longing for the change.[87]

A few observations may be made as a contribution to the interpretation of this well known development. Some students of Islam have interpreted the choice of Jerusalem as a reflection of the Prophet's desire "to model Islam more on Judaism";[88] others denied any such intention on the part of the Prophet.[89] Despite the potentially sensitive nature of the idea that the Prophet adopted details of Jewish and Christian rituals into Islam, it is remarkable that the Muslim tradition itself preserved references to the Prophet's desire to conciliate the Jews. We read that the Prophet was commanded after the *hijra* to pray toward Jerusalem "in order to come to an agreement with the Jews", or, at least, "to win their hearts" (... *thumma lammā hājara umira bi-'l-ṣalāt ilā al-ṣakhra ta'allufan li-'l-yahūd*).[90] Elswhere it is said that the *qibla* was not determined by God, but was left to the Prophet's discretion; it was he who chose Jerusalem (*inna al-tawajjuha ilā bayt al-maqdis kāna bi-'jtihādihi ᶜalayhi al-salām*) with this conciliatory purpose in mind. In a similar vein, the Prophet is reported to have prayed in the direction of Jerusalem so that the Jews "believe in him, follow him and abandon the *ummī* Arabs" (*li-yu'minū bihi wa yattabiᶜūhu wa yadaᶜū bi-dhālika al-ummiyyīn min al-ᶜarab*). Like the Meccans during the Satanic verses episode, the Jews are also described as being glad (*fa-fariḥat al-yahūd*) when the Prophet prayed in the direction of Jerusalem.[91] There are even some faint echoes of joint prayers of Muslims and Jews in the direction of Jerusalem,[92] similar to al-Ṭabarī's account of the joint prayer between Muslims and polytheists after the recitation of the Satanic verses by the Prophet. According to other traditions, the Jews interpreted the choice of Jerusalem as the *qibla* of the Muslims as a Muslim declaration of intent to join the Jewish religion in its entirety. The *qibla* was changed in order to belie these expectations (... *li-allā yaḥtajja al-yahūd ᶜalaykum bi-'l-muwāfaqa fī al-qibla fa-yaqūlūna: qad wāfaqūnā fī qiblatinā fa-yūshiku an yuwāfiqūnā fī dīninā*).[93]

[86] "... turn your face towards the Holy Mosque; and wherever you may be, turn your faces towards it ..."
[87] See Ṭabarī, *Jāmiᶜ al-bayān*, vol. 2, p. 19 (on Qur'ān 2:144).
[88] W. M. Watt, *Muḥammad, Prophet and Statesman*, Oxford: Oxford University Press, 1961, p. 99.
[89] See Goitein, "al-Ḳuds", *EI²*, vol. 5, p. 323b.
[90] Bayḍāwī, *Anwār al-tanzīl*, vol. 1, p. 89 (on Qur'ān 2:136); M. J. Kister, "Do not assimilate yourselves ...", *Jerusalem Studies in Arabic and Islam* 12(1989), p. 329, note 30.
[91] Ṭabarī, *Jāmiᶜ al-bayān*, vol. 2, pp. 4–5 (on Qur'ān 2:142); Ibn Kathīr, *Tafsīr*, vol. 1, pp. 333, 338.
[92] See Ibn al-Murajjā, *Faḍā'il bayt al-maqdis*, p. 97, ll. 5–6: "The Jews were delighted when he (i.e. the Prophet) and the People of the Book prayed in the direction of Jerusalem, but when he turned his face to the direction of the Kaᶜba, they disapproved of it" (*wa kānat al-yahūd yuᶜjibuhum idh kāna* [*yuṣallī*] *qibala bayt al-maqdis wa ahla 'l-kitāb fa-lammā wallā wajhahu qibala al-bayt ankarū dhālika*). It seems that the *wāw* preceding *ahl al-kitāb* is the *wāw al-maᶜiyya.*
[93] Ibn Taymiyya, *Iqtiḍā' al-ṣirāṭ al-mustaqīm*, vol. 1, p. 88.

A comparable development is described regarding the Muslim fast. When the Prophet came to Medina, it is said that he saw the Jews fasting on the tenth of the first month (*ʿāshūrāʾ*, *yom ha-kippurim*) and imposed this fast on the Muslims as well. Later Qurʾān 2:185 was revealed, obligatory fasting during the month of Ramaḍān was imposed and *ʿāshūrāʾ* was demoted to the status of a voluntary fast.[94] Similarly, the Prophet initially wanted to call to prayer with "a horn like the horn of the Jews" (*fa-hamma rasūl Allāh ... an yajʿala būqan ka-būq al-yahūd*); then he came to dislike the idea and resolved to use a wooden board (*nāqūs*)[95] like the Christians. Finally, he instituted the call to prayer by human voice on the basis of a dream seen by the Companion ʿAbd Allah b. Zayd b. Thaʿlaba and confirmed by ʿUmar b. al-Khaṭṭāb.[96]

These traditions reflect a fairly significant effort on the part of the Prophet to attract the People of the Book in general, and the Jews of Medina in particular. This is, of course, a well known theme in scholarly discussions of early Islam, but recently published material sheds additional light on it. Muslim tradition seems to contain an early layer according to which Jews and Christians were actually considered part of the Muslim community. The Ḥanbalī jurist al-Khallāl (d. 311 A.H. / 923 A.D.)[97] opens the chapter on the non-Muslim religions in his *al-Jāmiʿ* with a scathing refutation of a tradition, which reads: "The Jews and the Christians belong to the community of Muḥammad" (*inna al-yahūd wa al-naṣārā min ummati Muḥammad*). He adduces a report by Abū Bakr al-Marwadhī,[98] who asked Ibn Ḥanbal about this *ḥadīth*. Ibn Ḥanbal became so furious that his colors changed: in his view, "this is an extremely filthy idea which should not be discussed" (*hādhihi masʾala qadhira jiddan lā yutakallamu fīhā*). He even doubted that a Muslim would stoop so low as to transmit it.[99]

Ibn Ḥanbal's righteous indignation in the third century A.H. is understandable, but it stands to reason that this rarely quoted and surprising tradition does indeed reflect a phase in the early period of Islam when the boundaries of the community were not yet clearly defined. Attempts to blur the communal boundaries are said to have been made on both sides of the future divide, and echoes of these attempts have been preserved in the Islamic tradition. In connection with Qurʾān 3:97,[100] several sources contain a report according to which the Prophet attempted to induce members of all religions to participate in the Muslim *ḥajj*, but all except the

94 Bukhārī, *Ṣaḥīḥ*, *Kitāb al-Ṣawm*, p. 69; S. Bashear, "*ʿĀshūrāʾ*, an early Muslim fast." *Zeitschrift der deutschen morgenländischen Gesellschaft* 141 (1991), pp. 281–316.

95 See "Nāḳūs", *EI²*, s.v. (F. Buhl).

96 Ibn Hishām, *al-Sīra al-nabawiyya*, Beirut 1990, vol. 2, pp. 115–116.

97 H. Laoust, "al-Khallāl", *EI²*, s.v.; Ibn Abī Yaʿlā, *Ṭabaqāt al-Ḥanābila*, Cairo: Maṭbaʿat al-sunna al-muhammadiyya, 1952, vol. 2, pp. 12–15 (no. 582); Ziāuddin Aḥmad, "Abū Bakr al-Khallāl...".

98 Abū Bakr al-Marwadhī was a prominent associate of Aḥmad b. Ḥanbal. He died in 275 A.H. See Ibn Abī Yaʿlā, *Ṭabaqāt al-Ḥanābila*, vol. 1, pp. 56–63 (no. 50).

99 Khallāl, *Ahl al-milal*, pp. 53–57; Ibn Ḥanbal, *Masāʾil*, vol. 3, p. 206 (no. 1658).

100 "...It is a duty of all men towards God to come to the House a pilgrim, if he is able to make his way there..."

Muslims refused.[101] According to a frequently quoted tradition, the Jews reacted to Qur'ān 3:85, which reproaches "those who seek a religion other than Islam", by saying: "We are Muslims" (*fa-naḥnu muslimūn*).[102] The *ḥadīth* which aroused Ibn Ḥanbal's indignation should be read in conjunction with the extensive discussion of the so-called "Constitution of Medina" (*ᶜahd al-umma*). In that document, certain Jewish groups are recognized as "a community belonging to the believers" (*ummatun min al-mu'minīn*),[103] though their connection with the Prophet himself is left unspecified. If we take into account that even the less explicit formulation of the "Constitution" needed tortuous explanations in later periods,[104] we can easily understand the indignation of Aḥmad b. Ḥanbal at the extremely explicit wording of our *ḥadīth*.

The issue also seems relevant to the development "from believers to Muslims" which Donner has recently suggested as a way to interpret the emergence of the early Muslim community. In a tentative manner, Donner takes the position that the early community led by Muḥammad was a community of "believers" in one God which may have included some Jews and Christians. At this stage, the first half of the *shahāda*, attesting to the non-existence of deities other than Allah, faithfully represented the essential beliefs of Muḥammad's followers. Only later they were transformed into a *Muslim* community which excluded Jews and Christians, added the second half of the *shahāda* and placed great stress on the unequivocal acknowledgment of Muḥammad's prophethood. Donner dates the second stage of this development to the third quarter of the first century A.H.[105] This seems much too late. It is unlikely that the inclusion of some Jews and Christians in the community of believers (or, even, in the "community of Muḥammad") could have survived the decision to expel the Jews from Medina and the exclusion from Islam of the seemingly Jewish elements discussed above. The late Qur'ānic verse enjoining military struggle against the People of the Book (Qur'ān 9:29) also speaks against Donner's late dating of the crystallization of Islam as an exclusive, confessional community. While Donner's perception of a process transforming "believers to Muslims" seems acceptable in principle, it is, I think, preferable to fix the date of the change in the later years of the Prophet in Medina. This is the period when the transformation of Islam into a totally independent faith and its disengagement from the former religions took place.

[101] Saᶜīd b. Manṣūr, *Sunan*, vol. 3, p. 1074 (no. 515); Ṭabarī, *Jāmiᶜ al-bayān*, vol. vol. 4, p. 46.

[102] See Saᶜīd b. Manṣūr, *Sunan*, vol. 3, p. 1063 (no. 506) and the numerous places mentioned by the editor.

[103] See U. Rubin, "The Constitution of Medina", *Studia Islamica* 62 (1985), pp. 5–23 and the sources mentioned there.

[104] See U. Rubin, "'The Constitution of Medina'", especially pp. 19–20.

[105] See Fred M. Donner, "From believers to Muslims: confessional self-identity in the early Islamic community", in Lawrence I. Conrad, ed., *Studies in late antiquity and early Islam, IV: Patterns of communal identity*, Princeton: Darwin Press, forthcoming. I wish to thank Professor Donner for placing a preprint of his paper at my disposal. See also M. J. Kister, "... illā bi-ḥaqqihi ..." and my "Conditions of conversion in early Islam.", in A. Destro, and M. Pesce, eds., *Ritual and ethics: patterns of repentance*. Larnham, MD: University Press of America, 2003, pp. 63–83, in press.

V

With the gradual but speedy disengagement of Islam from Judaism and Christianity, described in the previous section, the demarcation lines between the various religions became sharp and unmistakable. The dichotomy of belief versus infidelity and of believers versus unbelievers progressively became a major theme in the Muslim scripture. Since the early stages of their history, Muslims have come to believe earnestly that Islam was the only true religion. It is the (or, perhaps, *the*) religion in the eyes of God who made it complete and gave it His approval.[106] It is therefore only natural that those who embraced it are superior to those who did not. The Muslims possess positive characteristics: they believe in Allah as the only, omnipotent God, who has no partner; they recognize the crucial role of Muḥammad, the Seal of the Prophets, in the spiritual history of mankind; they observe the commandments promulgated in the Qur᾽ān, behave according to the prophetic *sunna* and abide by the moral precepts of Islām. The infidels, on the other hand, deny the divine message, obstinately adhere to false beliefs and are steeped in moral depravity.[107] In contradistinction to the verses that we have quoted when describing the Prophet's overtures to the non-Muslims in the early Medinese period,[108] the Qur᾽ān now adopts a harsh tone. It now becomes only natural that humiliation should be inflicted on the People of the Book as a punishment for their obduracy. Islam was, of course, not alone in espousing such attitudes; they were part of what von Grunebaum called "the mood of (medieval) times", when "each civilization was convinced of its spiritual superiority, of possessing the unadulterated truth ..."[109]

The stellar qualities and upright behavior of the Muslims reflect on the nature of their religion and justify the Qur᾽ānic choice of the Muslims as "the best community ever brought forth to mankind."[110] In other Qur᾽ānic verses, the Muslims are explicitly described as exalted above others. In one verse, their exaltedness is a corollary of the Muslims' belief (*lā tahinū wa lā taḥzanū wa antum al-aᶜlawna in kuntum mu᾽minīn*);[111] in another, it is seen as a reason because of which Muslims should not be feeble or call for peace (*fa-lā tahinū wa tadᶜū ilā al-salm wa antum al-aᶜlawna* ...).[112] The purpose of Muḥammad's mission is described, in three essentially identical Qur᾽ānic verses, to make the true religion "prevail over all religion."[113] Conversely, humiliation and misery are inflicted on the unbelievers.[114]

106 Qur᾽ān 3:19, 5:3.

107 For an exhaustive analysis of this theme, see T. Izutsu, *Ethico-religious concepts in the Qur᾽ān*, Montreal: McGill University Press, 1966.

108 See above, note 83.

109 G. E. von Grunebaum, *Medieval Islam. A study in cultural orientation*. Chicago: University of Chicago Press, 1953, p. 7. See also above, Introduction, at notes 33–37.

110 Qur᾽ān 3:110. For an analysis of this idea and its connection to Muslim polemic against Judaism and Christianity, see Ben Shammai, "Raᶜyon ha-behira ...", *passim*.

111 Qur᾽ān 3:139 112 Qur᾽ān 47:35.

113 Qur᾽ān 9:33, 48:28, 61:9.

114 Qur᾽ān 2:61; 3:112; 9:29.

In the prophetic tradition and in the books of law, the motif of Muslim exaltedness gains an even more prominent position. The principle is expressed in the statement "Islam is exalted and nothing is exalted above it" (*al-Islām yaʿlū wa lā yuʿlā*),[115] and has ramifications in numerous fields of Muslim thought and practice. As we shall see later, it is the main reason for prohibiting Muslim women from wedding infidel husbands.[116] Those early traditionists who maintain (as a minority opinion) that unbelievers cannot inherit from Muslims but Muslims can inherit from unbelievers use a similar argumentation.[117] Ibn Rushd says that this group saw affinity between the laws of interfaith inheritance and interfaith marriages: "As we are allowed to marry their women but we are not allowed to give them our women in marriage – the same is the case with inheritance" (*wa shabbahū dhālika bi-nisāʾihim fa-qālū: kamā yajūzu lanā an nankiḥa nisāʾahum wa lā yajūzu lanā an nunkiḥahum nisāʾanā – ka-dhālika al-irth*).[118] When a Jew died, was survived by a Muslim brother of his and the question of inheritance was brought before Muʿādh b. Jabal, Muʿādh ruled that the Muslim should receive his Jewish brother's inheritance according to the purported prophetic dictum saying that "Islam increases" (*inna al-islām yazīdu*).[119]

The *al-islām yaʿlū ... ḥadīth* is also considered the reason substantiating the principle that non-Muslims' testimony is not admissible against Muslims, but the testimony of Muslims is valid against members of all religions.[120] Discussing the rules of testimony included in Qurʾān 2:282 and Qurʾān 65:2, al-Zarkashī says that "an unbeliever is not a person whose testimony is legally admissible" (*wa al-kāfir laysa bi-dhī ʿadlin*).[121] Even if an unbeliever is the only person who can provide evidence necessary for the adjudication of a certain event, the admissibility of his testimony is not generally accepted. According to Mālikī views as described in Saḥnūn's *Mudawwana*, the testimony of an unbeliever is not accepted even in such cases. For instance, if a Muslim died on a journey in the company of unbelievers

[115] Bukhārī, *Ṣaḥīḥ, Kitāb al-janāʾiz 80* (ed. Krehl, vol. 1, pp. 337–338). A variant version adds *ʿalayhi* at the end; see Rūyānī, *Musnad*, vol. 2, p. 37. Another version reads *al-islām yaẓharu wa lā yuẓharu ʿalayhi*; see Ibn ʿAbd al-Barr al-Namarī, *al-Tamhīd*, vol. 2, p. 22.

[116] See below, Chapter Five, section I.

[117] Ṣanʿānī, *Muṣannaf*, vol. 6, p. 106 (nos. 10144–10145); vol. 10, p. 339 (nos. 19294–19295); Khallāl, *Ahl al-milal*, pp. 502 (no. 1254), 523 (no. 1325); Khaṭṭābī, *Aʿlām al-ḥadīth*, vol. 4, p. 2295; *Fiqh Saʿīd b. al-Musayyab*, vol. 3, pp. 161–162; Ibn ʿAbd al-Barr al-Namarī, *Tamhīd*, vol. 9, p. 163; Cf. Shāshī, *Musnad*, vol. 3, pp. 275–276 (from the *musnad* attributed to Muʿādh b. Jabal).

[118] Ibn Rushd, *Bidāyat al-mujtahid*, Beirut: Dār al-fikr, vol. 2, p. 264 (*Maktabat al-fiqh wa uṣūlihi*, CD ROM edition, Turāth Company, ʿAmmān 1999). Cf. below, Chapter Five.

[119] Wakīʿ, *Akhbār al-quḍāt*, vol. 1, p. 99.

[120] Sarakhsī, *Mabsūṭ*, vol. 16, pp. 133–134; cf. Ṣanʿānī, *Muṣannaf*, vol. 6, p. 129 (no. 10229); vol. 8, pp. 356–357 (nos. 15525, 15529), pp. 358–359 (no. 15535); Saḥnūn, *al-Mudawwana al-kubra* vol. 5, p. 157, l. 12; Wakīʿ, *Akhbār al-quḍāt*, vol. 2, p. 256. It is noteworthy, however, that this principle is not universally accepted. According to some traditionists, when Qurʾān 5:109 speaks of witnesses eligible to testify on bequests and mentions "two men of equity among you or two others from another folk' (*dhawā ʿadlin minkum aw ākharāni min ghayrikum*), it means by "another folk" members of another religion, or People of the Book. See Ṭabarī, *Jāmiʿ al-bayān*, vol. 7, pp. 103–107; Ṣanʿānī, *Muṣannaf*, vol. 8, p. 360 (no. 15540); Jaṣṣāṣ, *Mukhtaṣar ikhtilāf al-ʿulamāʾ*, vol. 3, pp. 339–340 (no. 1470).

[121] Zarkashī, *Sharḥ* ... vol. 7, p. 324.

only, their testimony concerning the question whether the deceased made a bequest or not would not be accepted. Allowing the Muslim's bequest to lapse is apparently preferable to the acceptance of the testimony of his non-Muslim travel companions.[122] The Ḥanbalīs maintain, on the other hand, that this is an exceptional case in which a *kitābī* unbeliever's testimony is admissible. Qur᾿ān 5:106[123] is quoted in substantiation of this view.[124]

Certain rules concerning non-Muslim participation in *jihād* – a disputed issue in Muslim law and tradition – also reflect the idea of Muslim exaltedness. In some traditions, the Prophet is reported to have rejected the idea to seek assistance from a polytheist, or to receive help from one group of polytheists against another (…*fa-lā nastaᶜīnu bi-'l-mushrikīn ᶜalā 'l-mushrikīn*). These utterances are presented as the Prophet's response to requests by polytheists to join him in battle and thereby earn entitlement to a share in the spoils; they have no direct relevance to the question at hand.[125] Elsewhere the Prophet is reported to have received assistance from a group of Jews in his wars and is said to have given them an equal share of the booty. This egalitarian tradition was adopted as a legal norm by al-Awzāᶜī, al-Zuhrī, Aḥmad b. Ḥanbal (according to one report), Sufyān al-Thawrī, Isḥāq b. Rāhwayhi and "people on the frontier and people who were knowledgeable about major military expeditions" (*ahl al-thughūr wa ahl al-ᶜilm bi-'l-ṣawā᾿if wa al-buᶜūth*).[126] However, a sizeable segment of legal opinion stipulated that assistance from non-Muslims may be sought only if they are subject to the law of Islam (*idhā kāna ḥukm al-islām huwa al-ẓāhir ᶜalayhim*) and fight under its flag. If they are in such a subordinate position, it is not forbidden to seek their help because it is like seeking help from dogs. On the other hand, help may not be sought from non-Muslims who are independent. Hence, during the battle of Uḥud, the Prophet refused to cooperate with an autonomous (*kānū ahla manᶜatin, kānū mutaᶜazzizīna fī anfusihim*) Jewish group, rejecting the idea of getting assistance from non-Muslims.[127] Abū Ḥanīfa, (Sufyān) al-Thawrī, al-Awzāᶜī, Mālik b. Anas and al-Shāfiᶜī are reported to have allowed using one group of polytheists in fighting other polytheists only if they are employed in menial jobs (*illā an yakūnū*

[122] Saḥnūn, *al-Mudawwana al-kubrā*, vol. 5, pp. 156–157.

[123] "O believers, the testimony between you when any of you is visited by death, at the bequeathing, shall be two men of equity among you; *or two others from another folk …*"

[124] Ibn Ḥanbal, *Masā᾿il*, vol. 1, p. 218 (no. 793; but on p. 219 Ḥasan al-Baṣrī is quoted as disallowing the testimony of scriptuaries in any circumstances); Zarkashī, *Sharḥ* … vol. 7, pp. 324, 338, 341. See also ibid., pp. 339–340 and Wakīᶜ, *Akhbār al-quḍāt*, vol. 1, 286–287 for an episode in which Abū Mūsā al-Ashᶜarī acted according to this rule; cf. ibid., vol. 1, pp. 281.

[125] See Ibn Ḥanbal, *Musnad*, vol. 6, p. 149; vol. 3, p. 454; Dārimī, *Sunan*, vol. 2, p. 151 (*Kitāb al-siyar* 54) and further references in Wensinck, *Concordance*, s.v. *ᶜ-w-n* (vol. 4, p. 443, infra).

[126] Ibn Qudāma, *Mughnī*, vol. 8, p. 414, supra; Ṣanᶜānī, *Muṣannaf*, vol. 5, pp. 188–189 (nos. 9328–9330); Ibn Ḥazm, *Muḥallā*, vol. 7, p. 391; Ibn ᶜAbd al-Barr al-Namarī, *al-Tamhīd*, vol. 12, p. 37; Zarkashī, *Sharḥ*…, vol. 6, pp. 497–498; Cf. Shāfiᶜī, *Kitāb al-umm*, vol. 4, pp. 372–373. This view is relevant to the *ᶜahd al-umma*; see Rubin, "The Constitution of Medina", *Studia Islamica* 52 (1985), p. 12, note 35.

[127] Sarakhsī, *Sharḥ kitāb al-siyar al-kabīr*, vol. 4, pp. 1422–1423 (no. 2751); idem, *Mabsūṭ*, vol. 10, p. 24, ll. 4–5.

khadaman wa nawātiya).[128] According to the view of Abū Ḥanīfa, Mālik b. Anas, al-Shāfiᶜī and a second view attributed to Aḥmad b. Ḥanbal – a non-Muslim warrior does not receive a regular share of the spoils, but only a small ex-gratia payment (*lā yushamu lahu bal yurḍaḥu lahu*),[129] or no payment at all.[130]

Islamic exaltedness is a well known leitmotif in the *sharᶜī* injunctions concerning the *dhimmī*s: they are not to build houses higher than those built by the Muslim; they are denied the privilege of riding horses because of the height and respectability of these animals; they are not to be appointed to positions in which they would hold authority over the affairs of Muslims.[131] On the other hand, it is permissible to show friendliness to a *dhimmī* by visiting him when he is sick, though some sources specify that Islam must be offered to him on such an occasion.[132] While non-Muslim religious worship was allowed, worshipers were obliged to keep a low profile, not to pray loudly, not to display their religious symbols in the open and to behave in all matters in an inconspicuous, subdued manner. In general, they must at all times behave toward the Muslims with a deference reflecting their lowly station in society. Reading the relevant material in the Muslim sources, one has frequently the impression that the humiliation of the unbeliever is more important than his conversion.[133]

Conversely, the Muslims are required not to place themselves, or the symbols of their religion, in a position of inferiority. In keeping with this principle, the Prophet is reported to have prohibited the carrying of the Qurᵓān by small military units into enemy territory, for fear that the infidels would treat it with contempt. According to some, the prohibition does not apply to a big army, because then the danger of humiliation does not exist.[134] The fourteenth-century Mālikī scholar Ibn al-Ḥājj al-ᶜAbdarī used the *al-islām yaᶜlū wa lā yuᶜlā ᶜalayhi* tradition to

[128] See Ibn ᶜAbd al-Barr al-Namarī, *Tamhīd*, vol. 12, p. 36; Khallāl, *Ahl al-milal*, pp. 317–319 (nos. 663–670); Ibn Qudāma, *Mughnī*, vol. 8, pp. 414 supra, 415, l. 12. Zarkashī, *Sharḥ* ..., vol. 6, pp. 497–498.

Nawātiya (sg. *nūtī*) means "sailors." The sailors were considered the lowest ranking soldiers in Muslim armies and the term is used here in a pejorative sense. See D. Ayalon, "The Mamlūks and naval power. A phase of the struggle between Islam and Christian Europe", *Princeton Near East Paper 20*, section I (no pagination); see also "Baḥriyya", (*EI*², vol. 1, p. 946a) where Ayalon mentions that *usṭūlī*, "a man of the navy", was an insult in the Ayyūbid and Mamlūk periods.

[129] Zarkashī, *Sharḥ* ..., vol. 6, pp. 497–498 (no. 3384); Ibn Qudāma, *Mughnī*, vol. 8, p. 414, ll. 4–6.

[130] Sarakhsī adduces a rare tradition according to which the Prophet availed himself of the assistance of Banū Qaynuqāᶜ against Banū Qurayẓa, but did not give them any share of the spoils. See Sarakhsī, *Mabsūṭ*, vol. 10, p. 23, ll. 17–19; cf. This was also the view of Ibn Ḥazm; see *Muḥallā*, vol. 7, p. 391.

[131] Khallāl, *Ahl al-milal*, p. 195 (no. 331) and numerous places in the standard works on the *dhimmī*s.

[132] Khallāl, *Ahl al-milal*, pp. 291–293.

[133] The ways in which Muslim law provided for the humiliation of non-Muslim inhabitants of the Muslim state have been discussed extensively and we can keep our treatment of this subject brief. The best single medieval source for these matters is Ibn Qayyim al-Jawziyya's *Aḥkām ahl al-dhimma*. In modern research, a substantial amount of relevant material can be found in Tritton, *The caliphs and their non-Muslim subjects*, in Fattal, *Le statut légal des non-musulmans en pays d'Islam* and in Lewis, *The Jews of Islam*.

[134] Ibn Abī Zayd al-Qayrawānī, *Kitāb al-jihād*, p. 27; Ibn ᶜAbd al-Barr al-Namarī, *al-Tamhīd*, vol. 15, pp. 253; Sarakhsī, *Mabsūṭ*, vol. 10, p. 29, ll. 10–15;

substantiate his opposition to Muslims traveling to infidel territory where they would be placed in a subordinate position.[135] Iyās b. Muᶜāwiya, the *qāḍī* of Baṣra during the reign of ᶜUmar b. ᶜAbd al-ᶜAzīz (d. 121 A.H. / 739 A.D.),[136] is reported to have opposed travel to infidel territory to such an extent that he deprived merchants who traveled to India or traded in Persian villages of the right to give testimony in court: these merchants compromised their religion and integrity by placing themselves in an inferior situation vis-à-vis the unbelievers and by taking interest from their Zoroastrian business partners (*ammā 'lladhīna yarkabūna al-baḥr fa-innahum yarkabūna ilā al-hind ḥattā yugharrara bi-dīnihim wa yumakkinū ᶜaduwwahum minhum min ajl ṭamaᶜ al-dunyā … wa ammā 'lladhīna yatjurūna fī qurā Fāris fa-inna al-majūs yuṭᶜimūnahum al-ribā … fa-abaytu ujīzu shahādatahum li-ajl al-ribā…*).[137]

In addition to the unquestionable exaltedness of Islam, in some sources a hierarchy between the non-Muslim religions can also be discerned. A discussion of such a hierarchy can be found in Ibn Qayyim al-Jawziyya whose *Aḥkām ahl-al-dhimma* is probably the single most comprehensive medieval work on the law applicable to the *dhimmī*s. In his perception, Islam is followed, in descending order, by Christianity, Judaism, Zoroastrianism and polytheism. In assigning to each community its proper place in this hierarchy, the number of prophets in which it believes is an important consideration. As is well known from Islamic prophetology, the number of prophets who were sent by Allah to deliver the divine message is enormous and only Muslims believe in them all: starting with Adam, the first prophet, and culminating with Muḥammad who brought the prophetic missions to a close.[138] According to Ibn Qayyim al-Jawziyya's understanding, Christianity is second to Islam in the hierarchy of religions. It is considered better than Judaism because Christians believe in both Moses and Jesus, while Jews do not include Jesus in their list of prophets. Al-Sarakhsī contends, on the other hand, that monotheistic Judaism is better than Christianity which believes in the trinity.[139] According to all views, the Zoroastrians are one rung lower on the ladder than the Jews,[140] because they do not believe in any prophet mentioned in the Qurᵓān and according to most early jurists do not have a revealed book.[141] The superiority of the Christian People of the Book over the Zoroastrians was the reason because of which the Muslims rejoiced at the Byzantine victory over the Persians,

135 Ibn al-Ḥājj, *Mudkhal*, vol. 3, p. 105.

136 See "Iyās b. Muᶜāwiya", *EI*², s.v. (Ch. Pellat).

137 Wakīᶜ, Akhbār al-quḍāt, vol. 1, p. 359.

138 See Friedmann, *Prophecy continuous*, pp. 50ff.

139 Sarakhsī, *Mabsūṭ*, vol. 5, 48, ll. 10–13.

140 See, for instance, Sarakhsī, *Mabsūṭ*, vol. 5, p. 44, line 14: … *li-anna al-yahūdiyya idhā qūbilat bi-'l-majūsiyya fa-'l-majūsiyya sharr* …. While speaking about a scriptuary who converted to Zoroastrianism, Ibn Qudāma maintains that this conversion cannot be allowed to stand, because the scriptuary in question "moved to a religion inferior to his (previous) one" (… *li-annahu intaqala ilā anqaṣa min dīnihi*). See *Mughnī*, vol. 6, p. 593, ll. 10–11.

141 See below, Chapter Two, section IV.

mentioned in Qurʾān 30:3–4.[142] The lowest of all are the *mushrikūn*, who not only disbelieve in the prophets, but also worship deities in addition to Allah.[143]

VI

We have indicated that the idea of Muslim exaltedness is the background for numerous *sharʿī* regulations concerning the *dhimmīs*. Many of these have been extensively discussed in scholarly literature and we have therefore referred to them only briefly. A relevant issue that has not received the attention it deserves is the reflection of Islamic exaltedness in laws concerning retaliation and blood-money.

Discussions of *lex talionis* (*qiṣāṣ*) and of blood-money (*diya*) provide Muslim traditionists and jurisprudents with ample opportunity to express their views on the hierarchy of religions. In contradistinction to the material covered in the previous section, here we have no unanimity of opinion among the *madhāhib*. While three schools of law maintain that the inferiority of the unbeliever should be a decisive factor in determining the law regarding the questions at hand, the Ḥanafīs provide a cogent argument supporting the *dhimmīs*' equality with respect to the laws of *qiṣāṣ* and the payment of blood-money.[144]

The Qurʾānic *lex talionis* is phrased in two fashions which gave rise to two different interpretations of the law when the slain person is a non-Muslim. Sūra 2:178 reads: "O those who believe! The law of retaliation was prescribed to you concerning slain persons: the free for the free, the slave for the slave, the woman for the woman ..." On the other hand, Sūra 5:45 reads: "We prescribed therein for them (i.e., in the Tawrāt for the Children of Israel): life for life (*al-nafs bi-'l-nafs*), eye for eye, nose for nose, ear for ear, tooth for tooth ..." The former verse stipulates that retaliation should be directed against a person whose social status is comparable to that of the slain one, while the latter seems to disregard the social standing of the persons involved. We shall see later how this difference was used with respect to the question at hand. Qurʾān 5:45 is problematic also from another point of view: since the law included in it is described as having been imposed on the Children of Israel, some jurists assert that it is not valid for the Muslims.

The *ḥadīth* literature also addresses the issue. One of the traditions which the Prophet is reported to have confided to ʿAlī b. Abī Ṭālib reads:

> The blood of the believers is equal, the lowliest of them can promise protection on their behalf, and they are all united against the others. Verily, a believer is not to be killed for (killing) an unbeliever and he who has an agreement (with the Muslims) shall not be

[142] Ṭabarī, *Jāmiʿ al-bayān*, vol. 21, pp. 16–18.

[143] Ibn Qayyim al-Jawziyya, *Aḥkām ahl al-dhimma*, pp. 394–397.

[144] R. Peters is apparently unaware of this variety of legal opinion when he states that "Non-Muslim lawful residents in the Abode of Islam do enjoy protection of life, property and freedom." This statement needs to be qualified in view of the discussion that follows. See Peters, "Islamic law and human rights: a contribution to an ongoing debate", in *Islam and Christian-Muslim relations* 10 (1999), p. 9.

killed while the agreement is in force (*al-muʾminūna tatakāfaʾu dimāʾuhum wa yasʿā bi-dhimmatihim adnāhum wa hum yadun ʿalā man siwāhum; alā lā yuqtalu muʾminun* (or *muslimun*) *bi-kāfirin wa lā dhū ʿahdin fī ʿahdihi*).[145]

In a speech which the Prophet is reported to have delivered after his takeover of Mecca in 630 A.D., he said:

The Muslims are united against the others, their lives are equal ..., a believer is not to be killed for (the killing of) an unbeliever, and the blood-money of an unbeliever is half that of a Muslim ...(*al-muslimūn yadun ʿalā man siwāhum tatakāfaʾu dimāʾuhum ... lā yuqtalu muʾminun bi-kāfirin diyat al-kāfir niṣf diyat al-muslim*).[146]

On the other hand, some of the earliest collections of *ḥadīth* preserved a tradition according to which the Prophet ordered the execution of a Muslim who had killed a *dhimmī*, saying that "it is most appropriate that I live up fully to my (promise of) protection" (*anā aḥaqqu* [or *awlā*] *man waffā bi-dhimmatī* [or *bi-dhimmatihi*]).[147]

[145] Ibn Ḥanbal, *Musnad*, vol. 1, pp. 119, 122; Ṣanʿānī, *Muṣannaf*, vol. 10, pp. 98–99 (nos. 18502–18510); Abū Dāwūd, *Sunan, Kitāb al-jihād* 147 (ed. 1972, vol. 3, p. 185); Bukhārī, *Ṣaḥīḥ, Kitāb al-diyāt* 31 (vol. 4, pp. 326–327); Ibn Māja, *Sunan, Kitāb al-diyāt* 21 (ed. 1349, vol. 2, p. 145); Nasāʾī, *Sunan, Kitāb al-qasāma*, ed. 1988, vol. 3, p. 984; Tirmidhī, *Ṣaḥīḥ*, vol. 6, pp. 180–181; Dāraquṭnī, *Sunan*, vol. 3, p. 131 (no. 155); Bayhaqī, *Sunan*, vol. 8, pp. 28–30 (also: *lā yuqtalu muʾminun bi-mushrikin*); Wensinck, *Concordance*. vol. 5, p. 282a.

According to some commentators, Qurʾān 17:33 is also relevant to this issue when it says that the heir of a wrongfully slain person is given authority (to demand retaliation), but "he should not exceed the bounds in killing" (*fa-lā yusrifu fī al-qatl*). Taking the life of a Muslim for killing an unbeliever is deemed excessive; see Muqriʾ, *al-Nāsikh wa al-mansūkh*, p. 39.

[146] Ibn Ḥanbal, *Musnad*, vol. 2, pp. 180 infra, 192, 211, 215; Ṣanʿānī, *Muṣannaf*, vol. 10, pp. 92–95 (nos. 18473–18490); Tirmidhī, *Ṣaḥīḥ*, vol. 6, p. 182. A similar formulation can be found in the "Constitution of Medina": "A believer shall not kill a believer because of (his killing of) an unbeliever" (*lā yaqtulu muʾmimun muʾminan fī kāfirin*). See Abū ʿUbayd, *Kitāb al-amwāl*, p. 203, and R. B. Serjeant, "The *Sunna Jāmiʿah*, pacts with the Yathrib Jews and the *taḥrīm* of Yathrib", *BSOAS* 41 (1978), p. 17. In some traditions, the *diya* of the unbeliever is one third of the full amount, and its payment is coupled with temporary banishment of the culprit from his tribal territory.

[147] Ṣanʿānī, *Muṣannaf*, vol. 10, p. 101 (no. 18514); Abū Dāwūd, *Marāsīl*, pp. 207–208 (nos. 250–251); Yaḥyā b. Ādam, *Kitāb al-kharāj*, p. 110 (no. 238); Dāraquṭnī, *Sunan*, vol. 3, pp. 134–135 (nos. 165–167); Khallāl, *Ahl al-milal*, pp. 399–400 (no. 908). The following *ḥadīth* (p. 400, no. 909) changes the significance of the story completely by saying that it concerned the killing of a *dhimmī* by another *dhimmī*.

Most sources used here do not mention the name of the Muslim in question. Al-Māwardī (*al-Ḥāwī al-kabīr*, vol. 12, p. 10) observes that it was ʿAmr b. Umayya. This identification makes the whole story problematic. ʿAmr b. Umayya al-Ḍamrī was a Companion. He was close to the Prophet and was sent by him on several important missions. However, the historical and biographical literature does not mention that he was executed by Muḥammad for killing a *dhimmī*; on the contrary, we read that he died a natural death during the reign of Muʿāwiya. See Ibn Saʿd, *Kitāb al-ṭabaqāt al-kabīr*, vol. 4, pp. 182–183; Bukhārī, *al-Taʾrīkh al-kabīr*, vol. 3, part 2, pp. 307–308; Ṭabarī, *Taʾrīkh al-rusul wa al-mulūk*, index; Ibn al-Athīr, *Usd al-ghāba*, Cairo: al-Maktaba al-Islāmiyya, 1863–1865, vol. 4, p. 86; Ibn ʿAsākir, *Taʾrīkh madīnat Dimashq*, Beirut: Dār al-fikr, 1996, vol. 45, pp. 418–431 (no. 5314); Mizzī, *Tahdhīb al-kamāl*, vol. 21, pp. 545–547 (no. 4328); ʿAsqalānī, *Iṣāba*, vol. 4, 602–603; ʿAsqalānī, *Tahdhīb al-tahdhīb*, Beirut: Dār al-fikr, 1984–1988, vol. 8, p. 6; Kister, "O God, tighten thy grip on Muḍar...", at pp. 251, 257, 261–264. Al-Baghawī (*Sharḥ al-sunna*, vol. 6, pp. 129–130), who mentions ʿAmr b. Umayya al-Ḍamrī's full name (including the *nisba*), uses this discrepancy in order to discredit our tradition in its entirety. The same attitude is adopted by ʿAynī, *ʿUmdat al-qārī*, vol. 2, p. 161, ll. 25–26. It is of course possible that ʿAmr b. Umayya mentioned in the biographical literature was not the same man as his namesake whose execution for killing a *dhimmī* is said to have been mandated by the Prophet.

He is also is reported to have said that "whoever kills someone who has a contract (with the Muslims), will not smell the scent of Paradise" (*man qatala nafsan muᶜāhadan lam yariḥ rāʾiḥat al-janna*), and this has been taken to mean that killing a *dhimmī* should be avenged.[148] In a similar vein, we have a number of traditions in which the Prophet fixed the *diya* payable to the relatives of a slain *dhimmī* at 1000 dīnār, which is the full amount.[149] One of the most important of these traditions, which allows us to interpet the existence of disparate reports concerning the amount of blood-money payable for the slaying of a *dhimmī* as a result of historical development, is reported by ᶜAbd al-Razzāq al-Ṣanᶜānī on the authority of Maᶜmar and al-Zuhrī. According to this tradition, the *diya* for slaying a Jew, a Christian or a Zoroastrian was equal to that of a Muslim until the days of ᶜUthmān. Muᶜāwiya did not change the law, but left only half the *diya* in the hands of the slain *dhimmī*'s relatives, and appropriated the other half for the public treasury. It was the Umayyad caliph ᶜUmar b. ᶜAbd al-ᶜAzīz who reduced the *diya* of a *dhimmī* to one half. He also annulled the appropriation for the treasury, considering it unjust.[150]

These verses and traditions are the principal source material used in the debate concerning the question whether a Muslim ought to be killed in retaliation for killing an infidel. The Ḥanafīs answer this question in the affirmative as far as the *dhimmī*s are concerned.[151] Their view is based on episodes from early Islamic history, on the non-restrictive phrasing of some relevant verses and traditions, as well as on an extensive analysis of the reasons for instituting the law of *qiṣāṣ*.

The most general argument of the Ḥanafīs is based on the statement in Qurʾān 2:179: "In retaliation there is life for you ..." This verse clarifies that the purpose of retaliation is the preservation of human life; once the *dhimmī*'s life was made inviolable by the *dhimma* contract, he deserves to be protected by the mechanism of *qiṣāṣ*. The *ḥadīth* according to which the lives of the Muslims are equal to each other does not mean that they are not equal to the lives of the *dhimmī*s.[152] Al-Jaṣṣāṣ mentions the famous tradition about the three reasons because of which a Muslim's life may be taken: one of them is intentional killing, punished by retaliation (... *aw qatala ᶜamdan fa-ᶜalayhi al-qawad*).[153] The tradition does not

148 Bukhārī, *Ṣaḥīḥ, Kitāb al-diyāt* 30 (ed. Krehl, vol. 4, p. 326); Ṣanᶜānī, *Muṣannaf*, vol. 10, p. 102 (nos. 18521–18522).

149 Abū Dāwūd, *Marāsīl*, p. 215 (no. 264). For similar traditions, attributed to the Prophet's companions and other persons of the first century, see Ṣanᶜānī, *Muṣannaf*, vol. 10, pp. 95–98 (nos. 18491–18501).

150 Ṣanᶜānī, *Muṣannaf*, vol. 10, pp. 95–96 (no. 18491).

151 Al-Jaṣṣāṣ mentions the following jurists as supporters of this view: Abū Ḥanīfa, Abū Yūsuf, Muḥammad (b. al-Ḥasan al-Shaybānī), Zufar, Ibn Abī Laylā and ᶜUthmān al-Battī. See Jaṣṣāṣ, *Aḥkām al-Qurʾān*, vol. 1, p. 163. Ibn Qudāma (*al-Mughnī*, vol. 7, p. 652) adds to the list (ᶜĀmir) al-Shaᶜbī, Ibrāhīm al-Nakhaᶜī and the *ahl al-raʾy* in general. On the other hand, ᶜAbd al-Razzāq has al-Shaᶜbī express the opposite opinion. See Ṣanᶜānī, *Muṣannaf*, vol. 9, p. 473 (nos. 18059–18060)

152 Jaṣṣāṣ, *Aḥkām al-Qurʾān*, vol. 1, pp. 167–168.

153 Nasāʾī, *Sunan*, vol. 7, p. 103. The two other reasons are illicit sexual relations of a *muḥṣan* and apostasy.

specify that the victim must be a Muslim.[154] Neither is such specification included in Qurʾān 17:33, which is also understood as referring to retaliation.[155] Both al-Jaṣṣāṣ and al-Sarakhsī relate that the Prophet himself ruled on a certain occasion that a Muslim who killed a *dhimmī* was liable to *qiṣāṣ*. Other episodes also reflect the Ḥanafī interpretation, but show that in many cases ways were devised to spare the lives of the Muslim culprits. ʿUmar is reported to have ruled that a Muslim who killed a *dhimmī* from al-Ḥīra should be killed in retaliation, but when he learned that the Muslim in question was a horseman (and therefore indispensable as a warrior), he ordered that a blood-money agreement be reached with the slain person's surviving relatives. Some traditions only maintain that ʿUmar changed his verdict, but do not mention the reason for the change or the substitution of *qiṣāṣ* by *diya*.[156] The famous case of ʿUbayd Allāh b. ʿUmar, who killed al-Hurmuzān for the latter's alleged complicity in the murder of his father ʿUmar b. al-Khaṭṭāb, ended in a similar fashion: ʿUthmān pardoned ʿUbayd Allāh and paid blood-money to al-Hurmuzān's survivors.[157] Al-Sarakhsī concludes this section of his discussion by relating another episode in which ʿAlī ruled in favor of a *dhimmī*'s right to *qiṣāṣ*, but this was once again averted by payment of *diya*. ʿAlī commented: "We gave you blood-money – while you are paying the *jizya* so that your lives and property be equal to ours" (*aʿṭaynākum al-diya wa tabdhulūna al-jizya li-takūna dimāʾukum ka-dimāʾinā wa amwālukum ka-amwālinā*).[158] ʿAlī seems to be critical of this arrangement, though this interpretation of his statement is not the only possible one.

Perhaps the most significant episode which exemplifies the Ḥanafī view of *qiṣāṣ* – but also the difficulty of putting it into practice – is connected with Abū Yūsuf (d. 182 A.H. / 798 A.D.), the *qāḍī al-quḍāt* of the early ʿAbbāsīs. It is related that Abū Yūsuf ordered *qiṣāṣ* against a Muslim who killed a *dhimmī*. Trying to save the culprit's life, his relatives approached Abū Yūsuf, lashing out at him and accusing him of the wrongful intention to kill a Muslim for killing an infidel. Abū Yūsuf decided to consult Hārūn al-Rashīd, who instructed him to find a legal loophole in order to avoid the Muslim's execution and to stave off possible public

[154] Jaṣṣāṣ, *Aḥkām al-Qurʾān*, vol. 1, p. 164 infra. Jaṣṣāṣ quotes another version of this tradition: *qatlu nafsin bi-ghayri nafsin*.

[155] "Whoever is slain unjustly, We have appointed to his next-of-kin authority; but let him not exceed in slaying …"

[156] Ṣanʿānī, *Muṣannaf*, vol. 10, p. 102 (no. 18520).

[157] Jaṣṣāṣ, *Aḥkām al-Qurʾān*, vol. 1, pp. 164–165; Shaybānī, *Kitāb al-aṣl*, vol. 4, part 2, pp. 488–491; Ṣanʿānī, *Muṣannaf*, vol. 10, p. 100 (nos. 18509–18510); Sarakhsī, *Mabsūṭ*, vol. 26, pp. 132, ll. 22–133, l. 7; Khwārizmī, *Jāmiʿ masānīd al-imām al-aʿẓam*, vol. 2, pp. 177–178. According to a tradition recorded by Khallāl (*Ahl al-milal*, p. 398), ʿUmar b. al-Khaṭṭāb reprieved the Muslim who killed the *dhimmī* from al-Ḥīra not because of his martial qualities, but because of the prophetic *ḥadīth* (*lā yuqtalu muʾminun bi-kāfirin*), which came to his attention. Bayhaqī (*Sunan*, vol. 8, p. 32) records a version according to which ʿUmar's instructions arrived after the culprit had already been put to death. A tradition in which ʿUmar b. ʿAbd al-ʿAzīz was the person who ordered *qiṣāṣ* against a Muslim who killed a *dhimmī* (and the verdict was carried out) is recorded by Ṣanʿānī, *Muṣannaf*, vol. 10, pp. 101–102 (no. 18518).

[158] Sarakhsī, *Mabsūṭ*, vol. 26, p. 133, ll. 5–8. A slightly different version of this tradition can be found in Bayhaqī, *Sunan*, vol. 8, p. 34.

commotion. Acting upon the caliph's instructions, Abū Yūsuf demanded that the relatives of the slain *dhimmī* furnish proof that he had been paying the *jizya* willingly and that his *dhimma* was therefore valid; he made this demand in view of the contention that the *dhimmī* had refused to pay his tax and this was the cause of his killing. The survivors could not provide the proof; the *qiṣāṣ* was averted and payment of *diya* was ordered instead. This is a significant example of public and governmental pressure which resulted in reversing a judicial decision and saved a Muslim from being subjected to the full rigor of the law.[159]

Let us now turn to the legal analysis of the question by the Ḥanafīs. The term *qiṣāṣ* carries the notion of equality; it is explained in the dictionaries as "doing to someone what he has done, such as killing, amputation (of limbs), beating or inflicting an injury" (... *an yafᶜala bihi mithla fiᶜlihi min qatlin aw qaṭᶜin aw ḍarbin aw jarḥ*).[160] This clearly means that the retaliatory act should be identical in nature to the injury sustained. Nevertheless, the Ḥanafīs devote their attention not only to this, but also to the question whether the notion of equality can be upheld when the culprit is a Muslim and the victim is not.

Since *qiṣāṣ* involves taking a person's life, the equality which is necessary for its imposition should relate to this element. This principle of al-Sarakhsī's legal thinking is formulated in the following manner: "*Qiṣāṣ* is based on 'equality in life', because it entails destruction of a life" (... *al-qiṣāṣ yaᶜtamidu al-musāwāt fī al-ḥayāt li-annahu izhāq al-ḥayāt*). This means that the only element which is necessary for the imposition of *qiṣāṣ* is that the life of the victim be as inviolable as the life of the culprit (*wa innamā tataḥaqqaqu al-musāwāt fī dhālika sharᶜan li-wujūd al-tasāwī fī ḥaqn al-dam*). This is clearly the situation regarding the *dhimmī*: the *dhimma* contract is a substitute for Islam as far as the protection of the *dhimmī*'s life is concerned.[161] The Qurʾānic verses that deny the equality between believers and infidels (and serve to support the view that a believer cannot be killed for killing an infidel[162]) should be understood as describing the inequality of

[159] Sarakhsī, *Mabsūṭ*, vol. 26, p. 131, ll. 15–20; Māwardī, *al-Ḥāwī al-kabīr*, vol. 12, pp. 15–16; Māwardī, *al-Aḥkām al-sulṭāniyya*, p. 304 (the editor's emendation of *ṣiḥḥat al-dhimma* to *ṣiḥḥat al-tuhma* is uncalled for; Fagnan's translation (p. 495) is also incorrect); Kardarī, *Manāqib Abī Ḥanīfa*, p. 407; Baghdādī, *Taʾrīkh Baghdād*, Cairo, Maṭbaᶜat al-saᶜāda, 1931, vol. 14, pp. 253–254. On p. 254, Baghdādī quotes a limerick written for the occasion and severely critical of Abū Yūsuf's initial verdict:

yā qātila l-muslimi bi-'l-kāfiri / jurta wa mā 'l-ᶜādilu ka-'l-jāʾiri
yā man bi-Baghdāda wa aṭrāfihā / min fuqahāʾi nnāsi aw shāᶜiri
jāra ᶜalā ddīni Abū Yūsufa / idh yaqtulu 'l-muslima bi-'l-kāfiri
fa-'starjiᶜū wa 'bkū ᶜalā dīnikum / wa 'ṣṭabirū fa-'l-ajru li-ṣṣābiri

"O killer of Muslim for an infidel! / You have done wrong and a just man differs from a wrongdoer.
O jurists and poets in Baghdād and its surroundings!
Abū Yūsuf wronged the religion / by killing a Muslim for an infidel.
Say: 'Surely we belong to God and to Him we return' (Qurʾān 2:151), weep for your religion / and be steadfast, for the steadfast are rewarded."

[160] Ibn Manẓūr, *Lisān al-ᶜarab*, s.v. *q-ṣ-ṣ* (ed. Beirut 1956, vol. 7, p. 76b).

[161] Sarakhsī, *Mabsūṭ*, vol. 26, pp. 133, l. 23 – 134, l. 1; Marghīnānī, *Hidāya*, vol. 4, pp. 1606–1607; Qurṭubī, *al-Jāmiᶜ li-aḥkām al-Qurʾān*, vol. 2, pp. 231–232.

[162] For Shāfiᶜī's argument to this effect, see Sarakhsī, *Mabsūṭ*, vol. 26, p. 131, ll. 20–22.

the two groups in the hereafter. The case is substantially the same as the case of a man killing a boy or a woman, a slave killing a free man or of a woman killing a man. All are liable to *qiṣāṣ* because their lives are equally protected (*li-wujūd al-musāwāt baynahumā fī al-ḥayāt*).[163] Elsewhere it is explained that Qur'ān 5:45 (*al-nafs bi-'l-nafs ...*) abrogated Qur'ān 2:178 (*al-ḥurr bi-'l-ḥurr ...*) and the Ḥanafīs used the phrase *al-nafs bi-'l-nafs* (which seems to disregard differences in social status between the culprit and his victim) in Qur'ān 5:45 to support their view that a Muslim is to be killed for intentionally killing a *dhimmī*.[164] As for the argument that the phrase *al-nafs bi-'l-nafs* is not binding on the Muslims because it is part of the law imposed on the Jews, the Ḥanafīs reject it by saying that if such laws are mentioned in the Qur'ān, they remain valid unless there is proof of their abrogation.[165]

The protection of a *dhimmī*'s life by the *qiṣāṣ* mechanism is a corollary of the *dhimma* contract; it is not based on the perception that all human lives are of equal value. The Ḥanafīs therefore do not extend this protection to infidels who are not *dhimmī*s. Consequently, a Muslim – or, for that matter, a *dhimmī* – is not liable to *qiṣāṣ* if he kills a *musta'min* who does not enjoy permanent protection in *dār al-islām* (*fa-'l-musta'min ghayru muḥrizin nafsahu bi-dār al-islām ᶜalā al-ta'bīd*), and may take up arms against the Muslims after his return to *dār al-ḥarb*. According to al-Sarakhsī, this is also the meaning of the prophetic tradition according to which a Muslim is not to be killed for killing an unbeliever: the unbeliever intended here is a *ḥarbī*.[166] In a similar vein, al-Jaṣṣāṣ argues that the *dhimma* contracts were made only after the takeover of Mecca in 630. Hence there were no *dhimmī*s when the Prophet uttered the sentence *lā yuqtalu mu'minun bi-kāfirin* on that occasion, and his pronouncement must have been directed to non-*dhimmī* unbelievers.[167]

The Ḥanafī scholar al-Ṭaḥāwī perceives the same meaning in the sentence *lā yuqtalu mu'minun bi-kāfirin wa lā dhū ᶜahdin fī ᶜahdihi*. In his view, this should be understood as saying that "a believer and a person having a contract (of protection) with the Muslims are not to be killed for (the killing of) an unbeliever." The unbeliever in question is a *ḥarbī* who has no contractual relationship with the Muslims and is therefore not protected by the *qiṣāṣ* mechanism like his *dhimmī* coreligionist. Despite the word-order of the text, the person having a contractual

[163] Sarakhsī, *Mabsūṭ*, vol. 26, p. 131, ll. 3–14.
[164] ᶜAynī, *ᶜUmdat al-qāri'*, vol. 24, p. 40; cf. Jaṣṣāṣ, *Aḥkām al-Qur'ān*, vol. 1, p. 164 supra.
[165] Sarakhsī, *Mabsūṭ*, vol. 26, p. 60, ll. 1–4; Sarakhsī, *Uṣūl*, vol. 2, p. 100 (the view is attributed here to Abū al-Ḥasan al-Karkhī). In Ṣanᶜānī, *Muṣannaf*, vol. 9, pp. 489–490 (no. 18134), this view is attributed also to Ibn al-Musayyab who is reported to have said concerning Qur'ān 5:45: *fa-hādhihi al-āya lanā wa lahum*; cf. ᶜAynī, *ᶜUmdat al-qārī*, vol. 2, p. 161, l. 16. See also above, section III of the present chapter.
[166] Sarakhsī, *Mabsūṭ*, vol. 26, p. 134, ll. 16ff; Marghīnānī, *Hidāya*, vol. 4, p. 160; Qudūrī, *Mukhtaṣar*, p. 184, l. 13. For an attribution of this view to Abū Ḥanīfa, see Māwardī, *al-Ḥāwī*, vol. 12, p. 11. Māwardī mentions in the same place the view of (ᶜĀmir) al-Shaᶜbī who thought that a Muslim may be killed for killing a *kitābī*, but not for killing a Zoroastrian.
[167] Jaṣṣāṣ, *Aḥkām al-Qur'ān*, vol. 1, p. 166; ᶜAynī, *ᶜUmdat al-qārī*, vol. 2, p. 162, ll. 10–16.

relationship with the Muslims should be grammatically attached (*maᶜṭūf*) to the believer; otherwise the sentence would mean that the person under Muslim protection cannot be killed (*lā yuqtalu … dhū ᶜahdin fī ᶜahdihi*) under any circumstances. This conclusion is patently absurd: evidently, a person enjoying the Muslim protection is not immune from retaliation if he kills a Muslim.[168]

Al-Shāfiᶜī adopted a diametrically opposed stance on this issue. In his view, a believer is not to be killed for killing an unbeliever under any circumstances. This rule is valid whether the killer is a free man, a slave or a woman. According to one source, some Shāfiᶜīs maintained that even an apostate from Islam is not to be killed for killing a *dhimmī*, because "the laws of Islam remain valid with respect to him, he is obliged to perform the commandments and is required to revert to Islam" (*qāla baᶜḍ aṣḥāb al-Shāfiᶜī: lā yuqtalu al-murtadd bi-'l-dhimmī … li-anna aḥkām al-islām fī ḥaqqihi bāqiya bi-dalīl wujūb al-ᶜibādāt ᶜalayhi wa muṭālabatihi bi-'l-islām*).[169] The purpose of the killing is also immaterial and the believer's immunity from retaliation is not invalidated even if he killed the unbeliever in order to take possession of his property or in the course of highway robbery.[170] On the other hand, if the robbery was not accompanied by homicide which is punishable by death, al-Shāfiᶜī seems to support the imposition of the other penalties for robbery on Muslims who robbed *dhimmī*s (… *wa idhā qaṭaᶜa al-muslimūn ᶜalā ahl al-dhimma ḥuddū ḥudūdahum law qaṭaᶜū ᶜalā al-muslimīn illā annī atawaqqafu fī an aqtulahum in qatalū aw uḍamminahum al-diya*).[171] The *ḥadīth* according to which a believer is not to be killed for killing an unbeliever is al-Shāfiᶜī's principal substantiation of his position. The punishment inflicted on a believer who killed an infidel is *taᶜzīr* and imprisonment. The *taᶜzīr* must not reach the level of a *ḥadd*, and the imprisonment must not last longer than a year. On the other hand, if an infidel kills a believer, he is to be killed whether he is a *dhimmī*, a *ḥarbī* or a *mustaʾmin*. If Allah allowed killing a believer for killing another believer, the killing of an infidel for the same offense is even more justified.[172] The principle guiding al-Shāfiᶜī in this matter was clearly formulated by al-Māwardī: retaliation is practiced against the lowly for killing the eminent,

[168] Ṭaḥāwī, *Mushkil al-āthār*, vol. 2, pp. 92–95.

[169] Shīrāzī, *Muhadhdhab*, vol. 3, p. 172; Ibn Qudāma, *al-Mughnī*, vol. 7, p. 658.

[170] This is Shāfiᶜī's view as expressed in his works (see the following note). Al-Māwardī agrees that this is Shāfiᶜī's well known (*mashhūr*) view; he points out, however, that in one place, Shāfiᶜī favored killing a Muslim who killed an infidel during a robbery, because "killing of robbers is a right of God which must be fully respected and may not be forgiven; in this case the killing of a Muslim or of an infidel is the same" (*hādhā mimmā astakhīru 'llāha fīhi an yuqtala bihi li-anna fī qatl al-ḥarrāba haqqan li-'llāhi … yajibu an yustawfā wa lā yajūzu al-ᶜafw ᶜanhu fa-'stawā fīhi qatl al-muslim wa al-kāfir*). Killing in other circumstances is "a right of man" (*ḥaqqun li-ādamī*) which may be forgiven and lapses in case of an infidel. See Māwardī, *al-Ḥāwī al-kabīr*, vol. 12, p. 16 infra.

[171] Shāfiᶜī, *Kitāb al-umm*, vol. 4, p. 419, ll. 15–16. For penalties for highway robbery which is not accompanied by homicide, see J. Schacht, *Introduction to Islamic Law*, Oxford: The Clarendon Press, 1964, pp. 180–181.

[172] Shāfiᶜī, *Kitāb al-umm*, vol. 6, p. 57; Shāfiᶜī, *Aḥkām al-Qurʾān*, vol. 1, pp. 273–275. For a similar view of Ibn Ḥazm, see *al-Muḥallā*, vol. 10, p. 427–428.

but not against the eminent for killing the lowly (*fa-yuqtaṣṣu min al-adnā bi-'l-aᶜlā wa lā yuqtaṣṣu min al-aᶜlā bi-'l-adnā*).[173] ᶜAṭāʾ al-Maqdisī, a Shāfiᶜī *faqīh* whom Ibn al-ᶜArabī al-Mālikī met in Jerusalem at the end of the eleventh century A.D., maintained that the element of equality which is inherent in the concept of *qiṣāṣ* "does not exist between a Muslim and an infidel because infidelity lowered his standing and diminished his rank" (*wa lā musāwāt bayna al-muslim wa al-kāfir fa-inna al-kufr ḥaṭṭa manzilatahu wa waḍaᶜa martabatahu*).[174] Perceiving Muslims as exalted above the infidels is, again, the conceptual basis for determining the law.

In an attempt to undermine the Ḥanafī reasoning, al-Shāfiᶜī argues that the *mustaʾmin*, for whose killing a believer may not be killed even according to the Ḥanafīs, also has a contract with the Muslims: his *amān* is materially not different from the *dhimma* contract. Addressing the Ḥanafī interpretation of *al-nafs bi-'l-nafs*, al-Shāfiᶜī points out that the verse is not to be interpreted as having general validity, because it does not cover cases where a freeman kills a slave or a man kills a woman.[175] Furthermore, Qurʾān 5:45, in which this expression appears, is seen by al-Shāfiᶜī as a law imposed on the Children of Israel and, as such, is not binding on the Muslims (*hādhā khabarun ᶜan sharᶜi man qablanā wa sharᶜu man qablanā laysa sharᶜan lanā*). Another argument leading to the same conclusion is that since the Children of Israel were a homogeneous community and had no *dhimmī*s, the retaliation mentioned in the verse must have been intended to cover murders within their community only. Therefore, even if the verse is valid for the Muslims, it relates, by analogy, only to murders within the Muslim community.[176] As for the traditions alleging that the Prophet himself ordered the killing of a Muslim in retaliation for killing an infidel, the Shāfiᶜīs maintain that these traditions were related by unreliable transmitters and cannot be trusted.[177]

The Ḥanbalīs thought along similar lines and shuddered at the idea that a non-Muslim would be treated equally to a Muslim in this matter, in glaring disregard of the prophetic *ḥadīth* to the contrary. In their view, the *dhimmī*'s life is not permanently protected and resembles that of a *ḥarbī*. If, however, the *dhimmī* is killed by another *dhimmī*, the killer is liable to *qiṣāṣ*.[178] According to Ibn Ḥanbal,

173 Māwardī, *al-Ḥāwī al-kabīr*, vol. 12, p. 11. See also Māwardī, *al-Aḥkām al-sulṭāniyya*, p. 303; Shīrāzī, *Muhadhdhab*, vol. 3, p. 171.

174 Ibn al-ᶜArabī, *Aḥkām al-Qurʾān*, vol. 1, pp. 61–62.

175 Shāfiᶜī, *Kitāb ikhtilāf al-ḥadīth*, (in *Kitāb al-umm*, vol. 9), pp. 643–645. As is well known, this is not a rule accepted by all early *fuqahāʾ*.

176 Qurṭubī, *al-Jāmiᶜ li-aḥkām al-Qurʾān*, vol. 6, p. 139; Ibn al-ᶜArabī, *Aḥkām al-Qurʾān*, vol. 2, p. 622–623; Ibn al-Jawzī, *al-Muṣaffā*, p. 16. For a similar, if less explicit, view of Aḥmad b. Ḥanbal, see Khallāl, *Ahl al-milal*, p. 396. See also Ibn Ḥazm, *al-Muḥallā*, vol. 10, p. 426. For an *uṣūlī* discussion of the validity of pre-Islamic laws for Muslims, see Ibn Ḥazm, *al-Iḥkām fī uṣūl al-aḥkām*, pp. 943–973 (the issue of *lā yuqtalu muʾminun bi-kāfirin* is dealt with on p. 951) and above, section III of the present chapter.

177 Māwardī, *al-Ḥāwī al-kabīr*, vol. 12, pp. 14–15; Qurṭubī, *al-Jāmiᶜ li-aḥkām al-Qurʾān*, vol. 2, pp. 231–232.

178 Ibn Ḥanbal, *Masāʾil*, vol. 3, p. 60 (no. 1339); Khallāl, *Ahl al-milal*, pp. 394–395 (nos. 895–896); Ibn Qudāma, *al-Mughnī*, vol. 7, p. 652. For the prophetic *ḥadīth* in question, see above, at notes 145 and 146 to this chapter.

this ruling does not change even if the killer later embraces Islam, because he was not a Muslim when he committed the murder (*yuqtalu bihi li-annahu qatalahu wa huwa naṣrānī fa-laysa yadraʾu ʿanhu al-islāmu ʾl-qatla*).[179] In a comparable vein, Ibn Ḥanbal maintained that a Muslim who vilified a Jew or a Christian should be subjected to discretionary punishment (*yuʾaddab*, or *yuʿazzar*), but not to the more severe *ḥadd*. Some *tābiʿūn*, mentioned by Ibn Ḥanbal, maintained that he should not be punished at all. We are told that the *ḥadd* is imposed to protect the Muslim because of his purity, "and what connection does a *dhimmī* have with this?" (*inna al-ḥadda innamā huwa li-ʾl-muslim li-ṭahāratihi – fa-ʾl-dhimmī mā lahu wa li-hādha*).[180] In a similar vein, ʿĀmir al-Shaʿbī is reported to have exempted a Muslim from any punishment for vilifying a Christian: the polytheism tainting the Christian is more offensive than the contents of any vilification may be (*fīka aʿẓamu min hādhā: al-shirk*)[181] and therefore, apparently, he is not entitled to any protection against vilification. Moreover, a Muslim who vilified a Jewish or Christian woman will suffer the *ḥadd* punishment only if the woman in question is married to a Muslim or has a Muslim child; according to another version, even in such a case he will not be subjected to the *ḥadd*, because, in his view, "a Muslim should not be flogged for (insulting) an infidel" (*fa-lam yara an yujlada muslimun bi-kāfirin*). According to another report, the offending Muslim should be subjected to *taʾdīb*.[182]

VII

An issue closely related to *qiṣāṣ* is the question of blood-money (*diya*) payable in certain cases of murder to the surviving relatives of the victim. Muslim jurists discuss the issue in great detail and devote much attention to cases when the killer and his victim belong to different social groups.[183] In this context, the question of *diya* payable to the relatives of a slain non-Muslim figures prominently. The schools of law display a considerable variety of opinion on this matter. Let us start with Ibn Ḥazm whose view is not shared by other classical jurists: according to him, a Muslim is not liable for the payment of any blood-money if he killed an

[179] Ibn Ḥanbal, *Masāʾil*, vol. 2, p. 429 (no. 845). The view of the Mālikī scholar Ashhab b. ʿAbd al-ʿAzīz (d. 819) was the same: *suʾila ʿan naṣrāniyyayn qatala aḥaduhumā ṣāḥibahu thumma aslama al-qātil. qāla: yuqtalu bihi*. See *Majālis Ashhab b. ʿAbd al-ʿAzīz, al-juzʾ al-awwal*, p. 11. Manuscript Qayrawān. I am grateful to Dr. M. Muranyi for this reference.

[180] Khallāl, *Ahl al-milal*, pp. 345–347 (nos.750–757, 759–762). The translated passage is on p. 345, ll. 16–17, and on p. 347, ll. 12–13.

[181] Wakīʿ, *Akhbār al-quḍāt*, vol. 2, pp. 415 infra, 428.

[182] Khallāl, *Ahl al-milal*, pp. 343–344 (nos. 743–747); p. 345 (no. 753), p. 346 (no. 757), p. 366 (no. 810), ll. 7–8. In contradistinction to the reports surveyed above, al-Khallāl also quotes a tradition according to which ʿIkrima (d. 723 A.H.) said that he would have flogged a Muslim who vilified a Jewish or a Christian woman. See ibid., p. 346 (no. 761).

[183] For initial information on *diya* and related matters, see "Diya", *EI*², s.v. (E. Tyan); "Ḳatl" and "Ḳiṣāṣ", *EI*², s.vv. (J. Schacht).

infidel. It is immaterial whether the killing was intentional or by mistake. Ibn Ḥazm reaches this conclusion by a close reading of Qur'ān 4:92: the whole verse stipulates the compensation to be paid when a believer is slain, and the words "whoever kills a believer by mistake" (*wa man qatala mu'minan khaṭa'an*) are crucial for understanding the phrase "if he belongs to a people with whom you have an agreement" (*wa in kāna min qawmin baynakum wa baynahum mīthāqun*). Contrary to other interpretations, Ibn Ḥazm maintains that the slain person intended in the latter phrase is also a believer and no *diya* is payable if he is not. Nevertheless, the killing of a *dhimmī* without just cause (*bi-ghayri ḥaqqin*) is a reprehensible act (*munkar*), and as such should be corrected by the imprisonment of the culprit. The period of incarceration is not specified. As for the traditions reporting that the Prophet himself ordered the payment of *diya* in such cases, Ibn Ḥazm regards them unreliable because of their weak *isnād*.[184]

The Mālikīs and the Ḥanbalīs follow the prophetic *ḥadīth* according to which the *diya* payable for killing a Jew or a Christian is half the *diya* payable for killing a Muslim. According to another tradition, the *diya* of a Jew or a Christian is 4000 dirhams, or one third of the full amount. This is said to be the view of ᶜUmar b. al-Khaṭṭāb, ᶜUthmān b. ᶜAffān and al-Shāfiᶜī. Aḥmad b. Ḥanbal is said to have thought first that the *diya* for killing a Jew or a Christian should be a third of the full amount, but later changed his mind and supported the higher amount.[185] As for the Zoroastrians, the *diya* for their killing was fixed at 800 dirhams, or 6.66% of the full amount. The rule regarding polytheists and other "scriptureless" persons who were given *amān* was the same. In a rarely quoted tradition, ᶜUmar b. ᶜAbd al-ᶜAzīz equated the *diya* of the Zoroastrians with that of the People of the Book, referring to the famous *ḥadīth* stipulating that the Zoroastrians should be treated like the People of the Book (*sunnū bihim sunnata ahl al-kitāb*),[186] but the Ḥanbalīs rejected this reasoning and asserted that this tradition refers to the payment of the *jizya* only.[187] Al-Shāfiᶜī supported the idea of unequal *diyāt* by verses which deny the equality between believers and infidels, such as Qur'ān 32:18 and 59:20.[188] It was also supported by analogy with the rules concerning the reduction of blood-money by half when the slain person is a woman: according to a prophetic *ḥadīth*, women are "deficient in intelligence and religion" (*nāqiṣāt al-ᶜaql wa al-dīn*), while infidels have no (true) religion at all. Consequently, if the deficiency inherent in femininity brings about the reduction of the *diya*, such a reduction is certainly justified for an infidel (... *nuqṣān al-kufr fawqa nuqṣān al-unūtha wa idhā kānat*

[184] Ibn Ḥazm, *al-Muḥallā*, vol. 10, pp. 422, 434–436.

[185] Khallāl, *Ahl al-milal*, pp. 384–388 (nos. 856–859, 863–865, 869, 872).

[186] See below, Chapter Two, section IV.

[187] Khallāl, *Ahl al-milal*, pp. 392–393 (nos. 882–887), p. 394 (nos. 891–894); Ibn Qudāma, *al-Mughnī*, vol. 7, p. 796.

[188] "What? Is he who has been a believer like unto him who has been ungodly? They are not equal." "Not equal are the inhabitants of the Fire and the inhabitants of Paradise. The inhabitants of Paradise – they are the triumphant."

al-diya tanquṣu bi-ṣifat al-unūtha fa-bi-'l-kufri awlā).[189] The deficiency inherent in infidelity is compounded when aggravated by the absence of a heavenly book (*wa yatafāḥashu al-nuqṣān idhā 'nḍamma ilā kufrihi ᶜadam al-kitāb*); this argument is used to explain the extremely low amount of blood-money specified by most jurists for killing a Zoroastrian.[190]

An interesting variation on these rules is adduced by the Ḥanbalīs. Having said that the blood-money of a free *kitābī* is half that of a free Muslim, they add that if the *kitābī* was murdered intentionally, the *diya* is doubled because it is imposed instead of retaliation (*wa in qutilū ᶜamdan uḍᶜifat al-diya ᶜalā qātilihi al-muslim li-izālatihi al-qawada* [*wa hākadhā ḥakama ᶜUthmān b. ᶜAffān*]). The same rule is applied if a Zoroastrian is killed intentionally; the *diya* for his killing is, in such a case, 1600 dirhams.[191] Thus, the blood-money paid for the intentional killing of a *kitābī* is the same as that paid for the unintentional killing of a Muslim.

Similarly to the question of *qiṣāṣ*, the Ḥanafīs have a distinct opinion on the question of blood-money as well. Following some of the earliest traditionists and jurisprudents, such as al-Zuhrī, ᶜAṭāᵓ b. Abī Rabāḥ and Mujāhid, they maintain that the blood-money payable for killing a Muslim and a *dhimmī* is the same.[192] Al-Jaṣṣāṣ substantiates this view by a painstaking analysis of Qurᵓān 4:92 which deals with the various cases in which blood-money is payable. In his view, the person described in the verse as "belonging to a people with whom you have a treaty" (*wa in kāna min qawmin baynakum wa baynahum mīthāq*) must be an unbeliever having a contractual relationship with the Muslims. The *diya* mentioned in the verse had a fixed value, well known among the Arabs of the period. Since the term *diya* is employed regardless of the religious affiliation of the slain person, the same amount is payable in both cases. Traditions supporting the opposite view are not to be trusted for various reasons.[193] In a similar vein, al-Sarakhsī argues that the *diya* of the *dhimmī*s, whether People of the Book or not, is the same as the *diya* of

[189] Tirmidhī, *Sunan*, vol. 6, pp. 182–183; Bayhaqī, *Sunan*, vol. 8, pp. 100–101; Jaṣṣāṣ, *Aḥkām al-Qurᵓān*, vol. 2, p. 290; Sarakhsī, *Mabsūṭ*, vol. 26, p. 84, ll. 18ff (the last quoted passage is from this source); Marghīnānī, *Hidāya*, vol. 4, pp. 178–179; Mālik b. Anas, *Muwaṭṭaᵓ*, p. 864; Saḥnūn, *al-Mudawwana al-kubrā*, vol. 6, p. 395; Ibn ᶜAbd al-Barr al-Namarī, *al-Tamhīd*, vol. 17, p. 359; Shāfiᶜī, *Kitāb al-umm*, vol. 6, pp. 136–137; Shīrāzī, *Muhadhdhab*, vol. 3, p. 213; Ibn Kathīr, *al-Masāᵓil al-fiqhiyya*, pp. 185–186; Ibn Ḥanbal, *Masāᵓil*, vol. 2, pp. 229–233 (nos. 809–819), pp. 241–242 (nos. 832–835), vol. 3, p. 59 (no. 1338), p. 172 (no. 1586); Khallāl, *Ahl al-milal*, p. 383 (no. 852), p. 385 (no. 860) – ᶜUmar's view; pp. 385–386 (nos. 861–862) – ᶜUthmān's view; Ibn Qudāma, *al-Mughnī*, vol. 7, p. 793; Ibn Qudāma, *al-Kāfī*, vol. 4, p. 16. A concise and lucid summary of the various views can be found in Māwardī, *al-Ḥāwī*, vol. 12, pp. 308–309 (on Jews and Christians), and pp. 311–313 (on Zoroastrians and others).

[190] Sarakhsī, *Mabsūṭ*, vol. 26, p. 85, ll. 4–5; Ṣanᶜānī, *Muṣannaf*, vol. 6, pp. 126–127 (nos. 10213–10220). Except for al-Shāfiᶜī, the early jurists maintained that though the Zoroastrians were *ahl al-dhimma*, they were not People of the Book. See below, Chapter Two, section IV.

[191] *Mukhtaṣar al-Khiraqī*, p. 180; Khallāl, *Ahl al-milal*, pp. 389–391, 392–393 (nos. 873–879, 888–889; Ibn Qudāma, *al-Mughnī*, vol. 7, p. 795; Māwardī, *al-Ḥāwī*, vol. 12, p. 308. The tradition on which this ruling is based is recorded in Bayhaqī, *Sunan*, vol. 8, p. 33.

[192] For a convenient survey of the divergent views on this issue among the early traditionists, see Ṭabarī, *Jāmiᶜ al-bayān*, vol. 5, pp. 208–214; Khallāl, *Ahl al-milal*, p. 383 (nos. 853–854).

[193] Jaṣṣāṣ, *Aḥkām al-Qurᵓān*, vol. 2, pp. 290–291, 298.

the Muslims. He quotes traditions to this effect from the period of the Prophet and ascribes this view to Abū Bakr and ᶜUmar as well.[194] By concluding the *dhimma* contract, the *dhimmī*s bound themselves by the laws of Islam as far as social relationships are concerned, and the rules of justice observed among the Muslims are equally valid for them (*wa hādhā li-annahum bi-ᶜaqd al-dhimma iltazamū aḥkām al-islām fīmā yarjiᶜu ilā al-muᶜāmalāt fa-yathbutu fīmā baynahum min al-ḥikma mā huwa thābitun bayna al-muslimīn*).[195] Ibrāhīm al-Nakhaᶜī, ᶜĀmir al-Shaᶜbī and *aṣḥāb al-raʾy* are willing to go even further when they say that the *diya* of a Zoroastrian equals the *diya* of a Muslim "because (the Zoroastrian) is a free and inviolable human being, akin to a Muslim" (*diyatuhu ka-diyat al-muslim li-annahu ādamī ḥurr maᶜṣūm fa-ashbaha al-muslim*).[196]

VIII

The material surveyed in the preceding section deals with matters of retaliation and blood-money. In more general terms, it deals with the extent of protection afforded by Islam to the various religious groups inhabiting the Muslim state. It enables us to study the notions of equality and inequality between these groups and to gain an insight into the development of these notions during the first centuries of Islam. It is important also for understanding the Muslim tradition's perception of equality before the law.

It should be pointed out that equality before the law was, in principle, a notion well known among early Muslim traditionists. Rejecting an appeal for clemency on behalf of an apparently well-connected woman who was guilty of theft, the Prophet is reported to have said that

> the perdition of those who had been before you was brought about by the fact that when a nobleman among them committed theft they let him go, but when a humble man did the same, they punished him. By Him to Whose hands the soul of Muḥammad is (entrusted), if Fāṭima the daughter of Muḥammad committed theft, I would cut her hand (*fa-innamā ahlaka al-nāsa qablakum annahum kānu idhā saraqa fīhimi 'l-sharīfu tarakūhu wa idhā saraqa fīhimi 'l-ḍaᶜīfu aqāmū ᶜalayhi al-ḥadd; wa 'lladhī nafsu Muḥammadin bi-yadihi, law anna Fāṭima bint Muḥammad saraqat – la-qaṭaᶜtu yadahā*).[197]

As we already know, the enunciation of this principle did not preclude the controversy concerning the standing of non-Muslims in this regard, and the *ḥadīth*

[194] Traditions to this effect are conveniently listed in Bayhaqī, *Sunan*, vol. 8, pp. 102–103, though the Shāfiᶜī compiler has reservations about their authenticity.

[195] Sarakhsī, *Mabsūṭ*, vol. 26, p. 84, ll. 14–18; p. 85, ll. 5ff; Qudūrī, *Mukhtaṣar*, p. 187, l. 10. Traditions supporting this view are listed also in Jaṣṣāṣ, *Aḥkām al-Qurʾān*, vol. 2, pp. 291–293; Ibn ᶜAbd al-Barr al-Namarī, *al-Tamhīd*, vol. 17, pp. 359–360; Ibn Qudāma, *al-Mughnī*, vol. 7, pp. 793–794. For the usage of *ḥikma* in the sense of "equity, or justice in judgment or judicial decision", see Lane, *Lexicon*, s.v. (vol. 2, p. 617c). Cf. Marghīnānī, *Hidāya*, vol. 4, pp. 178–179.

[196] Ibn Qudāma, *al-Mughnī*, vol. 7, p. 796.

[197] Bukhārī, *Ṣaḥīḥ*, *Kitāb al-maghāzī* 53 (ed. Krehl, vol. 3, p. 145); Ibn Taymiyya, *Iqtiḍāʾ al-ṣirāṭ*, vol. 1, pp. 294–296.

literature has faithfully preserved the diversity of relevant opinion. We have seen, first of all, the unqualified and strikingly humanistic approach attributed to Ibrāhīm al-Nakhaᶜī and ᶜĀmir al-Shaᶜbī, according to whom even "a Zoroastrian is a free and inviolable human being, akin to a Muslim".[198] The Ḥanafīs reach a similar conclusion from a different premise: in their view, the protection accorded to the *dhimmī*s results from their contract with the Muslims, rather then from an inherent human right. It is the payment of *jizya* which entitles the *dhimmī* to the protection of his life and limb rather than his humanity. Therefore, while a *dhimmī* is protected by the *qiṣāṣ* mechanism and the blood-money payable for his murder is the same as that payable to the surviving relatives of a slain Muslim, such protection is not extended to a *mustaᵓmin* who is not a permanent resident of *dār al-islām*, does not pay *jizya* and, consequently, does not enjoy the same level of protection. Next come the Mālikīs, who maintain that a Muslim may be killed for killing an unbeliever only if the *dhimmī* was murdered treacherously (*ghīlatan*);[199] in other cases, they award half the blood-money to the surviving relatives of the slain *dhimmī*. The Ḥanbalīs also fixed the amount of blood-money at one half, but stipulated that if the murder was intentional, the full *diya* will be paid, because in this case it is a substitute for retaliation. Al-Shāfiᶜī maintained that a Muslim may not be killed for killing an unbeliever under any circumstances, and fixed the amount of blood-money payable to his surviving relatives at one third of the amount payable for slaying a Muslim. At the far end of the spectrum stands Ibn Ḥazm: according to him, a Muslim is never liable for payment of any blood-money if he killed an infidel.

It seems that all these views – with the exception of Ibn Ḥazm's stance rejecting the payment of any *diya* for slaying a *dhimmī* – existed simultaneously among the Muslim traditionists and jurists in the first and second centuries. Perhaps the most conspicuous example of the various views existing side by side in one compilation is ᶜAbd al-Razzāq al-Ṣanᶜānī's *Muṣannaf*. It is noteworthy that al-Ṣanᶜānī, in contradistinction to most traditionists and jurists, records the contradictory traditions on the issue at hand without trying to promote one view at the expense of another.[200] The compilers of al-Shāfiᶜī's *Musnad* have also not refrained from recording the tradition according to which the Prophet ordered the execution of a Muslim for killing a *dhimmī*, though al-Shāfiᶜī himself rejected it as spurious.

The material is not sufficient to enable us to chart the development of the relative importance of these various views with certainty. It stands to reason, however, that the idea of equal application of *qiṣāṣ* to slayers of Muslims and

[198] But see Māwardī, *al-Ḥāwī al-kabīr*, vol. 12, p. 11 where Shaᶜbī is quoted as saying that a Muslim is to be killed for killing a *kitābī*, but not for killing a Zoroastrian.

[199] Mālik b. Anas, *al-Muwaṭṭaᵓ*, p. 864; Saḥnūn, *al-Mudawwana al-kubrā*, vol. 6, p. 427; Jaṣṣāṣ, *Aḥkām al-Qurᵓān*, vol. 1, p. 163, ll. 21–22; ᶜAynī, *ᶜUmdat al-qārī*, vol. 2, p. 161, l. 15. For another usage of the term *ghīla*, see below, Chapter Four, at note 129.

[200] This could be added to Motzki's arguments in favor of the basic authenticity of Ṣanᶜānī's work. See Motzki, "The *Muṣannaf* of ᶜAbd al-Razzāq …", passim.

non-Muslims alike was more favorably viewed in the earliest period of Islam.[201] It seems to reflect a time when the self-confidence of the Muslim community and its conviction of exaltedness had not yet fully developed. If this interpretation is correct, the case of *qiṣāṣ* does not stand alone: it can be compared with similar development of early Muslim thinking in other fields.[202]

Eventually, the view according to which the *dhimmīs* are equally protected by the *qiṣāṣ* mechanism and the full *diya* is payable for their murder came to be held by the Ḥanafī school alone. Consequently, the *ḥadīth* literature bears witness to a systematic delegitimization of traditions supporting the Ḥanafī stance. This was done in several ways. The most common one was to impugn the trustworthiness of ᶜAbd al-Raḥmān b. al-Baylamānī who is the last link in the *isnād* of the tradition supporting the equal application of *qiṣāṣ* to slayers of Muslims and non-Muslims alike. It was also argued that the *ḥadīth* in question is *mursal* and therefore unworthy of much credence. This was done in many classical collections of *ḥadīth* as well as in the *rijāl* literature;[203] some modern Muslim editors and scholars have followed suit.[204] Another way to achieve the same objective was to contend that this tradition dates from an early stage of Muḥammad's career; as such it was abrogated when the Prophet said, in his last sermon, that a Muslim is not to be killed for killing an infidel.[205] In a further attempt to discredit the egalitarian position, Zufar b. al-Hudhayl, a prominent jurist of the Ḥanafī school,[206] is shown as abandoning this view in favor of the opposite one without any attempt to defend it.[207] The invective heaped on the Ḥanafīs in Ibn Ḥazm's *al-Muḥallā* seems to be the most extreme denunciation of their position.[208] And the tradition in which the

201 See Ṣanᶜānī, *Muṣannaf*, vol. 10, pp. 97–98 (no. 18498): "… The blood-money of every unbeliever having a contract is equal to the blood-money of the Muslims, males and females. This was the *sunna* at the time of the Prophet …" (*ᶜaqlu kulli muᶜāhidin min ahl al-kufr wa muᶜāhidatin ka-ᶜaql al-muslimīn dhukrānihim wa ināthihim; jarat bi-dhālika al-sunna fī ᶜahd rasūl Allāh …*).

202 See my *Prophecy continuous*, pp. 49–53, where I tried to explain the gradual replacement of Muslim views asserting the equality of all prophets with the unshakable belief in the superiority of Muḥammad along similar lines. See also Chapter Six.

203 Dāraquṭnī, *Sunan*, vol. 3, pp. 134–135 (no. 165); Bayhaqī, *Sunan*, vol. 8, pp. 30–31; Māwardī, *al-Ḥāwī al-kabīr*, vol. 12, pp.14–15; Zarqashī, *Sharḥ al-Zarkashī ᶜalā Mukhtaṣar al-Khiraqī*, vol. 6, pp. 64–66 (nos. 2912–2913); Ibn Abī Ḥātim al-Rāzī, *Kitāb al-jarḥ wa al-taᶜdīl*, vol. 2, part 2, p. 216 (Ibn Abī Ḥātim's judgment is rather moderate; he considers ᶜAbd al-Raḥmān only *layyin*); Dhahabī, *Dīwān al-ḍuᶜafāʾ wa al-matrūkīn*, vol. 2, p. 92 (no. 2426); Dhahabī, *Mīzān al-iᶜtidāl*, Beirut: Dār al-kutub al-ᶜilmiyya, 1995, vol. 4, p. 264 (no. 4832); Ibn Qayyim al-Jawziyya, *al-Manār al-munīf*, p. 35; ᶜAsqalānī, *Tahdhīb al-tahdhīb*, vol. 6, pp. 135–136 (no. 305); Jazāʾirī, *Kitāb takhrīj al-aḥādīth al-ḍiᶜāf*, Beirut: Dār al-kutub al-ᶜilmiyya, 1990, p. 278 (no. 629); al-Mizzī, *Tahdhīb al-kamāl fī asmāʾ al-rijāl*, vol. 17, pp. 8–12; ᶜAynī, *ᶜUmdat al-qārī*, vol. 2, p. 161, ll. 21–26.

204 See the note of Ḥusayn Muʾnis in his edition of Yaḥyā b. Ādam's *Kitāb al-kharāj*, p. 110, note. 1; and of Aḥmad Muḥammad Shākir in his edition of the same work (Cairo, 1347 A.H.), p. 76, note 1. See also Sāᶜātī, *Badāʾiᶜ al-minan*, vol. 2, p. 252, note 1 and Zaydān, *al-Qiṣāṣ wa al-diyāt*, p. 54 infra.

205 Māwardī, *al-Ḥāwī al-kabīr*, vol. 12, p. 10; Baghawī, *Sharḥ al-sunna*, vol. 6, p. 130.

206 See on him N. Tsafrir, *The spread of the Ḥanafī school in the western regions of the ᶜAbbāsid caliphate up to the end of the third century A.H.*, Princeton, 1993 (unpublished Ph. D. dissertation), pp. 41ff; ᶜAbd al-Sattār Ḥāmid, *al-Imām Zufar b. al-Hudhayl, uṣūluhu wa fiqhuhu*, Baghdād: Wizārat al-awqāf, 1979.

207 Bayhaqī, *Sunan*, vol. 8, p. 31.

208 See Ibn Ḥazm, *al-Muḥallā*, vol. 10, pp. 428, 431.

Prophet was reported to have equated the *diya* of a Muslim with that of a *dhimmī* suffered a similar fate: it was relegated to the collections of so-called forged *aḥādīth*.[209]

The struggle between the two viewpoints concerning the protection accorded to non-Muslims was conducted on several levels. On the level of principle, the question was whether the idea of Islamic exaltedness should be a factor in deciding the question at hand. According to the prevalent opinion, a Muslim should not be executed for slaying a non-Muslim; this is comparable to the ruling according to which a Muslim should not be flogged for slandering a Christian[210] and a free man should not be executed for slaying a slave. The issue was also addressed with the tools of *ḥadīth* criticism: the prophetic tradition rejecting *qiṣāṣ* against a Muslim for killing an infidel was considered trustworthy, while the opposite one came to be considered spurious. The Ḥanafī view assigning decisive importance to the contractual obligation of the Muslim state to protect the *dhimmī*s had to succumb to the now irresistible power of *ḥadīth*. Finally, there was also a struggle on the practical level: public pressure was applied to prefer the interests of individual Muslims, as part of the dominant community, over the abstract principle of equality before the law. Combined together, these factors brought about the marginalization of the egalitarian position. With the significant exception of the Ḥanafī school, which eventually came to prevail over a substantial part of the Muslim world, *lā yuqtalu muʾminun bi-kāfirin* came to be the dominant view in *fiqh* and *ḥadīth*. On the question of *qiṣāṣ*, the idea of Islamic exaltedness gained the upper hand as the decisive factor in the determination of the law.[211]

[209] Ibn al-Jawzī, *Mawḍūʿāt*, vol. 3, p. 127; Suyūṭī, *al-Laʾāliʾ al-maṣnūʿa*, vol. 2, pp. 188–189; Jazāʾirī, *Kitāb takhrīj al-aḥādīth al-ḍiʿāf*, p. 278–279 (no. 628, 630); Qurṭubī, *al-Jāmiʿ li-aḥkām al-Qurʾān*, vol. 2, pp. 231–232.

[210] Wakīʿ, *Akhbār al-quḍāt*, vol. 2, pp. 420, 428 infra.

[211] For a modern scholar's adoption of this view, see Zaydān, *al-Qiṣāṣ wa al-diyāt*, p. 54. On the question of *diya* when the victim is a *dhimmī*, Zaydān has adopted the egalitarian, Ḥanafī view; see ibid., pp. 206–207.

CHAPTER TWO

Classification of unbelievers

The religious history of mankind and its religious diversity has been a central theme in Muslim tradition since the earliest stages of its development. A copious literary genre, known in Arabic as *al-milal wa al-niḥal,*[1] came into existence and included detailed treatment of Jewish, Christian and Muslim sects, as well as extensive descriptions of the religions and philosophies of Iran, India and Greece. The present book is not concerned with this relatively late literary genre, but rather with the same topic as treated in Qur^ʾānic exegesis, *ḥadīth* and jurisprudence. Here the issue of religions other than Islam is treated on a much more limited scope and is restricted to the religious traditions encountered by the Muslims in the nascent stage of their history: polytheism, Judaism, Christianity, Zoroastrianism and some of their offshoots.

I

The non-Muslim religious communities mentioned in the Qurʾān are the Banū Isrāʾīl and the Jews (*yahūd*),[2] the Christians (*naṣārā*), the Zoroastrians (*majūs*), the Ṣābiʾa, and the polytheists who associate other deities with Allah (*mushrikūn*). As far as revealed books are concerned, we hear, in addition to the Tawrāt and the Injīl, about the "scrolls of Abraham and Moses" (*ṣuḥuf Ibrāhīm wa Mūsā*), the "first scrolls" (*al-ṣuḥuf al-ūlā*), "the books of the ancient people" (*zubur al-awwalīn*), the zabūr of David, commonly identified with the Psalms, and – outside the Qurʾān – "the scrolls of Shīth."[3] In extra-Qurʾānic literature, there are also the "heretics" (*zanādiqa*, sg. *zindīq*), frequently equated with the Manichaeans, and the Samaritans. In various contexts, all these are subsumed under the more general categories of infidels (*kuffār*, sg. *kāfir*), scriptuaries (*ahl al-kitāb*), the "protected

[1] See above, Chapter One, note 2.
[2] For the distinction between these two groups, see below, at the end of section II of this chapter.
[3] Qurʾān 3:163, 4:162, 17:55. 20:133, 21:105, 26:196, 53:36, 80:13, 87:18–19; Māwardī, *al-Ḥāwī al-kabīr*, vol. 9, p. 226; Ibn Qudāma, *al-Mughnī*, vol. 8, pp. 501, 590–591; Ibn Qayyim al-Jawziyya, *Aḥkām ahl al-dhimma*, vol. 2, pp. 432–433.

people" (*ahl al-dhimma* or *dhimmīs*) and the inhabitants of areas under infidel rule (*ahl al-ḥarb* or *ḥarbīs*). In some sources we also have the larger category of "the people who have an agreement" with the Muslims (*ahl al-ᶜahd*). These are divided into *dhimmīs* (*ahl al-dhimma*), "people of the armistice" (*ahl al-hudna*) and "people who received guarantee of safety" (*ahl al-amān*). The people of armistice live outside the Muslim territory, are not ruled by Muslims and their only obligation is to refrain from waging war against the Muslims. The people who received guarantee of safety (*mustaʾminūn*) are those who stay in the Muslim area temporarily, do not settle and are not obliged to pay *jizya*. These may be envoys, merchants, seekers of refuge and visitors.[4]

Ahl al-dhimma, *ahl al-ᶜahd* and *ahl al-ḥarb* are concepts defining the relationship between these groups and the Muslims in terms of Islamic law; the rest of the terms define the groups in question in terms of their religious beliefs. There is some overlapping between these categories: the scriptuaries who live under Muslim rule are at the same time infidels and *dhimmīs*: they agreed to live under Islamic rule and received permanent protection from the Muslims. The scriptuaries who live beyond the frontiers of *dār al-islām* are infidels but not *dhimmīs*: since they have not been awarded the protection of the Muslim community, they are *ḥarbīs*, or *ahl al-hudna*. Jews and Christians are considered scriptuaries, though there is some discussion of the question whether polytheistic elements entered into their systems of belief. At times an ethnic characterization is added to the religious one, and the jurists speak of Arab Christians and of Arab Jews; these two groups are ethnically unrelated to the ancient Children of Israel (*banū Isrāʾīl*) and some jurists draw legal conclusions from this assessment of their genealogy. With regard to the Zoroastrians, the prevalent (but not the sole) opinion is that they are not scriptuaries; nevertheless, they are unanimously considered *dhimmīs*. There is also some debate regarding the question whether polytheists (*mushrikūn*) can be given the status of *dhimmīs*, and whether there is any difference between Arab *mushrikūn* and polytheists of other ethnic affiliations. The purpose of the following analysis is to clarify the various considerations which come into play when non-Muslims are classified into sub-categories for various purposes of administration or law.

At the outset, let us consider the Muslim views of the infidel world in general. There is, first of all, a notion according to which all of it is, at least for certain purposes, a single entity. Speaking of the laws governing the inheritance of a person who converted from one non-Muslim religion to another and died, al-Shāfiᶜī (d. 204 A.H. / 820 A.H.) says that members of his family (who retained their original religion) are entitled to inherit from the deceased "because all infidelity is

[4] For material on *amān* and *mustaʾminūn*, see "Amān", *EI*², s.v. (J. Schacht); W. Heffening, *Das islamische Fremdenrecht bis zu den islamisch-fränkischen Staatsverträgen. Eine rechtshistorische Studie zum fiqh*, Osnabrück: Biblio Verlag, 1975; Ibn Qayyim al-Jawziyya, *Aḥkām ahl al-dhimma*, p. 475–476; cf. Māwardī, *al-Ḥāwī al-kabīr*, vol. 9, p. 306. For the classification of the unbelievers in the Ottoman period, when the term *kāfir* related only to Christians and did not include the Jews, see Lewis, *The Muslim discovery of Europe*, pp. 171–184.

one religion ... in the same way as Islam is (one) religion" (*li-anna al-kufr kullahu millatun wāḥida ... kamā al-islām milla*).[5] This view is also used in support of the idea that conversion from one non-Muslim faith to another is devoid of any significance and Muslims should therefore pay no attention to such kind of religious change.[6] Nevertheless, al-Shāfiʿī stated elsewhere that a person who converted from one infidelity to another should lose his rights as a *dhimmī* and be expelled from *dār al-islām*.[7] Furthermore, al-Shāfiʿī's perception of the infidel world as a single entity did not prevent him from differentiating between various groups of infidels as far as the payment of the *jizya* is concerned.[8] The Ḥanafī jurist al-Sarakhsī (died probably in 483 A.H. / 1090 A.D.) says in a similar vein that, from the vantage point of Muslim law, marriage between Jews, Christians and Zoroastrians is permissible because they belong to one religious community even if their beliefs differ (*hum ʿalā millatin wāḥida wa in ikhtalafat niḥaluhum*): they are united by their *shirk* and by their denial of Muḥammad's prophethood. Their mutual relationship can be compared to the relationship between the adherents of the various schools of Muslim law. They are therefore allowed to testify against each other and inherit from each other.[9] The Ḥanafī jurists al-Jaṣṣāṣ (d. 370 A.H. / 981 A.D.) and al-Sarakhsī see support for this view in the Qurʾānic expression "To you your religion and to me mine" (*lakum dīnukum wa lī dīnī*)[10] which does not make any distinction between the various types of infidelity. Even if adherents of the various religions differ from each other in their particular beliefs, when compared to the Muslims they are all one community because of their rejection of Muḥammad's prophethood.[11]

[5] Shāfiʿī, *Kitāb al-umm*, vol. 4, p. 261, ll. 2–3; vol. 6, p. 66, ll. 13ff; Jaṣṣāṣ, *Mukhtaṣar ikhtilāf al-ʿulamāʾ*, vol. 4, pp. 449–450 (no. 2138). Shāfiʿī's statement is necessary because of the general principle in Muslim laws of inheritance: members of two different religions do not inherit from each other. See also Nazwī, *Muṣannaf*, vol. 11, p. 197: "All infidelity is one religion; likewise, all Islam is one religion" (*al-kufr kulluhu milla wāḥida wa ka-dhālika al-islām kulluhu milla wāḥida*); Ṣanʿānī, *Muṣannaf*, vol. 6, pp. 17, 130; vol. 8, p. 360; Ibn Kathīr, *Tafsīr*, vol. 7, p. 393. This is also one of the views attributed to Aḥmad b. Ḥanbal (see Ibn Qudāma, *al-Mughnī*, vol. 6, p. 295); for Ibn Ḥanbal's other view, see below. Cf. also Qalʿajī, *Mawsūʿat fiqh Sufyān al-Thawrī*, p. 115. Cf. B. Lewis, *The Muslim discovery of Europe*, p. 63. Lewis does not discuss the variety of approaches to the homogeneity or heterogeneity of the non-Muslim world; see below.

[6] See Shāfiʿī, *Kitāb al-umm*, vol. 2, p. 367, lines 6–7: *wa law irtadda naṣrānī ilā majūsiyya aw majūsī ilā naṣrāniyya lam nastatibhu wa lam naqtulhu li-annahu kharaja min kufrin ilā kufrin ...*

[7] See *Kitāb al-umm*, vol. 4, p. 260, lines 11–13 and Jaṣṣāṣ, *Mukhtaṣar ikhtilāf al-ʿulamāʾ*, vol. 3, p. 508, no. 1656.

[8] For a discussion of this issue, see below, section VI.

[9] Sarakhsī, *Mabsūṭ*, vol. 5, p. 44; vol. 30, p. 31. See also vol. 5, p. 48, where Sarakhsī speaks about conversions from one non-Muslim religion to another and says that such a change of religion does not require any action on part of the Muslims "because all infidelity is one religion" (*li-anna al-kufra kullahu millatun wāḥida*). See also Abū Yūsuf, *Kitāb al-āthār*, p. 171 (no. 781) and Wakīʿ, *Akhbār al-quḍāt*, vol. 2, p. 415.

[10] Qurʾān 109:6.

[11] Jaṣṣāṣ, *Aḥkām al-Qurʾān*, vol. 3, pp. 585–586 (on Qurʾān 109:6); cf. Jaṣṣāṣ, *Mukhtaṣar ikhtilāf al-ʿulamāʾ*, vol. 4, p. 449 (no. 2138); Sarakhsī, *Mabsūṭ*, vol. 30, p. 32; Ibn Kathīr, *Tafsīr*, vol. 7, p. 393 (on Qurʾān 109:6).

Regarding the views of Mālik b. Anas, the reports are contradictory. In a discussion concerning the validity of inheritance divided according to non-Muslim laws between heirs who were non-Muslims at the time of the legator's death, Mālik maintains that such a division is valid regardless of the religious affiliation of the deceased and of his heirs,

> since the laws concerning infidelity do not change because of the variety of infidel religions ... According to Mālik and all his associates, the infidels are equal – whether they are Zoroastrians or People of the Book – in that the Muslims fight them, impose *jizya* upon them and allow them to retain their religion. Allah the Exalted combined them all under his threat and consigned them to the Fire forever. The term "infidelity" is used for all of them and no distinction should be made between any of their laws unless there is a proof to this effect ... (*wa li-ʾanna al-kufr lā taftariqu aḥkāmuhu li-'khtilāfi adyānihi ... wa ʿinda Mālik wa jamīʿ aṣḥābihi anna ahl al-kufr kullahum sawāʾ – majūsan kānū aw kitābiyyīn – fī muqātalatihim wa ḍarb al-jizya ʿalayhim wa qabūlihim minhum wa iqrārihim ʿalā dīnihim wa qad jamaʿahum Allah ʿazza wa jalla fī al-waʿīd wa al-takhlīd fī al-nār wa shamalahum ism al-kufr fa-lā yufarraqu bayna shayʾin min aḥkāmihim illā mā qāma al-dalīl ʿalayhi ...*).[12]

Discussing, on the other hand, the question of cross-religious inheritance, Mālik is among the jurists who maintain that Jews, Christians and Zoroastrians cannot inherit from each other, because the Prophet said that members of different communities do not inherit each other (*lā yatawārathu ahl millatayn shattā*) and because "infidelity consists of separate religions."[13]

In a similar vein, Ibn Ḥanbal (d. 241 A.H. / 855 A.D.) thought that "infidelity consists of different religious communities whose adherents do not inherit from each other" (*inna al-kufr milalun mukhtalifa lā yarithu baʿḍuhum baʿdan*). This view is in conformity with the tradition of the Prophet who is reported to have said that adherents of different religions do not inherit from each other. The distinctiveness of the various religions is indicated by the Qurʾānic usage which frequently mentions them separately.[14] The Ḥanbalī *qāḍī* Abū Yaʿlā (d. 458 A.H. / 1066 A.D.)[15] took a similar view: "infidelity consists of three communities: Judaism, Christianity and the religion of the others whose common feature is that they do not possess a book" (*al-kufru thalāthu milalin: al-yahūdiyya, al-naṣrāniyya wa dīnu man*

[12] Ibn ʿAbd al-Barr al-Namarī, *al-Tamhīd*, vol. 2, p. 53. In the Mālikī school the situation seems to be less clear. In *al-Mudawwana al-kubrā*, Mālik is reported to have been silent on the issue of cross-religious inheritance, but Saḥnūn (d. 240 A.H. / 854 A.D.) quotes traditions which imply that his own view was the same as that of Ibn Ḥanbal: members of different (non-Muslim) communities do not inherit from each other. See Saḥnūn, *Mudawwana*, vol. 3, p. 389. This was also the view of some Shāfiʿīs who differed in this respect from the eponymous founder of their schoool. See Sarakhsī, *Mabsūṭ*, vol. 30, p. 31.

[13] Ibn ʿAbd al-Barr al-Namarī, *al-Tamhīd*, vol. 9, p. 170.

[14] *lā yatawārathu ahlu millatayni bi-shayʾ* (or *shattā*). See Khallāl, *Ahl al-milal*, p. 406 (no. 927; but see no. 929 where Ibn Ḥanbal is reported to have allowed inheritance between Jews and Christians); Sarakhsī, *Mabsūṭ*, vol. 30, pp. 31–32; Ibn Qayyim al-Jawziyya, *Aḥkām ahl al-dhimma*, vol. 2, pp. 446–447.

[15] See *EI*², s.v. Ibn al-Farrāʾ (H. Laoust).

ᶜadāhum yajmaᶜuhum annahum lā kitāba lahum).[16] The Ḥanbalī jurist Ibn Qudāma (d. 620 A.H. / 1223 A.D.), on the other hand, rejects the validity of this perception: he maintains that the non-possession of a book is a negative criterion (*waṣf ᶜadamī*, "description based on an absence") which cannot serve as a useful basis for categorization. A category created on such a basis is meaningless, because its constituent parts differ from each other in numerous respects. Religions such as Zoroastrianism, idolatry or sun worship do not form a homogeneous group and should be considered distinct from each other.[17] Ibn Qayyim al-Jawziyya (d. 751 A.H. / 1350 A.D.) counted five non-Muslim groups: the Jews, the Christians, the Zoroastrians, the Ṣābiᵓans and the polytheists. This is based on Qurᵓān 22:17 and on a statement of Ibn ᶜAbbās who is reported to have said: "The religions are six: one belongs to the Merciful and five to Satan" (*al-adyān sitta wāḥidun li-'l-Raḥmān wa khamsatun li-'l-shayṭān*).[18]

Ibn Abī Laylā (d. 148 A.D. / 765 A.H.) took a more nuanced view of the non-Muslims. He discerned basic affinity between the Jews and the Christians, because they believe in the unity of God and in the prophethood of Moses, and allowed cross-religious inheritance between them; but he rejected such a possibility between these two monotheistic communities and the dualistic Zoroastrians.[19] Similar was the view of the early Syrian jurist al-Awzāᶜī (d. 157 A.H. / 774 A.D.) who thought that all (non-Muslim) communities are divided into People of the Book and *majūs*. Whoever is not a *kitābī* belongs to the *majūs*. He specifically included the Khazars and the people of Ādharbayjān in this category.[20]

II

The main body of Muslim religious tradition has always displayed a keen interest in the comparative description, analysis and criticism of religions other than Islam. Judaism and Christianity have received the lion's share of Muslim attention. From the Muslim vantage point, these two religions have much in common. Together with Jāhilī polytheism, they were the religions which Islam faced at the nascent stage of its development. Conceived of in the earliest days of Islam, the Muslim perception of Judaism and Christianity was inspired by the interpretation of abundant Qurᵓānic material. The well known Muslim view is that Jews and Christians are

[16] Ibn Qudāma, *al-Mughnī*, vol. 6, pp. 296–298; Ibn Abī Shayba, *Muṣannaf*, vol. 2, p. 187; Ibn Qayyim al-Jawziyya, *Aḥkām ahl al-dhimma*, vol. 2, p. 446; Jubūrī, *Fiqh al-imām al-Awzāᶜī*, vol. 2, p. 150. This is also one of the views ascribed to Ibn Abī Laylā. See Ibn ᶜAbd al-Barr al-Namarī, *Tamhīd*, vol. 9, p. 170.

[17] Ibn Qudāma, *al-Mughnī*, vol. 6, p. 296.

[18] Ibn Qayyim al-Jawziyya, *Hidāyat al-ḥayārā*, pp. 23–24; Ṭabarī, *Jāmiᶜ al-bayān*, vol. 17, p. 129; Rāzī, *al-Tafsīr al-kabīr*, vol. 23, p. 17 (on Qurᵓān 22:17). In Zamakhsharī's *Kahshāf* (vol. 3, p. 8) the tradition speaks of five religions: four belong to Satan and one to the Merciful; this version results from the idea that the Ṣābiᵓūn are a kind of Christians (*juᶜila al-Ṣābiᵓūn maᶜa al-naṣārā li-annahum nawᶜun minhum*). Cf. also Rāzī, *al-Tafsīr al-kabīr*, vol. 3, p. 98.

[19] Sarakhsī, *Mabsūṭ*, vol. 30, pp. 31, 32.

[20] Ṭabarī, *Kitāb ikhtilāf al-fuqahāᵓ*, pp. 200–201.

People of the Book (*ahl al-kitāb*); those of them who are subject to Islamic jurisdiction, pay the poll tax (*jizya*), and agree to live in accordance with the Muslim laws concerning them are considered as "protected people" (*ahl al-dhimma*). Muslims may marry their women, may consume meat slaughtered by them and should allow them to retain their respective faiths. The Samaritans are treated as a Jewish group because they observe the laws of the Tawrāt.[21] In the earliest books of law, the Christians are mentioned as one group, but Ibn Qudāma al-Maqdisī, who lived in Jerusalem and Damascus during the Crusades, enumerates various Christian denominations, such as the Jacobites, the Nestorians, the Melchites, the Franks (*Faranjiyya*), the Byzantines and the Armenians.[22] The detailed reference to the local Christian groups is understandable; however, the inclusion of the Franks who can hardly be considered as "protected" by the Muslims is rather surprising.

A closer examination of early Muslim tradition and law will reveal, however, that this commonly known view does not represent the whole spectrum of Muslim legal opinion. Let us start our discussion with the uncommon views of Ibn Ḥazm whose criteria for inclusion of non-Muslims in the *dhimmī* category are very restrictive. Those who moved from one *kitābī* religion to another; those who moved from infidelity to a *kitābī* religion after the mission of the Prophet; and those who counted Muslims among their ancestors, even in the distant past, will not be allowed to retain their faith and must face the alternatives of Islam or the sword. Ibn Ḥazm connects this perception to the *fiṭra ḥadīth:* Islam is the religion of every newborn and the Prophet stipulated that those who change their religion should be killed. In other words, in his view all non-Muslims are considered apostates if there is no evidence to the contrary.[23] Therefore only people who were explicitly allowed to retain a non-Muslim religion are eligible for the payment of *jizya* and the concomitant *dhimmī* status.[24] Furthermore, Ibn Ḥazm is willing to grant the People of the Book *dhimmī* status only if they agree to recognize Muḥammad as a Messenger of God to the Muslims (or to the Arabs) and refrain from injuring his honor. In his view, People of the Book who maintain that Muḥammad was not a prophet at all should be killed.[25]

[21] Ṣanʿānī, *Muṣannaf*, vol. 6, p. 74 (no. 10043); Abū Yūsuf, *Kitāb al-kharāj*, pp. 122 supra, 128 infra; Shāfiʿī, *Kitāb al-umm*, vol. 4, p. 259, ll. 15–17; vol. 5, p. 10, ll. 7–8; Jaṣṣāṣ, *Mukhtaṣar ikhtilāf al-ʿulamāʾ*, vol. 3, p. 206 (no. 1304); Ibn Qayyim al-Jawziyya, *Aḥkām ahl al-dhimma*, vol. 1, pp. 90–92, 245, 431; Ibn Qudāma, *Mughnī*, vol. 6, p. 590; vol. 8, p. 362, 496; Bayhaqī, *Sunan*, vol. 7, p. 173. For the same view as expressed in *fatwā*s from the Ottoman period, see E. Mittwoch, "Muslimische Fetwās über die Samaritaner," *Orientalische Literaturzeitung* 29 (1926), pp. 845–849.

[22] Ibn Qudāma, *Mughnī*, vol. 8, p. 496 infra.

[23] For a full discussion of the *fiṭra* tradition, see Chapter Three, section VIII.

[24] Ibn Ḥazm, *al-Iḥkām*, vol. 2, pp. 889–890.

[25] Ibn Ḥazm, *Muḥallā*, vol. 7, p. 371. One should mention in this context the Jewish sect known as the ʿĪsāwiyya, which is said to have emerged during the reign of the Umayyad caliph ʿAbd al-Malik b. Marwān (reigned 685–705 A.D.) and maintained that Muḥammad was a prophet, but his mission was not directed at the Jews who ought to retain their ancestral laws. See "Īsāwiyya", *EI*^{2}, s.v. (S. Pines) and Y. Erder, "The doctrine of Abū ʿĪsā al-Iṣfahānī and its sources", *Jerusalem Studies in Arabic and Islam* 20 (1996), pp. 162–199. For a similar requirement directed at the Jews and the Christians in ninth century Spain, see Janina N. Safran, "Identity and differentiation in ninth-century al-Andalus", *Speculum* 7 (2001), pp. 589–590. I am grateful to Professor David Wasserstein for this reference.

Some early Muslims and prominent jurists also maintain that not all Jews and Christians can be regarded *dhimmīs*. They assert that mere adherence to the Jewish or Christian faith is not sufficient in order to gain the status of "protected people". According to their view, two further interrelated criteria ought to be investigated in order to rule on the status of the groups in question: the time at which they accepted Judaism or Christianity, and their ethnic affiliation. The time since which the Jews and Christians have belonged to their respective communities is important because at a certain point the adherents of these two faiths corrupted the divine message delivered to them by Moses and Jesus respectively. The time at which this corruption (*taḥrīf, tabdīl*) took place is not clearly indicated, though certain passages give the impression that sometime after the coming of Jesus both religions were already corrupt.[26] Certain jurists maintain that after this corruption took place, it was not legitimate anymore to embrace Judaism or Christianity. Those who converted to these two religions at this late stage are therefore ineligible for *dhimmī* status. And it is certainly not legitimate to embrace any religion other than Islam after the coming of the Prophet Muḥammad. This is analogous to the well known rule according to which Muslims do not destroy non-Muslim places of worship which had existed prior to the Muslim conquest, but non-Muslims are not allowed to construct new synagogues or churches in areas under Muslim rule.

The conversion date of the Jews and the Christians is related to the question of their ethnic affiliation. Classical jurists and commentators postulate the existence of two groups among them. The first includes the descendants of Banū Isrā'īl who received divine revelation through Moses and Jesus. The second is ethnically unrelated to the Banū Isrā'īl; it consists of Jews and Christians of mostly Arab descent whose ancestors did not embrace their respective religions at the time of their revelation to Moses and Jesus, but rather converted at a later date. Some traditionists have considered this a factor in determining the eligibility of these groups for *dhimmī* status and asserted that the Qur'ānic regulations concerning the People of the Book relate only to the descendants of the Banū Isrā'īl, and are not applicable to members of other ethnic groups who embraced Judaism or Christianity. Some make a distinction between the various elements of *dhimmī* status: it is possible, for instance, that certain Jews and Christians will be allowed to pay the *jizya* and retain their religion, but the meat slaughtered by them and their women will be forbidden to the Muslims. The issue comes up frequently in Muslim jurisprudence. Early works of *fiqh* indicate that conversion to Judaism and Christianity in the pre-Islamic period had been fairly extensive and it is evident that the jurists and traditionists were well aware of the existence of numerous Jews and Christians of Arab extraction in the Arabian peninsula during the Jāhilī period.[27] With easily

[26] See, for example, Ibn Taymiyya, *Majmū' fatāwā*, vol. 35, p. 225.

[27] This apparently widespread phenomenon can be seen as a background for the material assembled by M. Lecker in a series of articles on individual and tribal conversions, based on historical, biographical and geographical literature. See his "Ḥudhayfa b. al-Yamān and 'Ammār b. al-Yāsir ..."; "The conversion of Ḥimyar to Judaism ..."; "Judaism among the Kinda and the *ridda* of Kinda", *JAOS* 115 (1995), pp. 635–650; "On Arabs of the Banū Kilāb executed together with the Jewish Banū Qurayẓa", *JSAI* 19 (1995), pp. 66–72; *Muslims, Jews and Pagans*, pp. 41–45. See also M. Gil, "The origins of the Jews of Yathrib," *JSAI* 4 (1984), pp. 203–224.

discernible gloom, al-Shāfiʿī recounts that entire Arab tribes "perished" by converting to Christianity or Judaism before the coming of Islam (*intawat qabāʾilu min al-ʿarab qabla an yabʿatha 'llāhu rasūlahu Muḥammadan … wa yunzila ʿalayhi al-furqān*).[28] Elsewhere he speaks of Jewish and Christian Arabs whose original religion was the *Ḥanīfiyya*, then they strayed into idolatry, and only later embraced the religion of the People of the Book.[29] This is apparently the reason why a part of the Jews who lived in Medina and its vicinity were ethnically Arabs.[30] The Banū Naḍīr are said to have been a subtribe of the Judhām who embraced Judaism (… *wa hum fakhdhun min Judhām illā annahum tahawwadū*).[31] Some Jews of Khaybar[32] and most Jews of the Yemen are described as Arabs (*wa ʿāmmatuhum ʿarab*) as well.[33] They are said to have embraced Judaism after the coming of Jesus;[34] this implies that they were of Arab descent. Ibn Taymiyya explicitly says that while some of the Jews of Yemen were related to Banū Isrāʾīl, others were Arabs.[35] And, in more general terms, we are told by Ibn Qudāma that many Christian and Jewish Arabs (*naṣārā al-ʿarab wa yahūd*[*u*]*hum*) lived in the lands of Islam during the era of the Prophet's companions.[36]

While the existence in the Arabian peninsula of numerous Jews and Christians of Arab extraction is not in dispute, the legal conclusions from this situation are divergent. The prevalent view affirms that differences in ethnicity or in the time of conversion should not have any effect on the standing of non-Muslims in Islamic law. Among the early proponents of this view, al-Ṭabarī mentions al-Ḥasan (al-Baṣrī, d. 110 A.H. / 728 A.D.), ʿIkrima (d. 105 A.H. / 723–724 A.D.), al-Shaʿbī (d. 103–110 A.H. / 721–728 A.D.), Saʿīd b. al-Musayyab (d. 94 A.H. / 713 A.D.), Ibn

[28] See Shāfiʿī, *Kitāb al-umm*, vol. 4, p. 244, ll. 11–12; *Mukhtaṣar al-Muzanī ʿalā al-Umm*, in Shāfiʿī, *Kitāb al-umm*, vol. 9, p. 292. I have translated *intawat* according to its meaning in the classical dictionaries, though they do not mention the *infaʿala* form of the root. The famous lexicographer Abū Manṣūr al-Azharī (d. 370 A.H. / 980 A.D.; see "al-Azharī", in *EI*², s.v. [R. Blachère]), who wrote a dictionary for the rare words used by Shāfiʿī, explains *intawā* as movement from the desert to settlements inhabited by Jews and Christians: *intawat ay intaqalat min bādiyatihā ilā ahl al-qurā fa-dānat bi-dīn ahl al-qurā min al-yahūdiyya wa al-naṣrāniyya fa-akhadha al-nabī … minhum al-jizya wa tarakahum ʿalā dīnihim kamā taraka ahl al-tawrāt wa al-injīl min banī Isrāʾīl.* See Azharī, *Kitāb al-zāhir fī gharīb alfāẓ al-Shāfiʿī*, printed in Māwardī, *al-Ḥāwī al-kabīr*, introductory volume, p. 382).

[29] Shāfiʿī, *Kitāb al-umm*, vol. 5, p. 10, ll. 10–12.

[30] Ibn Taymiyya, *Majmūʿ fatāwā*, vol. 35, p. 225: … *anna jamāʿatan min al-yahūd alladhīna kānū bi-'l-Madīna wa ḥawlahā kānū ʿaraban wa dakhalū fī dīn al-yahūd.*

[31] Yaʿqūbī, *Taʾrīkh*, vol. 1, pp. 49, 52. Cf. Gil, "The origins of the Jews of Yathrib", *JSAI* 4 (1984), p. 212, quoting this as well as other sources of similar content.

[32] In Nazwī's *Muṣannaf*, vol. 11, p. 132 we read: "Abū ʿAbd Allāh said: The Prophet did not take prisoner any Arab except the Arab Jews of Khaybar (*ma sabā rasūl Allāh … aḥadan min al-ʿarab illā ʿarab yahūd Khaybar*). See also Ibn Taymiyya, *Fatāwā*, vol. 35, p. 221: *sāʾir al-yahūd wa al-naṣārā min al-ʿarab*; and the cryptic statement of Vaglieri (in *EI*², s.v. "Khaybar", vol. 4, p. 1138a infra) according to whom the population of Khaybar consisted of "Jewish tribes and of Hebraised tribes."

[33] Shāfiʿī, *Kitāb al-umm*, vol. 4, p. 244, l. 15.

[34] Ibn Qayyim al-Jawziyya, *Aḥkām ahl al-dhimma*, vol. 1, p. 65. Ibn Qudāma (*al-Mughnī*, vol. 8, p. 515) speaks about people from Kināna and Ḥimyar who embraced Judaism (*man … tahawwada min Kināna wa Ḥimyar*).

[35] Ibn Taymiyya, *Fatāwā*, vol. 31, p. 380; cf. Ibn Qudāma, *al-Mughnī*, vol. 8, p. 499.

[36] Ibn Qudāma, *al-Mughnī*, vol. 8, p. 499.

Shihāb al-Zuhrī (d. 124 A.H. / 724 A.D.), Qatāda b. Diᶜāma (d. 117 A.H. / 735 A.D.) and others.[37] It is attributed also to Abū Ḥanīfa (d. 150 A.H. / 767 A.D.), Mālik b. Anas (d. 179 A.H. / 796 A.D.) and is the last (and therefore the authoritative) view reported about Ibn Ḥanbal.[38] Al-Shaybānī (d. 189 A.H. / 804 A.D.) seems to have held it as well: while discussing the permissibility of consuming meat slaughtered by Jews and Christians, he does not make any distinction between their various groups.[39] In a similar vein, al-Sarakhsī stipulates that a Muslim who has a *kitābī* wife must spend with her the same time which he spends with her Muslim counterpart, "whether she is ethnically related to the Children of Israel or not" (*isrāʾīliyya kānat aw ghayr isrāʾīliyya*).[40] The Ḥanbalī jurist Ibn Qayyim al-Jawziyya devotes a lengthy discourse to the substantiation of this stance.[41] All these scholars do not consider the time of conversion or ethnic affiliation as factors in determining eligibility for *dhimmī* status: all adherents to Judaism and Christianity, whatever the date of their (or their ancestors') conversion and whatever their lineage, are eligible for it. Numerous actions of the Prophet are cited in support of this opinion. The Prophet took *jizya* from the Jews of Yemen; they were for the most part Arabs who had embraced Judaism after the coming of Jesus, during the times of Tubbaᶜ, and from the Jews of Taymāʾ and Wādī al-Qurā. He also took *jizya* from the people of Najrān who were Arab Christians; according to some traditions, they were the first people to pay it. The same is true for Ukaydir, the ruler of Dūmat al-Jandal, who was an Arab and one of the Christian *ᶜibād*.[42] All these descriptions indicate that many Arab inhabitants of the peninsula embraced Judaism or Christianity in the Jāhiliyya, after these two faiths had already been corrupted and could no longer be considered as legitimate expressions of divine will. Nevertheless, the Prophet did not ask any one of these Jewish or Christian groups what was their genealogy and whether they had embraced their respective religions before his mission or after it, before the *naskh* and *tabdīl* or after it.[43] Qurʾān 5:5 in which all People

[37] Ṭabarī, *Jāmiᶜ al-bayān*, vol. 6, 101. Cf. Jaṣṣāṣ, *Mukhtaṣar ikhtilāf al-ᶜulamāʾ*, vol. 3, p. 206 (no. 1304) where ᶜIkrima's view is related by ᶜAṭāʾ b. al-Sāʾib.

[38] Ibn Taymiyya, *Majmūᶜ fatāwā*, vol. 7, p. 55; vol. 35, p. 219, 221, 224; Khiraqī, *Mukhtaṣar*, pp. 206–207. There is an obscure passage on this issue in Zarkashī, *Sharḥ*, vol. 6, pp. 469–470. Cf. also Ibn Abī Zayd al-Qayrawānī, *Kitāb al-jihād*, p. 450.

[39] Sarakhsī, *Sharḥ kitāb al-siyar al-kabīr*, vol. 1, p. 146. See also Jubūrī, *Fiqh al-imām al-Awzāᶜī*, vol. 1, pp. 462–463; vol. 2, pp. 28–29.

[40] Sarakhsī, *Mabsūṭ*, vol. 4, pp. 210, l. 23 – p. 211, l. 1.

[41] Ibn Qayyim al-Jawziyya, *Aḥkām ahl al-dhimma, vol. 1*, pp. 65–75.

[42] Sarakhsī, *Mabsūṭ*, vol. 10, p. 119; Ibn ᶜAbd al-Barr al-Namarī, *Tamhīd*, vol. 2, p. 124; Ibn Zanjawayhi, *Kitāb al-amwāl*, vol. 1, p. 129, no. 110; Ibn Qudāma, *al-Mughnī*, vol. 8, pp. 499, 515; Ibn Qayyim al-Jawziyya, *Aḥkām ahl al-dhimma*, vol. 1, pp. 3, 85; Zarkashī, *Sharḥ*, vol. 6, pp. 447–448 (no. 3322), pp. 581–582 (no. 3480). The historical tradition is not unanimous on this: according to some versions, Ukaydir embraced Islam, and if this is the case, the whole issue does not arise. For both versions see, for instance, Balādhurī, *Futūḥ al-buldān*, pp. 61–63.

[43] Ibn Taymiyya, *Majmūᶜ fatāwā*, vol 35, p. 222; Ibn Qayyim al-Jawziyya, *Aḥkām ahl al-dhimma*, vol. 1, p. 65. See also the lengthy discussion of the issue in Sarakhsī, *Mabsūṭ*, vol. 10, pp. 118–119. A short remark in *Mukhtaṣar al-Muzanī ᶜalā al-Umm*, in Shāfiᶜī, *Kitāb al-umm*, vol. 9, p. 296, lines 1–2, indicates that this Shāfiᶜī author also held this view in contradistinction to the eponymous founder of his school.

of the Book are treated as one group is also understood as supportive of this interpretation.[44] The law applicable to this issue is rooted in religion, not in genealogy (*ḥillu dhabāʾiḥihim wa munākaḥatihim murattab ʿalā adyānihim, lā ʿalā ansābihim*) or in the date of conversion.[45] An eloquent statement in support of this attitude is formulated by Ibn Taymiyya. He asserted that bringing genealogical considerations into the realm of religion would be contrary to the principles of Islam and a regression into the Jāhiliyya.[46]

The opposite view was supported by jurists for whom ethnicity was a factor in deciding the legal standing of non-Muslims. This group based their distinction between Christians in general and Christians of Arab extraction[47] on traditions concerning the Christian Arab tribe of Banū Taghlib.[48] These traditions are relevant to two legal issues: the possibility of including Arab Christians in the category of *ahl al-dhimma*, and the legality of wedding their women and consuming meat slaughtered by them. ʿUmar b. al-Khaṭṭāb maintained that Arab Christians were not People of the Book and was not prepared to leave them alone unless they embrace Islam; should they refuse, he was determined to kill them (*mā naṣārā al-ʿarab bi-ahl al-kitāb … wa mā anā bi-tārikihim ḥattā yuslimū aw aḍriba aʿnāqahum*).[49] According to another tradition, his view was more lenient: he was not certain whether the members of this Christian tribe were eligible for the status of *ahl al-dhimma*, or, being Arabs, they have to be treated as harshly as the Arab polytheists. Eventually, ʿUmar was swayed toward the more lenient view. His considerations included the fact that the Taghlib transferred to him some of their property; that they were, after all, Christians and not polytheists; and that the Prophet predicted that "Allah will protect the religion (of Islam) by means of Christians of (the tribe of) Rabīʿa on the banks of the Euphrates" (*inna Allāh … sa-yamnaʿu al-dīn bi-naṣārā min Rabīʿa ʿalā shāṭiʾ al-Furāt*).[50] ʿUmar interpreted this tradition as relating to the Taghlib and he imposed on them conditions of surrender. These conditions were harsher than those imposed on the Christian cities of Syria and Palestine: ʿUmar ruled that the Taghlib would be allowed to retain their religion, but would be forbidden to baptize their children. If they do baptize them, the agreement with them will be annulled. In other words, the religious tolerance with regard to the Taghlib would extend for one generation only. The material dealing with this issue seems to indicate that the Taghlib did not abide by ʿUmar's conditions, that they raised their children in Christianity and some

[44] Ibn Qudāma, *al-Mughnī*, vol. 8, p. 517; Ibn Taymiyya, *Majmūʿ fatāwā*, vol. 7, p. 55.

[45] Ibn Qayyim al-Jawziyya, *Aḥkām ahl al-dhimma*, vol. 1, p. 65.

[46] Ibn Taymiyya, *Majmūʿ fatāwā*, vol. 35, pp. 229–230.

[47] In order to avoid a possible misunderstanding, it would be useful to point out that classical Muslim traditionists and jurists use this term only for the Christian tribes who lived in the Arabian peninsula. The Christian inhabitants of other areas in the Middle East who espoused the Arabic language after the Muslim conquest and are now considered Christian Arabs are not included in this category as understood in the *ḥadīth* and *fiqh* literature.

[48] For basic information on Taghlib, see the extensive article of H. Kindermann, in *EI*[1], Supplement, s.v., and of M. Lecker, in *EI*[2], s.v.

[49] Shāfiʿī, *Kitāb al-umm*, vol. 4, p. 259, l. 11; ibid., vol. 2, p. 364, ll. 7–8.

[50] Ibn Sallām, *Kitāb al-amwāl*, p. 542 (nos. 1697–1698).

Muslims demanded therefore to resume the fighting against them.[51] It is noteworthy that according to a rarely quoted tradition, ᶜUmar did not allow any Jew or Christian to induct his children into his faith in the kingdom of the Arabs (… *anna ᶜUmar b. al-Khaṭṭāb kāna lā yadaᶜu yahūdiyyan wa lā naṣrāniyyan yunaṣṣiru waladahu wa lā yuhawwiduhu fī mulk al-ᶜarab*).[52]

The issue of Taghlib was unique also from another point of view. According to a repeatedly quoted tradition, the Taghlib were keenly aware of the humiliation connected with the payment of the *jizya* according to Qurʾān 9:29. They argued that they should not be subjected to this indignity because they were Arabs and as such should not be treated in this way.[53] Furthermore, they were a strong tribe and threatened to join the Byzantines if a satisfactory arrangement was not reached with them. On the basis of these considerations, ᶜUmar agreed to the suggestion of al-Nuᶜmān b. Zurᶜa[54] "to take from them *jizya*, calling it *ṣadaqa*" (*khudh minhum al-jizya bi-'smi al-ṣadaqa*).[55] He made peace with them stipulating that this *ṣadaqa* would be double the regular amount;[56] in other words, they would pay the amount that would be due from them if they paid the *jizya*, but would not suffer the indignity associated with it. The Taghlibīs are said to have fought for their honor as Arabs well into the Umayyad period. In a fascinating tradition, they are said to have asked the Umayyad caliph ᶜUmar b. ᶜAbd al-ᶜAzīz (r. 717–720) "to attach them to the Arabs" (*alḥiqnā bi-'l-ᶜarab*), apparently still thinking that their Arab ethnicity should bestow upon them all rights pertaining to their Muslim brethren. ᶜUmar

[51] Abū Yūsuf, *Kitāb al-kharāj*, pp. 121–135; Khiraqī, *Mukhtaṣar*, pp. 206–207; Ibn Qudāma, *al-Mughnī*, vol. 8, p. 513; Ibn Taymiyya, *Fatāwā*, vol. 7, p. 56; vol. 35, pp. 219–220, 223; Ibn Zanjawayhi, *Kitāb al-amwāl*, vol. 1, pp. 130–131, nos. 111, 113; Balādhurī, *Futūḥ*, p. 183.

[52] Ṣanᶜānī, *Muṣannaf*, vol. 6, pp. 48–49 (no. 9971); vol. 10, p. 319 (no. 19230), pp. 366–367 (no. 19389). What is exactly meant by "the kingdom of the Arabs" in this tradition is not clear at all.

[53] The idea that Arabs cannot be humiliated is mentioned in other contexts as well. It is said, for instance, that the Prophet did not take prisoners after the conquest of Mecca because "an Arab cannot be enslaved" (*lā riqqa ᶜalā ᶜarabī*). See Nazwī, *Muṣannaf*, vol. 1, p. 128. According to Sarakhsī, the underlying principle of this ruling has dire consequences: since Arabs cannot be enslaved and *jizya* cannot be imposed on them because of the ensuing humiliation, they must either embrace Islam or be killed (Sarakhsī, *Mabsūṭ*, vol. 10, p. 118). On the other hand, we read in the *Mudawwana* that Mālik b. Anas was not known to have expressed any view on this matter; according to al-ᶜUtaqī, in this respect the Arabs are to be treated like the non-Arabs (*qultu: a-raʾayta al-ᶜarab idhā subū hal ᶜalayhim al-riqq fī qawl Mālik? qāla: lam asmaᶜ min Mālik fīhim shayʾan wa lā aqūmu ᶜalayhi wa hum fī hādhā bi-manzilat al-aᶜājim*). See Saḥnūn, *al-Mudawwana al-kubrā*, vol. 2, p. 24, ll. 4–6.

[54] A tribal chief of Taghlib. As an enemy of Bakr b. Wāʾil and an envoy of the Persian king, he was involved in the events which led to the battle of Dhū Qār. See Ṭabarī, *Taʾrīkh al-rusul wa al-mulūk*, series I, pp. 1030, 1037 and *The history of Ṭabarī*, Albany: State University of New York Press, 1999, vol. 5 (translated and annotated by C. E. Bosworth), p. 370, note 903.

[55] Ibn Qudāma, *al-Mughnī*, vol. 8, p. 513. Cf. Balādhurī, *Futūḥ*, p. 181; Ṭabarī, *Taʾrīkh*, series 1, p. 2510

[56] Abū 'Ubayd, *Kitāb al-amwāl*, p. 541, no. 1694; Balādhurī, *Futūḥ*, pp. 181–183; Ibn Qudāma, *al-Mughnī*, vol. 8, pp. 499, 516; Ibn Qayyim al-Jawziyya, *Aḥkām ahl al-dhimma*, pp. 76–77; Zarkashī, *Sharḥ al-Zarkashī ᶜalā mukhtaṣar al-Khiraqī*, vol. 6, pp. 578–579 (with numerous references to other sources in the editor's note); see also Ibn Qayyim al-Jawziyya, *Aḥkām ahl al-dhimma*, pp. 78–79 according to whom ᶜUmar b. ᶜAbd al-ᶜAzīz (r. 717–720) reversed this ruling and insisted on levying the *jizya* from the Taghlib, apparently because in his times the Taghlib were no longer in the position to endanger the Muslims by threatening to join the Byzantines.

reacted sharply. He imposed on them the *dhimma* conditions in an extremely humiliating fashion; specifically, he deprived them of the right to wear turbans, a symbol of Arab — and Muslim — pride.[57] ᶜAlī b. Abī Ṭālib is also reported to have adopted a special position with regard to the Taghlib. He forbad the Muslims marrying Taghlibī women because he did not know whether this tribe had embraced Christianity before it was changed and corrupted or afterwards. He is also said to have supported the view that the Jews who are mentioned in the Qurᵓān are those whose ancestors had embraced their religion before the times of Jesus and before its abrogation (*naskh*) and corruption (*tabdīl*) of their religion.[58]

Among the early traditionists, ᶜAṭāᵓ b. Abī Rabāḥ (d. 114 or 155 A.H. / 732 or 733 A.D.) was supportive of ᶜAlī's view. He maintained that Christian Arabs are not People of the Book; People of the Book are only the Children of Israel who received the Tawrāt and the Injīl (*laysa naṣārā al-ᶜarab bi-ahl al-kitāb innamā ahl al-kitāb banū Isrāᵓīl* (*wa*) *alladhīna jāᵓathum al-tawrāt wa al-injīl fa-ammā man dakhala fīhim min al-nās fa-laysū minhum*).[59] He is reported to have thought that Muslims were permitted to wed only those *kitābī* women who are covered by this definition.[60] But the pride of place among the jurists who did not consider the Jews and the Christians as homogeneous entities belongs to al-Shāfiᶜī. He drew far-reaching conclusions from the existence in the peninsula of Arab adherents of Judaism and Christianity and asserted that Jews and Christians who are not ethnically related to the Banū Isrāᵓīl cannot be regarded as People of the Book absolutely, but only in a certain sense. He ruled, therefore, that it was lawful to levy from them the *jizya*,[61] and, presumably, to allow them to retain their religion, but under no circumstances were the Muslims permitted to marry Arab or Persian women who embraced Judaism or Christianity (... *fa-lam yakūnū ahla kitābin illā bi-maᶜnan lā ahla kitābin muṭlaq fa-lam yajuz – wa 'llāhu taᶜālā aᶜlam – an yunkaḥa nisāᵓu aḥadin*

[57] See Ibn Taymiyya, *Iqtiḍāᵓ al-ṣirāṭ al-mustaqīm*, vol. 1, p. 329: "A group of Taghlibīs came to visit ᶜUmar b. ᶜAbd al-ᶜAzīz, wearing turbans in the Arab fashion. They said: 'O Commander of the Faithful, attach us to the Arabs!' He said: 'Who are you?' They said: 'We are the sons of Taghlib.' He said: 'Are you then not from the inner core of the Arabs?' They said: 'We are Christians.' He said: 'Bring me a shear.' He cut their forelocks, threw the turbans (off their heads) and cut a span's length from the garment of each one of them, so that he use it as a girdle. He said: 'Do not ride saddles (*surūj*), but rather simple pads (*ukuf*) and suspend both your feet from the same side (of the riding animal).'" Cf. Ibn Qayyim al-Jawziyya, *Aḥkām ahl al-dhimma*, vol. 2, p. 742. For an exhaustive study of the turban and its significance in the Islamic tradition, see M. J. Kister, "'The crowns of this community ...' Some notes on the turban in the Islamic tradition." *Jerusalem Studies in Arabic and Islam* 24 (2000), pp. 217–245 (especially pp. 225, 229).

[58] Ibn Taymiyya, *Majmūᶜ fatāwā*, vol. 35, pp. 212, 219–220, 233; Ibn Qudāma, *Mughnī*, vol. 8, p. 517.

[59] Shāfiᶜī, *Kitāb al-umm*, vol. 5, p. 11, ll. 6–7.

[60] See Ṣanᶜānī, *Muṣannaf*, vol. 6, p. 72. The text is cryptic, but the meaning is not in any doubt: *qultu li-ᶜAṭāᵓ: naṣārā al-ᶜarab? lā yankiḥu al-muslimūn nisāᵓahum wa lā tuᵓkalu dhabāᵓiḥuhum, wa kāna lā yarā yahūda illā banī isrāᵓīl qaṭṭu* ... The last sentence means: "He thought that (from amongst) the Jews only (the women of) Banū Isrāᵓīl (can be married and only their food can be consumed)." On the terms *Yahūd* and *Banū Isrāᵓīl*, see below at notes 74 and 76. A similar tradition is attributed to Ibn ᶜAbbās: *lā tuᵓkalu dhabāᵓiḥu naṣārā banī Taghlib wa lā tunkaḥu nisāᵓuhum laysū minnā wa lā min ahl al-kitāb.* See Balādhurī, *Futūḥ*, pp. 181–182.

[61] Shāfiᶜī, *Aḥkām al-Qurᵓān*, vol. 2, pp. 53, 55; idem, *Kitāb ikhtilāf al-ḥadīth*, in Shāfiᶜī, *Kitāb al-umm*, vol. 9, p. 571, ll. 12–14. Cf. Abū ᶜUbayd, *Kitāb al-amwāl*, p. 26 (no. 63).

min al-ᶜarab wa al-ᶜajam ghayri banī Isrāʾīl dāna dīn al-yahūd wa al-naṣārā bi-ḥāl), and it was not legal to consume meat slaughtered by people belonging to these groups.[62] In a similar manner, al-Shāfiᶜī is said to have understood Qurʾān 5:5, which allows Muslims to marry scriptuary women, as applicable only to those who are ethnically Banū Isrāʾīl; it does not cover female members of other nations who joined the People of the Book by embracing their religion (… *man kāna dakhīlan fīhim min sāʾir al-umam mimman dāna bi-dīnihim*).[63]

Al-Shāfiᶜī was also resolved to prevent any further conversions to Christianity or Judaism. He maintained that *dhimmī* status can be given only to those Jews and Christians who (or whose forefathers) belonged to one of these religions before the coming of Islam. It can not be bestowed on those who embraced Judaism or Christianity during Muḥammad's mission or after it. According to his view, these "new" Jews and Christians should be given the options of embracing Islam or reverting to their former faith. A failure to abide by one of these alternatives would result in their expulsion from the land of Islam.[64] Al-Shāfiᶜī was apparently not willing to entertain the possibility that after the revelation of the Qurʾān there would be an increase in the number of those who deny the truth contained in it.[65]

It is fascinating to explore the reasons for al-Shāfiᶜī's decision to treat the Arab scriptuaries as a special category. The considerations which may have contributed to the development of his approach are indicated in a tradition attributed to ᶜUmar b. al-Khaṭṭāb. ᶜUmar is reported to have instructed one of his tax collectors to act harshly towards the Taghlib: since they are Arabs and not People of the Book, the chances of converting them are better.[66] According to this tradition, Arabs are more susceptible to conversion than others – possibly because Muḥammad was an Arab

[62] Shāfiᶜī, *Kitāb al-umm*, vol. 4, p. 259, ll. 8–9; cf. ibid., vol. 2, p. 364, lines 7–8; Shāfiᶜī, *Aḥkām al-Qurʾān*, vol. 2, p. 57; Ibn Qudāma, *al-Mughnī*, vol. 8, pp. 515, 517.

According to Aḥmad b. Ḥanbal, animals slaughtered by Abyssinian Christians may also not be consumed by Muslims, because some of the Abyssinians "slaughter with the(ir) nail(s)" (*hum naṣārā illā anna minhum qawman yadhbaḥūna bi-'l-ẓafar fa-lā yuʾkalu taᶜāmuhum*). See Khallāl, *Ahl al-milal*, p. 447 (no. 1049).

[63] Ṭabarī, *Jāmiᶜ al-bayān*, vol. 6, p. 101; Ṭabrisī, *Majmaᶜ al-bayān*, vol. 6, p. 32. Shāfiᶜī, *Kitāb al-umm*, vol. 5, p. 10, ll. 10–14. Shāfiᶜī does not make this distinction between the various types of the People of the Book when he discusses Qurʾān 5:5 in his *Aḥkām al-Qurʾān*, vol. 1, p. 187, and vol. 2, pp. 103, 184. See also Ghazālī, *Iḥyāʾ*, vol. 2, p. 36 infra.

[64] Shāfiᶜī, *Kitāb al-umm*, vol. 4, p. 260, ll. 6ff; Ibn Qayyim al-Jawziyya, *Aḥkām ahl al-dhimma*, vol. 1, p. 66 (quoting Muzanī's *Mukhtaṣar*); Jaṣṣāṣ, *Mukhtaṣar ikhtilāf al-ᶜulamāʾ*, vol. 3, p. 305 (no. 1304). For a similar view of a Ḥanbalī jurist, see Zarkashī, *Sharḥ al-Zarkashī ᶜalā Mukhtaṣar al-Khiraqī*, vol. 6, p. 567.

[65] For a possible application of this Shāfiᶜī distinction in the Ottoman period, see P. Wittek, "*Devshirme* and *sharīᶜa*", in *BSOAS* 17 (1955), pp. 271–278. Wittek argues that the Ottomans might have allowed themselves to recruit Balkan Christian children, forcibly convert them to Islam and use them as the Sultan's standing army – in flagrant contravention of their rights as *dhimmīs* – because they knew that the Albanians, the Serbs and the Bulgarians had all been converted to Christianity after the revelation of the Qurʾān and they must have known about the Shāfiᶜī distinction between various groups of Christians. While Wittek was not able to show positively that the Ottomans acted on the basis of the Shāfiᶜī distinction, his argument is intriguing. My attention to Wittek's work was drawn by Lewis, *Race and slavery in the Middle East*, p. 109, note 38.

[66] Abū Yūsuf, *Kitāb al-kharāj*, pp. 121, 135.

and the Qurʾān was revealed in Arabic.[67] Therefore more proselytizing efforts must be made with regard to the Arab Christians, and no easy alternative to conversion should be left available to them. It is more difficult to understand what is the intent of the statement that the Taghlib were not People of the Book: it seems to mean that since their affiliation with Christianity started relatively late, and hence the Injīl had not been revealed to them or to their ancestors in person, they can not be considered scriptuaries in the full sense of the word. Furthermore, their attachment to the faith may be weaker than that of their coreligionists who are not only Christians by faith, but are also ethnically related to the ancient Children of Israel. The jurists who think along these lines find support in a frequently quoted tradition of ᶜAlī who held a very low opinion of the Christian Arabs' religiosity: he commented derisively that the only commandment of their religion which they faithfully observed was the permissibility of imbibing wine.[68]

The Christian Arabs should therefore be treated, in al-Shāfiᶜī's view, differently from other *dhimmī*s: they should be allowed to retain their religion upon payment of *jizya*, but Muslims may not marry their women or consume meat slaughtered by them. A Mālikī scholar explained that this distinction stems from the different nature of these two issues: *jizya* is designed to punish and humiliate the People of the Book and therefore can be levied from all their groups, but the permission to marry *kitābī* women and consume their food is perceived as an honor which may be bestowed only on those who are People of the Book in the full sense: both religiously and ethnically.[69] According to another, Shāfiᶜī, explanation, the special regulations concerning the Christian Arabs stem from the fact that ᶜUmar b. al-Khaṭṭāb and the Prophet's companions were not sure whether they had embraced Christianity before its corruption or after it. They decided therefore that the lives of the Christian Arabs would be spared upon payment of *jizya* because blood should not be shed on a doubtful basis; but Christian Arab women would not be sought in marriage because sexual liaisons cannot be permitted when there is doubt concerning their legitimacy or propriety (*... naṣārā al-ᶜarab ka-Wajj wa Fihr wa Taghlib fa-hawlāʾi shakka fīhim ᶜUmar fa-shāwara fīhim al-ṣaḥāba fa-'ttafaqū ᶜalā iqrārihim bi-'l-jizya ḥaqnan li-dimāʾihim wa an lā tuʾkala dhabāʾiḥuhum wa lā tunkaḥa nisāʾuhum li-anna al-dimāʾ maḥqūna fa-lā tubāḥu bi-'l-shakk wa al-furūj maḥẓūra fa-lā tustabāḥu bi-'l-shakk*).[70]

[67] Cf. the explanation of E. Fagnan, *Le livre de l'impôt foncier*, Paris: Librairie Orientaliste, 1921, p. 186, note 1, who says: "Ce qu'il faut entendre dans ce sense que, étant Arabes, le seul Koran est pour eux le Livre révélé."

[68] Ibn Qudāma, *al-Mughnī*, vol. 8, p. 517; Ibn Taymiyya, *Majmūᶜ fatāwā*, vol. 35, p. 223; Ibn Qayyim al-Jawziyya, *Aḥkām ahl al-dhimma*, vol. 1, p. 87; Zarkashī, *Sharḥ*, vol. 6, p. 583 (no. 3481).

[69] Ibn ᶜAbd al-Barr al-Namarī, *Tamhīd*, vol. 2, pp. 116–117. Al-Namarī speaks here of a similar ruling with regard to the Zoroastrians, but the argumentation may be relevant also to the case at hand.

[70] Māwardī, *al-Ḥāwī al-kabīr*, vol. 9, p. 223. A similar argumentation can be found also in Ibn Qayyim al-Jawziyya, *Aḥkām ahl al-dhimma*, pp. 10–11.

Al-Shāfiʿī's category of Arab scriptuaries is significant also from a historical point of view. He deemed it necessary to create this legal category because he was aware of the fact that significant numbers of Arab Jews and Christians had existed in the peninsula. In view of the ample material concerning the tribe of Taghlib, the issue is better known with regard to Christian Arabs.[71] It is evident, however, that a similar situation obtained also with regard to the Jews. The existence of Judaism among the Arabs in the pre-Islamic period is, of course, well known and has been extensively discussed in research literature. Our sources indicate that conversions to Judaism and Christianity in the pre-Islamic period were of significant proportions, though we hear little of the way in which they occurred or of the reasons which may have brought them about.[72] Kister has drawn attention to a passage in al-Jāḥiẓ who praised Muḍar for being the only tribal group which was not permeated by Judaism, Christianity or Zoroastrianism and "knew only the religion of the Arabs, followed by Islam."[73] We have already noted al-Shāfiʿī's statement saying that whole Arab tribes "perished" by embracing Judaism or Christianity, and that most Jews of the Yemen were of Arab origin. Similar statements can be found in historical literature. Referring to a passage in al-Qalqashandī, Goitein drew attention to the view that the term *Banū Isrāʾīl* refers to "the ancient Jews by race", while *Yahūd* denotes Jews of other ethnic affiliation.[74] In our sources, Jewish influence among the Arabs is indicated in descriptions of the religious situation in the Jāhiliyya. Al-Masʿūdī, for example, reports that some Arabs "were inclined to Judaism and some to Christianity" (*wa minhum man māla ilā al-yahūdiyya wa al-naṣrāniyya*). Traditions about *ḥunafāʾ* who converted, or considered conversion, to Judaism or Christianity are well known. The standard commentaries on Qurʾān 2:256 speak about conversions to Judaism among the Arab inhabitants of pre-Islamic Medina.[75] A striking statement about significant numbers of converts to Judaism in the Jāhiliyya can be found in Abū al-Fidāʾ:

> The community of *Yahūd* is more inclusive than that of *Banū Isrāʾīl* because many Arabs, Byzantines, Persians and others became Jews without being (descendants of) *Banū Isrāʾīl;* indeed, *Banū Isrāʾīl* are the core in this religion while the others are strangers in it. Therefore every *yahūdī* is called *isrāʾīlī* (*wa ummat al-yahūd aʿammu*

[71] For a recent article on another Christian tribe, see I. Hasson, "Judhām entre la *Jāhiliyya* et l'Islam." *Studia Islamica* 81 (1995), pp. 5–42, especially pp. 20–21.

[72] Masʿūdī, *Murūj al-dhahab*, vol. 2, p. 252; and cf. Abū 'l-Fidāʾ, *Mukhtaṣar*, vol. 1, p. 98 infra; cf. Zarkashī, *Sharḥ al-Zarkashī ʿalā Mukhtaṣar al-Khiraqī*, vol. 6, pp. 581–582.

[73] Jāḥiẓ, *al-Radd ʿalā al-naṣārā*, in *Thalāth rasāʾil*, ed. Finkel, Cairo 1926, p. 15, quoted in M. J. Kister, "'O God, tighten thy grip on Muḍar…'", at pp. 242–243; reprinted in his *Society and religion from Jāhiliyya to Islam.* Variorum: London 1990. In the same passage, Jāḥiẓ gives a list of Arab tribes permeated by Judaism and Christianity. According to his description, Christianity was widespread among them, while Judaism was to be found among the Yaman and small fractions of Iyād and Rabīʿa. Most Jews were to be found in Yathrib, Ḥimyar, Taymāʾ, Wādī al-Qurā; these were "descendants of Hārūn rather than Arabs" (*min wuld Hārūn dūna al-ʿarab*). Contrast this with the passage from Ibn Taymiyya, *Majmūʿ fatāwā*, vol. 35, p. 225, quoted in note 30, above.

[74] Qalqashandī, *Ṣubḥ al-aʿshā*, Cairo: al-Maṭbaʿa al-amīriyya, 1918, vol. 13 (not 18), p. 253; see *EI*², s.v. "Banū Isrāʾīl" (vol. 1, p. 1022a).

[75] See M. Lecker, "ʿAmr b. Ḥazm al-Anṣārī …".

min banī Isrāʾīl li-anna kathīran min ajnās al-ʿarab wa al-rūm wa al-furs wa ghayrihim ṣārū yahūdan wa lam yakūnū min banī Isrāʾīl wa innamā banū Isrāʾīl hum al-aṣl fī hādhihi al-milla wa ghayruhum dakhīlun fīhā fa-li-dhālika yuqālu li-kulli yahūdī isrāʾīlī).[76]

Faint echoes of conversions to Zoroastrianism are also discernible in the traditional descriptions of the Jāhilī period. In a few traditions about him, the pre-Islamic Arab prophet Khālid b. Sinān al-ʿAbsī is credited with extinguishing a mobile fire which appeared in the land of the Arabs "who were lured by it and almost became Zoroastrians" (... *anna nāran ẓaharat fī arḍ al-ʿarab fa-'ftatanū bihā wa kānat tantaqilu fa-kādat al-ʿarab an tatamajjasa wa taghliba ʿalayhā al-majūsiyya*).[77] Ibn Qutayba speaks about Zoroastrianism in the tribe of Tamīm.[78] References to Arab Zoroastrians can occasionally be found in Qurʾānic exegesis.[79] And one could legitimately ask what were the ethnic origins of the Zoroastrians who lived in Hajar and al-Baḥrayn and are said to have been given the status of *ahl al-dhimma* by the Prophet. The spread of Judaism, Christianity (and Zoroastrianism?) among the Arabs was, in al-Shāfiʿī's view, significant enough to justify the creation of a special legal category for Jews and Christians who were of Arab ancestry and should therefore be treated differently from their coreligionists of non-Arab descent.

III

In the previous section we have discussed the status of the Jews and the Christians as scriptuaries. We have seen that most jurisprudents considered them as homogeneous groups, bestowing on all and sundry the same rights and obligations under Muslim law. Only al-Shāfiʿī deemed their ethnic provenance and the time of

[76] Abū 'l-Fidā, *Mukhtaṣar*, vol. 1, p. 87. See also Ibn Qutayba, *Maʿārif*, p. 621 who speaks about Judaism in Ḥimyar, Kināna, al-Ḥārith b. Kaʿb and Kinda.

[77] Masʿūdī, *Murūj al-dhahab*, vol.1, p. 75; Ibn al-Athīr, *al-Kāmil fī al-taʾrīkh*, vol. 1, p. 376; Jawād ʿAlī, *Taʾrīkh al-ʿarab qabl al-islām*, vol. 5, p. 367. Most accounts of Khālid b. Sinān do not contain an explicit reference to this issue and only describe Khālid's miraculous ability to enter into the fire, extinguish it and emerge unscathed. See, for instance, Ibn Ḥajar, *Iṣāba*, Cairo: Maṭbaʿat Nahḍat Miṣr, ca. 1971, vol. 2, p. 371. Ibn al-ʿAdīm (*Bughyat al-ṭalab fī taʾrīkh Ḥalab*, Frankfurt: Maʿhad taʾrīkh al-ʿulūm al-ʿarabiyya wa al-islāmiyya, 1986, vol. 7, p. 29) reads *tashtaʿilu* instead of *tantaqilu*. I owe this reference to my colleague Prof. Ella Landau-Tasseron; the possibility of this reading has also been brought up by Prof. M. Lecker. For an analysis of the traditions concerning Khālid b. Sinān, see Ella Landau-Tasseron, "Unearthing an Arabian prophet", *JSAI* 21 (1997), pp. 42–61.

[78] Ibn Qutayba, *Maʿārif*, p. 621. He also mentions al-Aqraʿ b. Ḥābis and Wakīʿ b. Ḥassān as Zoroastrians. See "al-Akraʿ b. Ḥābis" in *EI²*, s.v. (M. J. Kister); Ibn Qudāma, *al-Mughnī*, vol. 8, p. 515; Zarkashī, *Sharḥ al-Zarkashī ʿalā Mukhtaṣar al-Khiraqī*, vol. 6, pp. 581–582; and Jawād ʿAlī, *Taʾrīkh al-ʿarab qabl al-islām*, vol. 5, pp. 363–364; Chokr, *Zandaqa et zindīqs*, pp. 315–319.

[79] Referring to the views of the Mālikī scholars Ibn al-Qāsim, Ashhab and Saḥnūn, Qurṭubī says: "*Jizya* is taken from Arab Zoroastrians and from (the Zoroastrians?) of all other nations" (*tuʾkhadhu al-jizya min majūs al-ʿarab wa al-umam kullihā*). Ibn Wahb held a different opinion: "*Jizya* is not accepted from Arab Zoroastrians, but is accepted from other (Zoroastrians)" (*lā tuqbalu al-jizya min majūs al-ʿarab wa tuqbalu min ghayrihim*). See Qurṭubī, *al-Jāmiʿ li-aḥkām al-Qurʾān*, vol. 8, p. 45.

their conversion to be material factors in the determination of certain elements of their *sharʿī* status and reached the conclusion that Jews and Christians should be divided into two different categories on this basis. The nature of the Jewish and the Christian religious beliefs was not of central importance in these discussions; in a different context, however, these beliefs come in for sharp criticism which is essential for our inquiry into the classification of unbelievers in Muslim law and tradition.

It is a generally accepted notion that Islam considers Judaism and Christianity as monotheistic religions and bestows upon their adherents certain rights which it is not willing to grant to people affiliated with other faiths. In a certain sense this description of Islamic attitudes is true; Qurʾān 22:17 and 98:1, as well as other Qurʾānic verses in which the polytheists are mentioned separately from the People of the Book, serve as proof that the two groups should be considered distinct from each other.[80] However, this perception does not represent the whole spectrum of Muslim opinion. In the literature of tradition and in Qurʾānic exegesis, we repeatedly encounter the assertion that Jewish and Christian beliefs were contaminated with polytheistic elements. There is extensive discussion of the question what conclusions should be drawn from the existence of such elements when Muslims are called upon to determine their attitude to these two religions.

Let us start with an observation on the linguistic usage. Hawting has already noted correctly that "despite the distinction between Jews, Christians and *mushrikūn* made in some passages of the Qurʾān, it is sometimes impossible to maintain it in other Muslim texts, where *kufr* and *shirk* are imputed to Jews and Christians."[81] Numerous passages in the literature of jurisprudence and exegesis indicate that the term *mushrik* was often used for any non-Muslim. A clear example of this phenomenon can be found in al-Ṭabarī's commentary on Qurʾān 2:221: "Do not marry polytheist women until they believe ..." (*lā tankiḥū al-mushrikāt ḥattā yuʾminna* ...). Discussing the meaning of the verse, al-Ṭabarī says that according to some traditionists the verse was revealed with the intention of making all polytheist women forbidden to Muslims in marriage. He goes on to explain that it applies to all types of polytheists: idolaters, Jews, Christians, Zoroastrians and any other type (*fa-qāla baʿḍuhum: nazalat murādan bihā taḥrīmu nikāḥi kulli mushrika ʿalā kulli muslim min ayyi ajnāsi al-shirk kānat: ʿābidati wathan, aw kānat yahūdiyya aw naṣrāniyya aw majūsiyya aw min ghayrihim min aṣnāf al-shirk*). Only later, we are told, the prohibition to marry scriptuary women was abrogated by Qurʾān 5:5. Or, in another formulation, God "excluded the scriptuary women" (*istathnā nisāʾa ahl al-kitāb*) from the generality of polytheists.[82] Enumerating groups of people whom the Muslims should leave unharmed, Qatāda

[80] Ibn Qudāma, *al-Mughnī*, vol. 6, p. 590.
[81] Cf. Hawting, *The idea of idolatry*, pp. 82ff.
[82] Ṭabarī, *Jāmiʿ al-bayān*, vol. 2, p. 376 (for another formulation, see ibid., p. 377. This is not to say that this was the only understanding of the term: some commentators understood it as relating to idol worshipers only. See, for instance, Māwardī, *al-Ḥāwī*, vol. 9, p. 221: *wa dhahaba ghayruhu* (scil. *ghayr al-Shāfiʿī*) *min al-fuqahāʾ ilā anna ahl al-kitāb yanṭaliq ʿalā* (sic; probably a misprint for *ʿalayhi*) *ism al-kufr wa lā yanṭaliq ʿalayhi ism al-shirk* ... Ibn Qayyim al-Jawziyya maintains that in the Qurʾānic usage *ahl al-kitāb* are not included in the term *mushrikūn*. See his *Aḥkām ahl al-dhimma*, pp. 421, l. 17 – 422, l. 1.

mentions, among others, *zakāt*-paying Muslims and *jizya*-paying polytheists (*mushrik ᶜalayhi jizya*).[83] And ᶜUmar b. ᶜAbd al-ᶜAzīz who prohibited Jews and Christians from entering mosques is said to have quoted Qurᵓān 9:28 (... *innamā al-mushrikūna najas fa-lā taqrubū al-masjid al-ḥarām* ...) in support of his edict.[84]

Explicit statements according to which the term *mushrikūn* is comprehensive in its application to all non-Muslims can also be found. When ᶜAbd Allāh b. ᶜUmar wanted to substantiate his opposition to matrimony between Muslim males and *dhimmī* women, he is reported to have said: "A *kitābī* woman is an associationist" (*al-kitābiyya mushrika*).[85] Commenting on Qurᵓān 9:33, al-Shāfiᶜī asserts that *shirk* is a comprehensive term for two religions: the religion of the People of the Book, and the religion of the *ummiyyūn*, meaning the pre-Islamic Arabs.[86] Discussing Qurᵓān 2:221, he says that "the word *mushrik* is applied to the People of the Book and other polytheists" (*wa ism al-mushrik lāzim li-ahl al-kitāb wa ghayrihim min al-mushrikīn*).[87] The famous jurist al-Māwardī (d. 450 A.H. / 1058 A.D.), who wrote a voluminous exposition of Shāfiᶜī law, divides the polytheists into three groups: the People of the Book, meaning the Jews and the Christians; those who have no book, such as idolaters, sun worshipers, fire worshipers, worshipers of animals, believers in the eternity of the world and believers in the power of stars; and those who have a semblance of the book, such as the Ṣābiᵓa, the Sāmiriyya and the Zoroastrians.[88]

Certain beliefs of Jews and Christians are cited in support of their inclusion among the polytheists. The Prophet is reported to have considered the cross as an idol (*wathan*) and demanded that the Christian ᶜAdī b. Ḥātim take it off his neck when he came to meet him.[89] But the most important reason for the classification of Jews and Christians as polytheists is included in Qurᵓān 9:30–31: the Jews believe that ᶜUzayr is the son of God, the Christians believe that the *masīḥ* is the son of God, and both consider their sages and monks as lords beside Allah. Ibn ᶜUmar is reported to have said that no *shirk* is more opprobrious than if a woman says that her lord is Jesus.[90] It has also been argued that since the People of the Book denied the miracles performed by the messenger of God – and attributed them to some other entity – it is legitimate to use for them the term *shirk*.[91]

83 Ṭabarī, *Jāmiᶜ al-bayān*, vol. 10, pp. 78–79 (on Qurᵓān 9:5).

84 Ṭabarī, *Jāmiᶜ al-bayān*, vol. 10, p. 105; Suyūṭī, *al-Durr al-manthūr*, vol. 3, p. 227. Numerous other expressions which support our observation can be found in the literature. See, for instance, the sentence saying: *lam yakun bi-ḥaḍrat rasūl Allāh ... wa lā qurbahu wāḥidun min mushrikī ahl al-kitāb illā yahūd al-Madīna* ... in Shāfiᶜī, *Kitāb al-umm*, vol. 4, p. 242, l. 11.

85 Sarakhsī, *Mabsūṭ*, vol. 5, p. 210, l. 17.

86 Shāfiᶜī, *Aḥkām al-Qurᵓān*, vol. 2, p. 50: ... *jimāᶜ al-shirk dīnāni: dīn ahl al-kitāb wa dīn al-ummiyyīn*; Bayhaqī, *Sunan*, vol. 9, p. 179, l. 4; cf. Shāfiᶜī, *Aḥkām al-Qurᵓān*, vol. 2, p. 56: *wa ḥakama Allāh ... fī al-mushrikīna ḥukmayni: fa-ḥakama an yuqātala ahl al-awthān ḥattā yuslimū wa ahl al-kitāb ḥattā yuᶜṭū al-jizya in lam yuslimū*; Māwardī, *al-Ḥāwī al-kabīr*, vol. 9, p. 221.

87 Shāfiᶜī, *Kitāb al-umm*, vol. 5, p. 235, lines 13–14.

88 Māwardī, *al-Ḥāwī al-kabīr*, vol. 9, pp. 220–224; vol. 14, pp. 152ff.

89 Ṭabarī, *Jāmiᶜ al-bayān*, vol. 10, p. 114. Cf. Hawting, *The idea of idolatry*, p. 83.

90 Abū ᶜUbayd, *al-Nāsikh wa al-mansūkh*, p. 85, no. 144; Jaṣṣāṣ, *Aḥkām al-Qurᵓān*, vol. 1, p. 392; Ibn al-ᶜArabī, *al-Nāsikh wa al-mansūkh*, vol. 2, pp. 82–83; Ibn Taymiyya, *Majmūᶜ fatāwā*, vol. 14, p. 91; Ibn Qayyim al-Jawziyya, *Aḥkām ahl al-dhimma*, vol. 1, p. 188.

91 Māwardī, *al-Ḥāwī al-kabīr*, vol. 14, p. 152.

A more nuanced view of Jews and Christians is developed by Ibn Taymiyya in the framework of his polemics against the Shīʿa. In his view, there is no *shirk* in the basis of their religion, though some of them introduced into it polytheistic elements such as their attitude to their sages and monks. Therefore, if they are guilty of polytheistic tendencies, their polytheism is not absolute (*shirk muṭlaq*) but rather limited (*shirk muqayyad*). On the basis of this analysis, Ibn Taymiyya rejects the view of the Shīʿa who would prohibit marriage with Jewish and Christian women as a result of their classification as polytheists.[92]

IV

The only Qurʾānic reference to the Zoroastrians is in Sūra 22:17, where they are mentioned as one of the religions whom God will judge on the Last Day. The verse does not include any directive concerning their treatment by the Muslims and does not make any specific assessment of their religious standing. The scarcity of Qurʾānic material on this group is not difficult to understand: the Zoroastrians did not play a significant role during the period of the Prophet's activity in the Arabian peninsula. This situation was, however, not destined to last. After the conquest of Iran, the Zoroastrian issue came to the forefront of Muslim attention. The nature of the Zoroastrian faith and the way in which the Muslims should treat the Zoroastrians was extensively discussed in *ḥadīth*, *fiqh* and exegesis.

An infrequently quoted tradition, related on the authority of Ibn ʿAbbās, maintains that the Prophet decided to forbid the existence of Zoroastrianism under Islamic rule. We are told in it about an encounter between the Prophet and an unnamed Zoroastrian leader. When the man emerged from the meeting, he informed Ibn ʿAbbās that the Prophet had demanded the conversion of the Zoroastrians – otherwise they would be killed.[93] Echoes of opposition to the inclusion of the Zoroastrians among the *dhimmī*s can also be discerned in Muqātil's *Tafsīr*: here the *munāfiqūn* resent the Prophet's willingness to include the Zoroastrians of Hajar among the *jizya* payers while refusing to accord the same privilege to their own kith and kin.[94] Al-Khaṭṭābī writes in his commentary on Bukhārī in a similar vein. Analyzing the standard tradition on this issue,[95] al-Khaṭṭābī observes that ʿUmar would not have waited for ʿAbd al-Raḥmān b. ʿAwf's testimony regarding the Prophet's treatment of the Zoroastrians if the idea of levying *jizya* indiscriminately from all infidels had been widespread among the Companions (*yadullu*[96] *ʿalā anna*

92 Ibn Taymiyya, *Majmūʿ fatāwā*, vol. 32, p. 179; vol. 35, pp. 213–214; cf. Ibn Qayyim al-Jawziyya, *Aḥkām ahl al-dhimma*, vol. 1, p. 189.

93 Bayhaqī, *Sunan*, vol. 9, p. 190; Dāraquṭnī, *Sunan*, vol. 2, p. 155; Ibn ʿAbd al-Barr al-Namarī, *al-Tamhīd*, vol. 2, p. 125; cf. Levi Della Vida, "Madjūs" *EI*[1], s.v. (vol. 1, p. 98a).

94 Muqātil b. Sulaymān, *Tafsīr*, vol. 1, p. 214; the same tradition is found also in Saḥnūn, *Mudawwana*, vol. 2, p. 47, ll. 9–12.

95 See below, note 101.

96 The subject of the verb is the standard tradition instructing the Muslims to treat the Zoroastrians as they treat the People of the Book (*sunnū bihim sunnat ahl al-kitāb*).

ra'yahu wa ra'ya man ma'ahu min al-ṣaḥāba fī zamānihi anna al-jizya lā tuqbalu illā min ahl al-kitāb wa law kānat al-jizya fī ra'y al-ṣaḥāba maqbūlatan min jamī' aṣnāf ahl al-kufr lamā kāna li-tawaqqufi 'Umar wa man ma'ahu fī dhālika ma'nan).[97] We may conclude from these traditions that a segment of early Muslim opinion opposed the inclusion of the Zoroastrians in the *dhimmī* category.

Nevertheless, the Zoroastrians came to be treated as *ahl al-dhimma*. The decision to include them in this category is explained with unusual candor in a rarely quoted statement attributed to al-Ḥasan b. Abī al-Ḥasan.[98] When asked about the reason because of which the early Muslims allowed the Zoroastrians to retain their fire-temples, to continue practicing their idolatry and contracting their incestuous marriages, he said that this was the decision of al-'Alā' b. al-Khaḍramī[99] when he reached al-Baḥrayn. In this version, no reason is given for al-'Alā''s decision. In a second version, however, the reason for allowing the Zoroastrians to wed their mothers and sisters is given frankly and clearly:

> The *shirk* which they practice is worse than that. They were allowed to practice it for the sake of the *jizya* (*kataba 'Umar b. 'Abd al-'Azīz ilā 'Adī b. Arṭa'a yas'alu al-Ḥasan: lima khulliya bayna al-majūs wa nikāḥ al-ummahāt wa al-akhawāt? fa-sa'alahu fa-qāla: al-shirk alladhī hum 'alayhi a'ẓamu min dhālika wa innamā khulliya baynahu wa baynahum min ajl al-jizya*).[100]

The tradition that is quoted time and again in this context does not give any reason for the decision to include the Zoroastrians in the *dhimmī* category, but simply attributes it to the Prophet. According to it, 'Umar b. al-Khaṭṭāb did not take the *jizya* from the Zoroastrians until he was told by 'Abd al-Raḥmān b. 'Awf that the Prophet had levied it from the Zoroastrians of Hajar and had enjoined the Muslims to treat them as they would treat the People of the Book (*sunnū bihim sunnat ahl al-kitāb*). Some versions of this tradition seem to place the whole issue in an administrative context and make 'Umar say: "I do not know how to treat these people who are neither Arabs nor People of the Book ..." (*mā adrī mā aṣna'u bi-hawlā'i al-qawm alladhīna laysū min al-'arab wa lā min ahl al-kitāb* ...).[101] The decision to levy *jizya* from the Zoroastrians seems to have initially aroused some opposition, but eventually it carried the day; Ibn 'Abbās himself is made to say that the Muslims acted upon the tradition of 'Abd al-Raḥmān b. 'Awf and abandoned his own which was, after all, based on the report of a Zoroastrian

97 Khaṭṭābī, *A'lām al-ḥadīth*, vol. 2, pp. 1462.

98 This is the famous Ḥasan al-Baṣrī (d. 110 A.H. / 728 A.D.).

99 Al-'Alā' b. al-Ḥaḍramī was a companion of the Prophet who is said to have sent him on various missions to the eastern part of the peninsula. As a tax collector, he was instrumental in the Muslim takeover of al-Baḥrayn and 'Umān. See Ibn Sa'd, *Ṭabaqāt*, index; Ṭabarī, *Ta'rīkh al-rusul wa al-mulūk*, index.

100 Shāfi'ī, *Kitāb al-umm*, vol. 5, p. 10. The second version of the *ḥadīth* is in a note by the editor, apparently quoted from 'Abd al-Razzāq.

101 'Abd al-Razzāq al-Ṣan'ānī, *Muṣannaf*, vol. 6, p. 69; vol. 10, p. 325; for other versions, see Bukhārī, *Ṣaḥīḥ, kitāb al-jizya, bāb 1*; Abū Yūsuf, *Kitāb al-kharāj*, pp. 129–130; Ibn Zanjawayhi, *Kitāb al-amwāl*, vol. 1, pp. 136–145, nos. 122–132; Balādhurī, *Futūḥ al-buldān*, pp. 77, 267; and numerous places in the standard *ḥadīth* literature. See also *EI*[1] and *EI*[2], s.v. *madjūs*.

and not on the testimony of a respected Companion.[102] The tradition also preserved a letter from the Prophet to Mundhir b. Sāwā[103] in which the Zoroastrians are given the option of retaining their religion upon payment of the *jizya*.[104] The status of the Zoroastrians as *dhimmī*s was established in this way and does not seem to have ever been seriously challenged. Nonetheless, the laws governing social contacts between them and the Muslims were different from those concerning the Jews and the Christians: by agreement of all schools of law with the exception of Ibn Ḥazm,[105] Muslims were not allowed to wed Zoroastrian women or consume meat slaughtered by them.[106]

The justification for including the Zoroastrians in the category of *dhimmī*s was a subject of extensive discussion. The principal question discussed in this framework is whether the Zoroastrians are to be considered not only *ahl al-dhimma* but also *ahl al-kitāb*. ᶜAlī b. Abī Ṭālib, who considered himself a foremost expert on matters Zoroastrian, maintained that in the distant past they had possessed a book which they used to read and a body of religious knowledge (*ᶜilm*) which they used to study, but both were removed from their hearts as punishment for incest which their king had committed, while intoxicated, with his daughter (or sister).[107] Al-Shāfiᶜī is reported by numerous *fuqahā*ᵓ to have been inconsistent in his views on this issue: in some places he said that they did not possess a book, or had only a "semblance" of a book (*shubhat kitāb*), while elsewhere he is reported to have considered them People of the Book.[108] It is noteworthy, however, that in *Kitāb al-umm* and in *Aḥkām al-Qur*ᵓ*ān*, al-Shāfiᶜī expressed only the opinion that the Zoroastrians had possessed a book of their own and strongly rejected any other perception of their religious standing.[109] Since they lived in a remote area, the

[102] Bayhaqī, *Sunan*, vol. 9, p. 190.

[103] A tribal chief of Tamīm who was appointed by the Persians in the pre-Islamic period to control the Arab tribes in Hajar. See Ibn Saᶜd, *Ṭabaqāt*, vol. 1, part 2, p. 19, ll. 6–7; "Mundhir b. Sāwā", *EI*², s.v. (M. J. Kister).

[104] Saḥnūn b. Saᶜīd, *al-Mudawwana al-kubrā*, vol. 2, p. 47; Abū Yūsuf, *Kitāb al-kharāj*, p. 131; Ibn Zanjawayhi, *Kitāb al-amwāl*, vol. 1, pp. 118–119; Bayhaqī, *Maᶜrifat al-sunan wa al-āthār*, vol. 7, p. 118; Namarī, *Tamhīd*, vol. 12, pp. 63–65; M. J. Kister, "Concepts of authority in Islam", *JSAI* 18(1994), pp. 88–90.

[105] See below, Chapter Five, section II.

[106] According to a rarely quoted tradition, Saᶜīd b. al-Musayyab saw nothing wrong if a Zoroastrian slaughtered a sheep for a Muslim according to the latter's instructions. See Ibn ᶜAbd al-Barr al-Namarī, *al-Tamhīd*, vol. 2, p. 116 infra.

[107] Abū Yūsuf, *Kitāb al-kharāj*, p. 129; Ṣanᶜānī, *Muṣannaf*, vol. 6, pp. 70–71; Shāfiᶜī, *Kitāb al-umm*, vol. 4, p. 245 lines 12–17; *Musnad al-imām al-Shāfiᶜī*, in *Kitāb al-umm*, vol. 9, p. 429, lines 5–12; Shāfiᶜī, *Kitāb ikhtilāf al-ḥadīth*, in Shāfiᶜī, *Kitāb al-umm*, vol. 9, p. 572, ll. 15 ff.; Māwardī, *al-Ḥāwī al-kabīr*, vol. 14, p. 154; Ibn ᶜAbd al-Barr al-Namarī, *al-Tamhīd*, vol. 2, p. 120; Ibn Zanjawayhi, *Kitāb al-amwāl*, vol. 1, p. 149, no. 140; Ṭaḥāwī, *Mushkil al-āthār*, vol. 2, pp. 411–412; Suyūṭī, *al-Durr al-manthūr*, vol. 3, p. 229. According to a rarely quoted tradition, ᶜAlī drew from this the conclusion (unacceptable to all schools of law) that Muslims may wed Zoroastrian women. See Sarakhsī, *Mabsūṭ*, vol. 5, p. 211, ll. 2–4.

[108] Māwardī, *al-Ḥāwī al-kabīr*, vol. 9, p. 224; Ibn Kathīr, *Masā*ᵓ*il al-Shāfiᶜī*, p. 192; Shīrāzī, *Muhadhdhab*, vol. 3, p. 306; Bājī, *Muntaqā*, vol. 2, p. 177 lines 2–1 from bottom.

[109] It seems likely that the attribution of the other view to al-Shāfiᶜī stems from the fact that a considerable number of later Shāfiᶜīs supported the view of the other *madhāhib*, according to which the Zoroastrians were not to be considered People of the Book, and did not want to be out of step with their master.

people of Ḥijāz were not as familiar with their faith as they were with Judaism and Christianity. Their book may have been unknown to the early Muslims for this reason, but al-Shāfiʿī had no doubt that such a book had indeed existed. His view is clearly formulated in his *Kitāb ikhtilāf al-ḥadīth* where he said: "The Zoroastrians are People of a Book other than the Tawrāt and the Injīl. They forgot their book and corrupted it. (Nevertheless,) the Messenger of God allowed to take *jizya* from them" (*wa al-majūs ahlu kitābin ghayri al-tawrāt wa al-injīl wa qad nasū kitābahum wa baddalūhu fa-adhina rasūl Allāh fī akhdh al-jizya minhum*).[110] The erstwhile existence of this unidentified book was in Shāfiʿī's judgment the only justification for the Zoroastrians' inclusion in the category of *ahl al-dhimma* and for the legality of levying *jizya* from them.[111] This characterization of the Zoroastrians is related a general principle of al-Shāfiʿī's legal thought: the *sunna* cannot abrogate the Qurʾān.[112] Qurʾān 9:29 speaks only of the People of the Book as eligible to pay the *jizya*; if the Zoroastrians are allowed to join this category, they must also be People of the Book, otherwise the *sunna* changed a Qurʾānic rule and this is unacceptable. Only *ahl al-kitāb* can be considered *ahl al-dhimma* and can be allowed to retain their religion upon payment of the *jizya*.

Among other jurists, Abū Thawr (d. 240 A.H. / 854 A.D.)[113] is said to have supported the idea that the Zoroastrians were People of the Book, but details of his view are hard to come by.[114] Ibn Ḥazm (d. 456 A.H. / 1064 A.D.) argued that the Prophet would never have taken *jizya* from the Zoroastrians if he had not considered them People of the Book. Such a policy would be contrary to Qurʾān 9:29 according to which *jizya* is to be taken from the People of the Book only.[115]

Al-Shāfiʿī's view on the nature of the Zoroastrian religion was rejected by other early jurisprudents, who assert that the Qurʾān never mentions a Book revealed to the Zoroastrians. They draw support from Qurʾān 6:156, which explicitly says that only two communities had received revelation before the Muslims, and these were undoubtedly the Jews and the Christians. The tradition attributed to ʿAlī concerning the Zoroastrian book is said to be unreliable; but even if it is considered trustworthy, the book had been removed and the Zoroastrians can not claim to possess a book now. The Ḥanafī jurist al-Jaṣṣāṣ views the matter from a slightly different angle: "The Zoroastrians do not believe in anything found in the books revealed to God's prophets; they rather read the book of Zarādusht who was a self-styled prophet and a liar" (*fa-inna al-majūs lā yantaḥilūna shayʾan min kutub Allāh al-munazzala ʿalā anbiyāʾihi wa innamā yaqraʾūna kitāb Zarādusht wa*

110 Shāfiʿī, *Kitāb ikhtilāf al-ḥadīth*, in Shāfiʿī, *Kitāb al-umm*, vol. 9, p. 571, lines 8–9.

111 Shāfiʿī, *Aḥkām al-Qurʾān*, vol. 2, p. 54; idem, *Kitāb al-umm*, vol. 4, pp. 245–246; *Mukhtaṣar al-Muzanī ʿalā al-Umm*, in Shāfiʿī, *Kitāb al-umm*, vol. 9, pp. 292–293); Ṭaḥāwī, *Mukhtaṣar ikhtilāf al-ʿulamāʾ*, vol. 3, p. 207 (no. 1305); Bayhaqī, *Maʿrifat al-sunan wa al-āthār*, vol. 7, pp. 115–116; Bayhaqī, *Sunan*, vol. 9, pp. 188–189; Māwardī, *al-Ḥāwī al-kabīr*, vol. 9, pp. 224–226. Shāfiʿī's views on the "scrolls" mentioned in the Qurʾān are also relevant to this issue; see below, section VI.

112 See Shāfiʿī, *Risāla*, ed. Shākir, Cairo: Maṭbaʿat Muṣṭafā al-Bābī al Ḥalabī, 1940, p. 106 (no. 314); *Kitāb Ikhtilāf al-ḥadīth*, in *Kitāb al-umm*, vol. 9, pp. 572 infra – 573; Abū ʿUbayd, *Kitāb al-nāsikh wa al-mansūkh*, J. Burton's Introduction, pp. 23–24.

113 See on him "Abū Thawr", in *EI*², s.v. (J. Schacht) and Jabr, *Fiqh al-Imām Abī Thawr.*

114 Khallāl, *Ahl al-milal*, p. 470 (no. 1142).

115 Ibn Ḥazm, *al-Muḥallā*, vol. 7, pp. 404–405.

kāna mutanabbiyan kadhdhāban).[116] Furthermore, the tradition instructing the Muslims to "treat them as you treat the People of the Book" (*sunnū bihim sunnata ahl al-kitāb*) would be absurd if the Zoroastrians were themselves People of the Book. They are treated like the People of the Book only as far as the *jizya* is concerned.[117] The Zoroastrians are therefore not People of the Book; moreover, their belief in the two forces should be considered *shirk* par excellence. Aḥmad b. Ḥanbal is reported to have said that their religion is foul (*dīnuhum qadhir*)[118] and Ibn ᶜAbbās said that it was written by Satan.[119] Nevertheless, *jizya* is accepted from them and they are considered *ahl al-dhimma*. The generally agreed ruling that Muslims may not marry their women or consume meat slaughtered by them is an indication that they are not People of the Book, and the permissions included in Qurʾān 5:5 are therefore not applicable to them.[120]

It is clear from this argumentation that in contradistinction to al-Shāfiᶜī, the other schools of law do not consider the possession of a heavenly book as an indispensable requirement for a group's inclusion in the category of *ahl al-dhimma*. Thus, while no heavenly book was revealed to the Zoroastrians according to most early traditionists, there is practically no disagreement concerning their status as *ahl al-dhimma*.

V

The polytheists, or "associationists" as they should be properly called (*mushrikūn*), are the next major group to be considered in the framework of this enquiry. We have seen that in a certain sense this term may include all non-Muslims, but in this section we are going to consider the polytheists in a more restricted and much better known sense: the idolaters of Arabia and of the other regions into which Islam spread during its formative period.

116 Jaṣṣāṣ, *Aḥkām al-Qurʾān*, vol. 2, p. 400. Surprisingly enough, most jurists seem to have been totally unaware of the existence of sacred Zoroastrian literature.

117 Khallāl, *Ahl al-milal*, p. 468 (no.1134); p. 470 (nos. 1139–1141).

118 Khallāl, *Ahl al-milal*, p. 468 (no. 1135).

119 Khallāl, *Ahl al-milal*, p. 469 (no. 1136).

120 Ibn Qayyim al-Jawziyya, *Aḥkām ahl al-dhimma*, vol. 1, pp. 1–2, 6; Abū Yūsuf, *Kitāb al-kharāj*, p. 67; Ṭaḥāwī, *Mukhtaṣar ikhtilāf al-ᶜulamāʾ*, vol. 3, p. 207 (no. 1305); Sarakhsī, *Mabsūṭ*, vol. 10, p. 119; Ibn ᶜAbd al-Barr al-Namarī, *Tamhīd*, vol. 2, pp. 119–120; Ibn Taymiyya, *Majmūᶜ fatāwā*, vol. 32, pp. 186–188. The view that the Zoroastrians are not People of the Book is explicitly attributed to Mālik b. Anas and Abū Ḥanīfa in Bājī, *Muntaqā*, vol. 2, p. 172, lines 2–1 from bottom. Ibn Ḥanbal seems to have held a similar view: when asked about the permissibility of marrying Jewish and Christian women, he approved of the practice; when he was asked the same question about the Zoroastrians, he said: "I am not enthusiastic about anyone except the People of the Book (*lā yuᶜjibunī illā min ahl al-kitāb*). See his *Marwiyyāt*, al-Riyād: Maktabat al-Muʾayyad, 1994, vol. 2, p. 15; cf. Khallāl, *Ahl al-milal*, p. 468 (nos. 1134–1135). For the views of other Ḥanbalīs, see Zarkashī, *Sharḥ*, vol. 6, p. 446 (no. 3320). The statements of Cl. Cahen (*EI²*, s.v. "Dhimma", vol. 2, p. 227b), of G. Vajda (*EI²*, s.v. "Ahl al-kitāb", vol 1, p. 264a), of A. Heinen (in Kerber, ed., *Wie tolerant ist der Islam?*, p. 101) and of R.L. Nettler ("People of the Book", "Dhimmī", in *The Oxford Encyclopaedia of the Modern Islamic World*, s.vv.) who maintained that the Zoroastrians attained the status of *ahl al-kitāb* is therefore accurate only with regard to the views of al-Shāfiᶜī.

According to the generally accepted perception, Islam considered the Jews and the Christians as a separate group, designated them as People of the Book, and was willing to grant them a measure of tolerance that was not offered to polytheists and idolaters. Again, such a formulation is true to a certain extent, but it is far from adequate and it does not do justice to the variety of views expressed on this issue in the books of *ḥadīth*, law and exegesis. The matter was complicated by the fact that while the Qur'ān spoke only of Arab idolaters whom the Prophet encountered during his activities in the Arabian peninsula, the Muslims soon came into contact with other idolatrous religions in the vast regions of their newly established empire. Since these religions went unmentioned in the Qur'ān and received only scant attention in the *ḥadīth*, the early jurists were free to discuss the matter without the encumbrance of authoritative texts. This seems to have been one of the principal reasons for the existence of such a variety of views regarding the non-Arab idolaters; we shall see, however, that even with regard to their Arab counterparts the juristic perception was far from uniform.

The question of unity or diversity in the polytheistic world is discussed in those chapters of Muslim jurisprudence which deal with the payment of *jizya*. It is well known that the payment of *jizya* is based on Qur'ān 9:29 which stipulates that it is the People of the Book who are to be fought "until they pay the *jizya* out of hand, while being humiliated."[121] Nevertheless, some jurists entertain the possibility of levying *jizya* also from some – or all – polytheists and classify them on the basis of their eligibility to pay this tax and, consequently, to retain their religion.

It is to be expected that al-Shāfiʿī, for whom the whole infidel world was (for some purposes at least) one homogeneous entity, would treat the polytheists in the same way. And, indeed, he did not make any distinction between the various groups of polytheists and included them all in the category that must accept Islam or face death.[122] This was also the view of Ibn Ḥazm[123] and it is said to have been the prevalent view of the Ḥanbalīs as well.[124] Another group of jurists also considered the polytheists to be a single group, but derived from this perception a totally opposite conclusion, allowing to take *jizya* from all of them. The early Syrian jurist al-Awzāʿī (d. 157 A.H. / 774 A.D.)[125] expressed this view in a very straightforward and unequivocal manner.[126] According to one tradition, Mālik b. Anas held the same opinion and "thought that *jizya* is to be taken from all kinds of polytheists and deniers, Arabs or non-Arabs, Taghlibīs or Qurashīs, whoever they

121 This verse has been subject to numerous attempts at interpretation. To the bibliography included in Lewis, *The Jews of Islam*, p. 195, note 9, add now U. Rubin, "Qur'ān and Tafsīr: the case of *ʿan yadin*", *Der Islam* 70 (1993), pp. 133–144.

122 Shāfiʿī, *Kitāb al-umm*, vol. 4, p. 247, ll. 1–5; Bayḍāwī, *Anwār al-tanzīl*, vol. 1, p. 383; Ṭabarī, *Ikhtilāf al-fuqahā'*, p. 201; Māwardī, *al-Ḥāwī al-kabīr*, vol. 14, p. 153; Ibn Qudāma, *al-Mughnī*, vol. 8, p. 363 *supra*.

123 Ibn Ḥazm, *al-Muḥallā*, vol. 7, pp. 404–405.

124 Ibn Qudāma, *al-Mughnī*, vol. 8, pp. 362 line 1 from bottom – 363 lines 1–2; Zarkashī, *Sharḥ al-Zarkashī ʿalā mukhtaṣar al-Khiraqī*, vol. 6, p. 567. For the views of Ibn Ḥanbal himself, see below.

125 See "al-Awzāʿī", *EI²*, s.v. (J. Schacht).

126 Jubūrī, *Fiqh al-imām al-Awzāʿī*, pp. 524–525; Ibn al-Turkmānī, *al-Jawhar al-naqī*, vol. 9, p. 185; Ibn Taymiyya, *Majmūʿ fatāwā*, vol. 19, p. 19.

may be – except the apostates" (*...fa-innahu ra'ā anna al-jizya tu'khadhu min jamī' ajnās al-shirk wa al-jaḥd, 'arabiyyan aw 'ajamiyyan, taghlibiyyan aw qurashiyyan, kā'inan man kāna illā al-murtadd*).[127] Discussing the tradition in which the Prophet instructed the Muslims to treat the Zoroastrians as they treat the People of the Book, he said that in his eyes "all communities have the status of the Zoroastrians (*fa-'l-ummam kulluhā fī hādhā bi-manzilat al-majūs 'indī*). Giving examples of such communities, he mentioned the Fazāzina of southern Libya,[128] the Slavs (*Ṣaqāliba*),[129] the Abar,[130] the Turks and other non-Arabs who were not People of the Book.[131] And the Ḥanafī jurist al-Jaṣṣāṣ, like 'Abd al-Razzāq al-Ṣan'ānī, reports a curious tradition according to which "the Prophet ... made peace with idolaters upon payment of *jizya* – except those who were Arabs" (*... anna al-nabī ... ṣālaḥa ahl al-awthān 'alā al-jizya illā man kāna minhum min al-'arab*).[132] Since the term "idolaters" is normally not used for the Zoroastrians, one wonders who these idolatrous non-Arab contemporaries of the Prophet may have been. This tradition appears to have originated in order to provide a prophetic precedent for the later inclusion of non-Arab (especially Indian) polytheists in the category of *ahl al-dhimma*.

The tradition which is often cited in support of the idea that all polytheists ought to be considered as one group – eligible for the *jizya* – is referred to in the literature as "*ḥadīth* Burayda."[133] It includes instructions which the Prophet used to

[127] Qurṭubī, *al-Jāmi' li-aḥkām al-Qur'ān*, vol. 8, p. 45; Ibn 'Abd al-Barr al-Namarī, *al-Tamhīd*, vol. 2, pp. 117–118; Ṭaḥāwī, *Mukhtaṣar ikhtilāf al-'ulamā'*, Beirut: Dār al-bashā'ir al-islāmiyya, 1995, vol. 3, p. 484 (no. 1635). This is not the only view attributed to Mālik b. Anas; see Ṭabarī, *Ikhtilāf al-fuqahā'*, p. 200, where Mālik is reported to have said that only Arabs who are scriptuaries are allowed to pay *jizya*. The modern Muslim author 'Abd al-Karīm Zaydān, whose work deserves much more attention than it has hitherto received, maintains that this view should prevail; the refusal to take *jizya* from any non-Muslim means that he should be forced to embrace Islam and this would be contrary to Qur'ān 2:256: "There is no compulsion in religion" (*lā ikrāha fī al-dīn*). See his *Aḥkām al-dhimmiyyīn*, pp. 25–30. See also the comment of the modern Indian Muslim scholar Kāndhlawī in Sahāranpūrī, *Badhl al-majhūd fī ḥall Abī Dāwūd*, vol. 12, p. 119.

[128] See "Fazzān", in *EI²*, s.v. (J. Despois).

[129] For a survey of materials concerning the Slavs in Muslim sources, see "Ṣaqāliba", *EI²*, s.v. (P.B. Golden).

[130] The Abar are mentioned in the geographical literature, sometimes in conjunction with the Slavs and the Turks, but I was not able to identify them properly. See Ibn Rusta, *Kitāb al-a'lāq al-nafīsa*, Leiden: E. J. Brill 1891, p. 98; Mas'ūdī, *Kitāb al-tanbīh wa al-ishrāf*, Leiden: E. J. Brill 1893, pp. 32, 184, 191.

[131] Saḥnūn b. Sa'īd, *al-Mudawwana al-kubrā*, vol. 2, p. 46. This passage includes also a wording which could be interpreted differently, but Saḥnūn seems to prefer the more catholic interpretation. Again, this is not the only view attributed to Mālik. According to Ṭabarī (*Ikhtilāf al-fuqahā'*, p. 141), the Slavs and the blacks are not *majūs*; the *majūs* are only the Persians. The Slavs and the blacks are in his view of unknown religion and if someone buys a slave belonging to these groups, he should force him to embrace Islam.

[132] Ṣan'ānī, *Muṣannaf*, vol. 10, p. 326 (no. 19259); Jaṣṣāṣ, *Aḥkām al-Qur'ān*, vol. 3, p. 114 infra.

[133] Burayda b. al-Ḥuṣayb b. 'Abd Allāh ... al-Aslamī embraced Islam before the battle of Badr and was appointed by the Prophet to collect the taxes of his tribe. He participated in the battle of Mu'ta (see next note), lived for some time in Baṣra and died in Marw in 63 A.H. / 682 A.H. See Balādhurī, *Ansāb al-ashrāf*, Cairo: Dār al-ma'ārif 1959, vol. 1, p. 531; Mizzī, *Tahdhīb al-kamāl*, vol. 4, pp. 53–55; 'Asqalānī, *Tahdhīb al-tahdhīb*, vol. 1, pp. 378–379. His *Musnad* has now been published in *Musnad al-Rūyānī*, Cairo: Mu'assasat Qurṭuba, 1995, vol. 1, pp. 59–82, but our *ḥadīth* is not included in it.

issue when he sent one of his commanders on a military expedition. The tradition starts with the phrase: "When you encounter your enemy from amongst the polytheists, …" (*idhā laqīta ᶜaduwwaka min al-mushrikīn …*) and then lists the options to be offered to this enemy: conversion to Islam, or payment of the *jizya*.[134] Reaching in his discussion of this *ḥadīth* conclusions different from those of other Ḥanbalīs, Ibn Qayyim al-Jawziyya points out that the armies of the Prophet were mostly fighting Arab idolaters. It is therefore unacceptable to say that *jizya* was imposed only on the People of the Book: Qurʾān 9:29 imposed it on the People of the Book, and the prophetic *sunna* on all other infidels. Though Ibn Qayyim does not say so explicitly, the clear implication of his exposition is that, in principle, Arab polytheists are not to be treated differently from any other group of non-Muslims. They are, for example, similar to the Zoroastrians from whom the Prophet did take *jizya* though they were fire worshipers and "there was no difference between them and the idolaters" (*lā farqa baynahum wa bayna ᶜabadat al-awthān*). If no *jizya* was taken from idolaters – it is only because by the time Qurʾān 9:29 was revealed in year 9 A.H. "the whole peninsula had embraced Islam and no idolater remained in it" (*wa dhālika li-anna āyat al-jizya innamā nazalat ᶜāma Tabūk fī al-sana al-tāsiᶜa min al-hijra baᶜda an aslamat jazīrat al-ᶜarab wa lam yabqa bihā aḥadun min ᶜubbād al-awthān*).[135]

Other jurists distinguished between the polytheists on the basis of their ethnic origins. Abū Ḥanīfa and Abū Yūsuf divided the polytheists into two groups: the Arabs and the non-Arabs. In their view, the Arabs had no alternative except conversion to Islam. This conception could find support in the opinion of the first century traditionist Qatāda b. Diᶜāma (d. 117 A.H. / 735 A.D.) who maintained that "the Arabs had no (legitimate) religion and were, therefore, forced into embracing Islam by the sword" (*kānat al-ᶜarab laysa lahā dīn fa-ukrihū ᶜalā al-dīn bi-'l-sayf*).[136] The non-Arabs, on the other hand, had also the option of paying the *jizya*

[134] *Musnad al-imām al-Shāfiᶜi*, in *Kitāb al-umm*, vol. 9, pp. 428 infra – 429; Ibn Ḥanbal, *Musnad*, vol. 5, p. 352; Ibn Māja, *Sunan, Kitāb al-jihād 38* (no. 2858), vol. 2, pp. 953–954; Ibn Zanjawayhi, *Kitāb al-amwāl*, vol. 1, p. 122 (no. 102); Abū ᶜAwāna, *Musnad*, vol. 4, pp. 63–66 and numerous places in the standard *ḥadīth* literature.

Professor Ella Landau-Tasseron drew my attention to the fact that this tradition is mentioned in connection with the battle of Muʾta, where the enemies of the Muslims were mainly Byzantine Christians, supported by Bedouins of unclear religious affiliation (see Wāqidī, *Kitāb al-maghāzī*, p. 757). If we accept this provenance of the Burayda *ḥadīth*, the conclusions drawn from it regarding the eligibility of the polytheists for the *jizya* become problematic. Nevertheless, we should keep in mind the identification of Christians as polytheists in certain layers of the tradition (see above, section III); we should also remember that the battle of Muʾta took place beyond the boundaries of the Arabian peninsula where the legal situation with regard to the polytheists is different. It is also noteworthy that in Wāqidī's description of the battle, the enemies at Muʾta are routinely described as *mushrikūn* (see pp. 761, 763, 768; see also Ibn Saᶜd, *Ṭabaqāt*, vol. 2, part 1, pp. 92–94) though on p. 768 there is also a reference to Christian Arabs and to "a Byzantine" (*naṣārā al-ᶜarab, rajulun min al-Rūm*). In any case, the jurists who use this *ḥadīth* in support of the legitimacy of levying *jizya* from the polytheists do not pay any attention to these considerations, base their argument on the wording of the *ḥadīth* only and disregard its possible historical background.

[135] Ibn Qayyim al-Jawziyya, *Aḥkām ahl al-dhimma*, vol. 1, pp. 6–7; idem, *Hidāyat al-ḥayārā*, pp. 24–25. For a critique of this perception, see the last note in the present chapter.

[136] Ṭabarī, *Jāmiᶜ al-bayān*, vol. 3, p. 16 infra (on Qurʾān 2:256).

and retaining their faith. This is the view adopted by the Ḥanafī school, and was supported also by Mālik b. Anas who was willing, according to one view,[137] to accept *jizya* from "various faithless Turks and Indians" (*man lā dīna lahu min ajnās al-turk wa al-hind*) and supported Abū Ḥanīfa in treating the non-Arab polytheists with greater consideration than their Arab counterparts.[138] The same view was also attributed to Ibn Ḥanbal.[139] Ibn al-Jahm was more lenient with regard to the Arabs in general and maintained that only the Qurashīs have to be singled out and denied the possibility of paying the *jizya*. Two reasons were given to explain this: the Qurashīs are related to the Prophet and must therefore be spared the humiliation of *jizya*; or, *jizya* can not be levied from them because all Qurashīs embraced Islam when Mecca was conquered in 630. The implication of this is that if a Qurashī is found to be non-Muslim, he must be an apostate from whom *jizya* can not be collected according to any school of law.[140]

The nuanced attitude of the early jurists towards the polytheists calls for comment. The attitude of those who considered the whole polytheistic world as a monolithic entity with which there can be no compromise is not surprising in view of the strictly monotheistic content of the Qurʾānic revelation. However, the view that supports the collection of the *jizya* from any infidel, and the distinctions that were made by the Ḥanafīs and some Mālikīs between polytheists of various ethnic origins are remarkable. The harsh attitude to the Arab polytheists was explained by the fact that the Qurʾān was revealed in Arabic and its miraculous nature should have been evident to the Arabs more than to others. Furthermore, being the Prophet's kith and kin, they had the obligation to support him and respond to his call. Their rejection of Muḥammad's message is therefore deemed more reprehensible than the same behavior of other unbelievers.

VI

In our sources there are references to two additional religious groups which should be briefly discussed in this context. These are the Ṣābiʾa on the one hand, and the

[137] For Mālik's other view, see above, at note 131.

[138] Ṭabarī *Ikhtilāf al-fuqahā'*, p. 200; Abū Yūsuf, *al-Radd ʿalā siyar al-Awzāʿī*, Ḥaydarābād (Deccau): Lajnat iḥyāʾ al-maʿārif al-nuʿmāniyya, n.d., pp. 131–132; Abū Yūsuf, *Kitāb al-kharāj*, pp. 66–67; Sarakhsī, *Sharḥ kitāb al-siyar al-kabīr*, vol. 1, p. 189 (no. 212); Ibn ʿAbd al-Barr al-Namarī, *Tamhīd*, vol. 2, p. 118; Qaffāl, *Ḥilyat al-ʿulamā'*, vol. 7, pp. 695–696; Ibn Qudāma, *al-Mughnī*, vol. 8, pp. 363, 501. For the importance of this view for the development of Islam on the Indian subcontinent, see Y. Friedmann, "The temple of Multān. A note on early Muslim attitudes to idolatry", *Israel Oriental Studies* 2 (1972), pp. 176–182. Cf. Ibn Taymiyya, *Majmūʿ fatāwā*, vol. 20, p. 101, where it is stated, contrary to the other sources, that in Abū Ḥanīfa's view *jizya* can be taken even from Arab idolaters if they do not fight the Muslims. Ibn Abī Zayd al-Qayrawānī (*Kitāb al-jihād*, p. 450) thinks that *jizya* cannot be taken from Arab polytheists, but his argumentation is different: Allah did not allow the taking of *jizya* from them because He knew that they would embrace Islam.

[139] Ibn Qudāma, *al-Mughnī*, vol. 8, p. 500 infra; Zarkashī, *Sharḥ al-Zarkashī ʿalā Mukhtaṣar al-Khiraqī*, vol. 6, p. 449.

[140] Qurṭubī, *al-Jāmiʿ li-aḥkām al-Qurʾān*, vol. 8, pp. 45–46.

believers in the "scrolls of Ibrāhīm and Mūsā" (*ṣuḥuf Ibrāhīm wa Mūsā*), "the first scrolls" (*al-ṣuḥuf al-ūlā*), and the *zabūr* on the other.[141] According to some commentators, the Ṣābiʾa were the believers in the *zabūr*. In extra-Qurʾānic literature we also hear about the scrolls of Shīth. It should be pointed out that there was no actual community of believers in the various "scrolls", and the issue was discussed only because such believers were mentioned in the Qurʾān. As for the Ṣābiʾa, they did exist, of course; but the Muslim traditionists had only the vaguest information about them. Hence they held widely conflicting views about the religious standing of the Ṣābiʾa and discussed them also only because of their mention in the Qurʾān.

In the standard commentaries on the Qurʾān, the scrolls mentioned above are frequently understood as alternative names for the Tawrāt and the Injīl, though such an interpretation is problematic at least with regard to the scrolls of Ibrāhīm. If the scrolls were identified with these two books, there would be no room for this discussion. However, several commentators understand the scrolls to be distinct from the Tawrāt and the Injīl, and some jurists discuss the question of whether their adherents should be deemed People of the Book.

Ibn Ḥanbal observed (according to the *riwāya* of Ibn Manṣūr) that the Qurʾānic references to the People of the Book do not specify the books which are intended by this phrase; hence people who believe in any book revealed by God should be considered People of the Book and should be treated like the Jews and the Christians. Ibn Ḥanbal did not deal with the issue whether the scrolls in question have been preserved and who are their adherents. Ibn Qayyim al-Jawziyya, on the other hand, observed that in reality there do not exist people who believe in these scrolls (*fa-hādha al-qism muqaddar lā wujūda lahu*) to the exclusion of the Tawrāt and the Injīl; whoever believes in them, believes at the same time also in the Tawrāt and the Injīl or, at least, in one of them. Therefore, the Qurʾān never addressed these groups individually, but rather included them, by implication, with the other People of the Book.[142]

This Ḥanbalī view, however, did not enjoy universal acceptance. In the Shāfiʿī school, we have a difference of approach between al-Shāfiʿī himself and some of his successors. Al-Shāfiʿī used the Qurʾānic references to "the scrolls of Mūsā and Ibrāhīm" and to "the books of the ancient people" (*zubur al-awwalīn*) in order to boost his argument that God had revealed not only the Tawrāt, the Injīl and the Qurʾān, but numerous other books as well; the Zoroastrians could have therefore received a book of their own and should be considered People of the Book.[143] Later

[141] Qurʾān 20:133, 53:36, 80:13, 87:18–19. For an extensive survey and analysis of the literary issues related to this genre, see M. J. Kister, "'*Ḥaddithū ʿan banī isrāʾīla wa lā ḥaraja.*' A study of an early tradition", *Israel Oriental Studies* 2 (1972), pp. 215–239; and J. Sadan, "Some literary problems concerning Judaism and Jewry in medieval Arabic sources", in M. Sharon, ed., *Studies in Islamic history and civilization in honour of Professor David Ayalon*, Jerusalem: Cana Ltd., 1986, pp. 370–398.

[142] Ibn Qayyim al-Jawziyya, *Aḥkām ahl al-dhimma*, vol. 2, pp. 432–433. Cf. Zarkashī, *Sharḥ al-Zarkashī ʿalā Mukhtaṣar al-Khiraqī*, vol. 6, p. 449.

[143] Shāfiʿī, *Kitāb al-umm*, 4, p. 245, ll. 5ff; pp. 341, ll. 11 – 342, l. 6; *Kitāb ikhtilāf al-ḥadīth*, p. 154. For Shāfiʿī's perception of the Zoroastrians as People of the Book, see above, section IV.

Shāfiʿīs, on the other hand, were in the forefront of those who strove to restrict the eligibility for scriptuary status as much as possible. They used these verses in order to deny *dhimmī* status to the (non-existent) adherents of the various *ṣuḥuf*. Their argument was that divine revelation does not acquire the status of a book in the Qurʾānic sense unless it is "sent down" (… *anna al-kitāb mā kāna munazzalan*) like the Tawrāt, the Injīl and the Qurʾān; if it is not, as the Shāfiʿīs seem to assume with regard to the scrolls, it cannot be considered a book and is (merely) "revelation and inspiration" (*yakūnu waḥyan wa ilhāman*). Furthermore, even if these scrolls were "sent down", they included only exhortations and not commands and prohibitions (… *wa lākinnahā ishtamalat ʿalā mawāʿiẓ wa lam tashtamil ʿalā aḥkām wa hiya al-amr wa al-nahy*); these are, according to the Shāfiʿīs, an indispensable component of divine revelation, which bestows scriptuary status on its adherents.[144] In contradistinction to the view of Ibn Ḥanbal, the Ḥanbalī jurist Ibn Qudāma expressed the same view as the Shāfiʿīs.[145] The whole issue has never had much practical significance, but it is a reflection of the Shāfiʿī resolve to accord *dhimmī* status only to those communities who are unquestionably full fledged People of the Book.

The Ṣābiʾa appear three times in the Qurʾān. In verses 2:62 and 5:69, they are mentioned together with the Jews and the Christians in a favorable way, while in 22:17 they figure as one of the five communities (*inna 'lladhīna āmanū wa-'lladhīna hādū wa al-ṣābiʾīn wa al-naṣārā wa al-majūs wa-'lladhīna ashrakū*) whose fate Allah will determine on the Day of Judgment. The intricate problems related to the identity of the two groups who share the name Ṣābiʾa have been extensively treated in research literature and are beyond the scope of this study.[146] Our only concern is the way in which Muslim law and tradition views and classifies this group of non-Muslims. The great number and variety of definitions which can be found in the literature of *ḥadīth*, *fiqh* and *tafsīr* stems from the fact that the Muslim traditionists had no firm knowledge of the Ṣābiʾūn. They were obliged, nevertheless, to deal with them in order to explain the relevant references in the Qurʾān.[147] Perhaps the most telling example of the confusion about the Ṣābiʾa can be seen in the views attributed to al-Shāfiʿī. According to al-Māwardī's account, al-Shāfiʿī is said to have "suspended his judgment concerning them because of their dubious nature" (*fa-naẓara al-Shāfiʿī fī dīn al-Ṣābiʾīn wa al-Sāmira fa-*

[144] Ibn Qayyim al-Jawziyya, *Aḥkām ahl al-dhimma*, vol. 2, pp. 432–433; Māwardī, *al-Ḥāwī al-kabīr*, vol. 9, p. 226. Cf. Ṭabarī on Qurʾān 17:55 (vol. 15, p. 103) where the *zabūr* of David is described as follows: *laysa fīhi ḥalāl wa lā ḥarām wa lā farāʾiḍ wa lā ḥudūd*; a similar description can be found in Qurṭubī, *al-Jāmiʿ li-aḥkām al-Quʾrān* (vol. 5, p. 378, on Qurʾān 4:163), where it is also said that the *zabūr* of David included 150 Sūras (cf. the 150 Psalms of the Old Testament). In his commentary on Qurʾān 87:19, Qurṭubī describes the scrolls of Ibrāhīm as replete with proverbs (*amthāl*), and the scrolls of Mūsā as full with didactic stories (*ʿibar*). The same view is attributed to the Prophet himself in Ibn ʿAbd al-Barr al-Namarī, *al-Tamhīd*, vol. 9, p. 199.

[145] Ibn Qudāma, *al-Mughnī*, vol. 8, p. 497.

[146] For a summary of the research on this issue and an extensive bibliography, see "Ṣābiʾ", *EI*[2], s.v. (F.C. de Blois) and "Ṣābiʾa", *EI*[2], s.v. (T. Fahd).

[147] The bewildering variety of the views relative to the Ṣābiʾa was surveyed in J. D. McAuliffe, "Exegetical identification of the Ṣābiʾūn", *Muslim World* 72 (1982), pp. 95–106.

wajadahu mushtabihan fa-ᶜallaqa al-qawla fīhim li-'shtibāhi amrihim). In one place, he said that they were of the Jews and Christians (*innahum min al-yahūd wa al-naṣārā*), unless it is shown that they differ from them on fundamental commands and prohibitions; in another place, he concluded that they were, indeed, of them; in a third place, he refrained from expressing an opinion. In an apparent attempt to defend al-Shāfiᶜī against possible accusations of holding conflicting opinions on this issue, al-Māwardī explains that the variety of views attributed to al-Shāfiᶜī does not derive from his inconsistency, but rather from the existence of different types of Ṣābiʾa.[148] Standard commentaries on the Qurʾān deal with the nature of their religion; with the question whether they are scriptuaries or not, whether they are star-worshipers or not, and whether it is legal for Muslims to wed their women and consume meat slaughtered by them. Numerous examples of these discussions can be found in the literature; in the great majority of cases the issue is discussed in an extremely theoretical fashion, clearly indicating that the traditionists were dealing with a group of which they had only scant and vague information.[149] In the sources studied in preparation of this work, I have found only one concrete case of dealing with the Ṣābiʾa. The ᶜAbbāsī caliph al-Qāhir bi-'llāh (reigned 320–322 / 932–934) asked the *fuqahāʾ* for a *fatwā* concerning them; the Shāfiᶜī jurist Abū Saᶜīd al-Iṣṭakhrī (d. 328 A.H. / 939–940 A.D.)[150] ruled that that they cannot be allowed to retain their religion because they thought that "the sphere is alive and speaking" (*inna al-falak ḥayyun nāṭiq*) and that the seven planets are gods. The caliph ordered them to be killed, but desisted after they paid him a huge amount of money as ransom.[151]

VII

The present chapter focused almost exclusively on questions of Islamic tradition and law, and we have so far interpreted them on their own terms, following the views of the traditionists and taking into account the atmosphere permeating the relevant literature. Yet it seems that the data which were presented can be interpreted in a way which will shed some light on historical matters as well. The

[148] Māwardī, *al-Ḥāwī al-kabīr*, vol. 9, pp. 222–223; cf. Shāfiᶜī, *Aḥkām al-Qurʾān*, vol. 2, pp. 58–59. Cf. Ibn Qayyim al-Jawziyya, *Aḥkām ahl al-dhimma*, vol. 1, pp. 92–93.

[149] A good example of this material can be found in Bayhaqī, *al-Sunan al-kubrā*, vol. 7, p. 173. According to this passage, ᶜUmar b. al-Khaṭṭāb was told that the Ṣābiʾa observed the Sabbath, read the Tawrāt and do not believe in the Day of Resurrection. ᶜUmar ruled on the basis of this information that they belong to the People of the Book. According to a second passage on the same page, they pray in the direction of the *qibla* and pay the *khums* (!). On the basis of this, someone (it is not clear who is meant in the text) wanted to exempt them from the *jizya*, but he was informed that they worship the angels (and apparently desisted from his plan).

[150] For his biography, see Subkī, *Ṭabaqāt al-Shāfiᶜiyya al-kubrā*, ed. Maḥmūd Muḥammad al-Ṭanāḥī and ᶜAbd al-Fattāḥ Muḥammad al-Ḥilw, Cairo: Maṭbaᶜat ᶜĪsā al-Bābī al-Ḥalabī, 1965, vol. 3, pp. 230–233. I am grateful for this reference to my friend and colleague Dr. Nurit Tsafrir.

[151] Ibn Qayyim al-Jawziyya, *Aḥkām ahl al-dimma*, vol. 1, pp. 92–93; Māwardī, *al-Ḥāwī al-kabīr*, vol. 9, p. 224.

material surveyed and analyzed in the previous sections enabled us to discern a process by which the category of *jizya* payers, later designated *ahl al-dhimma*, was gradually expanded. At the Qur'ānic stage of its development, it included only the People of the Book, meaning the Jews and the Christians. Against slight resistance, the Zoroastrians were incorporated into the same category by a prophetic *ḥadīth* that reflected the administrative exigencies of the first Islamic century: ᶜUmar b. al-Khaṭṭāb complained that he did not know how to treat the Zoroastrians (whose land had just been conquered); and ᶜAbd al-Raḥmān b. ᶜAwf, a companion of the Prophet, provided a solution which must have been eminently suitable for the governance of the newly occupied territory of Iran. The Zoroastrians were included among the *dhimmī*s despite the fact that they were not considered scriptuaries by a great majority of the jurists, and despite the fact that their dualistic beliefs, their fire worship and some of their family laws must have been an anathema to the strictly monotheistic ideal of early Islam. The same was true with regard to the Berbers of North Africa from whom ᶜUthmān b. ᶜAffān is said to have levied the *jizya*[152] despite the fact that they were included in the inglorious list of peoples who rejected the idea of prophecy.[153] A rarely quoted tradition speaks about a group of black people who kept the Sabbath and circumcised their children, but were not otherwise related to Judaism. Saḥnūn ruled concerning them that if they have a Book, there would be no problem; if they do not have one, they will be treated like the Zoroastrians (*wa qāla fī ṭā'ifatin min al-sūdān yasbutūn wa yakhtatinūn lam yataᶜallaqū min al-yahūdiyya illā bi-hādhā. qāla: in kāna lahum kitāb, wa illā fa-lahum ḥukm al-majūs*).[154] The inclusion of these groups meant that the categories of *ahl al-kitāb* and *ahl al-dhimma* ceased to be synonymous and began to diverge. Equally important is the fact that the gradual expansion of the *dhimmī* category did not come to a halt even at this stage. Al-Awzāᶜī and Mālik b. Anas were willing to accommodate in it all infidels, not excepting even the idolaters. The Ḥanafīs opted for a slightly different approach and included all idolaters except those of Arab descent. This exception had little practical significance: when the legal development in question occurred, the whole Arabian peninsula had already embraced Islam, and in the perception of the jurists no Arab idolater remained in existence there or anywhere else. The exclusion of the Arab idolaters should therefore be seen as mere lip service to the uncompromising iconoclastic principle of Islam that was implemented in the Arabian peninsula, but inevitably fell into abeyance during the era of the great conquests. There is a fascinating parallel between the tradition describing the dilemma of ᶜUmar with regard to the Zoroastrians and a less known episode concerning the Indian idolaters. Muḥammad b. al-Qāsim, the youthful Muslim conqueror of an Indian town who also faced (at the beginning of the eighth century A.D.) the administrative problem of governing an area inhabited by

[152] Ṣanᶜānī, *Muṣannaf*, vol. 10, p. 326; Ibn ᶜAbd al-Barr al-Namarī, *al-Tamhīd*, vol. 2, p. 123; Khallāl, *Ahl al-milal*, p. 470 (no. 1143).
[153] Ibn Taymiyya, *Majmūᶜ fatāwā*, vol. 12, pp. 10, 334–335.
[154] Ibn Abī Zayd al-Qayrawānī, *Kitāb al-jihād*, p. 451. It is possible to understand this text as attributing this view to ᶜUmar b. al-Khaṭṭāb.

non-Muslims, uttered with admirable grasp of the situation a statement of momentous significance for the relationship between Islam and the adherents of Indian religions. He said: "The idol-temple is akin to the churches of the Christians, (to the synagogues of) the Jews and to the fire-temples of the Zoroastrians" (*mā al-buddu illā ka-kanāʾis al-naṣārā wa al-yahūd wa buyūt nīrān al-majūs*).[155] Though no prophetic sanction could be provided for this utterance, and though Muḥammad b. al-Qāsim did not enjoy a status which would induce the jurists to quote him as an authority, his statement became nevertheless the theoretical basis for an administrative inevitability: for reasons of state, the Hindūs had to be considered *ahl al-dhimma*.[156] The only way in which a small Muslim garrison could govern an area inhabited by a non-Muslim and idolatrous population was to allow that population to retain its traditions and interfere as little as possible in its affairs. There was no way to implement in India the policy applied to the idolaters of the Arabian peninsula. The course of action taken by the Muslim conquerors of Indian regions was the only feasible one, even if it was a far cry from the stern Qurʾānic stance against idolatry.[157] During the course of Indo-Muslim history, there were a few *ʿulamāʾ* who attempted to reclassify the Hindūs, determine that they were not eligible for *dhimmī* status and advised the Sultans to persecute them because of their polytheism. These demands were rejected by the Muslim rulers of India[158] and the Ḥanafī approach to the problem was allowed to stand.

The impression gained from the continual expansion of the category of *ahl al-dhimma* is that the relevant chapters in Islamic law, at least as represented by al-Awzāʿī, the Ḥanafīs and the Mālikīs, developed exactly as required by the phenomenal expansion of Islam during the first century of its history. It was not only Muslim practice which adapted itself to the changing requirements of a growing empire with diverse population; the legal thought of at least two schools of Muslim law went through a parallel process of adaptation. It is certainly not possible to accept the categorical statement of Paret who maintains that the commandment to kill the polytheists, included in Qurʾān 9:5, became authoritative for centuries after Muḥammad's death and says that in principle there is no pardon for polytheists in Islam.[159]

So far we have described the changes in the classification of unbelievers as a development in time. Yet it appears that the issue can be viewed also with a geographical perspective in mind. As long as the only idolaters encountered by the Muslims were inhabitants of the Arabian peninsula, the Muslims fought against

155 Balādhurī, *Futūḥ al-buldān*, ed. de Goeje, p. 439.

156 But not *ahl al-kitāb*; *pace* G. Vajda, *EI*², s.v. "Ahl al-kitāb", vol. 1, p. 264a.

157 Cf. Ibn Qayyim al-Jawziyya, *Aḥkām ahl al-dhimma*, vol. 1, p. 17, and the present author's "The temple of Multān", pp. 181–182.

158 See K. A. Nizami, *Some aspects of religion and politcs in India during the thirteenth century*, Bombay: Asia Publishing House, 1961, pp. 315–316; M. Habib and Afsar Umar Salim Khan, *The political theory of the Delhi Sultanate*, Allahabad: Kitab Mahall, n.d., pp. 46–52.

159 See his "Toleranz und Intoleranz im Islam", pp. 348–349: "Für Polytheisten gibt es im Islam grundsätzlich keinen Pardon. Wenn sie sich nicht zum Übertritt entschliessen, bleibt ihnen nur der Kampf auf Leben und Tod." Cf. also R. Gramlich in Kerber, ed., *Wie tolerant ist der Islam?*, p. 80.

them without compromise. This was caused not only by the Qur'ānic attitude to idolatry, but also by the ardent desire of early Islam to achieve religious uniformity in the peninsula. This desire is clearly reflected in the Qur'ān, in the biography of the Prophet and in the very frequently quoted tradition which stipulates that "no two religions will exist together in the Arabian peninsula" (*lā yajtamiʿu dīnāni fī jazīrat al-ʿarab*).[160] This being the case, the Muslims rejected not only the existence of idolatry on the peninsula, but also declared their intention to expel the Jews and the Christians from most of its territory. From this we can draw the conclusion that in the earliest stage of Muslim history, the stage which preceded the great conquests, Muslim policies were not informed by the distinction between Jewish or Christian monotheism on the one hand and Arab idolatry on the other, but rather by the urge to attain religious uniformity in the birthplace of Islam. Keeping this objective in mind, there was little difference between Judaism, Christianity or Arab idolatry. Once Islam became the sole religion in most of the peninsula, and the newly converted Muslim Arabs triumphantly emerged from their historical habitat, the religious considerations that demanded unflinching struggle against idolatry and other non-Muslim religions were replaced by the requirements of running a state and building an empire. These were the important matters in the period when classical Islamic law was being formulated, and this is the final stage of the development that we described in the previous sections: the Ḥanafī and the Mālikī schools, as well as al-Awzāʿī and some Ḥanbalīs – and according to some traditions Ibn Ḥanbal himself, – recognized all non-Muslims living under Muslim rule as *ahl al-dhimma*, even if they were idolaters. The Ḥanafī exclusion of Arab idolaters from this category was inconsequential; in the perception of the jurists at least, all members of this group had long vanished off the face of the earth.[161]

[160] Ṣanʿānī, *Muṣannaf*, vol. 6, p. 53; Ibn Abī Shayba, *Muṣannaf*, vol. 12, p. 271, no. 12797; p. 345, no. 13037; Abū ʿUbayd, *Kitāb al-amwāl*, p. 98, no. 272. Ibn Ḥanbal, *Musnad*, vol. 6, p. 275. Numerous traditions relevant to this issue are conveniently grouped together in Fākihī, *Akhbār Makka*, vol. 3, pp. 37–44.

In his classic work on the legal status of non-Muslims in Islamic lands, Fattal (*Le statut légal*, pp. 88–91) finds evidence of individual Jews and Christians living in the Arabian peninsula in the first centuries of Islam, and doubts, on this basis, the historicity of the Prophet's command to expel the non-Muslims from that area. Whatever the historical truth on this matter may be, the doctrine demanding religious uniformity in the peninsula is not in any doubt. It is also noteworthy that according to some views, the People of the Book are allowed to enter the Ḥijāz for short periods. See, for instance, Ibn Qayyim al-Jawziyya, *Aḥkām ahl al-dhimma*, vol. 1, p. 188.

[161] For a historian's critique of this perception, see Ella Landau-Tasseron, "From tribal society to centralized polity: an intepretation of events and anecdotes of the formative period of Islam", *JSAI* 24 (2000), pp. 204–205.

CHAPTER THREE

Is there no compulsion in religion?

> No compulsion is there in religion. Rectitude has become clear from error. So whoever disbelieves in idols and believes in God, has laid hold of the most firm handle, unbreaking; God is All-hearing, All-knowing.
>
> (Qurʾān 2:256)

I

Muslim attitudes to adherents of other faiths is usually the context for discussing religious tolerance in Islam. The prominence given to this aspect of the issue is understandable: in most periods of medieval Islamic history, Muslims wielded political power and were in the position to accord (or deny) tolerance to others. In the early period of Islam, few Muslims lived under non-Muslim rule and could be treated tolerantly – or intolerantly – by rulers belonging to other religious communities.[1] It is, however, significant to point out that the earliest manner in which religious intolerance manifested itself in Islamic history was the religious persecution endured by Muslims in Mecca before the *hijra*. In a certain sense, the twelve years between 610 and 622 in Islam can be compared to the first three centuries of Christian history. Though the suffering of these early Muslims for their faith lasted only for a short period of time and gained only limited importance in the Islamic ethos, an analysis of the question of religious tolerance in Islam cannot be complete without some reference to this nascent period of Islamic history. In the next chapter of the present study, we shall survey and analyze cases in which early Meccan Muslims were compelled to renege on their newly acquired faith. We shall also discuss the question what is expected of a Muslim who is exposed to religious coercion.[2] Here we shall therefore refrain from treating the religious situation of Muslims in Mecca before the *hijra*.

[1] Nevertheless, the *sharīʿa* does refer to problems concerning Muslims who live under non-Muslim rule. Naturally enough, these discussions treat mostly the duties of Muslims who live in *dār al-ḥarb* and the legitimacy of dwelling there rather than the obligations of the infidel power toward its non-Muslim subjects. See Khaled Abou el Fadl, "Islamic law and Muslim minorities: the juristic discourse on Muslim minorities from the second/eighth to the eleventh/seventeenth centuries." *Islamic law and society* 1 (1994), pp. 141–187.

[2] See Chapter Four, section IX.

II

In the conclusion of the preceding chapter, we have referred, in general terms, to the Muslim attitudes to non-Muslims in the Arabian peninsula and to the transformation of these attitudes after the successful establishment of the Muslim polity in Medina, and after the great conquests of Islam. It is now appropriate to describe these attitudes and their development in greater detail.

Islamic attitudes with regard to non-Muslims who lived in the peninsula underwent speedy and rather dramatic change during the lifetime of the Prophet. Muslim tradition depicts the period of Mecca and the first two or three years after the *hijra* to Medina as very different from the subsequent one. The views that the Prophet held in those early years of his activity can be gauged from a number of passages reflecting his thought.

Qur'ān 109:6 ("To you your religion, and to me mine"), which is dated to the first Meccan period[3] and should therefore be understood as addressing the polytheists of that city, takes cognizance of the unbridgeable gap between Islam and the religion of the Meccans. It seems to suggest that the only sensible way of action open to the two groups is to keep their religious affairs separate. Since the verse does not demand any action to suppress Meccan polytheism, it has sometimes been understood as reflecting an attitude of religious tolerance on the part of the Muslims;[4] yet if we take into account the harsh tone of the first five verses of Sūra 109 and the conditions prevailing in Mecca during the first years of Muḥammad's activity – when the Muslims were a small and persecuted minority in the city – it seems better to interpret this verse as a passionate plea to the Meccans to leave the Muslims alone, to refrain from practicing religious coercion against them.[5] In the earliest period of Mecca, the Muslims were not in a position to accord or deny tolerance to their non-Muslim compatriots.

Qur'ān 15:85 and 43:89, dated by Nöldeke to the slightly later "second" period of Mecca,[6] are also relevant. In contradistinction to Qur'ān 109:6, these verses clearly address the Prophet and enjoin him to turn away from those who do not believe. Qur'ān 15:85 reads: "Surely the Hour is coming; so pardon thou, with a gracious pardoning" (*fa-'ṣfaḥ al-ṣafḥ al-jamīl*); this injunction is related to the imminent approach of the Last Day. The connection between the two is not made clear in the text, yet the verse seems to mean that the Prophet may leave the unbelievers alone because God will soon sit in judgment and inflict on them the just punishment. In Qur'ān 43:88–89 we read: "And for his saying, 'My Lord, surely there are people who believe not' – yet pardon them (*fa-'ṣfaḥ ʿanhum*), and

[3] See Nöldeke–Schwally, *Geschichte des Qorāns*, vol. 1, p. 108.

[4] See, for instance, Ahmad, "Conversion from Islam", p. 3; Ḥasan al-Ṣaffār, *al-Taʿaddudiyya wa al-ḥurriyya fī al-islām*. Beirut: Dār al-bayān al-ʿarabī, 1990, p. 41.

[5] Zamakhsharī seems to be close to this understanding when he says commenting on this verse: *fa-idhā lam taqbalū minnī wa lam tattabiʿūnī fa-daʿūnī kifāfan wa lā tadʿūnī ilā al-shirk*. See *al-Kashshāf*, vol. 4, p. 293.

[6] Nöldeke–Schwally, *Geschichte des Qorāns*, vol. 1, pp. 129, 131–132.

say, 'Peace!' Soon they will know." Here the context is even less clear and does not give any indication concerning the reason for the divine command to leave the unbelievers alone.[7] We may assume, however, that the reason was the Prophet's limited ability to impose his will on his contemporaries, especially in the period prior to the *hijra*.

Then there is Qurʾān 10:99–100:

> And if thy Lord had willed, whoever is in the earth would have believed, all of them, all together. Wouldst thou then constrain the people, until they are believers? It is not for any soul to believe save by the leave of God; and He lays abomination upon those who have no understanding.

The verse seeks to convince the Prophet that matters of religious belief are in the hands of God, and that any attempt to spread his faith by coercion would be an exercise in futility. It also sounds as an attempt to allay the Prophet's distress at his initial failure to attract most Meccans to Islam: people believe only as a result of divine permission and the Prophet should not blame himself for their rejection of the true faith. If Allah chose not to impose true belief on all, then the Prophet, being a mere mortal, cannot attain religious uniformity in His stead. Despite prophetic efforts to the contrary, most people opt for clinging to unbelief.[8] The Qurʾān declares in numerous passages that prophets can only deliver the divine message; it is not within their power to assure its acceptance or implementation.[9]

Moving to the period immediately following the *hijra*, we should consider the famous document known as *ᶜahd al-umma* in which the Prophet stipulated the conditions under which the Jews would live in Medina and included a clause recognizing the fact that they have a distinct religion of their own: "The Jews have their religion and the believers have theirs" (*li-'l-yahūd dīnuhum wa li-'l-muʾminīna dīnuhum*).[10] Rubin has already referred to the affinity between this passage and Qurʾān 109:6.[11] Both accept the existence of religions other than Islam in the peninsula. The clause in *ᶜahd al-umma* bestows legitimacy on the existence

[7] Translation by Arberry. Some classical commentators, followed by a number of modern translators, understand the root *ṣ-f-ḥ* which appears in Qurʾān 15:85 and 43:89 in the sense of pardon or forgiveness. It is, however, unlikely that the Qurʾān would instruct the Prophet to "forgive" the unbelievers and this does not seem to be the primary meaning of the root. Ibn Manẓūr (*Lisān al-ᶜarab*, s.v. *ṣ-f-ḥ*, Beirut 1955, vol. 3, p. 515b) sees affinity between *ṣafaḥa ᶜan* and *aᶜraḍa ᶜan*. Zamakhsharī's commentary on Qurʾān 15:85 (*al-Kashshāf*, vol. 2, p. 397) reads: *fa-aᶜriḍ ᶜanhum wa-'ḥtamil mā talqā minhum iᶜrāḍan jamīlan bi-ḥilmin wa ighḍāʾ*. Even clearer are his comments on Qurʾān 43:89 (*al-Kashshāf*, vol. 3, p. 499: *fa-aᶜriḍ ᶜanhum yāʾisan ᶜan daᶜwatihim wa waddiᶜhum wa tārikhum*). The two verses discussed here should therefore be understood in way similar to Qurʾān 15:94 and 6:106: *aᶜriḍ ᶜan al-mushrikīn*, "turn away from the polytheists". Paret's note on Qurʾān 15:85 in *Kommentar und Konkordanz*, p. 279, is instructive. Forgiveness and pardon seem to be only secondary meanings of *ṣafaḥa*.

[8] See also Qurʾān 12:103, 16:37.

[9] Qurʾān 16:35, 82; 28:56, 29:18 and elsewhere. See also R. Paret, "Toleranz und Intoleranz im Islam," pp. 346–347.

[10] Abū 'Ubayd, *Kitāb al-amwāl*, p. 204.

[11] See U. Rubin, "The 'Constitution of Medina': some notes", *Studia Islamica* 62 (1985), p. 16, and note 45.

of the Jewish faith in Medina. It stands to reason that both passages reflect very early attitudes of nascent Islam, which had been willing, at that time, to tolerate the existence of other religions in the peninsula. This understanding can be supported by reference to Abū ᶜUbayd (d. 838–839 A.D. / 224 A.H.) who thought that the clause originated at a time when "Islam was not yet dominant and strong, before the Prophet was commanded to take *jizya* from the People of the Book" (*qabla an yaẓhara al-islām wa yaqwā wa qabla an yuʾmara bi-akhdh al-jizya min ahl al-kitāb*).[12]

These tolerant attitudes toward the non-Muslims of the Arabian peninsula were not destined to last. Banū Qaynuqāᶜ and Banū Naḍīr were expelled, and the men belonging to Banū Qurayẓa were massacred. Their women and children were taken into captivity. The Prophet also made up his mind to eradicate polytheism from the Arabian peninsula. The present work is not going to delve into the reasons which brought about these events. Nor are we going to comment on the often debated question why these three Jewish tribal units were not mentioned in the *ᶜahd al-umma*, or whether the break with the Jews resulted from political or religious considerations.[13] We shall rather concentrate on the description and analysis of the doctrine which came into being as a result of these developments and gave them religious sanction.

Early Muslim compendia of *ḥadīth* include a number of traditions according to which the Prophet decided to expel all non-Muslims from the Arabian peninsula. In some compendia we find traditions about the expulsion of the polytheists, and separate utterances about the expulsion of the Jews and the Christians.[14] The traditions are repeated in chapters dealing with various issues of religious law and appear in variant versions. Most of them deal with the expulsion of the Jews and the Christians from the areas of Medina, Khaybar and Najrān. The expulsion from Medina is said to have been carried out by the Prophet; he intended to expel the Jews of Khaybar as well, but allowed them to remain there on the condition that they continue to work the land and yield half of the agricultural produce to the Muslims. Eventually, ᶜUmar b. al-Khaṭṭāb carried out the Prophet's wish and expelled the Jews of Khaybar to Jericho and Taymāʾ.[15] Once this development took place, the clauses in *ᶜahd al-umma* bestowing legitimacy on the existence of the Jewish faith in Medina became problematic and had to undergo substantial reinterpretation, far removed from their primary meaning. According to Abū ᶜUbayd, the clauses which state that the Jews are *umma min al-muʾminīn* imply only that they must support the Muslims financially, while the clause stipulating that "the Jews

[12] Abū ᶜUbayd, *Kitāb al-amwāl*, p. 207.

[13] Cf. Paret, "Toleranz und Intoleranz ...", p. 350 infra.

[14] Sarakhsī, *Sharḥ al-siyar al-kabīr*, vol. 4, p. 1541 (no. 3069); Ibn Abī Shayba, *Muṣannaf*, vol. 12, p. 344 (nos. 13036–13037); Dārimī, *Sunan*, vol. 2, pp. 151–152; Ṭaḥāwī, *Mushkil al-āthār*, vol. 4, pp. 12–17.

[15] See Bukhārī, *Ṣaḥīḥ*, *Ijāra* 22 (vol. 2, pp. 55); *Ḥarth* 17 (vol. 2, p. 72); *Shurūṭ* 14, (vol. 2, p. 177); *Khums 19* (vol. 2, p. 290); *Jizya* 6 (vol. 2, pp. 294–299); *Maghāzī* 14 (vol. 3, p. 72); *Ikrāh* 2 (vol. 4, pp. 336); *Iʿtiṣām* 18 (vol. 4, p. 437); and Wensinck, *Concordance...*, s.v. *ajlā, akhraja*; Abū ᶜUbayd, *Kitāb al-amwāl*, pp. 98 (nos. 270–271), 99 (no. 276).

have their religion and the believers have theirs" only indicates that their religion is worthless (*ammā al-dīn fa-laysū minhu fī shay*ʾ).[16] Similar was the fate of Qurʾān 109:6, which was declared abrogated by Qurʾān 9:5 (*āyat al-sayf*), or interpreted as a threat against the polytheists.[17]

The *ḥadīth* literature does not deal very extensively with the reasons for the expulsion, but several observations may be made. When the Prophet decided to expel the Jews of Medina, he went with his companions to the Jewish school (*bayt al-midrās,* Hebrew: *bet ha-midrash*), promised them safety if they embraced Islam (*aslimū taslamū*), told them that the land belonged to Allah and His messenger and announced his intention to expel them. He also suggested that they sell their belongings.[18] According to a tradition reported by Mālik b. Anas, the last thing which the Prophet said before his death was: "May God fight the Jews and the Christians! They transformed the tombs of their prophets into mosques. Two religions will not remain in the land of the Arabs" (*lā yabqayanna dīnāni bi-arḍ al-ᶜArab*). The last sentence was also mentioned by ᶜUmar when he decided to expel the Jews from Khaybar.[19]

The tradition about the expulsion of the Jews from Medina, reported by Bukhārī, seems to imply that the reason for the Prophet's decision was his desire to take over their landed property. The traditions concerning the aftermath of the Banū Qurayẓa massacre also contain descriptions of distribution of land to the *muhājirūn*.[20] In most traditions of legal import, however, the reason given for the expulsion is the intention to bring about religious uniformity in the Arabian peninsula: the Prophet is reported to have said that no two religions would coexist there (*lā yajtamiᶜu dīnāni fī jazīrat al-ᶜarab*).[21] The reference to the Jews in this context is of particular significance: most Jews are monotheists, and if they are ordered to leave, the expulsion of other infidels follows as a matter of course.[22]

According to some traditions, the decision to expel the Jews and the Christians was the last decision taken by the Prophet before his death;[23] the implication of this

16 Abū ᶜUbayd, *Kitāb al-amwāl*, p. 207 (no. 218). These passages were already used and interpreted in Rubin, "The Constitution of Medina", *Studia Islamica* 62 (1985), pp. 19–20. See also Qur'ān 2:139, 28:55.

17 For a discussion of this development, see section IV of the present chapter.

18 Bukhārī, *Ṣaḥīḥ, Jizya* 6 (vol. 2, pp. 294–295).

19 Mālik b. Anas, *Muwaṭṭa*ʾ, vol. 2, pp. 892–893.

20 Cf. M. J. Kister, "The massacre of Banū Qurayẓa: a reexamination of a tradition", *JSAI* 8 (1986), pp. 61–96, at pp. 95–96 (= *Society and religion from Jāhiliyya to Islam*, Variorum Reprints, Aldershot 1990, VIII).

21 Ṣan'ānī, *Muṣannaf*, vol. 6, p. 53; Ibn Abī Shayba, *Muṣannaf*, vol. 12, p. 271 (no. 12797); p. 345 (no. 13037); Abū 'Ubayd, *Kitāb al-amwāl*, p. 98 (no. 272); Ibn Ḥanbal, *Musnad*, vol. 6, p. 275; in one tradition, the order to achieve religious uniformity does not apply to the Jews of Fadak and Najrān, and they seem to be excluded from those who are to be expelled; see Ṭaḥāwī, *Mushkil al-āthār*, vol. 4, p. 13.

22 ᶜAsqalānī, *Fatḥ al-bārī*, vol. 7, p. 80 (commenting on Bukhārī, *Ṣaḥīḥ, Jizya 6*, vol. 2, p. 294). It is not quite clear what ᶜAsqalānī means by saying that only most Jews are monotheists (*wa ka-anna al-muṣannif iqtaṣara ᶜalā dhikr al-yahūd li-annahum yuwaḥḥidūna Allāh taᶜālā illā al-qalīl minhum* ...), but see above, Chapter Two, section III.

23 Ibn Abī Shayba, *Muṣannaf*, vol. 12, pp. 344–345 (no. 13037); Ibn Ḥanbal, *Musnad*, vol. 6, p. 275; Ṭaḥāwī, *Mushkil al-āthār*, vol. 4, p. 12.

seems to be that this decision of his remains valid for ever, because nobody has the authority to revoke the Prophet's injunctions after his death. Nevertheless, ᶜUmar b. al-Khaṭṭāb allowed the Jews and the Christians to stay in Medina for no longer than three days, in order to enable them to sell food.[24] This permission was given in order to fulfill the needs of the Muslims, in the same way as the Prophet allowed the Jews of Khaybar to stay and work their land, until Muslims were able to take their place.[25]

The traditions concerning the expulsion of non-Muslims do not all use the same terms to define the area which they must be abandon. Sometimes only Medina is mentioned;[26] but in most cases the terms used are *arḍ al-ᶜArab, arḍ al-Ḥijāz, jazīrat al-ᶜArab, mulk al-ᶜArab*, Khaybar and Wādī al-Qurā.[27] Geographically speaking, these terms are not quite clear; some traditionists deem it therefore necessary to specify the boundaries of the area affected by the expulsion order.[28] There are also separate traditions about the expulsion of Christians from Najrān.[29] Regarding the Zoroastrians of 'Umān, there is a tradition according to which the conquering Muslims gave them the choice of embracing Islam or going into exile. The Zoroastrians chose to leave and abandoned their possessions, which were transformed into state lands (*ṣawāfī*).[30] On the other hand, the Yemen was not included in the areas that had to be evacuated by the non-Muslims.

The need for religious uniformity is discussed not only in relation to the Arabian peninsula. The basis for these discussions are prophetic traditions in which the need for religious uniformity is formulated in general terms and is not geographically restricted. In his *Sharḥ al-siyar al-kabīr*, the Ḥanafī scholar al-Sarakhsī (d. 1090) discusses the question whether it is permissible for the People of the Book to live in Muslim cities. He replies in the affirmative, because shared residence will, in his opinion, enable the People of the Book to see the beauty of Islam. He mentions, however, the view of al-Ḥalwāʾī,[31] who maintained that this rule applies

[24] Ṣan'ānī, *Muṣannaf*, vol. 6, pp. 53–54 (no. 9984).

[25] Ṭaḥāwī, *Mushkil al-āthār*, vol. 4, p. 15; ᶜAsqalānī, *Fatḥ al-bārī*, vol. 7, p. 64 (commenting on Bukhārī, *Ṣaḥīḥ, Khums* 10 (vol. 2, p. 290).

[26] Ibn Abī Shayba, *Muṣannaf*, vol. 12, p. 271 (no. 12797).

[27] Ṣan'ānī, *Muṣannaf*, vol. 6, pp. 53, 57–58; vol. 10, pp. 366–367 (no. 19389); Ibn Abī Shayba, *Muṣannaf*, vol. 12, pp. 344–345 (nos. 13036–13037); Sarakhsī, *Sharḥ al-siyar al-kabīr*, vol. 4, p. 1541; Ṭaḥāwī, *Mushkil al-āthār*, vol. 4, pp. 12–13.

[28] The geographical aspects need to be discussed separately. See the material referred to in the previous note.

[29] Ṣan'ānī, *Muṣannaf*, vol. 6, pp. 57–58 (9993–9995).

[30] Kister, "Land property and *Jihād*", p. 309, quoting al-Nazwī, *al-Muṣannaf*, vol. 19, p. 103.

[31] Abū Muḥammad ᶜAbd al-ᶜAzīz b. Aḥmad b. Naṣr Ṣāliḥ al-Ḥalwāʾī was known as *Shams al-aʾimma*, and seems to have been one of Sarakhsī's teachers. Samᶜānī describes him as the leader of *ahl al-raʾy* in Bukhārā. ᶜAbd al-ᶜAzīz b. Muḥammad al-Nakhshabī, who was his student, thought that al-Ḥalwāʾī really (*fī al-bāṭin*) was a supporter of *ahl al-ḥadīth*, though he issued *fatwās* according to the Ḥanafī *madhab* (*lam ashukka annahu ṣāḥib ḥadīth fī al-bāṭin ... min taᶜẓīmihi li-'l-ḥadīth ghayra annahu yuftī ᶜalā madhhab al-kūfiyyīn*). He died in 448 or 449 A.H. / 1056–57 A.D. and was buried in Kalābādh. See Samᶜānī, *Ansāb*, Beirut: Dār al-Jinān, 1988, vol. 2, p. 248; Salāḥ al-Dīn al-Munajjid's Introduction to Sarakhsī's *Sharḥ al-siyar al-kabīr*, vol. 1, p. 16; "Sarakhsī, Muḥammad b. Aḥmad", *EI*[2] s.v. (N. Calder).

only if the non-Muslims are few and their residence will not adversely affect Muslim rituals; if they are numerous, and their residence may have such an adverse effect, they are prevented from living in the city and are required to live in an area which is not populated by Muslims.[32] Seth Ward has drawn attention to the view of al-Ṭabarī, according to whom "the legal standing of all Islamic lands is the same as that of the Arabian peninsula" (... *anna ḥukma jamī*ᶜ *bilād al-islām ḥukmu jazīrat al-*ᶜ*Arab*).[33] ᶜAlī b. Abī Ṭālib is reported to have prohibited the Jews, the Christians and the Zoroastrians to live in Kūfa and instructed them to move to al-Ḥīra or Zurāra. Ibn ᶜAbbās is said to have supported this prohibition with regard to any Muslim town.[34] In a similar vein, we are told that "it is not right for two directions of prayer to exist in (one) country (*lā taṣluḥu qiblatāni fī arḍin wāḥida*).[35] Another tradition instructs the Muslims not to live together with the Jews and the Christians until they embrace Islam and not to live with the Nabateans in their land (*lā tusākinū al-yahūd wa al-naṣārā ilā an yuslimū; lā tusākinū al-anbāṭ fī bilādihim* ...).[36]

These traditions may be understood as extending the prohibition on the existence of non-Muslim religions beyond the boundaries of the Arabian peninsula and applying it to any Muslim town. It should be said, however, that these formulations have not become part of the established law; even al-Subkī, who included the above-mentioned view of al-Ṭabarī in his *Fatāwā,* rejected it and interpreted the prohibition as relating only to the Ḥijāz – unless the Muslim ruler decides that moving a certain group of *dhimmī*s from one city to another is in the best interests of the Muslims.[37] An unrestricted application of the prohibition would be incompatible with the main thrust of the well known laws concerning the obligations of non-Muslims living in *dār al-islām*. These laws would be meaningless if non-Muslim were not allowed to live in Muslim cities. Historically speaking, the rules implied in the geographically unrestricted traditions were rarely implemented beyond the boundaries of the Arabian peninsula; the non-Muslim communities living under Islam experienced far less expulsions and persecutions than Jews, or "deviant" Christians, living under medieval Christendom.[38]

[32] Sarakhsī, *Sharḥ al-siyar al-kabīr*, vol. 4, pp. 1536–1537 (no. 3020).

[33] Subkī, *Fatāwā*, vol. 2, p. 375 and Ward, "A fragment from an unknown work of al-Ṭabarī ...".

[34] Subkī, *Fatāwā*, vol. 2, p. 381.

[35] Tirmidhī, *Sunan*, vol. 3, p. 127; Abū Dāwūd, *Sunan*, vol. 3, p. 225 (*lā takūnu qiblatāni fī baladin wāḥid*); Ibn Ḥanbal, *Musnad*, vol. 1, pp. 223, ll. 9–10; 285, ll. 13–14; Ṭaḥāwī, *Mushkil al-āthār*, vol. 4, pp. 16–17; Subkī, *Fatāwā*, vol. 2, p. 382.

[36] Ibn 'Umar, *Musnad*, p. 29; Ibn Abī Shayba, *Muṣannaf*, vol. 12, p. 345 (no. 13039). Another formulation reads: "Do not live with the polytheists ..." (*lā tusākinū al-mushrikīn* ...) and al-Subkī maintains (*Fatāwā*, vol. 2, p. 375 infra) that in this *ḥadīth* the *dhimmī*s are included in the category of polytheists; on this inclusion see above, Chapter Two, section III.

[37] Ward, "A fragment from an unknown work by al-Ṭabarī ...", p. 415; Subkī, *Fatāwā*, vol. 2, pp. 383, 385.

[38] For exceptions, see B. Lewis, *The Jews of Islam*, pp. 121ff; Ward, "A fragment from an unknown work by al-Ṭabarī", pp. 417–418; S. D. Goitein, *Jews and Arabs*, pp. 74–75; J. Sadan, "The 'Latrines Decree'...", p. 174. Cf. Kedar, "Expulsion as an issue in world history."

III

Qur'ān 2:256, which serves as the motto of the present chapter, has become the *locus classicus* for discussions of religious tolerance in Islam. According to the "circumstances of revelation" (*asbāb al-nuzūl*) literature, it was revealed – surprisingly enough – in connection with the expulsion of the Jewish tribe of Banū Naḍīr from Medina in 4 A.H. / 625 A.D.[39] This expulsion was part of the process by which the Muslims established their dominance in the city. In contradistinction to Qur'ān 109:6, which seems to reflect a Muslim plea against religious coercion practiced against the early Muslims by the Meccan unbelievers, Qur'ān 2:256 appears to be addressing the Muslims themselves. The interpretation of the verse is, however, not without its share of problems. We may legitimately understand it as denying the feasibility of coercion in matters of religion rather than a command to refrain from it. The wording *lā ikrāha fī al-dīn* appears to favor such an interpretation. The connection between the absence of coercion and the notion that "rectitude has become clear from error" is not self-evident and it is not likely that the sophisticated interpretations of it by some classical commentators, followed (without acknowledgment) by R. Paret[40] could have been easily understood when the verse was first uttered by the Prophet. It is, nevertheless, evident that even if we do understand the first phrase of the verse as denying the feasibility of coercion rather than as an explicit command to refrain from practicing it, the verse is still more compatible with the idea of religious tolerance than with any other approach. Any Muslim who wanted to practice religious toleration throughout the centuries of Islamic history could use the verse as a divine sanction in support of his stance.[41] And in modern times the verse is being used constantly in order to substantiate the notion of religious tolerance in Islam.

On the other hand, the Qur'ān contain numerous verses enjoining *jihād*, which is routinely described as being fought "in the way of God" (*fī sabīl Allāh*) and is, in some cases, relevant to the issue of religious freedom. It is well known that the Qur'ānic material on *jihād* is not consistent. One verse, which is commonly considered as the first one to sanction *jihād*, speaks about religious coercion practiced against the early Muslims in Mecca. According to this verse, the Muslims were allowed to wage war because the polytheists had expelled them from their habitations only on account of their belief that their Lord was Allah (*alladhīna ukhrijū min diyārihim bi-ghayri ḥaqqin illā an yaqūlū rabbunā Allāh*); in other words, the polytheists deprived the Muslims of religious freedom.[42] In other verses, the war is "religious" in the sense that the enemies of the Muslims are

[39] Wāḥidī, *Asbāb al-nuzūl*, pp. 52–53 and numerous places in the standard *tafsīr* literature.

[40] See his *Der Koran: Kommentar und Konkordanz*, Stuttgart: Kohlhammer, 1981, on Qur'ān 2:256 and "Sure 2:256: *lā ikrāha fī d-dīni* ..." For a discussion of these interpretations, see below, section V of the present chapter.

[41] See below, section V of the present chapter and I. Goldziher, *Introduction to Islamic Theology and Law*, Princeton: Princeton University Press, 1981, pp. 32–36.

[42] Qur'ān 22:39–40.

described as "enemies of God"; nevertheless, the fighting is not waged for the purpose of religious coercion, and these verses need not concern us here.[43] Perhaps the most famous *jihād* verse demands the submission of the People of the Book and their payment of the *jizya*.[44] It requires the People of the Book to humble themselves before the Muslims and to pay a discriminatory tax, but it does not instruct the Muslims to convert their vanquished enemies in a forcible manner.

Several other verses, however, view the war waged by the Muslims as having a clearly religious goal of killing the unbelievers or expanding the Muslim faith. There are verses which call upon the Muslims to kill the polytheists. The "verse of the sword" (*āyat al-sayf*) enjoins the Muslims to "slay the idolaters wherever you find them, and take them and confine them, and lie in wait for them at every place of ambush." Only if they "repent, and perform the prayer and pay the alms" will they be left alone.[45] Qur'ān 48:16 may also be understood in this way: the expression *tuqātilūnahum aw yuslimūn* may refer to conversion to Islam, or to a military surrender. Thus both verses may indicate that the conversion of the enemies to Islam is the purpose of the war and the condition for its cessation. Two verses maintain that the war is being waged in order to achieve religious uniformity,[46] while Qur'ān 3:89 enunciates the principle that whoever desires a religion other than Islam, it will not be accepted from him.

IV

So far we have attempted to understand the pertinent verses in their original context, without reference to *tafsīr* or *ḥadīth*. It is now appropriate to analyze the way in which these verses were understood by Muslim scholars in the formative period of Islam. Their understanding, as reflected in the literature of tradition and exegesis, must be the mainstay of any discussion of religious tolerance and intolerance in early Islam.

Qur'ān 109 is understood to represent an uncompromising response to a Meccan offer of compromise: the leaders of Quraysh are said to have suggested to the Prophet the creation of a religion consisting of elements from their own beliefs as well as from Islam.[47] Needless to say, the idea of such a composite religion is preposterous from the point of view of Islam after its nascent period. The Sūra is unequivocal in its rejection of Meccan *shirk*, but it does not demand any action designed to effect its supression. The mainstream tradition was aware of the exegetical possibility to understand verse 6 ("To you your religion, and to me mine") as implying toleration of the Meccan religion. Fakhr al-Dīn al-Rāzī says

[43] Qur'ān 8:60–61. [44] Qur'ān 9:29. [45] Qur'ān 9:5.

[46] Qur'ān 2:193: "Fight them, till there is no persecution and the religion is God's ..." (*qātilūhum ḥattā lā takūna fitnatun wa yakūna al-dīn li-'llāh*) and Qur'ān 8:39: "Fight them, till there is no persecution and the religion is God's entirely" (*qātilūhum ḥattā lā takūna fitnatun wa yakūna al-dīn kulluhu li-'llāh*).

[47] Ibn Hishām, *Sīrat rasūl Allāh*, vol. 1, p. 239; Muqātil b. Sulaymān, *Tafsīr*, vol. 4, pp. 887–888.

that Sūra 109:6 is customarily used when Muslims conclude truce with others (*jarat ᶜādat al-nās bi-an yatamaththalū bi-hādhihi al-āya ᶜinda al-mutāraka*), but denounces such utilization of the verse. He also rejects the possibility that the verse allows the infidels to cling to their religion: the Prophet was sent to forbid infidelity, not to condone it.[48] Other commentators also agree implicitly that the verse may be understood as condoning infidelity, and solve the problem by asserting that it was abrogated by Qurʾān 9:5 ("the verse of the sword", *āyat al-sayf*), or is to be understood as a threat directed at the polytheists rather than as a verse indicating willingness for compromise. In this sense the verse is similar to Qur'ān 41:40 which reads: "Do what you want!"(*iᶜmalū mā shiʾtum*), or "Worship what you want apart from Him (*fa-'ᶜbudū mā shiʾtum min dūnihi*).[49] In the eyes of the exegetical tradition it is self-evident that these two verses cannot be understood at face value: the Qurʾān would never sanction, or implicitly condone, the worship of any deity except Allah.

Sūra 10:99 belongs to a group of verses that are perceived as responding to specific situations in the Prophet's life. According to the *asbāb al-nuzūl*, it was revealed in Mecca after the death of Muḥammad's uncle Abū Ṭālib in 619 A.D. This event is said to have affected the Prophet in two ways. His situation deteriorated because he lost his chief protector. On the other hand, he was deeply saddened by his failure to bring about his uncle's conversion to Islam: he strongly desired that the family of ᶜAbd al-Muṭṭalib become believers and be saved from punishment in hell.[50] The verse has also been intepreted from a theological point of view. According to Ibn ᶜAṭiyya,[51] Allah informed the Prophet in this verse that He had created some people destined for happiness and others for misery (*khalaqa ahlan li-'l-saᶜāda wa ahlan li-'l-shaqāwa*); had He wanted, He would have made them all believers. Nobody can decide the fate of anybody else (*lā qudrata li-aḥad ᶜalā al-taṣarruf fī aḥad*). The power to do this belongs to Allah alone; even the Prophet cannot change the divine decree and should not be aggrieved if in some cases he is not successful in spreading the faith. He should preach his message and be aware of the fact that he cannot be held responsible if some people reject it because the matter had been foreordained (*udᶜu wa lā ᶜalayka fa-'l-amr maḥtūm*).[52]

48 Rāzī, *Mafātīḥ al-ghayb*, vol. 32, p. 137. For the use of *mutāraka* in the sense of "truce", see Lane, *Lexicon*, s.v. *t-r-k*.

49 Qurʾān 39:15. See Muqātil b. Sulaymān, *Tafsīr*, vol. 4, p. 888; Muqriʾ, *al-Nāsikh wa al-mansūkh*, p. 206; Ḥaqqī, *Rūḥ al-bayān*, vol. 10, p. 527; *Tafsīr al-Khāzin*, Beirut: Dār al-fikr, 1979, vol. 6, p. 254.

50 Ibn Hishām, *Sīrat rasūl Allāh*, p. 277; Ṭabarī, *Taʾrīkh al-rusul wa al-mulūk*, series I, p. 1199. The death of Abū Ṭālib as an unbeliever, as well as traditions attempting to describe his faith at the moment of death in more favorable terms, have considerable significance in internal Muslim polemics. See Fred M. Donner, "The death of Abū Ṭālib", in John M. Marks and Robert M. Good, eds., *Love and death in the ancient Near East*, Guilford, Conn: Four Quarters Pub. Co., 1987, pp. 237–245.

51 Probably Abū Bakr Ghallāb b. ᶜAbd al-Raḥmān ... al-Muḥābirī al-Gharnāṭī al-Andalusī who died in 518 A.H. / 1124 A.D. See Dhahabī, *Tadhkirat al-ḥuffāẓ*, ed. F. Wüstenfeld, Göttingen, 1843, part III, p. 35 (no. 37).

52 Abū Ḥayyān, *al-Baḥr al-muḥīṭ*, vol. 5, p. 193 (for the author see "Abū Ḥayyān ... al-Gharnāṭī", *EI²*, s.v. (S. Glazer); Ṭabarī, *Jāmiᶜ al-bayān*, vol. 11, p. 173; Ibn al-Jawzī, *Zād al-masīr*, vol. 4, p. 67; Bayḍāwī, *Anwār al-tanzīl*, vol. 1, p. 425.

Divine predestination is used here as a philosophical basis for the conviction that an attempt to spread Islam (or another faith) forcibly is an exercise in futility. The verse is also understood as an indication that God did not want everybody to believe and is used as a proof against the views of the Qadariyya and the Muᶜtazila.[53]

Qurʾān 48:16, revealed after the Ḥudaybiyya treaty of 628,[54] is also relevant to our discussion: "You will be called against a people possessed of great might, to fight them or they surrender" (*sa-tudᶜawna ilā qawmin ulī baʾsin shadīd tuqātilūnahum aw yuslimūn*).[55] This verse poses two questions of interpretation: who are the people against whom the fighting will be waged, and what will be the purpose of the war. If *yuslimūn* is taken in its usual Qurʾānic sense of exclusive submission to Allah which is identical with conversion to Islam, the enemies are polytheists: various tribes against whom the Prophet himself fought, such as the Ghaṭafān or the Hawāzin at the battle of Ḥunayn. Assuming that the traditional dating of the Qurʾān is correct, this interpretation of the verse seems to be, historically, the only possible one. In this case, the declared purpose of the fighting is to bring about the conversion of the enemy and to accelarate the process of achieving religious uniformity in the Arabian peninsula. Some commentators understand the verse as a prediction of the *ridda* wars; such an interpretation is historically less appealing, but it does not affect the significance of the verse as suggested above. Others proffer a completely different exegetical possibility and understand the verse as a prediction of the later Muslim wars against the Persian and Byzantine empires. In this case *yuslimūn* is understood as "surrender" (*yanqādūn*): since the Persians and the Byzantines are included in the communities who are eligible to become *ahl al-dhimma*, they are not forced to embrace Islam if they surrender and agree to pay the *jizya*.[56]

Qurʾān 8:39 enjoins the Muslims to "fight … till there is no *fitna* and the religion is God's entirely".[57] The crucial word *fitna* is difficult and the commentators most usually explain it as "infidelity" or "polytheism" (*kufr, shirk*). It seems, however, that in this verse *fitna* conveys primarily the idea of the unbelievers trying to induce the Muslims to abandon their religion. This fits the primary meaning of

[53] Cf. R. Paret, "Toleranz und Intoleranz im Islam", pp. 346–347.
[54] Wāḥidī, *Asbāb al-nuzūl*, p. 255.
[55] The translation is by Arberry, through his usage of "surrender", is prejudging the issue under discussion.
[56] See Ṭabarī, *Jāmiᶜ al-bayān*, vol. 26, p. 84; Zamakhsharī, *Kashshāf*, vol. 3, p. 545; Ibn al-Jawzī, *Zād al-masīr*, vol. 7, pp. 431–432; Rāzī, *Mafātīḥ al-ghayb*, vol. 28, p. 81; Qurṭubī, *al-Jāmiᶜ li-aḥkām al-Qurʾān*, vol. 16, p. 248; Bayḍāwī, *Anwār al-tanzīl*, vol. 2, p. 268; Ibn Kathīr, *Tafsīr al-Qurʾān*, vol. 6, p. 340.
[57] See also Qurʾān 2:193. For recent discussions of the concept of *fitna*, see Abdul Qader Tayob, "An analytical survey of al-Ṭabarī's exegesis of the cultural symbolic construct of *fitna*", in G. R. Hawting and Abdul-Qader A. Shareef, *Approaches to the Qurʾān*, London: Routledge, 1993, pp. 157–172; and Humphrey J. Fisher, "Text centered research: *Fitna* as a case study and a way forward for guests in the house of African historiography", *Sudanic Africa* 5 (1994), pp. 225–260. A brief discussion of *fitna* in the Qurʾān is on pp. 232–234.

fatana and its usage in some early documents attributed to the Prophet.[58] It is also compatible with the historical context of early Islam, when the few Muslims were under constant pressure of their powerful adversaries to revert to their former faith. If our understanding is correct, the verse enjoins the Muslims to fight the infidels and weaken them to such an extent that they would no longer be capable of promoting apostasy among the Muslims.

The Qurʾānic commentators go far beyond this meaning of the concept. Though it is not easy to find an etymological justification for this, the prevalent understanding of *fitna* in exegesis is polytheism (*shirk*) or infidelity (*kufr*). Al-Ṭabarī quotes an exegetical tradition according to which the verse commands the Muslims to create a situation in which "no infidelity will coexist with your religion" (*lā yakūna maʿa dīnikum kufr*). He also stresses that even if the polytheists stop the fighting, the Muslims must fight them until they embrace Islam.[59] Qurʾān 2:193, 8:39 and 48:16 are to be primarily understood as a Qurʾānic command to achieve the exclusive dominion of Islam in the Arabian peninsula, by use of military force if necessary.

The desire to achieve religious uniformity is expressed also in the *ḥadīth*. Perhaps the most explicit tradition in which Islam enunciated this purpose reads:

> I was commanded to fight the people until they say: 'There is no god except Allah.' Once they have said this, they have rendered their lives and possessions inviolable by me, except on the ground of (unfulfilled) duties incumbent on them; it will be up to Allah to call them to account (*umirtu an uqātila al-nās ḥattā yaqūlū lā ilāha illā 'llāh wa idhā qālūhā ʿaṣamū minnī dimāʾahum wa amwālahum illā bi-ḥaqqihā wa ḥisābuhum ʿalā Allāh*).[60]

This tradition has been preserved in several versions which are essential for our understanding of its significance. The shortest and probably earliest version, which is quoted above, includes the minimal requirement for conversion: the affirmation of God's oneness. Kister has shown that soon afterward the second *shahāda*, attesting to the prophethood of Muḥammad, and the obligation to pray and pay the *zakāt* was added. The expanded version reads:

> I was commanded to fight the people until they say: 'There is no god except Allah, and Muḥammad is the messenger of Allah; and until they perform the prayer and pay the

[58] In the instructions issued by the Prophet with regard to the religious and fiscal policy to be followed in the Yemen, we read: "A Jew will not be induced to abandon his Judaism" (*lā yuftanu yahūdiyyun ʿan yahūdiyyatihi*). See Abū ʿUbayd, *Kitāb al-amwāl*, p. 27, no. 65, and a similar tradition in the following section (no. 66). See also Ṭabarī, *Jāmiʿ al-bayān*, vol. 9, p. 249: *iʾtamarat ruʾūsuhum an yaftinū man ittabaʿahu ʿan dīn Allāh min abnāʾihim* ... On the same page we read the phrase *ḥattā lā yaftura muʾminun ʿan dīnihi*; this is read in the Cairo 1327 edition (reprint Beirut, vol. 9, p. 162) *ḥattā lā yuftana muʾminun ʿan dīnihi*. See also Qurʾān 5:49; Ibn Qayyim al-Jawziyya, *Aḥkām ahl al-dhimma*, vol. 2, p. 698, and Suyūṭī, *al-Durr al-manthūr*, vol. 1, p. 206: *kāna al-islām qalīlan wa kāna al-muʾmin yuftanu fī dīnihi*. Blachère should be credited with conveying this meaning in his translation of Qurʾān 8:39 (*Le Coran. Traduction nouvelle*, Paris: G. P. Maisonneuve, 1949–1951, p. 835): "Combattez-les jusqua'à que ne subsiste plus de tentation [d'abjurer] ..." He is followed by Paret who reads: "Und kämpft gegen sie, bis niemand (mehr) versucht, (Gläubige zum Abfall vom Islam) zu verführen ..." This is also briefly alluded to in "Fitna", *EI*², s.v. (L. Gardet).

[59] Ṭabarī, *Jāmiʿ al-bayān*, vol. 2, p. 194; vol. 9, pp. 249–250.

[60] This tradition, and especially the expression *illā bi-ḥaqqihā*, has been exhaustively analyzed by M. J. Kister, in "... *illā bi-ḥaqqihi* ...". I follow his translation of *illā bi-ḥaqqihā* (p. 49).

poor-tax. If they do this, they have thereby rendered their lives and possessions inviolable by me ..." (*umirtu an uqātila al-nās ḥattā yaqūlū lā ilāha illā 'llāh wa inna Muḥammadan rasūl Allāh wa yuqīmū al-ṣalāt wa yu'tū al-zakāt fa-idhā fa'alū, 'aṣamū minnī ...*)

This version reflects the policy ascribed to Abū Bakr at the time of the *ridda* wars: he demanded that the rebellious tribes conform not only in the purely religious sense, but also pay their share in financing the nascent Muslim state.

The commentators on this *ḥadīth* deal with the question against which groups of people the Prophet was enjoined to fight in order to ensure their acceptance of Islam. A highly intricate passage discussing this issue is found in al-ʿAynī's *ʿUmdat al-qāri'*. According to al-Kirmānī,[61] whose opinion is quoted in the *ʿUmda*, the people against whom war must be waged are the polytheists; as for the People of the Book, they are not included because the fighting against them is terminated once they agree to pay the *jizya* according to Qur'ān 9:29. The version which al-ʿAynī quotes from al-Nasā'ī – *umirtu an uqātila al-mushrikīn* rather than *al-nās* – supports al-Kirmānī's understanding.[62] It is also possible that the *jizya* was imposed only after the Prophet pronounced the *ḥadīth* under discussion; al-Kirmānī seems to indicate that if this was the case, the tradition was directed at the time of its pronouncement to all people, but this meaning of it was abrogated by Qur'ān 9:29. Al-ʿAynī himself does not accept this interpretation. He maintains that *al-nās* refers to all mankind (*al-alif wa al-lām fī al-nās li-'l-jins*) and includes even the People of the Book who agreed to pay the *jizya*. This is why al-Ṭībī[63] said that *al-nās* is a general concept from which a specific group was singled out (*huwa min al-ʿāmm alladhī khuṣṣa minhu al-baʿḍ*). The preferred objective of the commandment (*al-qaṣd al-awlā min hādhā al-amr*) included in the *ḥadīth* can be understood from Qur'ān 51:56: "I have not created *jinn* and mankind except to serve Me." Al-ʿAynī's understanding of this verse seems to be that serving God is identical with embracing Islam, and Islam is, consequently, the purpose of creation. If someone is excluded from the commandment in certain circumstances because of an accidental reason, it does not gainsay the commandment's universal validity (*wa-in takhallafa minhu aḥadun fī baʿḍ al-ṣuwar li-ʿāriḍin, lā yaqdaḥu fī ʿumūmihi*). This can be inferred from the fact that fighting the polytheists can also be suspended if an armistice is concluded with them. By referring to this possibility, al-ʿAynī apparently intends to indicate that nobody would conclude from such a temporary suspension of hostilities that the general commandment to fight the polytheists until conversion is also void. Furthermore, the basic purpose of the *jizya* is to force the People of the Book to embrace Islam; the intention

[61] Muḥammad b. Yūsuf b. ʿAlī al-Kirmānī who died in 786 A.H. / 1384 A.D. The quotations may be from his *al-Kawākib al-darārī fī sharḥ al-Bukhārī*. See Brockelmann, *GAL*, I, p. 158; *GAL*, S I, pp. 211–212; Sezgin, *GAS*, I, p. 119.

[62] See Abū Dāwūd, *Sunan*, vol. 3, p. 61; Qasṭallānī, *Irshād al-sārī*, vol. 1, p. 108; ʿAynī, *ʿUmdat al-qāri'*, vol 1, p. 181, l. 10. The current edition of Nasā'ī does not contain the version mentioned here. It reads *umirtu an uqātila al-nās*, as usual. See Nasā'ī, *Sunan*, vol. 5, p. 14.

[63] Died in 743 A.H. / 1343 A.D. See Brockelmann, *GAL S* II, p. 67.

(*taqdīr*)[64] of Qur'ān 9:29 is "... until they embrace Islam or pay the *jizya*" (*fa-yakūnu al-taqdīr ḥattā yuslimū aw yu'ṭū al-jizya* ...).[65]

V

Let us now return to Qur'ān 2:256, which has become the prooftext for the idea of religious freedom in Islam and a substantial part of Muslim commentators include in their works traditions which are compatible with this interpretation. However, the verse has also been understood differently, and we shall attempt to survey the history of its interpretation since the earliest Qur'ānic commentaries.

Classical Muslim commentators treat Qur'ān 2:256 on several levels. In the earliest works of exegesis the verse is explained by alluding to its *asbāb al-nuzūl*: the commentators provide the perceived historical circumstances in which the verse was revealed. In this type of exegesis, the verse is understood as an injunction (*amr*) to refrain from the forcible imposition of Islam, though there is no unanimity of opinion regarding the precise group of infidels to which the injunction initially applied. There is also the related question whether the verse was later abrogated by the numerous verses enjoining *jihād* or not. Later commentators, some of whom are characterized by a pronounced theological bent of thought, treat the verse in a totally different manner, considering the question whether religious faith, being "an action of the heart" (*'amal al-qalb*), can be forcibly imposed in any case. Furthermore, if Islam were imposed on all mankind, it would change the nature of the world as "the abode of trial" (*dār al-ibtilā'*), a place where people are tested whether they are willing (or unwilling) to accept the true faith. Removing from human life the liberty to make religious choices would render the idea of reward and punishment in the hereafter – a cardinal principle of Muslim theology – meaningless.

In the first type of exegesis, the commentators relate the verse to a custom said to have been common among Arab women of Medina in the pre-Islamic period. Women whose children tended to die in infancy, or who bore only one child (*miqlāt*),[66] used to vow that if a child is born to them and survives, they would make him a Jew and let him live among the Jews in order to ensure his longevity.[67] Consequently, some of these children lived with the Jews when Islam came into being. When the Jews were about to be expelled from Medina, the Anṣār attempted to prevent the expulsion of their offspring. They argued that in the Jāhiliyya they had caused their children to adopt Judaism because they thought that this religion was better than theirs; now that Allah has honored them with Islam, they wanted to force their sons to embrace the new faith, so that they be permitted to stay in Medina with their biological parents. When they communicated their intentions to

[64] For *taqdīr* in this sense, see "Taḳdīr", *EI*², s.v. (A. Levin).
[65] Al-'Aynī, *'Umdat al-qāri'*, vol. 1, p. 181.
[66] For an explanation of this term, see Ibn Manẓūr, *Lisān al-'arab*, s.v. *miqlāt* (vol. 2, pp. 72–73).
[67] The connection between longevity and residing among the Jews is not explained in the traditions. See also Lecker, "'Amr b. Ḥazm ..."

the Prophet, he did not respond at first; then Qur'ān 2:256 was revealed, giving a clear, and negative, response to the request. Therefore, when the Banū Naḍīr were expelled from Medina by the Prophet, these sons of the Anṣār were given the choice to embrace Islam and stay, or to retain their adopted Jewish faith and leave the city with the other Jews. No compulsion was practiced against those who chose the latter alternative. A similar tradition is related about Anṣārī children who were suckled by women of Banū Qurayẓa.[68] Paradoxically enough, this backhanded tolerance resulted in the expulsion of its purported beneficiaries from their ancestral home town.

According to another tradition, which places the verse in a different context but understands it in an identical manner, the verse was revealed in connection with a certain Anṣārī called Ḥuṣayn (or Abū al-Ḥuṣayn)[69] whose two sons were converted to Christianity by Byzantine merchants who came to sell their goods in Medina. Following their conversion, the two sons left for Syria with the merchants. When this happened, their father asked the Prophet to pursue them and bring them back, apparently in order to cause them to embrace Islam again. On this occasion, Qur'ān 2:256 was revealed; consequently, the Prophet did not send anyone to pursue the two converts. The father developed a grudge against the Prophet because of the latter's failure to heed his request.[70] Elsewhere, the verse is said to have frustrated the attempts of an Anṣārī man to force a black slave of his to embrace Islam.[71] ᶜUmar b. al-Khaṭṭāb is reported to have interpreted and implemented Qur'ān 2:256 in a similar manner. He offered to his *mamlūk* (or *mawlā*) Wasaq al-Rūmī[72] to become his assistant in the management of Muslim affairs if he agreed to embrace Islam. When Wasaq refused, ᶜUmar left him alone, invoking Qur'ān 2:256. Similar was ᶜUmar's reaction when an old Christian woman refused to convert to Islam at his behest.[73]

[68] Ṭabarī, *Jāmiᶜ al-bayān*, vol. 3, pp. 14–16; Abū ᶜUbayd, *Kitāb al-nāsikh wa al-mansūkh*, pp. 96–99; Naḥḥās, *al-Nāsikh wa al-mansūkh*, vol. 2, p. 100; Bayhaqī, *Sunan*, vol. 9, p. 186; Ibn al-ᶜArabī, *Aḥkām al-Qur'ān*, vol. 1, p. 233; Ibn al-Jawzī, *Zād al-masīr*, vol. 1, p. 305; Qurṭubī, *al-Jāmiᶜ li-aḥkām al-Qur'ān*, vol. 3, p. 256; See also Saᶜīd b. Manṣūr, *Sunan*, vol. 3, pp. 957–960 (nos. 428–429) where the editor provides an extensive list of sources in which these traditions appear.

[69] See ᶜAsqalānī, *Iṣāba*, vol. 2, pp. 94–95 (no. 1760).

[70] Ṭabarī, *Jāmiᶜ al-bayān*, vol. 3, p. 15.

[71] Ṭabrisī, *Majmaᶜ al-bayān*, vol. 2, p. 305. The slave's name is given as Ṣabīḥ or Ṣubayḥ. Several *mawālī* bearing this name are mentioned in the biographies of the *ṣaḥāba*, but our story is not transmitted about any one of them. See Ibn al-Athīr, *Usd al-ghāba*, vol. 3, pp. 310–311; Ibn ᶜAbd al-Barr, *al-Istīᶜāb fī maᶜrifat al-aṣḥāb*, Cairo: Maṭbaᶜat Nahḍat Miṣr, n.d., vol. 2, p. 735.

[72] His exact name can not be established with any certainty. In Ibn Saᶜd's *Ṭabaqāt* (vol. 6, pp. 109–110) the name is Ussaq; in Abū ᶜUbayd's *Kitāb al-amwāl* (p. 35, no. 87) it reads Wussaq; in the same author's *Kitāb al-nāsikh wa al-mansūkh* (p. 282) it reads Washaq; and in Ibn Kathīr's *Tafsīr* (vol. 1, p. 552) it is Asbaq. The story is essentially the same in all these sources.

[73] Ibn Zanjawayhi, *Kitāb al-amwāl*, vol. 1, p. 145, no. 133; Abū ᶜUbayd, *Kitāb al-nāsikh wa al-mansūkh*, p. 282; Jaṣṣāṣ, *Aḥkām al-Qur'ān*, vol. 2, p. 44; Naḥḥās, *al-Nāsikh wa al-mansūkh*, vol. 2, p. 100; Suyūṭī, *al-Durr al-manthūr*, vol. 1, p. 330; Qurṭubī, *al-Jāmiᶜ li-aḥkām al-Qur'ān*, vol. 3, pp. 255–256; Abū Ḥayyān, *al-Baḥr al-muḥīṭ*, vol. 2, p. 251; for a slightly different version of the story, without mentioning the Qur'ānic verse, see Ibn Qayyim al-Jawziyya, *Aḥkām ahl al-dhimma*, vol. 1, p. 211. See also Saᶜīd b. Manṣūr, *Sunan*, vol. 3, pp. 962–963 (no. 431), where the editor provides a substantial number of additional sources for this tradition.

VI

The very general formulation of Qur'ān 2:256 left the field widely open for exegetical controversy concerning the significance of the verse. The commentators discuss the question whether the prohibition of religious coercion applies to all non-Muslims or only to some of them; a related issue is whether the ruling included in the verse was abrogated (*nusikha*) by a later revelation.

Concerning the question of abrogation (*naskh*), two exegetical trends can be discerned in the Qur'ānic commentaries. According to some traditionists and commentators,[74] Qur'ān 2:256 initially applied to all people, and was one of the "armistice verses" (*āyāt al-muwāda*ʿ*a*).[75] Eventually it was abrogated. Qur'ān 9:73[76] abrogated it with regard to the polytheists, and Qur'ān 9:29 did the same with regard to the People of the Book. According to numerous other traditions, it was abrogated by "the verse of the sword" (*āyat al-sayf*), a term normally used for Qur'ān 9:5.[77] In other words, Qur'ān 2:256 was revealed as universally valid and prohibited religious coercion with regard to all humanity. After the revelation of the two later verses, however, it was abrogated and the ruling included in it has not been in force ever since. This view of the doctrinal development can be supported, at least in part, by the jurists' perception of the history of Islam during the Prophet's lifetime: according to this perception, the Prophet fought the Arab *mushrikūn*, forced them to embrace Islam, and did not accept from them anything except conversion. It is inconceivable that the Prophet would have done this if he had been obliged to follow Qur'ān 2:256.

Both verses that are said to have abrogated Qur'ān 2:256 speak about *jihād*. It can be inferred from this that the commentators who consider Qur'ān 2:256 as abrogated perceive *jihād* as contradicting the idea of religious freedom. While it is true that religious differences are mentioned in both Qur'ān 9:29 and 9:73 as the reason because of which the Muslims were commanded to wage war, none of them envisages the forcible conversion of the vanquished enemy. Qur'ān 9:29 defines the purpose of the war as the imposition of the *jizya* on the People of the Book and their humiliation, while Qur'ān 9:73 speaks only about the punishment awaiting the infidels and the hypocrites in the hereafter, and leaves the earthly purpose of the war undefined. *Jihād* and religious freedom are not mutually exclusive by necessity; religious freedom could be granted to the non-Muslims

[74] Such as Ibn Masʿūd, Sulaymān b. Mūsā and Muqātil. See Abū ʿUbayd, *Kitāb al-nāsikh wa al-mansūkh*, p. 96; Ibn ʿĀshūr, *Tafsīr al-taḥrīr*, vol. 3, p. 27.

[75] Abū Ḥayyān, *al-Baḥr al-muḥīṭ*, vol. 2, p. 281.

[76] "O Prophet, struggle with the unbelievers and hypocrites, and be thou harsh with them; their refuge is Gehenna – an evil homecoming!"

[77] "Then, when the sacred months are drawn away, slay the idolaters wherever you find them, and take them and confine them, and lie in wait for them at every place of ambush. But if they repent, and perform the prayer, and pay the alms, then let them go their way; …" Qur'ān 9:5 is perceived as having abrogated an enormous number of verses. According to Ibn al-Bārizī (*Nāsikh al-Qur'ān wa mansūkhuhu*, pp. 22–24), it abrogated 114 verses in 53 Sūras. See also the list of such abrogated verses in al-Budhūrī, *Qabḍat al-bayān*, pp. 18–22; Muqri', *al-Nāsikh wa al-mansūkh*, p. 56.

after their defeat, and commentators who maintain that Qurʾān 2:256 was not abrogated freely avail themselves of this exegetical possibility with regard to the Jews, the Christians and the Zoroastrians. However, the commentators who belong to the other exegetical trend do not find it advisable to think along these lines, and find it necessary to insist on the abrogation of Qurʾān 2:256 in order to resolve the seeming contradiction between this verse and the numerous verses enjoining *jihād*.

Only toward the modern period, we find Qurʾānic scholars who see the doctrinal development in a completely different light. The twentieth-century North African commentator Ibn Āshūr (1879–1970 A.D.)[78] maintains that *jihād* with the purpose of conversion was enjoined only in the earliest period of Islam. This type of *jihād* is reflected in the tradition in which the Prophet said that he had been commanded to fight the people until they pronounce the *shahāda*.[79] In contravention of the whole exegetical tradition, Ibn Āshūr maintains that Qurʾān 2:256 is a very late verse: it was revealed, in his view, after the conquest of Mecca, after the subjugation of the Arabian peninsula by the Muslims, after its purification from polytheism and after the massive conversion of its inhabitants to Islam. Consequently, it is not abrogated. On the contrary: it is itself abrogating Qurʾānic verses and prophetic traditions according to which *jihād* was designed to bring about conversion. Since the revelation of Qurʾān 2:256, the purpose of *jihād* changed: its aim is now to expand the rule of Islam and induce the infidels to accept its dominion (*abṭala Allāh al-qitāla ʿalā al-dīn wa abqā al-qitāla ʿalā tawsīʿi sulṭānihi*). This is expressed by the concept of *dhimma*. The new situation is reflected in Qurʾān 9:29, where the unbelievers are required to submit and pay the *jizya*, but not to embrace Islam. Ibn Āshūr also maintains, again in contradiction to the mainstream tradition, that Qurʾān 9:29 abrogated Qurʾān 9:73 which does not mention the payment of *jizya* and could be understood as enjoining *jihād* for the purpose of conversion.[80] A similar view is expressed by al-Qāsimī (1866–1914)[81] who reaches the conclusion that "the sword of *jihād*, which is legitimate in Islam, ... is not used to force people to embrace the (Islamic) religion, but to protect the *daʿwa* and to ensure obedience to the just rule and government of Islam" (*ʿulima min hādhihi al-āya anna sayf al-jihād al-mashrūʿ fī al-islām ... lam yustaʿmal li-'l-ikrāh ʿalā al-dukhūl fī al-dīn wa lākin li-ḥimāyat al-daʿwa ilā al-dīn wa al-idhʿān li-sulṭānihi wa ḥukmihi al-ʿadl*).[82]

Let us now move to the other exegetical trend, represented by some of the most important early traditionists[83] and later endorsed by al-Ṭabarī.[84] Supporters of this

[78] For his biography and bibliography, see Dāghir, *Maṣādir*, vol. 3, pp. 57–59.
[79] See above, section IV. [80] Ibn Āshūr, *Tafsīr al-taḥrīr*, vol. 3, p. 26.
[81] See Dāghir, *Maṣādir*, vol. 3, pp. 1000–1005. [82] Qāsimī, *Maḥāsin al-taʾwīl*, vol. 3, p. 665.
[83] Qatāda b. Diʿāma, al-Ḥasan al-Baṣrī, ʿĀmir al-Shaʿbī, al-Ḍaḥḥāk. See Ibn ʿĀshūr, *Tafsīr al-taḥrīr*, vol. 3, p. 27. Qatāda's views on the issue can also be inferred from the fact that Qurʾān 2:256 does not appear among the abrogated verses from Sūrat al-Baqara enumerated in his *Kitāb al-nāsikh wa al-mansūkh*, pp. 32–38. Al-Zuhrī probably held the same opinion: Qurʾān 2:256 does not appear in his *al-Nāsikh wa al-mansūkh* either (the abrogated verses from Sūrat al-Baqara appear on pp. 18–22). For a general statement of the divergence of opinion regarding the verse, see Ibn al-Jawzī, *al-Muṣaffā*, p. 19. [84] Ṭabarī, *Jāmiʿ al-bayān*, vol. 3, p. 17.

trend maintain that the verse applied from the very beginning to the People of the Book only, and these were not forced to embrace Islam even after Qur'ān 9:29 had been revealed. We can quote, as an example, the view of Ḥasan al-Baṣrī, who explained the verse by saying: "The People of the Book are not to be coerced into Islam" (*lā yukrahu ahl al-kitāb ʿalā al-islām*).[85] In more general terms, the verse speaks only of a special group of infidels (*khāṣṣ min al-kuffār*) and nothing of it was abrogated. The Arabs (*hādha al-ḥayy min al-ʿArab*) were an *ummī* community and had no revealed book; according to some formulations, they had no (legitimate?) religion (*kānat al-ʿarab laysa lahā dīn*) and were therefore forced to embrace Islam. Nothing else was accepted from them. The early Muslim tradition is replete with statements in which the Prophet and his successors demanded time and again that the Arab tribes embrace Islam and offered them no alternative. Accordingly, Qur'ān 2:256 was never intended to allow for the continued existence of idolatry in the Arabian peninsula. Those who embraced Islam after their defeat in war were not to be considered converted forcibly (*lā taqūlū li-man dakhala fī al-dīn baʿda al-ḥarb annahu dakhala mukrahan li-annahu idhā raḍiya baʿda al-ḥarb wa ṣaḥḥa islāmuhu fa-laysa bi-mukrahin wa maʿnāhu lā tansibūhum ilā al-ikrāh*).[86] This tradition is evidently intended to eliminate any contradiction between the verse and the conversion of the Arab tribes defeated by the Muslims.

As for the *dhimmī*s (Jews, Christians or Zoroastrians), they are not forced to embrace Islam if they agree to pay the *jizya* or the *kharāj*. If they choose to ignore the truth of Islam after it is made clear to them, God will take care of their punishment in the hereafter, but no religious coercion is practiced against them on earth.[87] The validity of a forcible conversion is disputed. According to Abū Ḥanīfa, al-Shāfiʿī and Ibn Qudāma, if someone acts in contravention of this principle and illegitimately forces a *dhimmī* or a *mustaʾmin* into Islam, the latter's conversion is not valid unless he remained a Muslim voluntarily after the coercive force ceased. This opinion has practical significance: if a person was forcibly converted to Islam and later reverted to his former religion, he is not considered an apostate and may not be killed. Al-Shaybānī, on the other hand, maintains that such a person is "outwardly" (*fī al-ẓāhir*) a Muslim and ought to be killed if he reneges on Islam.[88]

A very restrictive interpretation is given to Qur'ān 2:256 by Ibn Ḥazm. He explains that the verse has no general validity and two important groups of people are not affected by the ruling included in it. The Prophet forced all those who were not People of the Book to embrace Islam or face the sword; and the Muslim community agreed that apostates should be forced to revert to Islam. Ibn Ḥazm also observes that the People of the Book mentioned in Qur'ān 9:29 died and others have come in their stead. Nevertheless, the Prophet extended the validity of the injunction against religious coercion to their descendants. The meaning of the verse is restricted (*makhṣūṣ*) by reliable texts (*nuṣūṣ*) mentioned above, and people

[85] Saʿīd b. Manṣūr, *Sunan*, vol. 3, p. 961 (no. 430).
[86] Rāzī, *Mafātīḥ al-ghayb*, vol. 7, p. 14, ll. 10–11; cf. Shaybānī, *Nahj al-bayān*, vol. 1, p. 330.
[87] Ṭabarī, *Jāmiʿ al-bayān*, vol. 3, p. 16; Ibn al-ʿArabī, *Aḥkām al-Qurʾān*, vol. 1, p. 233; Ibn al-Jawzī, *Zād al-masīr*, vol. 1, p. 305.
[88] Ibn Qudāma, *Mughnī*, vol. 8, p. 144 infra.

who are not explicitly covered by Qurʾān 9:29 come under the ruling of Qurʾān 9:5: "Kill the polytheists wherever you find them …"[89]

Ibn Ḥazm is not alone in interpreting Qurʾān 2:256 in such a restricted manner. The tenth-century traditionist al-Khaṭṭābī[90] maintained that the validity of verse is restricted to the specific story of the Jews in Medina; in general, it is incumbent upon the Muslims to force the infidels to embrace the true religion (*fa-inna ḥukm al-āya maqṣūrun ʿalā mā nazalat fīhi min qiṣṣat al-yahūd wa ammā ikrāhu al-kāfir ʿalā dīn al-ḥaqq fa-wājib wa li-hādhā qātalnāhum ʿalā an yuslimū aw yuʾaddū al-jizya wa yarḍaw bi-ḥukm al-dīn ʿalayhim*)[91] A similar approach to the verse is adopted by Ibn al-ʿArabī[92] in his *Aḥkām al-Qurʾān*. In his view, the verse only forbids forcing people to believe in falsehood; to force them to believe in the truth is a legitimate part of religion (*lā ikrāha – ʿumūmun fī nafyi ikrāhin bi-'l-bāṭil fa-ammā al-ikrāhu bi-'l-ḥaqq fa-innahu min al-dīn*). This is proven both by verses from the Qurʾān,[93] and by a prophetic tradition, according to which the Prophet was commanded to fight the people until they say that there is no god except Allah. This interpretation implies, of course, that Qurʾān 2:256 is valid, but forcible conversion to Islam is, nonetheless, legitimate. The author is not moved from his position by the argument that a person who is forced into professing something does not really believe in it. After the Prophet was given sufficient strength, he was ordered to call people to Islam by force (*umira bi-'l-duʿāʾ bi-'l-sayf*); such procedure is legitimate if sufficient warning is given in advance. Furthermore, it is possible that the people who were initially converted by force may have their belief strengthened when Islam prevails and as a result of their life among the Muslims. Should this not happen, on earth they will be treated according to their outward profession of faith, and Allah will settle the account with them on the Day of Judgment (*akhadhnā bi-ẓāhirihi wa-ḥisābuhu ʿalā Allāh*).[94]

The commentaries surveyed until now perceive *lā ikrāha fī al-dīn* as a command to refrain from the forcible imposition of Islam. In view of the phrase "Rectitude has become clear from error" included in Qurʾān 2:256, some of them reason that the truth of Islam is so self-evident that no one is in need of being coerced into it; and embracing Islam because of coercion would not benefit the convert in any case.[95] But this is not the only possible interpretation. According to

[89] Ibn Ḥazm, *al-Iḥkām*, vol. 2, p. 890.

[90] See *EI*², s.v. (Ed.). Al-Khaṭṭābī lived between 319/931 and 386/996 or 388/998.

[91] Khaṭṭābī, *Maʿālim al-sunan*, Ḥalab: al-Maṭbaʿa al-ʿilmiyya, 1933, vol. 2, p. 287. I am indebted to my colleague Vardit Tokatly for this reference. Cf. ʿAẓīmābādī, *ʿAwn al-maʿbūd*, vol. 7, p. 345.

[92] Abū Bakr Muḥammad b. ʿAbd Allah al-Maʿāfirī (468 A.H./1076 A.D. – 543 A.H./1148 A.D.), a Spanish Muslim jurist and traditionist. He belonged to the Mālikī *madhhab*, was a prolific author, and served for some time as a *qāḍī* in his native city of Seville. See Brockelmann, *GAL* S, I, p. 663; *EI*², s.v. (J. Robson). For an extensive biography, see Ibn al-ʿArabī, *al-Nāsikh wa al-mansūkh*, vol. 1, pp. 13–36.

[93] Qurʾān 2:193; 8:39.

[94] Ibn al-ʿArabī, *Aḥkām al-Qurʾān*, vol. 1, p. 233–234. A similar view was expressed by al-Khaṭṭābī in his *Maʿālim al-sunan*, printed on the margin of Abū Dāwūd's *Sunan*, ed. ʿIzzat ʿUbayd al-Daʿābis and ʿĀdil al-Sayyid, Ḥimṣ, 1971, vol. 3, p. 132.

[95] Ibn Kathīr, *Tafsīr*, vol. 1, p. 551. See also Ḥaqqī, *Rūḥ al-bayān*, vol. 1, pp. 406–407; Khusrawānī, *Tafsīr-i Khusrawī*, vol. 1, 335–337; Abū Saʿūd, *Tafsīr Abī Saʿūd*, vol. 1, p. 386.

another exegetical trend, Qur'ān 2:256 is not a command at all. It rather ought to be understood as a piece of information (*khabar*), or, to put it differently, a description of the human condition: it is designed to convey the idea that embracing a religious faith can only be the result of empowerment and free choice (*tamkīn, ikhtiyār*). It cannot be the outcome of constraint and coercion (*qasr, ijbār*).[96] Phrased differently, belief is "an action of the heart" in which no compulsion is likely to yield sound results (*li-anna al-ikrāh ᶜalā al-īmān lā yaṣiḥḥu li-annahu ᶜamal al-qalb*). Religious coercion would also create a theologically unacceptable situation: if people were coerced into true belief, their positive response to prophetic teaching would become devoid of value, the world would cease to be "an abode of trial" (*dār al-ibtilā'*),[97] and, consequently, the moral basis for the idea of reward and punishment would be destroyed. This argumentation uses the verse in support of the idea of free will.

VII

Despite Qur'ān 2:256 and its interpretations, Muslim traditionists and *fuqahā'* hold that certain groups of people may be forcibly converted to Islam. In Chapter Four, we shall devote some attention to religious coercion as applied to the apostates. Yet apostates are not the only group treated in this fashion. Women, children, prisoners of war and *ḥarbīs*[98] also belong to this category.

The debate concerning the forcible conversion of women seems to have been caused by restrictions placed in Muslim law on marriage and concubinage with non-Muslims. Qur'ān 2:221, which reads "Do not marry idolatresses, until they believe; a believing slave-girl is better than an idolatress, though you may admire her", can be understood in several ways. It may mean that Muslims are not permitted to marry females belonging to polytheistic communities; it also may mean that they may not take them as concubines or engage in any sexual relations with them. The term *mushrikāt* may also relate to Jewish or Christian women;[99] in that case, the problem is of even wider proportions. If the verse is interpreted as prohibiting both marriage and concubinage, it creates a significant problem: it would then appear as delegitimizing the Muslim captors' desire to forge relationships with their female captives.

96 Ibn al-Jawzī, *Zād al-masīr*, vol. 1, p. 306; Ṭabrisī, *Majmaᶜ al-bayān*, vol. 2, p. 306; Qāsimī, *Maḥāsin al-ta'wīl*, vol. 3, p. 665. This is the view expressed by R. Paret in his "Sure 2,256..."; Paret is apparently unaware of the fact that this interpretation had been proffered by medieval Muslim scholars.

97 Ibn al-Jawzī, *Zād al-masīr*, vol. 4, p. 67. For a similar analysis of Qur'ān 10:99, see above, section IV of the present chapter, and Ḥaqqī, *Rūḥ al-bayān*, vol. 4, p. 84. For al-Ḥasan al-Baṣrī using the same argument, see Ritter, "Studien ...", p. 76. Cf. McAuliffe, "Fakhr al-Dīn al-Rāzī on *āyat al-jizya* and *āyat al-sayf*", pp. 111–114. See also Zamakhsharī, *al-Kashshāf*, vol. 3, p. 461.

98 We shall not deal with this group in detail. Briefly, inhabitants of *dār al-ḥarb* who were not given *amān* may be legitimately coerced into embracing Islam. See Sarakhsī, *Mabsūṭ*, vol. 24, p. 57, ll. 12–13; Ibn Qudāma, *Mughnī*, vol. 8, p. 145, ll. 5–8.

99 See Chapter Two, section III.

Early Muslim *fuqahā*ʾ tackled this issue in ingenious ways. They accepted the notion of forcing these women to embrace Islam. Significantly enough, Qurʾān 2:256 ("No compulsion is there in religion …") is not mentioned in this context, and the jurists do not seem to be conscious of any contradiction between this verse and the forcible conversion of women. At the same time, they were aware of the possibility that they may fail to attain this objective if they act in the ordinary way. Some of them therefore devised special procedures that were not explicitly considered as substitutes for conversion, but were deemed sufficient to make sexual intercourse with the women in question licit.

The prevalent view of the jurisprudents is that sexual intercourse of any kind is not permissible with Zoroastrian or idolatrous women. According to some, a Muslim who has intercourse with such a woman is (from the religious view point) not better than the infidel woman herself. This being so, most *fuqahā*ʾ maintain that women belonging to these groups should embrace Islam before any intercourse can take place. If they refuse, they are used as servants, but sexual intercourse with them is not permitted.[100] This is evidently not an optimal solution, and numerous traditions maintain that women who refuse to embrace Islam willingly should be subjected to coercion. According to a report included in the *Jāmi*ᶜ of al-Khallāl (d. 311 A.H. / 923 A.D.), Ibn Ḥanbal maintained that

> if Zoroastrian and idolatrous women are taken prisoner, they are coerced into Islam; if they embrace it, sexual relations with them are permissible and they can (also) be used as maidservants. If they do not embrace Islam, they are used as maidservants but not for sexual relations (*wa idhā subīna* (sic) *al-majūsiyyāt wa ᶜabadat al-awthān ujbirna ᶜalā al-islām fa-in aslamna wuṭiʾna wa 'stukhdimna wa in lam yuslimna 'stukhdimna wa lam yūṭaʾna*).[101]

The contradiction inherent in this passage is evident: despite the unspecified coercive measures, some of the women in question resisted conversion and, consequently, the masters could not take full advantage of their services. If the only way to embrace Islam is pronouncing the declaration of faith, the conversion of a defiant woman may not be possible: it is not always feasible to force someone to utter the *shahāda*. According to a tradition transmitted on the authority of Ḥasan al-Baṣrī, the Muslims used various devices to attain their objective: they turned the Zoroastrian slave-girl toward the Kaᶜba, ordered her to pronounce the *shahāda* and to perform ablution. Her master then engaged in sexual relations after she had one menstruating period while in his house.[102] Others hold that the master must teach the slave-girl to pray, to purify herself and to shave her private parts before any

[100] Aḥmad b. Ḥanbal, *Masāʾil*, vol. 2, pp. 224–228; Ṣanᶜānī, *Muṣannaf*, vol. 7, pp. 195–196 (nos. 12751, 12754, 12755); Abū ᶜUbayd, *al-Nāsikh wa al-mansūkh*, pp. 95–98; Ibn Abī Shayba, *Muṣannaf*, vol. 4, pp. 177–178 (the text is corrupt in several places); vol. 12, pp. 245–247 (nos. 12701, 12702, 12708), pp. 248–249, (nos. 12715, 12716, 12718); Qurṭubī, *al-Jāmi*ᶜ *li-aḥkām al-Qurʾān*, vol. 3, p. 66.

[101] Khallāl, *Ahl al-milal*, p. 278 (no. 564); cf. Ibn Abī Shayba, *Muṣannaf*, vol. 4, pp. 177–179.

[102] ᶜAbd al-Razzāq, *al-Muṣannaf*, vol. 7, p. 196 (no. 12753); Abū 'Ubayd, *al-Nāsikh wa al-mansūkh*, p. 98; Qurṭubī, *al-Jāmi*ᶜ *li-aḥkām al-Qurʾān*, vol. 3, p. 67.

intercourse.[103] The participation of the girl in this procedure is minimal, and this wording may be interpreted as a considerable lowering of the conversion requirements so that the girl becomes eligible for sexual intercourse as expeditiously as possible. Among the early traditionists, only a few were willing to go beyond this and allow sexual relations with a Zoroastrian slave-girl without insisting on at least a semblance of conversion.[104]

Shāfiʿī's treatment of the issue is slightly different. Speaking of grown-up Zoroastrian or polytheist women taken into captivity, he maintains that no sexual relations with them are allowed before they embrace Islam, without bringing up the question of converting them forcibly. If the female captives are minor but were taken captive with at least one of their parents, the ruling is the same. If, however, the girl was captured without her parents, or one of her parents embraced Islam, she is considered a Muslim and is coerced into embracing it (*naḥkumu lahā bi-ḥukm al-islām wa nujbiruhā ʿalayhi*).[105] Once this happens, sexual relations with her are lawful. According to the *Mudawwana*, the ruling is similar: women who are capable of understanding what Islam is should be coerced into it and only then engaged in sexual relations. According to this passage, conversion consists of uttering the *shahāda*, performing the Muslim prayer, or "if she responds in an(other) way which also indicates that she responded (positively) and embraced Islam" (*aw ajābat bi-amrin yuʿrafu bihi ayḍan annahā ajābat wa dakhalat fī al-islām*).[106] Coercive measures should also be practiced against *kitābī* women who are married to Muslims and want to convert to a non-*kitābī* religion; if these measures fail by the end of the *ʿidda* period, the marriage is nullified.[107] Coercion is also recommended with respect to female captives of the Jewish and Christian faiths, but in these cases the women's refusal to convert does not result in the prohibition of sexual relations.[108]

[103] Ibn Abī Shayba, *Muṣannaf*, vol. 12, pp. 248–9 (no. 12717). Shaving the pudenda (*ḥalq al-ʿāna*) is said to have been customary in the ancient monotheistic faith (*fiṭra*), associated with Abraham. It therefore may serve as a symbol of conversion to Islam. In our context, I have not encountered references to female circumcision which may serve the same purpose. See M. J. Kister, "… 'and he was born circumcised' … Some notes on circumcision in *ḥadīth*", *Oriens* 34 (1994), pp. 21, 28, note 103 (= Concepts and ideas at the dawn of Islam, VII); idem, "'Pare your nails': a study of an early tradition," *The Journal of the Ancient Near Eastern Society of Columbia University 11 (Near Eastern Studies in memory of M. M. Bravmann)*, New York 1979, passim (= *Society and religion from Jāhiliyya to Islam*, X).

[104] See Ṣanʿānī, *Muṣannaf*, vol. 7, p. 197 (nos. 12758–12760); Abū ʿUbayd, *al-Nāsikh wa al-mansūkh*, p. 98 (end of no. 168, 169); Ibn Abī Shayba, *Muṣannaf*, vol. 4, pp. 178–179; vol. 12, p. 247 (nos. 12709, 12711). See also Chapter Five, section II, for the views of Ibn Qayyim al-Jawziyya who viewed the whole issue in a completely different fashion.

[105] Shāfiʿī, *al-Umm*, vol. 4, p. 389, ll. 8–11.

[106] Saḥnūn, *Mudawwana*, vol. 2, pp. 314, l. 22 – 315, l. 6. The passage is not entirely clear.

[107] Ibn Qudāma, *al-Mughnī*, vol. 6, p. 593.

[108] Aḥmad b. Ḥanbal, *Masāʾil*, vol. 2, p. 224; Khallāl, *Ahl al-milal*, pp. 277–278 (no. 564), 330 (no. 707); Ibn Abī Shayba, *Muṣannaf*, vol. 12, p. 247 (no. 12710); Abū Yūsuf, *Kitāb al-kharāj*, p. 207: *yuʿraḍu ʿalayhinna al-islām fa-in aslamna aw lam yuslimna wuṭiʾna wa 'stukhdimna wa ujbirnā ʿalā al-ghusl. qāla Abū Yūsuf: wa hādhā aḥsanu mā samiʿnā fī dhālika wa Allāh aʿlam.*

VIII

In the previous section we have discussed the permissibility of coercing women into Islam. Though this idea is frequently expressed in the books of law and we have attempted to understand its background, our sources rarely give the reasons for the distinct treatment of women in this field. From this point of view, forcible conversion of children is different. Some traditions imply that there is a connection between this issue and the religious status of the newborn, and also minor, child. This is an issue often discussed in the Muslim tradition. Two prophetic utterances relevant to it are repeatedly quoted in the collections of *ḥadīth*. In the first one, the Prophet was asked about the (afterlife of) polytheist children who die before growing up. He responded by saying that "God knows best what they were doing" (or "which commandments they performed") (*Allāh aᶜlam bi-mā kānū ᶜāmilīn*).[109] In other words, it is not known what is the religious status of a child who dies a minor. Following this non-committal answer, we find among the traditionists considerable reticence and unwillingness to rule on the issue.[110] Less cryptic and more important in our context is the *ḥadīth* according to which "every newborn is born in the natural condition; his parents transform him into a Jew, a Christian or a Zoroastrian" (*mā min mawlūdin illā yūladu ᶜalā al-fiṭra fa-abawāhu yuhawwidānihi aw yunaṣṣirānihi aw yumajjisānihi*).[111] In another formulation, though every child is born "on the *fiṭra*", he is judged to belong to the religion of his parents until he grows up, or, in the language of the tradition, "until he is of those whose tongues make their views clear" (*kullu mawlūdin min banī Ādam fa-huwa yūladu ᶜalā al-fiṭra abadan wa abawāhu yuḥkamu lahu bi-ḥukmihimā wa in kāna qad wulida ᶜalā al-fiṭra ḥattā yakūna mimman yuᶜabbiru ᶜanhu lisānuhu*).[112] Here the child is deemed to have the religious affiliation of his parents until he comes of age. As we shall see later, this has some significance.

The meaning of *fiṭra* was subject to divergent interpretations: sound nature prepared for the acceptance of (true) religion, which may be understood as meaning that every child is born with the potential to become a Muslim (*kullu mawlūdin yūladu musliman bi-'l-quwwa*); awareness of the existence of God the Creator; the felicity or misery for which God destined every newborn; and, finally, Islam.[113] In

[109] See Bukhārī, *Ṣaḥīḥ*, *Kitāb al-qadar* 3 (vol. 4, p. 252) and Wensinck, *Concordance...*, vol. 4, p. 376b for numerous other references.

[110] See, for instance, Ibn Ḥanbal's attempts to evade the issue in al-Khallāl, *Ahl al-milal*, pp. 73–74. See also ibid., p. 92 (no. 65), where Ibn Ḥanbal refuses to rule on the religious affiliation of a child born to a couple of his non-Muslim slaves. An extensive treatment of this issue can be found in Ibn Qayyim al-Jawziyya, *Aḥkām ahl al-dhimma*, pp. 609–656.

[111] Bukhārī, *Ṣaḥīḥ*, *Kitāb al-janāʾiz* 81 (vol. 1, p. 341).

[112] Ibn ᶜAbd al-Barr al-Namarī, *Tamhīd*, vol. 18, pp. 63, 87.

[113] A good account of these can be found in Subkī, *Fatāwā*, vol. 2, pp. 360–362. Ibn Taymiyya wrote a whole treatise on the issue of *fiṭra*: *Risāla fī al-fiṭra wa maᶜrifat Allāh*, printed in his *Majmūᶜat al-rasāʾil al-kubrā*, vol. 2, pp. 316–334. Another extensive treatment of the various attitudes to the *fiṭra* question can be found in Ibn Qayyim al-Jawziyya, *Aḥkām ahl al-dhimma*, pp. 523–609. See also Ibn ᶜAbd al-Barr al-Namarī, *Tamhīd*, vol. 18, pp. 70ff. and "Fiṭra", *EI*², s.v. (D. B. MacDonald). It must be pointed out, however, that some traditionists totally reject this interpretation by arguing

the version of the *ḥadīth* mentioned at the beginning of the present section, its meaning is not immediately evident. However, other versions leave little doubt regarding the meaning intended by numerous traditionists. In Muslim's *Ṣaḥīḥ* we read: *mā min mawlūdin yūladu illā wa huwa ᶜalā al-milla*. In another version, the last part of the tradition reads: ... *ᶜalā hādhihi al-milla ḥattā yubayyina ᶜanhu lisānuhu*.[114] "This religion" (*hādhihi al-milla*) is a clear reference to Islam. This is also the view of early commentators on Qurᵓān 30:30 where the term *fitraṭ Allāh* appears: both Muqātil b. Sulaymān and Mujāhid equate the *fiṭra* explicitly with Islam.[115] In *ḥadīth* and *fiqh* there are conclusions from this understanding of *fiṭra:* since the child in question is considered Muslim in principle, the Muslims are entitled, and perhaps required, to transform the principle into reality by coercing him, or her, into Islam.

The idea that Islam is the "natural" religion and children are, so to speak, born into it is an important factor in their treatment. Abū Ḥanīfa, Abū Yūsuf and the Ḥanbalīs maintained that a child taken into captivity without his parents is considered a Muslim.[116] Comparably, Aḥmad b. Ḥanbal maintained that a child prisoner must not be used for ransom: he is considered a Muslim because his captors are Muslims and, consequently, it is not permissible to return him to the polytheists (*lā yufādā bihim wa dhālika li-anna al-ṣabī yaṣīru musliman bi-islām sābīhi fa-lā yajūzu radduhu ilā al-mushrikīn*).[117] If a child is taken captive without his parents and dies, the Muslims pray at his funeral. They thus treat him as a Muslim though the child was born to non-Muslim parents and did not convert formally. Similarly, if a seven years old child or a slave-girl are taken into captivity, they are to be coerced into Islam. A young slave-boy who was raised in his Muslim master's house and declared himself a Christian when he grew up should be compelled to embrace Islam by beating and torture (*yujbaru ᶜalā al-islām bi-'l-ḍarb wa al-ᶜadhāb*), because he was raised by Muslims without the presence of his parents.[118]

that "Islam and belief consist of utterances by the tongue, belief in the heart and actions of the limbs; all these do not exist in a child." See Ibn ᶜAbd al-Barr al-Namarī, *Tamhīd*, vol. 18, pp. 70, 77, quoting Qurᵓān 16:78 ("And it is God who brought you forth from your mothers' wombs knowing nothing, and He appointed for you hearing and sights and hearts ...") in support of this view; cf. Adang, "Islam as the inborn religion of mankind", p. 408.

L. Krehl (in "Das islamische dogma von der *fiṭra* ...", *Festgruss an Rudolf von Roth*, Stuttgart: Kohlhammer, 1893, p. 167) has drawn attention to a comparable idea expressed by Tertullian concerning Christianity: *Anima humana a natura Christiana.*

114 Muslim, *Ṣaḥīḥ, Kitāb al-qadar* 23 (vol. 4, p. 2048).

115 Muqātil b. Sulaymān, *Tafsīr*, vol. 3, p. 412; Ṭabarī, *Jāmiᶜ al-bayān*, vol. 21, p. 40. This is also one of the meanings of the term given by Subkī (*Fatāwā*, vol. 2, p. 361 infra). In Ṭaḥāwī, *Mushkil al-āthār*, vol. 2, p. 165, *fiṭrat Allāh* is interpreted as *millat Allāh*. Cf. Ibn Qayyim al-Jawziyya, *Aḥkām ahl al-dhimma*, vol. 2, pp. 535–536.

116 See Shāfiᶜī, *al-Umm*, vol. 7, p. 599 (*Siyar al-Awzāᶜī*); Ibn Qudāma, *Mughnī*, vol. 8, p. 426; Zarkashī, *Sharḥ* ..., vol. 6, pp. 505–506; Ibn Qayyim al-Jawziyya, *Aḥkām ahl al-dhimma*, p. 509. According to Ibn Taymiyya (*Fiṭra*, p. 320), Ibn Ḥanbal's ruling was the same even if one of the parents was with the child. Only both parents can change the child's religious status; see below.

117 Ibn Qudāma, *Mughnī*, vol. 8, p. 376, infra.

118 Khallāl, *Ahl al-milal*, pp. 83–86 (nos. 41–48), 105 (no. 91), 109–110 (no. 103); Ibn Qayyim al-Jawziyya, *Aḥkām ahl al-dhimma*, pp. 512, ll. 1–2; p. 513, ll. 5–14.

It seems that this case is perceived as bearing affinity to that of an apostate: the boy was deemed Muslim while a minor, and tried to renege when he came of age. All these rulings are based on the premise that a child follows the non-Muslim religion of his parents only if both of them are there to raise him and "convert" him to their religion; if this condition is not fulfilled, the child reverts to his "original" faith of Islam. Therefore, a child taken into captivity with his parents is to become Muslim, by coercion if necessary, as soon as one of the parents converts to Islam. The same happens if the conversion of one parent takes place in a free non-Muslim family.[119]

In a similar vein, Muḥammad b. al-Ḥasan al-Shaybānī maintained that a child taken captive with his parents becomes a Muslim as soon as his parents die and he is brought to the abode of Islam.[120] According to the views of Aḥmad b. Ḥanbal as attributed to him by al-Khallāl, if Muslims find an abandoned infant in the Byzantine territory, they have to take him with them, even if there is no one to nurse him: the child is considered a Muslim and cannot be left in the hands of the Byzantines, lest they make him a Christian.[121] Similar is the case of a child who leaves the non-Muslim territory without his parents: he is to be coerced into Islam.[122] This ruling is valid even if the child leaves the *dār al-ḥarb* with the purpose of joining his Christian parents who reside in *dār al-islām*. Such a child is to be considered a Muslim,[123] apparently because the temporary separation between the child and his unbelieving parents brings about the cessation of their religious influence. Ibn Ḥanbal was not willing to allow the restoration of this influence when the child reunites with his parents and ruled that the child in question should not be allowed to revert to his parents' faith.

According to Abū Ḥanīfa, al-Shāfiʿī and Aḥmad b. Ḥanbal, the situation is different when a non-Muslim child is taken captive together with his parents. In this case, the child is not treated as a Muslim, apparently because the parents are presumed to have "converted" him – according to the *fiṭra ḥadīth* – to their own religion. Similarly, a Muslim master may not coerce into Islam the offspring born to a couple of his Christian slaves: his possession of the parents does not prevail over their parental influence.[124] However, this approach was not generally accepted. Al-Khallāl reports that in the Byzantine frontier areas the practice was different: the people there used to coerce minor captives into Islam even if they were taken into captivity together with their parents. According to al-Khallāl's report, the Syrian jurist al-Awzāʿī, well known for his support of the "living

[119] Khallāl, *Ahl al-milal*, pp. 100–101 (nos. 80–81).

[120] Sarakhsī, *Sharḥ Kitāb al-siyar al-kabīr*, vol. 5, p. 2269 (no. 4524).

[121] Khallāl, *Ahl al-milal*, pp. 82–83 (nos. 37–40); Ibn Qayyim al-Jawziyya, *Aḥkām ahl al-dhimma*, p. 511.

[122] Ibn ʿAbd al-Barr al-Namarī, *Tamhīd*, vol. 18, p. 140.

[123] Khallāl, *Ahl al-milal*, p. 90 (no. 61); Ibn Qayyim al-Jawziyya, *Aḥkām ahl al-dhimma*, pp. 516–517.

[124] Ṭabarī, *Ikhtilāf al-fuqahā'*, pp. 159–160; Ibn ʿAbd al-Barr al-Namarī, *Tamhīd*, vol. 18, p. 140. See also Khallāl, *Ahl al-milal*, p. 79 (no. 34) (where the child of polytheist parents is considered polytheist as a general rule; the question of captivity does not arise here), and pp. 95–96 (nos. 71, 72, 73); Ibn Qudāma, *Mughnī*, vol. 8, p. 427 supra; Zarkashī, *Sharḥ* ..., vol. 6, p. 506; Ibn Qayyim al-Jawziyya, *Aḥkām ahl al-dhimma*, p. 509–510; Shāfiʿī, *al-Umm*, vol. 7, p. 599 (*Siyar al-Awzāʿī*).

tradition", is said to have endorsed this stance. In his view, the fact that the minors are in the possession of Muslims bars their "conversion" to their parental religion (*idhā ṣāra al-sabyu fī mulk al-muslimīn fa-ḥukmuhu ḥukm al-islām li-anna al-mulk awlā bihi min al-nasab*).[125] Abū ᶜUbayd, who endorsed al-Awzāᶜī's stance, gives an additional reason in its support: the exaltedness of Islam, which should take precedence over the parental relationship.[126] The same ruling is attributed in some traditions to (Sufyān) al-Thawrī[127] Supporting al-Awzāᶜī's view, Ibn Ḥazm stipulates that the possession of the captive child by a Muslim master nullifies the influence of the child's parents who took him out of the natural religion, Islam.[128]

A very curious case, which countenances marriages with Zoroastrian and *kitābī* women[129] in which the children are to be coerced into Islam, is reported by al-Khallāl. He speaks of certain non-Muslims who used to give their daughters in marriage to Muslims on the condition that the male issue of these unions will become Muslims and belong to their Muslim fathers, while the females will be religiously affiliated with their non-Muslim mothers. These daughters are described in the text as "Jewish, Christian or Zoroastrian polytheistic females." Quoting the *fiṭra ḥadīth* in his support, Ibn Ḥanbal ruled that all offspring resulting from these unions should be coerced into Islam.[130] He deemed this agreement concerning the female issue of an interfaith marriage unacceptable because only if both parents of a child are non-Muslims can the child be considered a non-Muslim. The child's gender is immaterial in the determination of his religious affiliation.

The *fiṭra* tradition is seen relevant also for the determination of the religious status of *kitābī* or other non-Muslim orphans. Let us start again with the views of Ibn Ḥanbal. Quoting the *fiṭra* tradition, he asserts that a non-Muslim child whose parents (or father) died, is to be coerced into Islam.[131] His understanding seems to

125 Ibn ᶜAbd al-Barr al-Namarī, *Tamhīd*, vol. 18, p. 137; Shāfiᶜī, *Kitāb al-umm*, vol. 7, p. 599 (*Siyar al-Awzāᶜī*); Khallāl, *Ahl al-milal*, pp. 86–87, 95 (no. 71), 97 (no. 75); Ibn Qudāma, *Mughnī*, vol. 8, p. 426; Ibn Qayyim al-Jawziyya, *Aḥkām ahl al-dhimma*, p. 514, ll. 1–6; Ṭabarī, *Ikhtilāf al-fuqahāʾ*, p. 124. For Ibn Ḥanbal's opposition to this, see Ibn ᶜAbd al-Barr al-Namarī, *Tamhīd*, vol. 18, pp. 140–141. According to other reports of Awzāᶜī's views, the child captive becomes a Muslim only if he is sold and becomes the property of a Muslim. Ibn ᶜAbd al-Barr casts doubt on the veracity of this report. See Ibn ᶜAbd al-Barr al-Namarī, *Tamhīd*, vol. 18, p. 138.

126 Abū ᶜUbayd, *Kitāb al-amwāl*, p. 124; cf. Ibn ᶜAbd al-Barr al-Namarī, *Tamhīd*, vol. 18, p. 140: *wa 'lladhī yukhtāru minhu qawl al-Awzāᶜī li-anna dīna sayyidihi aḥaqqu bihi min abawayhi wa al-islām yaᶜlū wa lā yuᶜlā ᶜalayhi.*

127 Ibn ᶜAbd al-Barr al-Namarī, *Tamhīd*, vol. 18, pp. 138–139. According to another tradition, al-Thawrī concurred on this matter with Aḥmad b. Ḥanbal.

128 Ibn Ḥazm, *Muḥallā*, vol. 7, p. 379 (no. 947).

129 For the very few traditionists who allowed marriages with Zoroastrian women, see Chapter Five, at notes 149–151. For the prohibition of marriages with *mushrikāt* see Chapter Five, section V.

130 The passage in question deserves to be quoted in its entirety: *akhbaranā ᶜAbd Allāh b. Aḥmad qāla: saʾaltu abī ᶜan qawmin yuzawwijūna banātihim min qawmin ᶜalā annahu mā kāna min dhakarin fa-huwa li-'l-rajuli muslimun wa mā kāna min unthā fa-hiya mushrika yahūdiyya aw naṣrāniyya aw majūsiyya. qāla: yujbaru kullu hāʾulāʾi man abā minhum ᶜalā al-islām li-anna ābāʾahum muslimūn li-ḥadīth al-nabī ... "fa-abawāhu yuhawwidānihi wa yunaṣṣirānihi" – yuraddūna kulluhum ilā al-islām.* See Khallāl, *Ahl al-milal*, pp. 92 (no. 64).

131 Khallāl, *Ahl al-milal*, pp. 89–90 (no. 59), 97 (no. 76); Ibn Qayyim al-Jawziyya, *Aḥkām ahl al-dhimma*, p. 516 supra. Ibn Ḥanbal takes care to point out that in such a case the child in question is allowed to inherit from his parents before his conversion; otherwise one may argue that the

be based on a close reading of the text: since the *fiṭra* tradition speaks about the parents (in the dual form), it means that the living presence of both is essential for the "conversion" of the child to his ancestral non-Muslim faith; upon the death of both of them or one of them, the necessary religious influence is no longer being exerted and the child must revert to his original faith, Islam.[132] Ibn Qayyim al-Jawziyya admits that this view existed in the Ḥanbalī *madhhab*, but rejects it. According to him, Aḥmad b. Ḥanbal adopted this view only if the parents, or one of them, died in *dār al-islām*. Once the parents die, the dominant influence on the orphaned child's religion is his domicile (*dār*).[133]

This view is not accepted by most early jurists. Mālik b. Anas, al-Shāfiʿī and Abū Ḥanīfa thought that a non-Muslim child does not become Muslim because his parents died; according to Ibn Qayyim al-Jawziyya, the practice of the Prophet and of the early caliphs was based on this premise.[134] Mālik b. Anas was asked about the case of a man who embraced Islam while his children were about thirteen years of age and had not yet reached puberty. The man died and the question of his inheritance came up for decision. Mālik ruled that the decision must be postponed. If the children embrace Islam after reaching puberty, they will inherit from their father. If they decide to retain their non-Muslim religion, they should be allowed to do so, but their inheritance will go to the Muslims.[135] We may conclude from Mālik's disposition of this case that in his view the minor children of a Muslim are not necessarily Muslims themselves and therefore are not entitled to his inheritance before they reach puberty and resolve to embrace Islam. Should they reject this option, they are not entitled to inherit from their father because religious disparity bars inheritance.

The religion of a child born to non-Muslim parents one of whom later embraces Islam is a disputed matter in Muslim law and tradition. According to a *ḥadīth* included in Bukhārī's *Ṣaḥīḥ*, such a child follows the religion of the parent who embraced Islam, whether father or mother. The precedent quoted in substantiation of this ruling is that of Ibn ʿAbbās: since his mother embraced Islam, he was considered a Muslim though his father remained an infidel. Because of its exaltedness,

difference in religion between the newly converted child and his unbelieving parents would forestall the inheritance.

The present book is concerned almost exclusively with legal theory rather than with legal practice. It is, however, difficult to resist mentioning in this context the story of Abū al-Barakāt al-Baghdādī, the Jewish philosopher who converted to Islam in the twelfth century A.D. According to his biography in Ibn al-Qifṭī's *Taʾrīkh al-ḥukamāʾ* (p. 343), he agreed to convert only on the condition that his daughters – who remained Jewish – will be allowed to inherit his property. While Ibn Ḥanbal's ruling was designed to preclude economic harm from a convert to Islam, Abū al-Barakāt suceeded in doing the same for his daughters who chose to retain their Jewish faith. See S. Stroumsa, "On Jewish intellectuals who converted (to Islam) in the early Middle Ages under the rule of Islam." *Pe'amim* 42 (1990), p. 67 (in Hebrew).

132 Cf. Ibn Qudāma, *Mughnī*, vol. 8, p. 426, ll. 13–17. For implementation of this rule in modern Yemen, see B. Eraqi-Klorman, "The forced conversion of Jewish orphans in Yemen."

133 Ibn Qayyim al-Jawziyya, *Aḥkām ahl al-dhimma*, pp. 492, ll. 13 – 493, l. 2.

134 Ibn Qayyim al-Jawziyya, *Aḥkām ahl al-dhimma*, p. 492, ll. 1–9.

135 Saḥnūn, *Mudawwana*, vol. 2, pp. 308, l. 23 – 309, l. 4.

Islam prevails in such situations (*al-islām yaʿlū wa lā yuʿlā*).[136] This seemingly authoritative *ḥadīth* notwithstanding, the view expressed in it was not unanimously accepted. Shāfiʿī accepted it wholeheartedly and maintained that if the conversion of one parent occurs while the children are minors, they are considered Muslims. Shāfiʿī rejected any other view.[137] Ibn Ḥanbal was of the same opinion.[138] He ruled, for instance, that if a Jew who embraced Islam later gives his minor daughter in marriage to a Jew, the spouses must be separated and the girl is to be coerced into Islam because she was a minor when her father became a Muslim. The minor children of any non-Muslim who embraces Islam are to be treated in a similar manner.[139] According to one tradition, Mālik and Ibn Wahb[140] also accepted it. Ibn Ḥazm insists that this is the correct view, and lists ʿUthmān al-Battī, al-Awzāʿī, al-Layth b. Saʿd, al-Ḥasan b. Ḥuyayy, Abū Ḥanīfa and al-Shāfiʿī as its supporters.[141]

The views current in the Mālikī school were diverse. Ibn ʿAbd al-Barr al-Namarī states that according to the view which is "well-known in Mālik's school" (*al-mashhūr min madhhabihi*), the child belongs to the religion of his parents (or of his father if he was born from a religiously mixed union) until he grows up, makes up his mind and articulates his religious preference (*wa huwa ʿalā dīni abawayhi abadan ḥattā yablugha wa yuʿabbira ʿanhu lisānuhu*). Hence, no Muslim prayer is held for him if he dies. Captivity, whether in the company of the child's parents or alone, has no influence on his religious status: the child remains affiliated with his parental religion until he grows up and embraces Islam.[142] According to Ibn Mājishūn (d. 213–214 A.H. / 828–829 A.D.),[143] certain Mālikīs – including Mālik b. Anas himself – held that these rules were applicable only if the minor captives were not separated from their parents and did not fall into the possession of a Muslim by sale or division (of spoils); if this did happen, they were considered Muslims. The Mālikī scholar Ashhab is reported to have said that "minors have no religion, and therefore are to be coerced into Islam lest they follow a false religion" (*wa al-ṣighār lā dīna lahum fa-li-dhālika ujbirū ʿalā al-dukhūl fī dīn al-islām li-allā yadhhabū ilā dīnin bāṭil*).[144] Ibn ʿAbd al-Barr observes that this ruling is closer to the view of al-Awzāʿī than to that of Mālik b. Anas.[145] An unnamed Mālikī held that a child taken captive with his father is

[136] Bukhārī, *Ṣaḥīḥ*, *Kitāb al-janāʾiz* 80 (ed. Krehl, vol. 1, pp. 339–341); ʿAsqalānī, *Fatḥ al-bārī*, vol. 3, pp. 461–462. [137] Shāfiʿī, *Kitāb al-umm*, vol. 4, p. 381, ll. 8–12.

[138] Khallāl, *Ahl al-milal*, pp. 100–101 (no. 81).

[139] Khallāl, *Ahl al-milal*, pp. 101–104 (nos. 81–89), 107 (no. 96); cf. Saḥnūn, *Mudawwana*, vol. 2, p. 308, ll. 14–17 (see analysis in Chapter Five, section I).

[140] ʿAbd Allāh b. Wahb (125 A.H. / 743 A.D. – 197 A.H. / 812 A.D.), an Egyptian *faqīh* and a long time associate of Mālik b. Anas. See, for him, the seminal study of M. Muranyi, *ʿAbd Allāh b. Wahb, Leben und Werk*.

[141] Ibn Ḥazm, *Muḥallā*, vol. 7, pp. 376–378 (no. 945). Elsewhere Abū Ḥanīfa and al-Shāfiʿī are said to have adopted a different view: if the father remains an unbeliever, the child follows him. See Ibn Qudāma, *Mughnī*, vol. 8, p. 426. For a detailed study of Ibn Ḥazm's views of various matters connected with the *fiṭra ḥadīth*, see Adang, "Islam as the inborn religion of mankind."

[142] Ibn ʿAbd al-Barr al-Namarī, *Tamhīd*, vol. 18, pp. 135, 141.

[143] See for him, Muranyi, *Beiträge* ..., p. 33 and index.

[144] Qurṭubī, *al-Jāmiʿ li-aḥkām al-Qurʾān*, vol. 3, p. 257 (on Qurʾān 2:256).

[145] Ibn ʿAbd al-Barr al-Namarī, *Tamhīd*, vol. 18, pp. 136–137.

not to be coerced into Islam until he (grows up and) understands what Islam is. However, if he refuses to embrace Islam when he comes of age, he is to be coerced into it by non-fatal beating (*aḍribuhu mā dūna nafsihi*).[146]

According to traditions found in the *Mudawwana*, Mālik b. Anas held that the conversion to Islam of a father or of a mother in a non-Muslim marriage has no bearing on the religious affiliation of their children. A question directed to Mālik dealt with the case of a non-Muslim who embraced Islam, but did not intervene in the religious status of his children (*aqarrahum*). When the children reached the age of about twelve years, they refused to embrace Islam. Mālik ruled that they should not be forced into it;[147] his decision seems to have been based on the premise that the father's conversion while the children were minor does not alter their religious status. Shāfiᶜī also mentions the existence of a view according to which children who were born polytheists will retain this religion until they make their wishes known (*aw qawlun thānin: annahum idhā wulidū ᶜalā al-shirk kānū ᶜalayhi ḥattā yuᶜribū ᶜan anfusihim*) and the conversion of the father to Islam does not transform the children's religious status. This may be a reference to the view of Mālik mentioned above.[148] In a similar vein, the conversion of the mother to Islam is also immaterial: the children retain the non-Muslim religion of the father.[149] It seems that this view was not generally accepted in the Mālikī school: the *Mudawwana* passage quoted in the previous note subsequently says that other traditionists (also of the Mālikī school?) expressed an opposite opinion and said that the children in question "are to be coerced: they are Muslims. This is the prevalent view among the Medinese (scholars)" (*yujbarūna wa hum muslimūn wa huwa akthar madhāhib al-madaniyyīn*).[150] It is also noteworthy the the ruling according to which the child follows the religion of his mother even if the father embraced Islam is described by al-ᶜAynī as *shādhdh*, unattested in the Mālikī school.[151]

IX

The last category of persons whose forcible conversion is discussed in the books of tradition and law are prisoners of war.[152] The Qurʾān refers to this group in

146 Khallāl, *Ahl al-milal*, p. 87 (no. 52). 147 Saḥnūn, *Mudawwana*, vol. 2, p. 309, ll. 4–7.

148 Shāfiᶜī, *Kitāb al-umm*, vol. 4, p. 381, ll. 8–13.

149 Saḥnūn, *Mudawwana*, vol. 2, pp. 307, l. 21 – 308, l. 3.

150 Saḥnūn, *Mudawwana*, vol. 2, p. 309, ll. 7–8. The text has *al-maraniyyīn*. I am indebted to M. Muranyi for the suggested emendation.

151 ᶜAynī, *ᶜUmdat al-qāriʾ*, vol. 8, p. 168; Ibn Ḥazm, *Muḥallā*, vol. 7, p. 376, ll. 20–21.

152 Scholarly literature on the treatment of prisoners of war in Islamic law and tradition is meagre. Basic details and some relevant anecdotes may be found in Khadduri, *War and peace in the law of Islam*, Baltimore: The Johns Hopkins Press, 1955, pp. 126–130. The article by Troy S. Thomas, "Prisoners of war in Islam: a legal inquiry" (*The Muslim World* 87 (1997), pp. 44–53) has a promising title, but uses only secondary or translated material, does not survey even the few Qurʾānic verses relevant to the issue, does not refer to any Qurʾānic commentary and consequently reaches untenable conclusions. For an analysis of some modern Muslim views, see S. H. Hashmi, "Saving and taking life in war: three modern Muslim views", *The Muslim World* 89 (1999), pp. 174–176.

several verses. Sūra 2:85 contains a critical but rather obscure reference to the ransom of prisoners as practiced among the Children of Israel. Sūra 33:26 mentions a battle against the People of the Book whom the Muslims defeated with divine help; they slew some of their enemies and took others captive. This is normally understood as a reference to the massacre of Banū Qurayẓa.[153] These two verses have only marginal significance for the development of the law concerning prisoners of war. More important are Qurʾān 8:67 and 47:4. The first verse stipulates that "it is not for a prophet to have prisoners until he make wide slaughter in the land. You desire the chance goods of the present world, and God desires the world to come …" The second instructs the believers to smite the necks of the unbelievers; "then, when you have made wide slaughter among them, tie fast the bonds; then set them free, either by grace or ransom, till the war lays down its loads."

In the preceding passage we have used Arberry's rendition of the verses in question. In translating the verb *athkhana* by "making wide slaughter", Arberry follows several standard commentators, such as al-Ṭabarī,[154] Bayḍāwī[155] and Zamakhsharī.[156] According to Muqātil b. Sulaymān, the verb is used in a different sense and means to "subdue by the sword and defeat".[157] Whatever its precise meaning may be, it is clear that taking of prisoners is not allowed before Muslim victory is decisively assured.

In view of this Qurʾānic material, the treatment of prisoners was a disputed matter in Islamic tradition since its very beginning. The controversy is exemplified in the standard accounts of the aftermath of the battle of Badr in which – so the historical tradition tells us – the Muslims took seventy unbelievers captive. In the ensuing consultation concerning their fate, Abū Bakr suggested to ransom them for three reasons: they were the Muslims' kinsmen (and therefore should not be killed), the ransom will be a source of strength for the Muslims and God may eventually guide the released prisoners to Islam. ʿUmar b. al-Khaṭṭāb, on the other hand, suggested to execute them because they mistreated the Prophet and were the leaders of infidelity; according to some traditions, he even suggested that the execution be carried out by each prisoner's Muslim relative – apparently in order to make clear that since the coming of Islam the ties of kinship were superseded by the solidarity of believers. ʿAbd Allāh b. Rawāḥa[158] supported ʿUmar's view and advised to burn the prisoners in a ravine full of firewood. Taking into consideration the fact that the Muslims were at that time destitute, the Prophet ruled

[153] For an extensive survey and analysis of traditions relevant to this event and for pertinent bibliography, see M. J. Kister, "The massacre of Banū Qurayẓa …".

[154] *Jāmiʿ al-bayān*, vol. 10, p. 42 (on 8:67): *ḥattā yuthkhina fī al-arḍ: … ḥattā yubāligha fī qatl al-mushrikīn fīhā wa yaqhurahum ghalabatan wa qasran …*

[155] *Anwār al-tanzīl*, vol. 1, p. 374 (on Qurʾān 8:67): *ḥattā yuthkhina fī al-arḍ: yukthira al-qatl wa yubāligha fīhi ḥattā yudhilla al-kufr wa yuqilla ḥizbahu wa yuʿizza al-islām wa yastawliya ahluhu.*

[156] *Al-Kashshāf*, vol. 2, p. 168 (on 8:67): *wa maʿnā al-ithkhān: kathrat al-qatl wa al-mubālagha fīhi …*

[157] Muqātil b. Sulaymān, *Tafsīr*, vol. 4, p. 44 (on Qurʾān 47:4): *athḫantumūhum: qahartumūhum bi-'l-sayf wa ẓahartum ʿalayhim.* See also Hamidullah, *Muslim conduct of state*, p. 213 who translates *athkhana* by "route".

[158] See "ʿAbd Allāh b. Rawāḥa", *EI²*, s.v. (A. Schaade).

in favor of Abū Bakr.[159] The Prophet's policy after the conquest of Mecca was the same, though he ordered the execution of four prisoners whom he held responsible for certain serious transgressions.[160] The controversy on the issue of prisoners is said to have continued during the first century of Islam: al-Ḥasan (al-Baṣrī), ᶜAṭāᵓ (b. Abī Rabāḥ) and Saᶜīd b. Jubayr[161] disliked the killing of prisoners because of Qurᵓān 47:4, while ᶜUmar b. ᶜAbd al-ᶜAzīz and ᶜIyāḍ b. ᶜUqba[162] held the opposite view.[163] The commentators and traditionists use the Badr episode and the other views of early Muslims as a springboard for extensive discussions concerning the treatment to be meted out to prisoners of war.

Muslim tradition maintains that Islamic law concerning prisoners of war differs from that which was current among the pre-Islamic communities. According to a repeatedly quoted tradition, taking of spoils and of prisoners was forbidden to all prophets who had been sent to promulgate the divine message before Muḥammad. In the communities which preceded the Muslims, it was customary to collect and burn the spoils, and to kill the prisoners.[164] Taking prisoners and enslaving them or accepting ransom for their release is perceived as a result of the captors' desire for worldly possessions, "while God desires for you the finery of Paradise ... as a recompense for killing them".[165] With the advent of Islam, however, a change in divine attitude set in. Standard Qurᵓānic commentaries understand the relevant Qurᵓānic verses as a reflection of this change. During the battle of Badr, the law was still the same as that which had been imposed on the previous prophets and Muslims were not allowed to release their prisoners; at that time, they were few,[166] their overall victory was not yet certain and they should have instilled fear in the hearts of their enemies by executing the prisoners. As we have seen above, the Prophet decided differently and Qurᵓān 8:67 is understood as criticizing him for releasing the prisoners for ransom before the Muslims were allowed to do so by

159 Abū ᶜUbayd, *Kitāb al-amwāl*, pp. 113–115; Ṭabarī, *Taᵓrīkh*, series I, pp. 1354–1355; Wāḥidī, *Asbāb al-nuzūl*, pp. 160–162; Jaṣṣāṣ, *Aḥkām al-Qurᵓān*, vol. 3, pp. 89–90; Qurṭubī, *al-Jāmiᶜ li-aḥkām al-Qurᵓān*, vol. 7, p. 403 (on Qurᵓān 8:67).

160 Abū ᶜUbayd, *Kitāb al-amwāl*, pp. 106–107.

161 Saᶜīd b. Jubayr was an important transmitter of *ḥadīth*, closely associated with Ibn ᶜAbbās and famous for his expertise in inheritance law. He participated in the insurrection of Ibn al-Ashᶜath and was executed by al-Ḥajjāj in 94 or 95 A.H. / 712–714 A.D. See Ibn Saᶜd, *Ṭabaqāt*, vol. 6, p. 184, ll. 23–28, 185; Dhahabī, *Siyar aᶜlām al-nubalāᵓ*, Beirut: Muᵓassasat al-risāla, 1985, vol. 4, pp. 321–343; ᶜAsqalānī, *Tahdhīb al-tahdhīb*, vol. 4, pp. 11–13;

162 ᶜIyāḍ b. ᶜUqba was the son of ᶜUqba b. Nāfiᶜ, the famous warrior who played an important role in the Muslim conquest of North Africa (see "ᶜUqba b. Nāfiᶜ", *EI*², s.v. (V. Christides)). ᶜIyāḍ himself belongs to the *tābiᶜūn* and participated in the invasion of Spain. See Maqqarī, *Nafḥ al-ṭīb*, Beirut: Dār Ṣādir, 1968, vol. 3, p. 10 (no. 9); al-Mizzī, *Tahdhīb al-kamāl*, vol. 34, p. 60.

163 Abū Yūsuf, *Kitāb al-kharāj*, p. 195; Ibn Qudāma, *Mughnī*, vol. 8, pp. 372–373; Zarkashī, *Sharḥ ...*, vol. 6, pp. 463–464; Saḥnūn, *Mudawwana*, vol. 2, p. 11 infra.

164 Muqātil, *Tafsīr*, vol. 2, pp. 125–126; cf. Jaṣṣāṣ, *Aḥkām al-Qurᵓān*, vol. 3, p. 89, ll. 4–5: "Spoils were not permitted to people with black heads (?) before you. When a prophet and his companions took spoils, they used to collect them (in one place) and fire would descend from the sky to consume them" (*lam taḥilla al-ghanāᵓim li-qawmin sūd al-ruᵓūs qablakum kāna al-nabī idhā ghanima huwa wa aṣḥābuhu jamaᶜū ghanāᵓimahum fa-tanzilu min al-samāᵓ nārun fa-taᵓkuluhā*).

165 Ṭabarī, *Jāmiᶜ al-bayān*, vol. 10, p. 42.

166 Abū ᶜUbayd, *Kitāb al-amwāl*, p. 116 (no. 313), p. 128 (no. 342).

Qur'ān 47:4. The same idea seems to be reflected in the vision in which the Prophet saw the divine punishment to be inflicted on the Muslims because of the ransom they took.[167] Qur'ān 8:68 says that the Muslim would have been severely punished for what they did if there had not been a (later) divine decree (*law lā kitābun min Allāh sabaqa la-massakum fīmā akhadhtum ʿadhābun ʿaẓīm*); the Qur'ān is silent regarding its contents, but the commentators assert that it contained God's permission for the Muslims to take spoils and prisoners. Qur'ān 8:69 explicitly permits the Muslims to enjoy their spoils, while Qur'ān 47:4 permits giving the prisoners quarter or releasing them for ransom after making "wide slaughter" among them. And the *ḥadīth* suggests that taking of spoils (and prisoners) is one of six things by which the prophet Muḥammad was preferred to his predecessors in the prophetic office.[168]

The preceding survey indicates that the Qur'ān and its commentators were mainly interested in the question whether prisoners of war should be killed, used for ransom or unconditionally released. In extra-Qur'ānic literature some attention is given also to the possibility of their conversion. In a tradition which can be interpreted as relevant to our topic, the Prophet is seen smiling. When asked by his companions what was the reason for his smile, he said that he saw people led into Paradise in fetters. When asked who these people were, he said: "(They were) people whom the Emigrants took prisoner and caused them to embrace Islam" (*qawmun yasbīhim al-muhājirūn fa-yudkhilūnahum fī al-islām*). According to another version, they were captive Persians; according to a third, they were "people led into Paradise against their will" (*yusāqūna ilā al-janna wa hum kārihūn*).[169] Elsewhere there are rather categorical statements about black and Slav prisoners and slaves: they are to be forcibly converted to Islam. The reasoning behind this verdict is that the Slavs and the blacks "have no religion" (*lā dīna lahum, lā yuʿlamu mā dīnuhum*), apparently meaning that they have no religion which the Muslims deem legitimate; in addition, they are not strongly attached to their religion and are unlikely to resist conversion.[170] As for other prisoners, the schools of law are not of one mind concerning their treatment. According to the Ḥanafī view, polytheistic prisoners have a powerful incentive to embrace Islam: barring an explicit guarantee of safety (*amān*), conversion to Islam is the only barrier between them and their execution. The classical formulation of this attitude to the

[167] Ṭabarī, *Ta'rīkh*, series I, pp. 1354–1355; Abū ʿUbayd, *Kitāb al-amwāl*, p. 115–116 (no. 307). *Pace* Watt and McDonald (*The History of Ṭabarī*, vol. 7, p. 81) who translate ... *ʿuriḍa ʿalayya ʿadhābukum* by "It was laid before me that I should punish them ..."

[168] See Tirmidhī, *Ṣaḥīḥ, Kitāb al-manāqib 18* (vol. 2, p. 390): "I was preferred to the [other] prophets by six things: I was given the ability to speak concisely, I was aided by fear [with which Allah struck my enemies, [taking of] spoils was made lawful for me (*uḥillat lī al-ghanā'im*), the earth was made for me into a mosque and a purifying [substance], I was sent to all people and the prophets were sealed with me." For further references to this tradition, see Friedmann, *Prophecy continuous*, p. 54, note 18.

[169] Haythamī, *Majmaʿ al-zawā'id*, vol. 5, 333.

[170] Jaṣṣāṣ, *Aḥkām al-Qur'ān*, vol. 3, p. 113, l. 20; Ṭabarī, *Ikhtilāf al-fuqahā'*, pp. 141 infra – 142; Khallāl, *Ahl al-milal*, p. 329 (no. 703). See also Chapter Four, section I (at note 18) where the religious status of the apostate is discussed in similar terms.

polytheistic prisoners is that "nothing is accepted from them except Islam or the sword" (*lā yuqbalu minhum illā al-islām aw al-sayf*).[171] Al-Shāfiʿī said that "any grown-up polytheist who refuses to embrace Islam or to pay the *jizya* is to be killed" (*yuqtalu kullu mushrikin bālighin idhā abā al-islām aw al-jizya*).[172] The Ḥanafī school seems to have adopted the same attitude to non-polytheist prisoners as well. Substantiating their position, the Ḥanafīs report that Abū Bakr issued stern directives concerning two Byzantine – presumably Christian – prisoners. He instructed their captors not to release them even if their ransom amounted to two bushels of gold; they should be killed unless they embrace Islam (*lā tufādūhumā wa in uʿṭītum bihimā muddayni min al-dhahab wa lākin uqtulūhumā aw yuslimā*). The possibility of giving them *dhimmī* status and exacting *jizya* from them does not arise. Al-Sarakhsī learns from this tradition that ransoming prisoners for money or material goods is forbidden and they must be killed if they do not embrace Islam. The Prophet allowed to ransom the polytheists captured in the battle of Badr only because the event had occurred before the revelation of Qurʾān 8:67 and 9:5, in which the permission to take ransom or release the prisoners unconditionally was abrogated.[173] Ibn Qudāma maintains that a prisoner who embraced Islam avoids death, but becomes a slave; if this happens, his status becomes identical to female prisoners who also become slaves, but may not be killed. According to Ibn Qudāma, al-Shāfiʿī held the same opinion according to one of the views reported from him, while according to the other he allowed the *imām* to chose any of the three options except execution.[174] Mujāhid[175] maintained, on the other hand, that a prisoner who embraced Islam becomes a free man, though his property becomes spoils of the Muslims.[176] If the prisoners are male People of the Book and ask to be released on the condition of paying the *jizya*, this saves them from execution according to the Shāfiʿīs, but their women remain spoils of the Muslims. Ibn Qudāma maintains that the Muslims are not obliged to grant this request and may kill them.[177]

171 See Sarakhsī, *Sharḥ al-siyar al-kabīr*, vol. 3, pp. 1030 (no. 1902), 1035 (no. 1910) and countless other places in the literature of *ḥadīth* and *fiqh*. See also ibid., vol. 3, p. 1025 (no. 1890): "… safety from execution is established only by a guarantee of safety or (Muslim) belief" (*al-amn ʿan al-qatl innamā yathbutu bi-'l-amān aw bi-'l-īmān …*). According to another formulation of the Ḥanafī attitude, the options for the prisoners are execution or enslavement. See Bayḍāwī, *Anwār al-tanzīl*, vol. 2, p. 261 (on Qurʾān 47:4).

172 Shāfiʿī, *Kitāb al-umm*, vol. 4, p. 409, l. 2. See above, Chapter Two, section III, for the usage of *mushrik* for both polytheists and scriptuaries.

173 Sarakhsī, *Mabsūṭ*, vol. 10, p. 24, ll. 8ff; Sarakhsī, *Sharḥ al-siyar al-kabīr*, vol. 3, p. 1030 (no. 1902).

174 Ibn Qudāma, *Mughnī*, vol. 8, p. 374. It is not quite clear what these three options are. Al-Khiraqī's *Mukhtaṣar*, of which the *Mughnī* is a commentary, mentions five options available to the *imām* with regard to prisoners of war: (1) to kill them, (2) to give them quarter (*manna ʿalayhim*) and release them without receiving anything in return, (3) to release them for money, (4) to return them as ransom (for Muslim prisoners), and, (5) to enslave them. Hence there are four options, except the execution, which lapses with the prisoner's conversion. See Ibn Qudāma, *Mughnī*, vol. 8, p. 372; Shāfiʿī, *Kitāb al-umm*, vol. 4, p. 363, ll. 9–10; p. 413, ll. 10–11; Khiraqī, *Mukhtaṣar*, p. 200; Zarkashī, *Sharḥ …*, vol. 6, pp. 458, 466.

175 Mujāhid b. Jabr al-Makkī, an important scholar of *tafsīr*, who died between 100 and 104 A.H. / 718–722 A.D. See "Mudjāhid b. Djabr al-Makkī", *EI*², s.v. (A. Rippin).

176 Shāfiʿī, *Kitāb al-umm*, vol. 4, p. 362, ll. 11–12.

177 Ibn Qudāma, *Mughnī*, vol. 8, p. 375.

The Mālikī school makes a distinction between prisoners who are grown-up People of the Book and all other prisoners, whether they are minor People of the Book, or idolaters and Zoroastrians regardless of age. Grown-up People of the Book are not to be forced into Islam,[178] but Zoroastrians and idolaters are. According to al-Qurṭubī, the reason for this distinction is utilitarian: the captor cannot derive full advantage from idolatrous or Zoroastrian captives because he considers them impure, and, consequently, is not allowed to eat from their slaughter or to engage their women sexually. He is therefore allowed to coerce them into Islam. The views of Mālik b. Anas and of Ashhab (b. ᶜAbd al-ᶜAzīz, d. 204 A.H. / 819 A.D.)[179] were the same.[180]

We may say in conclusion that conversion, forcible or otherwise, is not a focal point in the chapters of *fiqh* discussing the treatment of prisoners of war. The question does not arise in the tradition describing the treatment of the Meccan prisoners taken at Badr; since this episode has become, together with the relevant Qurʾānic verses, foundational for the development of pertinent laws, the issue is only rarely treated by the *muḥaddithūn* and the *fuqahāʾ*. Two observations are, nevertheless, in order. The wars of the Prophet against the tribes of Arabia are clearly beyond the scope of the present work, but it is noteworthy that the historical tradition describing them maintains that the Muslims routinely demanded the conversion of their adversaries with the formula "Embrace Islam and you will be safe" (*aslimū taslamū*).[181]

The veiled threat included in this sentence notwithstanding, the prophetic tradition disregarded the inferior standing of the vanquished vis-à-vis the victors and stated, in a rather backhanded manner, that people converted after suffering a military defeat should not be deemed converted forcibly.[182] Though most of them were not prisoners of war in the formal sense, the tradition seems to have some relevance to the issue at hand. It also constitutes and attempt to remove any possible contradiction between Qurʾān 2:256 and the policies ascribed to the Prophet in the Arabian peninsula.

178 According to a manuscript variant to the text, the same rule holds for minor People of the Book. See al-Qurṭubī, *al-Jāmiᶜ li-aḥkām al-Qurʾān* (ed. Cairo: Dār al-shaᶜb, n.d.), vol. 2, p. 1089, note 3.

179 See, for him, Muranyi, *Beiträge…*, index; idem, *Die Rechtsbücher des Qairawāners Saḥnūn b. Saᶜīd*, index.

180 Qurṭubī, *al-Jāmiᶜ li-aḥkām al-Qurʾān*, vol. 3, p. 257 (on Qurʾān 2:256). The substantial chapter in Saḥnūn's *Mudawwana* (vol. 2, pp. 9–12) includes no reference to forcible conversion of prisoners of war.

181 See, for instance, Ṣanᶜānī, *Muṣannaf*, vol. 5, p. 377 (no. 9739); Ṭabarī, *Taʾrīkh*, Series I, p. 1724; Fākihī, *Akhbār Makka*, vol. 5, p. 214; ᶜAsqalānī, *Iṣāba*, vol. 3, p. 363 (no. 3933); vol. 6, p. 69 (no. 7879).

182 See above, at note 86 in the present chapter.

CHAPTER FOUR

Apostasy[1]

I

Despite Qur'ān 2:256 and its prevalent intepretation, Muslim books of tradition and jurisprudence include extensive chapters on groups of people who should be forced to accept Islam. We have already surveyed the views of Muslim jurists concerning idolaters of various ethnic affiliations, as well as women, children and prisoners of war in certain circumstances. Another group against whom religious coercion is to be applied are the apostates (*murtaddūn*), people who had been Muslims but renounced their faith.[2]

In order to become a Muslim, one has to pronounce the twofold declaration of faith (*shahāda*), affirming the oneness of Allah and the prophethood of Muḥammad. Though the conditions of conversion are not the same for members of all religions and the issue is more complex than it seems to be in the general expositions of Islam,[3] the double declaration of faith is, in the overwhelming majority of cases, an indispensable condition for joining the Muslim fold. The simplest manner of leaving Islam is, naturally enough, an explicit conversion to another religion. In addition to this, retraction of the two declarations of faith, or of one of them, would also signify the believer's decision to fall away from the faith. And, indeed, the jurists maintain that denial of the *shahāda* is the foremost indication of apostasy. It is, however, not the only one. Whoever claims prophethood after the completion of Muḥammad's mission, or gives support to such a claimant, becomes also an apostate: such claims contradict the idea of the finality of Muḥammad's

[1] This work is not concerned with the modern Muslim views on apostasy. A thorough discussion of these can be found in A. E. Mayer, *Islam and Human Rights*, pp. 163–187. See also Peters and de Vries, "Apostasy in Islam", pp. 9–25; Abu Sahlieh, "Le délit d'apostasie aujourd'hui ..."; Abdullahi Ahmad an-Naim, "The Islamic law of apostasy and its modern applicability: a case from the Sudan", *Religion* 16 (1986), pp. 197–224. For a survey of some modern discussions of the topic in Egypt, see Ṭāḥūn, *Ḥurriyyat al-ʿaqīda fī al-sharīʿa al-islāmiyya*, Cairo, 1998, pp. 350–388 and Aḥmad al-Suyūfī, *Muḥākamat al-murtaddīn*, n.p., n.d.

[2] The chapters on apostasy in the books of Islamic tradition and law deal with numerous subjects which are outside the scope of this study, such as the question of the apostates' inheritance, the disposition of their property and the dissolution of their marriages. In this chapter we shall not deal with these issues, unless they have some relevance to the general theme of the present work. Some material concerning the dissolution of apostates' marriages is discussed in Chapter Five, sections II and IV.

[3] For details, see Friedmann, "Conditions of conversion in early Islam".

prophethood which became so central to Islamic creed.[4] In his compendium of Ḥanbalī *fiqh*, Ibn Qudāma (d. 620 A.H. / 1223 A.D.) gives a long list of transgressions which amount in his view to apostasy. In addition to the retraction of the *shahāda*, they include

> vilifying Allah the Exalted or His Prophet,[5] falsely impugning the honor of the Prophet's mother,[6] denying the Book of Allah or a part of it,[7] (denying) one of His prophets or one of His books, rejecting a manifest and agreed upon commandment such as the five pillars (of Islam),[8] or making licit a well known and agreed-upon prohibition, such as wine, pork, carrion, blood,[9] illicit intercourse and the like. If these occurred because of the person's ignorance,[10] his being a recent convert to Islam, or his awakening from

[4] Ibn Qudāma, *Mughnī*, vol. 8, p. 150. The historical examples of such claimants given by Ibn Qudāma are those of Musaylima and Ṭulayḥa b. Khuwaylid al-Asadī. See "Musaylima", *EI*², s.v. (W. Montgomery Watt) and "Ṭulayḥa", *EI*², s.v. (Ella Landau-Tasseron). For more examples from the classical period, see Friedmann, *Prophecy continuous*, pp. 65–68. The modern Aḥmadī movement was excommunicated by the Muslim mainstream for the same reason.

[5] See section VIII of the present chapter.

[6] Ibn Taymiyya (*al-Ṣārim al-maslūl*, p. 301) attributes this view to the early Ḥanbalī scholar al-Khiraqī (d. 334 A.H. / 945–46 A.D.); see his *Mukhtaṣar*, p. 193 supra. The *qadhf* of the Prophet's mother probably relates to her being an unbeliever. This offense is taken extremely seriously because it stains the Prophet's genealogy; see *Sharḥ al-Zarkashī*, vol. 6, p. 319 infra. The issue is alive even in modern times. For the case of a Pakistani man who was sentenced to death for saying that the Prophet was an infidel before the age of forty and that his parents died as infidels, see Y. Friedmann, *Prophecy continuous*, Preface to the Second Printing, by Zafrira and Yohanan Friedmann, at note 17, New Delhi: Oxford University Press, 2002.

Some Muslim scholars coped with the problem of the Prophet's parents (who died as unbelievers before their son was called to prophethood) with the help of a tradition according to which God resurrected both of them so that they have the opportunity to become believers. This was an "irregular" event, generated in order to honor the Prophet (*... alā tarā anna nabiyyanā akramahu Allāh ... bi-ḥayāt abawayhi lahu (?) ḥattā āmanā bihi ... wa 'ntafaʿā bi-'l-īmān baʿd al-mawt ʿalā khilāf al-qāʿida ikrāman li-nabiyyihi ...*). See *Ḥāshiyat Ibn ʿĀbidīn*, Beirut: Dār al-fikr, 1386 A.H., vol. 4, p. 231 (CD ROM edition, ʿAmmān: Turāth Company, 1999).

[7] Al-Ashʿarī reports in his *Maqālāt al-islāmiyyīn wa 'khtilāf al-muṣallīn* (ed. Ritter, Istanbul: Maṭbaʿat al-dawla, 1929, vol. 1, p. 96) that a group of the Khawārij maintained that Sūrat Yūsuf was not part of the Qurʾān; he says, however, that he was not able to verify this report. Similarly, there is a report about Hāshim al-Awqaṣ who doubted whether Qurʾān 111 was included in the heavenly, original, version of the Qurʾān (*al-lawḥ al-maḥfūẓ*), because of its predestinarian content. See J. van Ess, *Traditionistische Polemik gegen ʿAmr b. ʿUbayd: zu einem Text des ʿAlī b. ʿUmar ad-Dāraquṭnī*. Beirut and Wiesbaden: Franz Steiner Verlag, 1967, p. 10 (text), p. 16 (translation) (I am indebted to my colleague Vardit Tokatly for this last reference); idem, *Theologie und Gesellschaft*, Berlin and New York: Walter de Gruyter, 1991, vol. 1, p. 33; vol. 2, p. 107 and index s.v. Hāshim (b.) al-Awqaṣ. Ibn Qudāma may be referring here to views of this kind.

[8] Abandonment of prayer is a case in point. The numerous traditions according to which a person who abandons prayer may be considered an infidel and the discussion of this matter in the books of *fiqh* and *ḥadīth* deserve separate treatment. See, for instance, Nasāʾī, *Sunan*, vol. 1, pp. 231–232: "The covenant between us and them is (based on) prayer; whoever abandons it, becomes an infidel" (*inna al-ʿahd baynanā wa baynahum al-ṣalāt fa-man tarakahā fa-qad kafara*). For additional traditions in this vein, see Wensinck, *Concordance ...*, s.v. *taraka*. In *fiqh*, see Khiraqī, *Mukhtaṣar*, p. 189.

[9] Shāfiʿī does not agree with this: these are transgressions which may be inadvertently committed by Muslims who believe that these things are forbidden and they do not cease being Muslims as a result of committing them. See Nawawī, *al-Majmūʿ sharḥ al-Muhadhdhab*, vol. 18, p. 7.

[10] According to the Shāfiʿī jurist al-Shīrāzī, the ruling would not be the same in the case of a person who ate pork or drank wine without making this a part of his belief (*min ghayr iʿtiqād*). In other words, infringement of these dietary laws in a non-provocative way, in a way which is not designed to show the person's mockery or disregard for the *sharīʿa*, does not amount to apostasy. See Shīrāzī, *Muhadhdhab*, vol. 3, p. 256.

insanity and the like – he does not become an unbeliever but is apprised of the law (concerning these matters) and of its proof. If he persists, he becomes an unbeliever, because the proofs of these manifest matters are evident in the Book of Allah and in the *sunna* of His Prophet. The denial (of these matters) does not come forth except from someone who gives the lie to the Book of God and to the *sunna* of His Prophet" (*wa al-ridda taḥṣulu bi-jaḥd al-shahādatayn aw iḥdāhumā, aw sabb Allāh taᶜālā, aw rasūlihi ṣalᶜam, aw qadhf umm al-nabī ṣalᶜam, aw jaḥd kitāb Allāh taᶜālā, aw shayʾin minhu, aw shayʾin min anbiyāʾihi, aw kitābin min kutubihi, aw farīḍatin ẓāhira mujmaᶜ ᶜalayhā ka-'l-ᶜibādāt al-khams aw istiḥlāl muḥarram mashhūr ujmiᶜa ᶜalayhi ka-'l-khamr wa al-khinzīr wa al-mayta wa al-dam wa al-zinā wa naḥwihi. fa-in kāna dhālika li-jahlin minhu aw li-ḥadāthat ᶜahdihi bi-'l-islām aw li-ifāqatin min junūnin aw naḥwihi lam yakfur wa ᶜurrifa ḥukmahu wa dalīlahu fa-in aṣarra ᶜalayhi kafara li-anna adillata hādhihi al-umūr al-ẓāhira ẓāhiratun fī kitāb Allah wa sunnati rasūlihi fa-lā yaṣduru inkāruhā illā min mukadhdhibin li-kitāb Allāh wa sunnati rasūlihi*).[11]

The legal status of apostates is substantially different from those who had never joined the Muslim fold. Defining the difference, the jurists speak of two kinds of infidelity: "original" (*kufr aṣlī*) and "new" (*kufr ṭāriʾ*). It is felt that the crime of apostasy, or "new infidelity", is worse than its "original" counterpart. The following tradition can give us the sense of revulsion towards apostasy which permeates the literature of *ḥadīth* and *fiqh*. The second century *faqīh* Wakīᶜ b. al-Jarrāḥ (d. 197 A.D. / 812 A.H.)[12] explained why a Muslim is allowed to marry a fifth wife at once if one of his four wives apostatized; he said that "(apostasy) is like death" (*huwa bi-manzilat al-mawt*).[13] Abū Yūsuf voices the same opinion when he stipulates that the property of an apostate who migrated to *dār al-ḥarb* should be divided between his heirs because "his migration to *dār al-ḥarb* is like his death" (*wa luḥūquhu bi-dār al-ḥarb bi-manzilati mawtihi*).[14] Denying the truth of Islam after having acknowledged it at some point is deemed more abhorrent than being persistent in its denial ab initio (*fa-inna al-inkār baᶜda al-iqrār aghlaẓ min al-iṣrār fī al-ibtidāʾ ᶜalā al-inkār*).[15] In Ibn Taymiyya's formulation, "the apostate is more crude in his infidelity than an original unbeliever" (*al-murtadd aghlaẓu kufran min al-kāfir al-aṣlī*).[16] The attitude to the second type of infidels is therefore much harsher than to the first one. As we shall see later, killing the unrepentant apostate is mandatory, while an "original" unbeliever is killed only if he is a combatant; furthermore, the life of the latter may be spared in various ways: by giving him safe-conduct (*amān*), concluding a truce, according him the status of a

[11] Ibn Qudāma, *al-Kāfī*, vol. 4, p. 60. For a considerably longer and substantially different list of transgressions leading to apostasy, taken from *Majmaᶜ al-anhur*, a work of the seventeenth-century Ḥanafī scholar ᶜAbd al-Raḥmān b. Muḥammad Shaykhzāda (d. 1078 A.H. / 1667 A.D.), see Peters and de Vries, "Apostasy in Islam", pp. 3–4.

[12] See Sezgin, *GAS*, vol 1, pp. 96–97; N. Tsafrir, "Semi-Ḥanafīs and Ḥanafī biographical sources", *Studia Islamica* 84 (1996), pp. 67–85, at p. 70.

[13] Khallāl, *Ahl al-milal*, p. 502 (no. 1255).

[14] Abū Yūsuf, *Kitāb al-kharāj*, p. 181. For similar views expressed in late Ḥanafī sources, see Krscmárik, "Beiträge…", pp. 92–93; Marghīnānī, *Hidāya*, vol. 2, p. 874 infra. See also below, Chapter Five, beginning of section III.

[15] Sarakhsī, *Mabsūṭ*, vol. 10, p. 109; ᶜAynī, *Bināya*, vol. 6, p. 697.

[16] Ibn Taymiyya, *al-Ṣārim al-maslūl*, p. 321.

dhimmī, enslaving him, giving him quarter or releasing him for ransom.[17] These options are not open to an apostate.

The apostate has a special standing also from another point of view. Several jurists contend that an apostate "has no religion" (*lā dīna lahu, lā millata lahu*). This seems to imply that only people whose religions are recognized by the Muslims as legitimate are deemed "to have a religion." Since the Muslims are not willing to allow the apostate to retain the religion to which he converted, he is considered to be "faithless." Therefore he is not entitled to perform actions which are deemed to be religious in nature, such as marriage or slaughtering for food.[18]

Historically speaking, this perception of the difference between the two types of unbelievers lies in the notion that after the conversion of the Arab polytheists, Islam has not sought to impose itself on those who did not want to accept it, but, at the same time, it was not willing to condone an increase in the number of infidels by allowing Muslims to abandon their true faith, or by allowing the infidels to spread their false religions.

The idea that conversion to Islam ought to be irreversible developed as a result of the desire to protect the integrity of the early Muslim community. Both in Mecca and Medina, the community experienced instability and faced various dangers. On the one hand, the Muslim tradition maintains that numerous people and whole tribes joined the Muslim fold while the Prophet was still alive, and the Qur'ān does not hide its happiness while referring to these conversions.[19] On the other hand, we also have verses reflecting less favorable developments. On several occasions the Qur'ān refers to non-Muslims attempting to induce apostasy among Muslims.[20] It is evident that some of these attempts were crowned with success. The Qur'ān mentions people who abandoned Islam and reverted to their former faith; those of them who did this willingly are condemned in a harsh and vindictive tone. There is a sense of resentment at the idea that someone who had perceived the truth of Islam and joined it only a short time ago could be swayed into reverting to idolatry or another false religion. The Qur'ān therefore asserts that the endeavors of the unrepentant apostates will fail, Allah will visit them with His wrath and will send valiant warriors against them; however, the main punishment of those who abandoned Islam will be inflicted upon them, according to the Qur'ān, in the hereafter.[21] It is evident that in

17 Ibn Taymiyya, *al-Ṣārim al-maslūl*, p. 325.

18 Sarakhsī, *Mabsūṭ*, vol. 5, p. 48; vol. 10, p. 99. It is not clear what Sarakhsī means when he says in vol. 10, p. 99, ll. 19–20 that the apostate has no *milla munfiʿa*. See also Marghīnānī, *Hidāya*, vol. 2, pp. 872, 876; ʿAynī, *Bināya*, vol. 6, p. 715. We may mention in this context the expression "faithless Turks and Indians" (*man lā dīna lahu min ajnās al-turk wa al-hind*), attributed to Mālik b. Anas; in this case, however, these "faithless" people are allowed to retain their (non-existent?) religions if they agree to pay the *jizya*. See Friedmann, "The temple of Multān", p. 181.

19 Qur'ān 110:2: "When comes the help of God, and victory, and you see men entering God's religion in throngs, then proclaim the praise of your Lord ..."

20 Qur'ān 2:109 ("Many of the People of the Book wish they might restore you as unbelievers, after you have believed ..."), 217. See also Chapter Three, section IV.

21 Qur'ān 2:217; 3:86, 90; 4:137; 5:54; 9:74; 16:106; 47:25. Ṭabarī (*Jāmiʿ al-bayān*, vol. 3, pp. 342–344) quotes traditions according to which Qur'ān 3:90 refers to the Jews and the Christians, but this does not seem to be the primary meaning of the text. Verses such as Qur'ān 2:217 ("And if any

these verses the Qur'ān has in mind persons who embraced Islam at some stage, but later abandoned their faith.[22]

The *ḥadīth* and the *fiqh* literatures provide us with further details concerning the instability of the early Muslim community. At times military failure was instrumental in weakening the loyalty of the newly converted Muslims. The early traditionist and commentator, Muqātil b. Sulaymān (d. 150 A.H. / 767 A.D.), suggests that the faith of some Muslims was shaken following their defeat at Uḥud (*wa dhālika ḥīna huzimū yawma Uḥud shakka unāsun min al-muslimīn fa-qālū mā qālū*).[23] Among the few persons whose execution the Prophet ordered during the takeover of Mecca in 630 A.D. were three men described in some sources as apostates: ʿAbd Allah b. Saʿd b. Abī Sarḥ (who was eventually reprieved); ʿAbd Allah b. Khaṭal who embraced Islam, and became a tax collector (*muṣaddiq*), but later reverted to *shirk;* Miqyas b. Ṣubāba[24] who (wrongfully?) killed an Anṣārī for the accidental killing of his brother and subsequently returned to Quraysh as an apostate.[25] Only some versions of these traditions say explicitly that the executions were ordered because of the apostasy of the persons in question, but a number of jurists have seen them as a prophetic precedent substantiating the legality of capital punishment for apostates.[26] The tradition about Furāt b. Ḥayyān is slightly different: according to one version, the Prophet wanted to execute him because he was a spy for Abū Sufyān; according to another, the reason for the Prophet's verdict was his apostasy. Furāt eventually repented and was reprieved. A case with an unclear ending is that of a certain Nabhān: the man apostatized, and the Prophet asked him to repent four times. In one source, we are not told the conclusion of this episode.[27] In other sources, he is said to have apostatized and repented several times and was reprieved by the Prophet.[28]

of you turn back from their faith and die in unbelief – their works will bear no fruit in this life and in the Hereafter they will be companions of the Fire and will abide therein") seem to address members of the early Muslim community. See also "Ḳatl", *EI*², s.v. (J. Schacht).

It may be noted here that some jurists attempt to support the death penalty for apostates by the Qur'ān. Sarakhsī (*Mabsūṭ*, vol. 10, p. 98, ll. 17–18) mentions in this connection Qur'ān 48:16, though this verse does not speak of apostates by any stretch of the imagination, and the expression quoted (*tuqātilūnahum aw yuslimūn*) does not speak of the death penalty. It is an instance of the jurists' desire to find Qur'ānic substantiation for *sharʿī* regulations which developed independently of the Qur'ān.

22 For a detailed survey of the Qur'ānic material on apostasy, see Griffel, *Apostasie und Toleranz*, pp. 24–34. 23 Muqātil, *Tafsīr*, vol. 1, p. 485 (on Qur'ān 5:54)

24 In Ibn Taymiyya, *al-Ṣārim al-maslūl*, pp. 110, 113 we have Miqyas b. Ḥubāba; the editor prefers this reading on the basis of Fayrūzābādī, *al-Qāmūs al-muḥīṭ* s.v. q-y-s.

25 Mūsā b. ʿUqba, *Maghāzī*, pp. 273 infra – 275; Ibn Hishām, *Sīrat rasūl Allah*, pp. 818–820; Abū ʿUbayd, *Kitāb al-amwāl*, pp. 107–108 (no. 296–297); Ibn Saʿd, *Ṭabaqāt*, vol.1, part 2, pp. 97, 98, 101, 102; Abū Dāwūd, *Sunan*, vol. 3, pp. 79–80 (*Kitāb al-jihād, bāb qatl al-asīr wa lā yuʿraḍu ʿalayhi al-islām*); Fākihī, *Akhbār Makka*, vol. 5, pp. 219–220; Ṭabarī, *Ta'rīkh al-rusul wa al-mulūk*, series 1, pp. 1639–1640; Ṭaḥāwī, *Mushkil al-āthār*, vol. 2, pp. 225–227; Māwardī, *al-Ḥāwī al-kabīr*, vol. 12, p. 8; Bayhaqī, *Sunan*, vol. 8, p. 205; Ibn Taymiyya, *al-Ṣārim al-maslūl*, pp. 110–115, 127–128, 134–136; ʿAsqalānī, *Iṣāba*, Cairo 1970, vol. 4, p. 109 (no. 4714); cf. Kraemer, "Apostates, …" p. 38.

26 See, e.g., Shāfiʿī, *Kitāb al-umm*, vol. 1, p. 431. 27 Bayhaqī, *Sunan*, vol. 8, p. 197.

28 According to the version quoted in Haythamī (*Majmaʿ al-zawā'id*, vol. 6, p. 262), Nabhān apostatized three times; when he was about to be killed, he pronounced the *shahāda* again and was set free. For a similar account, see ʿAsqalānī, *Iṣāba*, vol. 6, pp. 419–420 (no. 8684).

The behavior of all these persons was perceived as betraying a relationship forged with the Prophet. In this respect, the apostates resemble the Arab polytheists who are also seen as disregarding their kinship with the Prophet and are therefore judged more harshly than polytheists of other ethnic affiliations: their being Arabs makes their transgression more reprehensible than that of their non-Arab counterparts. The apostates transgressed against the Prophet's religion, while the Arabs who refused to join it in the first place violated their duty to support their kith and kin (... *li-anna al-murtaddīn ka-mushrikī al-ᶜarab fa-inna ūlāʾika junāt ᶜalā qarābat rasūl Allāh ... wa hāʾulāʾi ᶜalā dīnihi*).[29]

The episodes related above indicate that the Muslim tradition makes a sustained effort to demonstrate that the Qurʾānic view according to which apostasy is punishable only in the hereafter began to change while the Prophet was still alive. The change was formalized in the *ḥadīth* literature where we have an unequivocal ruling with regard to this issue. It stands to reason that the Bedouin insurrection against the nascent Muslim state after the Prophet's death was the background for this development. The new attitude, which effectively transfers the punishment for apostasy from the hereafter to this world, is reflected in several utterances repeatedly attributed to the Prophet in the earliest collections of tradition. The most frequently quoted of these reads: "Whoever changes his religion, kill him" (*man baddala* (or *man ghayyara*) *dīnahu fa-'qtulūhu* or *fa-'ḍribū ᶜunuqahu*). In another formulation, taking into account the idea that a person forced to abandon Islam is not considered an apostate, the Prophet is reported to have said: "Whoever willingly disbelieves in God after he has believed, kill him" (*man kafara bi-'llāhi baᶜda īmānihi ṭāʾiᶜan fa-'qtulūhu*).[30] In a different context, reverting to infidelity after belief (*kufr baᶜda īmān*) is one of the three reasons for which a Muslim's blood may be shed with impunity.[31] The person liable for capital punishment is sometimes described in slightly more general terms: "he who abandons his religion and leaves the community" (*al-tārik li-dīnihi al-mufāriq li-'l-jamāᶜa*).[32] Such a formulation allowed some jurists to include among those whose blood may be shed not only apostates in the strict sense of the word, but also those who separated themselves from the Muslim community or rebelled against it: the Khawārij, the "innovators" (*ahl al-bidaᶜ*) and rebels of various kinds (*ahl al-baghy, al-muḥāribūn wa mā ashbahahum*). According to these jurists, the *man baddala ...*

[29] Sarakhsī, *Mabsūṭ*, vol. 10, p. 117.

[30] Mālik b. Anas, *al-Muwaṭṭaʾ*, vol. 2, p. 736 (*kitāb al-aqḍiya* 18); Abū Yūsuf, *Kitāb al-kharāj*, p. 179; ᶜAbd Allah b. Wahb, *al-Muwaṭṭaʾ*, *kitāb al-muḥāraba*, pp. 26–27 (back pagination); Ṣan'ānī, *Muṣannaf*, vol. 10, p. 168 (nos. 18705–18706); Bukhārī, *Ṣaḥīḥ*, vol. 4, p. 329 (*Kitāb istitābat al-murtaddīn* 2); Ibn Māja, *Sunan*, vol. 2, p. 848, (*Kitāb al-ḥudūd*, 2); Abū Dāwūd, *Sunan*, vol. 4, p. 126 (no. 4351), (*Kitāb al-ḥudūd*, 1); Nasāʾī, *Sunan*, vol. 7, p. 105; Ṭaḥāwī, *Mushkil al-āthār*, vol. 4, p. 63; Sarakhsī, *Sharḥ al-siyar al-kabīr*, vol. 5, p. 1938; Nazwī, *Muṣannaf*, vol. 11, p. 189. Cf. Griffel, *Apostasie und Toleranz*, pp. 51–52 who gives cogent reasons for an early dating of this *ḥadīth*.

[31] The other two are illicit sexual intercourse of a *muḥṣan*, and unjustified homicide. See, for instance, al-Shāfiʿī, *Kitāb al-umm*, vol. 6, p. 219; Bayhaqī, *Sunan*, vol. 8, p. 202. Ṣanᶜānī's formulation is: *innamā yuḥillu dama muslimin thalāthun: kufrun baᶜda īmān, aw zinaw baᶜda iḥṣān aw qatlu nafsin bi-ghayri nafsin.* See his *Muṣannaf*, vol. 10, p. 167 (no. 18701).

[32] Bayhaqī, *Sunan*, vol. 8, p. 194.

ḥadīth applies to all these groups: the apostate *stricto sensu* changed his religion in its entirety, while the others changed a part of it (... *al-murtadd ghayyara kull al-dīn wa ghayruhu min al-mufāriqīn baddala baᶜḍahu*).[33]

Most classical jurists agree that the execution of the unrepentant apostate is the proper punishment for his transgression. While apostasy is frequently considered a *ḥadd*, the procedure followed in punishing it is different from the one used with regard to the other *ḥudūd*. Theft, highway robbery, illicit intercourse and wine drinking have to be proved according to the accepted rules of evidence; the punishment is then inflicted. In case of apostasy, the offender is given – according to most jurists – the opportunity to repent. This is so because in contradistinction to other *ḥudūd*, apostasy is a result of a declaration which can be revoked by a contradictory one. A fornicator who repents remains a fornicator, but an apostate who repents is no longer an unbeliever.[34] "Asking the apostates to repent" (*istitābat al-murtaddīn*) is therefore a standard theme in the books of *ḥadīth* and jurisprudence.[35] The jurists debate the appropriate manner in which the apostate should be asked to repent and the length of time which he should be allowed to consider his decision. Detailed discussion is devoted to the question whether this procedure is mandatory (*wājib*) or desirable (*mustaḥabb*). Both views can be substantiated by reference to appropriate *aḥādīth*.[36]

Abū Ḥanīfa is among those who maintain that asking apostates to repent is only desirable. The *man baddala* ... *ḥadīth* specifies the death penalty for apostates and does not mention the obligation to ask for their repentance before inflicting it. If someone kills an apostate before the latter was asked to repent, he is not accountable for the killing. This is understood to support Abū Ḥanīfa's view: if asking apostates to repent had been mandatory, a penalty would have been stipulated for the failure to provide them with the repentance option (*wa hal yajibu an yustatāba aw yustaḥabbu – fīhi qawlāni; aḥaduhumā lā yajibu li-annahu law qutila qabla al-istitāba lam yaḍmanhu al-qātil wa law wajabat al-istitāba la-ḍaminahu*). Though ᶜUmar b. al-Khaṭṭāb dissociated himself from the action of those who killed the apostates of Tustar (see below), he did not impose on them any penalty, nor did he require them to pay compensation to the surviving relatives of the slain persons. This is what he would have done if making the repentance option available to the apostates had been obligatory. The Ḥanafī jurist al-Marghīnānī thinks along similar lines. He maintains that the repentance option is desirable rather than mandatory because the call to Islam must have reached the apostate and he is therefore presumed to know what his obligations are. Al-Marghīnānī also thinks

33 Qurṭubī, *Mufhim*, vol. 5, pp. 39–40; cf. Nawawī, *Sharḥ Ṣaḥīḥ Muslim*, vol. 11, p. 177 (*Kitāb al-qasāma, bāb mā yubāḥu bihi dam al-muslim*).

34 Ṭaḥāwī, *Mushkil al-āthār*, vol. 4, p. 64. It would appear that the same rule may apply also to the crime of *qadhf*; it may be argued that a person who retracts his slanderous accusation is no longer a slanderer. I have not yet investigated the question whether such a view is expressed in some of the sources.

35 See, for instance, Bukhārī, *Ṣaḥīḥ*, vol. 4, pp. 327–334.

36 See Abū Dāwūd, *Sunan*, vol. 4, p. 182 (nos. 4355–4357; no. 4355 is mistakenly marked as 4359) and Griffel, *Apostasie und Toleranz*, pp. 53–55.

that an apostate who does not use the repentance option promptly should be killed at once since "it is not permissible to postpone a legal obligation because of an uncertain matter" (*li-annahu lā yajūzu taʾkhīr al-wājib li-amrin mawhūm*), the uncertain matter being the possible repentance and reconversion of the apostate. In light of the traditions mentioned above, it is not necessary to postpone the execution. The apostate has, in al-Marghīnānī's view, the status of a *ḥarbī* infidel whom the call to Islam had reached in the past and who should therefore be killed without delay.[37] Al-Māwardī also refers to this view: he explains that, according to one view, an apostate who does not repent at once should be killed instantly "so that the fulfilment of God's right is not delayed" (*li-allā yuʾakhkhara li-'llāhi ʿazza wa jalla ḥaqqun*).[38] In a similar vein, al-Sarakhsī maintains that forgoing the repentance option was reprehensible in the early period when many people were recent converts to Islam (*ḥadīthu ʿahdin bi-'l-islām*) and may have entertained doubts about their new faith; in Sarakhsī's own time, however, when Islam became established and its truth manifest, apostasy may still be the result of doubt, but stems most likely from foolhardiness (*taʿannut*). It is probable that someone with a doubt will request time to reconsider; if he does not do that, it is an indication of his foolhardiness and he may be executed at once. Even in such a case, it is desirable to provide him with the repentance option, but it is not mandatory.[39]

The opposite idea, according to which it is mandatory to provide the apostate with the repentance option, is said to be supported by Qurʾān 8:38,[40] which commands the Prophet to ask the infidels to desist from what they were doing while promising them forgiveness, and making no distinction between "original" infidels and apostates. It can also find support in another understanding of the Tustar episode: if asking the apostates to repent had not been mandatory, ʿUmar would not have dissociated himself from the slaying of the apostates without giving them the opportunity to repent.[41]

ʿAṭāʾ (b. Abī Rabāḥ), Ibrāhīm al-Nakhaʿī, Mālik b. Anas, Sufyān al-Thawrī, al-Awzāʿī, Isḥāq (b. Rāhawayhi), *aṣḥāb al-raʾy* and Aḥmad b. Ḥanbal (according to one tradition) viewed the repentance option as mandatory. Nevertheless, some jurists who prefer to follow the literal wording of the *man baddala ... ḥadīth* do

[37] Marghīnānī, *Hidāya*, vol. 2, pp. 871–872; ʿAynī, *Bidāya*, vol. 6, pp. 697–699. Ibn Taymiyya (*al-Ṣārim al-maslūl*, p. 321) maintains that the well known and the prevalent (*mashhūr*) view of the whole Ḥanafī *madhhab* is that asking an apostate to repent is only desirable.

[38] Māwardī, *al-Aḥkām al-sulṭāniyya*, p. 75.

[39] Sarakhsī, *Mabsūṭ*, vol. 10, p. 99, ll. 10–16.

[40] "Say to the unbelievers, if they give over He will forgive them what is past; ..."

[41] Shīrāzī, *Muhadhdhab*, vol. 3, p. 257; Nawawī, *al-Majmūʿ sharḥ al-Muhadhdhab*, vol. 18, p. 11. Nawawī gives a list of the early traditionists who supported each option. ʿUbayd b. ʿUmayr, Ṭāwūs, Ḥasan (al-Baṣrī), Ibn al-Mundhir, Aḥmad b. Ḥanbal (according to one tradition) and the *aṣḥāb al-ẓāhir* supported the idea that asking the apostates to repent was desirable only. He thinks that Bukhārī also supported this view because he quotes verses from the Qurʾān which say that repentance will not help the apostates. The verses are Qurʾān 2:217, 3:86–90, 100, 4:137, 5:54 and 16:106–110; cf. ʿAsqalānī, *Fatḥ al-bārī*, vol. 15, p. 295. While it is true that most of these verses either do not mention repentance or say that it will not help (Qurʾān 3:90), one has to remember that Bukhārī's chapter is entitled *kitāb istitābat al-murtaddīn* (Bukhārī, *Ṣaḥīḥ*, vol. 4, p. 327), a *bāb* in it is entitled *bāb ḥukm al-murtadd wa al-murtadda ... wa-'stitābatihimā* (ibid., p. 328), and Qurʾān 3:89 does refer to the efficacy of repentance.

not think that the repentance option is legally binding at all and maintain that the apostate is to be executed at once. On the other end of the severity scale, there are a limited number of traditions indicating that the punishment of choice for apostates is imprisonment. This infrequently expressed view can be supported by asserting that the repentance option is not limited in time and the apostate should be given for ever the opportunity to repent.

Let us treat the last mentioned views first. Several collections of *ḥadīth* relate a tradition according to which six men from the tribe of Bakr b. Wāʾil apostatized during the conquest of the Persian city of Tustar[42] and joined the polytheists. When ᶜUmar b. al-Khaṭṭāb received the report that they had been killed, he expressed his displeasure and said: "I would have suggested that they enter through the door from which they had gone out. If they had done it, I would have accepted it from them; if not, I would have placed them in prison" (*kuntu ᶜāriḍan ᶜalayhim al-bāb alladhī kharajū minhu an yadkhulū fīhi fa-in faᶜalū dhālika qabiltu minhum wa illā 'stawdaᶜtuhum al-sijn*).[43] In al-Ṣanᶜānī's version, the manner of their being killed is not clear; according to al-Bayhaqī, they were killed in battle against the Muslims. Whatever the truth, it is clear that ᶜUmar stipulates imprisonment rather than execution as the punishment of choice for apostasy. Similarly, Sufyān al-Thawrī and Ibrāhīm al-Nakhaᶜī are reported to have given the apostate an opportunity to repent for ever;[44] or, in another formulation, "as long as there is hope for his repentance" (*yuʾajjal mā rujiyat tawbatuhu*).[45] Al-Nakhaᶜī is willing to give this privilege even to apostates who repeat their transgression.[46] Al-Ḥasan b. Ḥayy maintained that an apostate is to be given an opportunity to repent "even if he repented one hundred times" (*yustatābu al-murtadd wa in tāba miʾata marra*).[47] The same view is reported of the Ḥanafī jurist Abū al-Ḥasan al-Karkhī.[48] In other words, and despite the *man baddala ... ḥadīth* mentioned above, these jurists were willing to forego the infliction of capital punishment for apostasy. Ibn Qudāma is quick to observe that this view contradicts the *sunna* and the *ijmāᶜ* because it means that in practical terms the apostate will never be killed.[49]

42 See "Shushtar", *EI*², s.v. (J. H. Kramers – [C. E. Bosworth]).

43 Ṣanᶜānī, *Muṣannaf*, vol. 10, pp. 165–166 (no. 18696); Ibn Abī Shayba, *Muṣannaf*, vol. 12, p. 266 (no. 12783); Khallāl, *Ahl al-milal*, pp. 488–489 (nos. 1201, 1204), 490–491 (nos. 1208–1209); Ṭaḥāwī, *Mukhtaṣar ikhtilāf al-ᶜulamāʾ*, vol. 3, p. 503 (no. 1651); Bayhaqī, *Sunan*, vol. 8, p. 207.

44 Ṣanᶜānī, *Muṣannaf*, vol. 10, p. 166; Bayhaqī, *Sunan*, vol. 8, p. 197, ll. 21–22; Nazwī, *Muṣannaf*, vol. 11, p. 190; Ibn Qudāma, *al-Mughnī*, vol. 8, pp. 125 infra – 126 supra; Dimashqī, *Raḥmat al-umma*, p. 491; ᶜAynī, *Bināya*, vol. 6, p. 699.

45 Ibn Taymiyya, *al-Ṣārim al-maslūl*, p. 321.

46 Sarakhsī, *Sharḥ kitāb al-siyar al-kabīr*, vol. 5, p. 1939 (no. 3883).

47 Ṭaḥāwī, *Mukhtaṣar ikhtilāf al-ᶜulamāʾ*, vol. 3, p. 502 (no. 1651). On al-Ḥasan (b. Ṣāliḥ b. Ṣāliḥ) b. Ḥayy, see Mizzī, *Tahdhīb al-kamāl*, vol. 6, pp. 177–191 (no. 1238). He died in 169 A.H. / 785 A.D. (for the date of his death, see p. 190).

48 ᶜAynī, *Bināya*, vol. 6, p. 700. Al-Karkhī lived between 260 A.H./ 873 A.D. and 340 A.H./ 951 A.D. He is described as the "head of the Ḥanafīs" and the teacher of Abū Bakr al-Jaṣṣāṣ. His *Risāla fī al-uṣūl* is printed together with *Kitāb taʾsīs al-naẓar* by Abū Zayd ᶜUbayd Allah b. ᶜUmar b. ᶜĪsā al-Dabūsī al-Ḥanafī, Cairo n.d. His biography, adapted from *Kitāb aᶜlām al-akhyār wa Tāj al-tarājim* is on p. 79. See also Sezgin, *GAS*, vol. 1, p. 444.

49 Ibn Qudāma, *al-Mughnī*, vol. 8, p. 126 line 1; cf. ᶜAynī, *Bināya*, vol. 6, p. 699.

Traditions reflecting an opposite point of view are reported by Aḥmad b. Ḥanbal. According to these, God will not accept the repentance of someone who became an infidel after he had been a Muslim (*inna Allāh … lā yaqbalu tawbata ᶜabdin kafara baᶜda islāmihi*).[50] This tradition is similar to the Qurʾānic verses on the fate of the apostates in the hereafter and does not entail inevitable conclusions for their treatment in this world. Other utterances are more explicit in this regard. Ḥasan al-Baṣrī, Ṭāwūs[51] and the *ahl al-ẓāhir* are reported to have said that it is not necessary to ask the apostate to repent and he should be killed at once.[52] Al-Shāfiᶜī also mentions the existence of jurists who refused to accept the repentance of apostates, at least those of them who were born Muslims.[53] Al-Ṭaḥāwī explains that those who oppose the repentance option for apostates view their execution as a *ḥadd*: since the punishment for the other *ḥudūd* cannot be set aside by repentance, the punishment for apostasy cannot be revoked by it either.[54]

Most jurists reject the two opinions mentioned above and maintain that the apostate must be asked to repent and should be surrendered to the executioner only if he refuses to comply. According to one source, al-Shaybānī is reported to have advocated the execution of apostates without reference to the repentance option, but elsewhere he asserts that Islam should be offered to the apostate before any action is taken against him.[55] Al-Ṭaḥāwī holds the same opinion.[56] Though the plain wording of the *man baddala … ḥadīth* does not provide a basis for the repentance option, some jurists maintain that the *ḥadīth* should be understood as referring only to someone who persists in the abandonment of Islam for another religion.[57] Aḥmad b. Ḥanbal is reported to have defined change of religion as "persistence in polytheism; as for him who repents, it is not a change" (*al-tabdīl al-iqāma ᶜalā al-shirk; fa-ammā man tāba fa-lā yakūnu tabdīlan*).[58] Furthermore, the prevalent view is that the *man baddala … ḥadīth* should be read in conjunction with numerous other traditions which portray both the Prophet and the first *khulafāʾ* as providing the repentance option to apostates whom they encountered.

[50] Aḥmad b. Ḥanbal, *Musnad*, vol. 5, pp. 2, 3, 5; vol. 4, p. 446.

[51] Ṭāwūs b. Kaysān al-Ḥawlānī al-Hamdānī died in 106 A.H. / 724 A.D. See *Aᶜyān al-Shīᶜa* (ed. Muḥsin al-Amīn, Beirut n.d.), vol. 36, p. 325.

[52] Nazwī, *Muṣannaf*, vol. 11, p. 190; Ṭaḥāwī, *Mukhtaṣar ikhtilāf al-ᶜulamāʾ*, vol. 3, p. 489 (no. 1638); ᶜAsqalānī, *Fatḥ al-bārī*, vol. 15, p. 295; cf. also Ṣanᶜānī, *Muṣannaf*, vol. 10, p. 164 (no. 18694) and Ibn Taymiyya, *al-Ṣārim al-maslūl*, p. 321 where this view is attributed also to ᶜUbayd b. ᶜUmayr. Aḥmad b. Ḥanbal is also said to have held this view, but the Ḥanbalī *madhhab* is said to have adopted the repentance option; see Ibn Qudāma, *al-Kāfī*, vol. 4, pp. 60–61. See also Ibn Qudāma, *al-Mughnī*, vol. 8, p. 124 infra.

[53] Shāfiᶜī, *Kitāb al-umm*, vol. 6, p. 229, line 11.

[54] Ṭaḥāwī, *Mushkil al-āthār*, vol. 4, pp. 63–64.

[55] Sarakhsī, *Sharḥ Kitāb al-siyar al-kabīr*, vol. 5, p. 1938 (no. 3881); Shaybānī, *Kitāb al-siyar al-kabīr*, p. 197.

[56] Ṭaḥāwī, *Mukhtaṣar*, p. 258; *Mukhtaṣar ikhtilāf al-ᶜulamāʾ*, vol. 3, p. 501 (no. 1651).

[57] Abū Yūsuf, *Kitāb al-kharāj*, p. 179: *wa maᶜnā ḥadīth al-nabī … ay man aqāma ᶜalā tabdīlihi*. For a list of early jurists who thought that the apostate must be asked to repent, see Ibn Qudāma, *al-Mughnī*, vol. 8, p. 124 infra. A substantial discussion supporting this view can be found also in Ibn Taymiyya, *al-Ṣārim al-maslūl*, pp. 314–320.

[58] Khallāl, *Ahl al-milal*, pp. 485–492 (nos. 1194–1200, 1202–1204, 1208, 1209, 1211).

The Prophet is said to have accepted the repentance of several persons who abandoned Islam.[59] ᶜUmar b. al-Khaṭṭāb is reported to have stipulated that an apostate should be imprisoned for three days; one should give him food and drink in order to reconcile him to Islam, and only then ask him to repent. ᶜUmar made this ruling after he heard that some Muslims had executed an apostate in a hurried manner.[60] Regarding a group of apostates, ᶜUthmān b. ᶜAffān instructed Ibn Masᶜūd to demand their repentance and kill those who refuse.[61] There are various views regarding the question how much time should be allocated for this purpose: some say that the apostate is to be asked to repent three times; others maintain that he is to be allowed three days, one month, or three months.[62] According to instructions attributed to ᶜUmar b. ᶜAbd al-ᶜAzīz, the apostate should be subjected to a series of increasingly menacing actions, such as binding him and placing a lance on his heart, until he repents.[63] The Shāfiᶜī jurist Ibn Surayj (d. 235 A.H. / 849–50 A.D.)[64] thought that the apostate should not be dispatched with the sword, but rather beaten to death with a stick: such a slow method might provide him with an additional opportunity to repent.[65] Some jurists explain that the repentance option is necessary because apostasy frequently occurs as result of misunderstanding (*li-'ᶜtirāḍi shubha*) and, therefore, the execution should not be carried out before an attempt is made to remove that misunderstanding.[66]

Al-Shāfiᶜī not only supports the idea that providing the apostate with the repentance option is mandatory, but also draws concrete conclusions from this juridical stance. He maintains that if an apostate is brought to the place of execution, declares the twofold *shahāda* but is, nonetheless, killed by a governor who does not think that an apostate should be given the opportunity to repent – his inheritance goes to his Muslim heirs and his executioner must atone for the killing and pay blood-money to the slain apostate's family; furthermore, but for the *shubha*, he would be liable for retaliation (... *fa-mīrāthuhu li-warathatihi al-muslimīn wa ᶜalā qātilihi al-kaffāra wa al-diya wa lawlā al-shubha la-kāna ᶜalayhi al-qawad*).[67] Whoever injures an apostate before asking him to repent suffers discretionary punishment (*taᶜzīr*) if the apostate repents and later dies of his wounds, although there is no *qawad* or *diya*.[68] This is in sharp contrast to the view of Abū

[59] Bayhaqī, *Sunan*, vol. 8, pp. 197, 207; al-Nasā'ī, *Sunan*, vol. 7, p. 107; Māwardī, *al-Ḥāwī al-kabīr*, Beirut 1994, vol. 13, p. 156; Ṭaḥāwī, *Mushkil al-āthār*, vol. 4, pp. 64–65.

[60] Ṣanᶜānī, *Muṣannaf*, vol. 10, pp. 164–165, no. 18695; Ibn Ḥanbal, *Masāʾil*, vol. 2, pp. 473–475 (nos. 1191–1192). [61] Māwardī, *al-Ḥāwī al-kabīr*, vol. 13, pp. 158–159.

[62] Ṣan'ānī, *Muṣannaf*, vol. 10, p. 164 (nos. 18690–18693); Māwardī, *al-Aḥkām al-sulṭāniyya*, p. 75; Nazwī, *Muṣannaf*, vol. 11, p. 190; ᶜAsqalānī, *Fatḥ al-bārī*, vol. 15, p. 295. According to Abū Yūsuf (*Kitāb al-kharāj*, p. 180), the notion of asking the apostate to repent three times (or for three days?) is based on a tradition attributed to the Prophet himself.

[63] Abū Yūsuf, *Kitāb al-kharāj*, p. 182.

[64] See on him *EI*², s.v. (J. Schacht).

[65] Māwardī, *al-Aḥkām al-sultāniyya*, p. 75.

[66] Māwardī, *al-Ḥāwī al-kabīr*, vol. 13, p. 159; Ibn Qudāma, *al-Kāfī*, vol. 4, p. 61; Marghīnānī, *Hidāya*, vol. 2, p. 871.

[67] Shāfiᶜī, *Kitāb al-umm*, vol. 4, p. 416, ll. 8–9. Cf. *Kitāb al-umm*, vol. 1, pp. 430–431; Māwardī, *al-Ḥāwī al-kabīr*, vol. 13, p. 159; Sarakhsī, *Mabsūṭ*, vol. 10, p. 99.

[68] *Mukhtaṣar al-Muzanī ᶜalā al-Umm*, in Shāfiᶜī, *Kitāb al-umm*, vol. 9, p. 275, ll. 12–13.

Ḥanīfa who argued that since there was no penalty for killing an apostate without providing him with the repentance option, the provision of this option was not mandatory but only desirable.[69]

As a rule, repentance of an apostate is effected by his pronouncing the twofold *shahāda* and is identical in this respect to the conversion of an unbeliever who had never been a Muslim.[70] This rule is applied to someone who became an apostate by disclaiming Allah's oneness and Muḥammad's prophethood in a straightforward and absolute manner. There could, however, be cases of apostasy to specific religious groups who were willing to acknowledge the prophethood of Muḥammad, but they did it in a sense unacceptable to Muslims. With respect to such apostates, the mere pronouncing of the *shahāda* is not deemed sufficient. If, for instance, the apostate joined a community which believed that Muḥammad was a prophet but his mission was directed to the Arabs alone rather than to all humanity, he must add to the *shahāda* an affirmation of the Prophet's universal mission and renounce all religions except Islam.[71] If he joined a group which inteprets the *shahāda* as predicting the appearance of a prophet bearing the name Muḥammad in the future, he must declare that the Prophet Muḥammad who had already been sent is, indeed, the prophet in whom he believes. Similarly, it is not acceptable for a repentant apostate, or for a first-time convert, to attest that "the prophet is the messenger of Allah" (... *anna al-nabī rasūl Allah*) because he may mean somebody other than the Prophet Muḥammad.[72] In other words, he must not be allowed to make equivocal statements which have a Muslim ring, but which, in effect, hide beliefs far removed from Islam. On the more lenient side, an apostate who joined mainstream Judaism (which rejects the prophethood of Muḥammad without any qualification) and then pronounced the second part of the *shahāda* only, is judged a Muslim. The first part of the *shahāda* is not required of him because monotheism is, with regard to the Jews, an established fact (*li-anna tawḥīd Allāh thābit fī*

[69] See above, at note 39.

[70] Such a person is called in the jurists' parlance an "original unbeliever" (*kāfir aṣlī*).

[71] About Jewish groups who were willing to acknowledge Muḥammad's prophethood in this restricted sense, see Sarakhsī, *Sharḥ kitāb al-siyar al-kabīr*, vol. 5, p. 2265 (no. 4519). In particular, one should mention in this context the Īsāwiyya, a Jewish sect which is said to have emerged during the reign of ᶜAbd al-Malik b. Marwān (reigned 685–705) and maintained that Muḥammad was a prophet, but that his mission was not directed at the Jews. See "ᶜĪsāwiyya", *EI²*, s.v. (S. Pines); and Y. Erder, "The doctrine of Abū ᶜĪsā al-Iṣfahānī and its sources". See also Shīrāzī, *Muhadhdhab*, vol. 3, p. 258.

In *Sharḥ al-Ṭaḥāwī* (quoted in al-ᶜAynī, *Bināya*, vol. 6, pp. 700–701; I have not been able to locate the passage in Ṭaḥāwī himself) there is an interesting observation concerning this issue. Only Jews and Christians who live among Muslims speak about the Prophet being sent to the Arabs alone, and therefore must declare their belief in the universality of Muḥammad's prophethood in order to make their conversion acceptable. Ṭaḥāwī seems to understand that such formulations serve as a tool to minimize the friction between the Jews and the dominant Muslim faith. By perceiving the mission of Muḥammad as directed solely to the Arab ethnic group, these Jews could at the same time acknowledge Muḥammad's prophethood and justify their refusal to embrace Islam. Jews and Christians who live in the Abode of War do not entertain such beliefs; hence, in their case, the mere pronouncing of the twofold *shahāda* is a sufficient indication of their conversion to Islam.

[72] Ibn Qudāma, *al-Kāfī*, vol. 4, p. 62; Ibn Qudāma, *al-Mughnī*, vol. 8, pp. 142–143; Shīrāzī, *Muhadhdhab*, vol. 3, p. 258.

ḥaqqihi). On the other hand, if he joined a non-monotheist group such as the Christians, the Zoroastrians, or the idolaters, he will not be accepted as a Muslim without pronouncing both parts of the *shahāda*.[73]

In the same manner, removal of all ambiguity is required of a person who became an apostate by the denial of a certain commandment. Such an apostate can not reconvert by merely uttering the *shahāda*: he must also reaffirm his commitment to that commandment. Or, if he apostatized by denying a prophet, or a verse from the Qur᾽ān, or a heavenly book, or an angel, or by allowing something forbidden, he must renounce the cause of his apostasy in addition to the general declaration of faith.[74] Ḥasan (al-Baṣrī?) reports that some (unnamed) jurists consider it desirable that the apostate resume his status as a Muslim by performing the pilgrimage, if he had performed it before renouncing Islam. It seems that according to this view, apostasy invalidates some commandments fulfilled before it.[75] Mālik b. Anas is reported to have supported this view, asserting that a repentant apostate must make up for the prayer and the fasting which he had missed during his apostasy. Aḥmad b. Ḥanbal stipulated that an apostate who had performed the pilgrimage before his apostasy should perform it again after his repentance.[76] Al-Shāfiᶜī maintained that the apostate must make up for all the prayers, alms and days of fasting which he missed during his apostasy.[77] Contradictory views on this are reported from Abū Ḥanīfa: according to one report, he maintained that apostasy does not invalidate a pilgrimage performed before it, and the repentant apostate is therefore not obliged to go on pilgrimage again. According to another report, Abū Ḥanīfa held the opposite view.[78]

Manifestly Muslim behavior may in some cases be deemed an indication of repentance. An apostate (or, for that matter, any infidel) who prays in the Muslim manner is a case in point. The Ḥanbalī jurist Ibn Qudāma maintains that such a person becomes a Muslim, whether he prays in public or in private, in *dār al-islām* or in *dār al-ḥarb*. Al-Shāfiᶜī is less forthcoming: he is willing to agree to this only if the person in question prays in *dār al-ḥarb*, because prayer in *dār al-islām* may be the result of precautionary dissimulation (*taqiyya*) or hypocrisy (*riyā᾽*).[79]

II

The literature of jurisprudence deals in detail with several distinctions concerning the apostates. For a number of jurists, the identity of the apostate is an important

[73] Ibn Qudāma, *al-Kāfī*, vol. 4, p. 62; Ibn Qudāma, *al-Mughnī*, vol. 8, p. 142.
[74] Ibn Qudāma, *al-Mughnī*, vol. 8, p. 142; Shīrāzī, *Muhadhdhab*, vol. 3, p. 258.
[75] See Ṣanᶜānī, *Muṣannaf*, vol. 6, p. 107 (no. 10148). The text of this passage is in some doubt.
[76] Khallāl, *Ahl al-milal*, p. 512 (nos. 1285–1286).
[77] Shāfiᶜī, *Kitāb al-umm*, vol. 1, pp. 148–149.
[78] Māwardī, *al-Aḥkām al-sulṭāniyya*, p. 75.
[79] Ibn Qudāma, *Mughnī*, vol. 8, pp. 143–144; Shīrāzī, *Muhadhdhab*, vol. 3, p. 258. Ibn Qudāma argues that other commandments do not have the same significance, but his arguments on this matter are not very clear or cogent.

factor in determining the treatment to be meted out to him. Some maintain that all apostates are to be treated alike; others think that an apostate who had been Muslim by birth should not be treated in the same way as a Muslim by conversion;[80] and that the fate of a female apostate should not be the same as that of her male counterpart.

ᶜAṭāᵓ (b. Abī Rabāḥ), Ibn ᶜAbbās, al-Layth b. Saᶜd and some of al-Shāfiᶜī's associates[81] thought that repentance of an apostate who had been Muslim by birth cannot be accepted.[82] This seems to have been also the view of Mālik b. Anas.[83] Mālik felt that the apostasy of someone who was born a Muslim is a more severe transgression than that of a person who was not. Reverting to a religion that one experienced in the past is in his view slightly more understandable than choosing a false religion with which one had never been associated. On the other hand, the religious commitment of someone who was born a Muslim should be stronger than that of a neophyte and his punishment should therefore be of greater severity.[84] Perceiving a similar correlation between the degree of a person's commitment to Islam and the severity of his punishment for apostasy, Abū Ḥanīfa ruled that an apostate who had become Muslim merely by the conversion of one of his parents is not to be executed for apostasy because of the presumed weakness of his commitment to Islam (*in ṣāra musliman bi-islāmi aḥadi abawayhi lam yuqtal bi-'l-ridda li-ḍuᶜfi islāmihi*).[85] Abū Ḥanīfa apparently felt that the circumstances of such a person's conversion, the fact that he never made a conscious decision to become a Muslim and lived at least a part of his life in a non-Muslim household, explain (and to an extent justify) the tenuous nature of his bond with Islam. These are extenuating circumstances, which serve as grounds for not punishing this person to the full extent of the law. In a similar vein, al-Shaybānī would dispense with capital punishment in the case of a minor who abandoned Islam and would replace it with (indefinite?) imprisonment. This ruling remains in effect even after the person in question reached maturity and remained infidel. The reason is that he did not make a decision to become a Muslim as a mature person,[86] and therefore is not to be considered an apostate in the full sense of the word.

80 In the Shīᶜī tradition, apostasy of a Muslim by birth is called *fiṭrī*, while apostasy of a Muslim by conversion is called *millī*. For a discussion of this issue in Shīᶜī jurisprudence, see M. Ayoub, "Religious freedom …", at pp. 86–87. I have not encountered these terms in the Sunnī sources used in the preparation of the present work.

81 Shāfiᶜī, *Kitāb al-umm*, vol. 1, p. 430; vol. 6, p. 229; Māwardī, *al-Ḥāwī al-kabīr*, vol. 13, p. 158. I understand Shāfiᶜī's *man wulida ᶜalā al-fiṭra* to mean a Muslim by birth.

82 Ibn ᶜAbd al-Barr al-Namarī, *Tamhīd*, vol. 5, p. 311; Ṭaḥāwī, *Mukhtaṣar ikhtilāf al-ᶜulamāᵓ*, vol. 3, p. 502 (no. 1651); Māwardī, *al-Ḥāwī al-kabīr*, vol. 13, pp. 151, 158; Dimashqī, *Raḥmat al-umma*, p. 491; ᶜAsqalānī, *Fatḥ al-bārī*, vol. 15, p. 295. An opposite view of ᶜAṭāᵓ is reported in Nazwī, *Muṣannaf*, vol. 11, p. 190. This seems to be also the view of Ibn Qudāma; see Ibn Taymiyya, *al-Ṣārim al-maslūl*, pp. 300–301. Cf. Kraemer, "Apostates, …" p. 42.

83 The text has: *ḥakā al-Shāfiᶜī ᶜan baᶜḍ ahl al-madīna wa aḥsibuhu Mālikan*. See Māwardī, *al-Ḥāwī al-kabīr*, vol. 13, p. 151. See also a remark in Shāfiᶜī, *Kitāb al-umm*, vol. 6, p. 233: *qāla al-Rabīᶜ: idhā qāla: baᶜḍ al-nās, fa-hum al-mashriqiyyūn; wa idhā qāla baᶜḍ aṣḥābinā aw baᶜḍ ahl baladinā, fa-huwa Mālik.*

84 Māwardī, *al-Ḥāwī al-kabīr*, vol. 13, p. 151.

85 Māwardī, *al-Ḥāwī al-kabīr*, vol. 13, p. 151.

86 Shaybānī, *Kitāb al-siyar*, p. 224 infra; and cf. Shāfiᶜī, *Kitāb al-umm*, vol. 6, pp. 222–223.

Al-Shāfiᶜī categorically rejects these distinctions. His arguments are supported by the plain meaning of the two relevant traditions: the *man baddala … ḥadīth* and the tradition about the three transgressions which make the shedding of a Muslim's blood licit. Both indicate that the substitution of infidelity for true belief is the sole reason for the culprit's execution. There is no discussion of his personal history. Furthermore, the Prophet, Abū Bakr and ᶜUmar b. al-Khaṭṭāb all ordered the killing of apostates. While al-Shāfiᶜī does not say so explicitly, this statement seems to support his argument because these early apostates must have been Muslims by conversion rather than by birth.[87] A Muslim by conversion has the same rights and obligations as any other Muslim; it is therefore not legitimate to make a distinction between him and other Muslims with regard to the punishment for apostasy.[88] According to the early Ḥanbalī jurist al-Khallāl (d. 311 A.H.), the uniform treatment of all apostates was also the last – and therefore the authoritative – view of Ibn Ḥanbal; it should be mentioned, however, that according to some reports Ibn Ḥanbal was not willing to provide apostates who had been Muslims by birth with the repentance option.[89] According to one report, he held this opinion even with regard to female apostates who were Muslims by birth.[90]

III

The ruling with regard to female apostates is a subject of some controversy. Early jurists have widely differing views on the question whether female apostates are to be treated in the same way as their male counterparts. One substantial body of legal opinion supports the idea that they must not be killed. This view finds support in a tradition of Ibn ᶜAbbās who said: "Women are not to be killed when they renounce Islam. They are to be imprisoned, summoned to Islam and forced to embrace it" (*lā yuqtalu al-nisāʾ idhā hunna 'rtadadna ᶜan al-islām wa lākin yuḥbasna wa yudᶜayna ilā al-islām wa yujbarna ᶜalayhi*).[91] Jurists who favor this view base their opinion on the Prophet's general prohibition to kill women and children; this prohibition is frequently found in traditions that purport to reflect the rules of warfare established by the Prophet. Haythamī also quotes a prophetic tradition that makes a clear distinction between apostates of the two genders: an unrepentant male apostate is to be killed, while a similar female is to be asked to repent – though it is not clear what happens in case she stands by her refusal.[92] Furthermore, in respect of the female apostate, many jurists envisage an option that they do not deem legitimate, or feasible, in respect of her male counterpart: forcing her

[87] Shāfiᶜī, *Kitāb al-umm*, vol. 1, pp. 430–431; vol. 6, p. 222, l. 6; see also *Mukhtaṣar al-Muzanī ᶜalā al-Umm*, in Shāfiᶜī, *Kitāb al-umm*, vol. 9, p. 275, lines 5–7.

[88] Māwardī, *al-Ḥāwī al-kabīr*, vol. 13, p. 151; Māwardī, *Aḥkām sulṭāniyya*, p. 74.

[89] Khallāl, *Ahl al-milal*, pp. 493–494 (nos. 1217–1221).

[90] Khallāl, *Ahl al-milal*, p. 503 (no. 1256).

[91] Abū Yūsuf, *Kitāb al-kharāj*, pp. 180 infra – 181; Cf. Kraemer, "Apostates, …" p. 44.

[92] Haythamī, *Majmaᶜ al-zawāʾid*, vol. 6, p. 263.

to embrace Islam.[93] The other group of jurists, those who maintain that the treatment of male and female apostates should be identical, find support for their view in the all-inclusive wording of the *man baddala … ḥadīth* and in the general principle that the *ḥudūd* punishments are inflicted on the culprits regardless of their gender. They also quote a tradition according to which the Prophet treated a certain Umm Marwān who renounced Islam in the same way as he would treat a male person in the same situation: he ordered that she be asked to repent and that she should be executed in case of refusal.[94] Furthermore, in some versions of the famous instructions of the Prophet to Muᶜādh b. Jabal, Muᶜādh is told to kill unrepentent apostates regardless of gender.[95]

According to al-Sarakhsī's *Mabsūṭ* and other books of *fiqh*, Abū Ḥanīfa was the chief protagonist of the view that a female apostate should not be killed. The historical precedent for this ruling is the tradition according to which Abū Bakr enslaved the women and children of the tribe of Banū Ḥanīfa[96] and presented ᶜAlī b. Abī Ṭālib with a slave-girl who eventually gave birth to Muḥammad b. al-Ḥanafiyya. According to al-Sarakhsī's report, Abū Ḥanīfa maintained that a female apostate should be imprisoned and forced to embrace Islam again. Time and again she should be given thirty-nine lashes, then returned to prison until she repents or dies. Al-Shaybānī portrays Abū Ḥanīfa's views as more lenient: she should be imprisoned until she embraces Islam again. No coercive measures are mentioned by him.[97] Shaybānī was also opposed to the killing of the female apostate; Abū Yūsuf vacillated but finally gave his support to his associates in the Ḥanafī *madhhab*.[98] Qatāda (b. Diᶜāma) entertained the same opinion: according to him, a woman who reneged on Islam should be enslaved (*tustaʾmā*).[99]

Abū Ḥanīfa employs some ingenuity to refute the argument according to which the very phrasing of the *man baddala … ḥadīth* indicates its applicability to both genders. Though the phrase *man baddala dīnahu* refers, from the grammatical point of view, to both men and women, it should not be interpreted according to the strict rules of grammar, or according to its apparent (*ẓāhir*) meaning: if it is understood in this way, one would be obliged to interpret all other aspects of its meaning according to the same principle. In that case, it would have to be understood also as relating to any change of religion – even when abandonment of Islam is not

93 See also above, Chapter Three, section VII.

94 Bayhaqī, *Sunan*, vol. 8, p. 203; Ibn Qudāma, *al-Mughnī*, vol. 8, p. 123; Nazwī, *Muṣannaf*, vol. 11, p. 196.

95 ᶜAsqalānī, *Fatḥ al-bārī*, vol. 15, p. 297.

96 As is well known, the Banū Ḥanīfa who took active part in the so-called *ridda* wars are deemed by many jurists to have committed apostasy after the death of the Prophet.

97 Shaybānī, *Kitāb al-siyar al-kabīr*, p. 204; Abū Yūsuf, *Ikhtilāf Abī Ḥanīfa wa Ibn Abī Laylā*, pp. 199–200; Jaṣṣāṣ, *Mukhtaṣar ikhtilāf al-ᶜulamāʾ*, vol. 3, p. 471 (no. 1624); Māwardī, *al-Aḥkām al-sulṭāniyya*, p. 75; Marghīnānī, *Hidāya*, vol. 2, p. 872–873; Ibn Taymiyya, *al-Ṣārim al-maslūl*, p. 253; ᶜAsqalānī, *Fatḥ al-bārī*, vol. 15, p. 293; ᶜAynī, *Bināya*, vol. 6, pp. 701–702; For a discussion of rules concerning female apostates in the Shīᶜī tradition, see M. Ayoub, "Religious freedom and the law of apostasy in Islam", p. 87.

98 Jaṣṣāṣ, *Mukhtaṣar ikhtilāf al-ᶜulamāʾ*, vol. 3, p. 471 (no. 1624).

99 Khallāl, *Ahl al-milal*, p. 498 (nos. 1235–1236)

involved. This is clearly not the case: there is certainly no capital punishment for embracing Islam, and even a change from one non-Muslim religion to another is not punishable by death. If the strict semantic meaning of the *man baddala … ḥadīth* is clearly not intended for all types of religious change which can be understood from it, it cannot be intended for apostates of both genders either. Abū Ḥanīfa deems the formulation of the *ḥadīth* to be of the *'āmmun laḥiqahu khuṣūṣ* type: a general formulation conveying a particular meaning. Despite the all-inclusive meaning of *dīn* ("religion") and *man* ("whoever"), in this *ḥadīth*, the word *dīn* means only Islam, and the particle *man* refers only to those who have a potential for fighting. Women are presumed not to possess such a potential. The female apostates who were killed in the earliest days of Islam were done to death only because they fought against the Muslims or incited others to fight. The implication of Abū Ḥanīfa's argument is that mere apostasy would not have resulted in their execution.

Abū Ḥanīfa further substantiates his views on this issue by discussing the primary reason for the punishment of apostasy. While it is true that abandonment of Islam and insistence on reverting to another religion are extremely serious transgressions, they are between man and God (*bayna al-ᶜabd wa bayna rabbihi*) and the recompense for them is to be meted out in the hereafter. This can be seen from the fact that apostasy is different from the *ḥudūd*: the *hudūd* punishments cannot be rescinded, while the punishment for apostasy can be evaded by repentance. The punishments for apostasy inflicted in this world are legitimate measures of public policy (*siyāsāt mashrūᶜa*), designed to protect the people's interests. The killing of an unrepentant apostate is designed to stop him from fighting the Muslims. Women normally have no fighting ability. Femininity is, therefore, the female apostate's "protector."[100] The Prophet therefore prohibited the killing of women, and this prohibition applies both to a female infidel who never was a Muslim and to a female apostate.[101]

Thus, in Abū Ḥanīfa's analysis, apostasy has two aspects. It is a religious transgression to be punished by God in the hereafter; it is also a political crime, likely to be followed by rebellion.[102] Only this latter aspect of apostasy is punished here and now. Hence female apostates, who lack fighting potential and are unlikely to rebel, should not suffer capital punishment.

[100] This is a formulation attributed to Abū Ḥanīfa by Ibn al-ᶜArabī al-Mālikī: (*al-marʾa idhā 'rtaddat*) … *lā tuqtal li-anna āṣimahā maᶜahā wa huwa al-unūtha.* See his *Kitāb al-qabas*, vol. 3, p. 909.

[101] Sarakhsī, *Mabsūṭ*, vol. 10, pp. 108–110; cf. Shaybānī, *al-Jāmiᶜ al-ṣaghīr*, p. 251; Ṣanᶜānī, *Muṣannaf*, vol. 10, p. 177 (no. 18731); Ibn Qudāma, *al-Mughnī*, vol. 8, p. 123; Dimashqī, *Raḥmat al-umma*, p. 491; cf. Māwardī, *al-Ḥāwī al-kabīr*, vol. 13, p. 156, where Māwardī adduces further arguments which can be used in favour of Abū Ḥanīfa's stance. A list of jurists who supported Abū Ḥanīfa's view is found in ᶜAsqalānī, *Fatḥ al-bārī*, vol. 15, p. 293. There is some variety of views among them: ᶜAlī thought that the female apostate should be enslaved; ᶜUmar b. al-Khaṭṭāb wanted to sell her to another country. In view of these references, Griffel (*Apostasie und Toleranz*, p. 73, note 20) is mistaken when he says that the *ḥadīth* forbidding the killing of female apostates does not appear in later collections.

[102] For a similar modern interpretation of apostasy and its punishment, see Sachedina, *The Islamic roots of democratic pluralism*, pp. 98–101.

Special formulations regarding a slave-girl apostate can be found in Ḥanafī literature. According to al-Shaybānī, the rules applicable to a slave-girl differ from those applied to a free woman. As we have seen, a free woman is imprisoned until she repents. The imprisonment of a slave-girl, on the other hand, can be dispensed with. If her owners need her services, she should be surrendered to them, they employ her and force her to embrace Islam again. Al-Sarakhsī's interpretation of this rule is remarkably utilitarian: the reason for a female apostate's imprisonment is "a right of Allah"; yet the right of the master to enjoy her services is given precedence over the right of Allah to have her incarcerated until she enters the fold of Islam again (*li-anna ḥabsahā li-ḥaqq* (or *la-ḥaqqu*) *Allāh taᶜālā wa ḥaqqu al-mawlā fī khidmatihā yuqaddamu ᶜalā ḥaqq Allāh fī ḥabsihā*).[103] A similar view is attributed to Abū Ḥanīfa.[104]

The opposite view on the issue of female apostates is represented by al-Shāfiᶜī. Any mature person who abandons Islam, regardless of gender, must be asked to repent and be put to death in case of refusal. Al-Shāfiᶜī provides a systematic argument to support his ruling and to undermine the Ḥanafī one. He also maintains that the abovementioned tradition of Ibn ᶜAbbās is weak[105] and is contradicted by traditions according to which both the Prophet and Abū Bakr ordered the execution of female apostates.[106] Al-Shāfiᶜī repeatedly makes use of the argument from grammar: the particle *man* in the *man baddala ... ḥadīth* refers to men and women alike. In a series of imaginary polemical exchanges with an unnamed opponent, he attempts to show that the prophetic prohibition to kill old people, monks and women applies to unbelievers against whom Muslims waged battles in the Abode of War, but is not applicable to persons who had been Muslims and renounced their faith. He forces his opponent to admit that a Muslim man who apostatizes and becomes a monk is not to be spared capital punishment despite the prophetic prohibition to kill monks. The reason is that the punishment for apostasy is akin to a *ḥadd* and as such cannot be abolished. Al-Shāfiᶜī then clinches the argument by showing that the *ḥadd* punishments are applied equally to men and women.[107]

On the imposition of death penalty on female apostates, Aḥmad b. Ḥanbal, Mālik b. Anas, Ibn Abī Laylā, Abū Yūsuf (before he changed his view and lent his

[103] Sarakhsī, *Sharḥ kitāb al-siyar al-kabīr*, vol. 5, p. 1938 (no. 3882). Cf. also Shaybānī, *al-Jāmiᶜ al-ṣaghīr*, p. 251, and Sarakhsī, *Mabsūṭ*, vol. 10, p. 112.

[104] ᶜAsqalānī, *Fatḥ al-bārī*, vol. 15, p. 293, l. 13.

[105] Shāfiᶜī, *Kitāb al-umm*, vol. 1, p. 435; vol. 6, p. 234; Shīrāzī, *Muhadhdhab*, vol. 3, pp. 256–257; Nawawī, *al-Majmūᶜ sharḥ al-Muhadhdhab*, vol. 18, p. 10.

[106] Bayhaqī, *Sunan*, vol. 8, pp. 203–204; Ṣanᶜānī, *Muṣannaf*, vol. 10, p. 172 (no. 18728).

[107] Shāfiᶜī, *Kitāb al-umm*, vol. 1, pp. 428–429, 435–436; vol. 6, pp. 234–235; Māwardī, *al-Ḥāwī al-kabīr*, vol. 13, p. 155; Shīrāzī, *Muhadhdhab*, vol. 3, pp. 256–257. For traditions supporting Shāfiᶜī's view, see Ṣanᶜānī, *Muṣannaf*, vol. 10, p. 176 (nos. 18725–18727); Abū ᶜUbayd, *Kitāb al-amwāl*, pp. 180–181, no. 484: *fa-'stawā ḥukm al-rijāl wa al-nisāʾ fī al-irtidād li-anna rasūl Allāh ... qāla: man baddala ... fa-hādhā yaᶜummu al-rijāl wa al-nisāʾ al-dhakar wa al-unthā*; Ibn Abī Shayba, *Muṣannaf*, vol. 12, p. 279 (nos. 12825–12858); Jaṣṣāṣ, *Mukhtaṣar ikhtilāf al-ᶜulamāʾ*, vol. 3, pp. 471–472 (no. 1624); Bayhaqī, *Sunan*, vol. 8, pp. 203–204; Sarakhsī, *Mabsūṭ*, vol. 10, pp. 108–109; Nazwī, *Muṣannaf*, vol. 11, p. 196. For comparable arguments of Aḥmad b. Ḥanbal, see Khallāl, *Ahl al-milal*, pp. 496–497.

support to that of Abū Ḥanīfa) and several other early jurists are of the same view as al-Shāfiᶜī. Furthermore, if the woman in question was born Muslim, Ibn Ḥanbal even sees no need to ask for her repentance before putting her to death (*fa-in kānat wulidat ᶜalā al-fiṭra qutilat wa lā 'stutībat*).[108] The equal application of the death penalty on apostates of both sexes was, according to some sources, the view of most early jurists (*al-jumhūr*).[109] Ibn al-ᶜArabī al-Mālikī proffers a rather original explanation for this ruling. He suggests that a woman is protected not by her femininity, as Abū Ḥanīfa would have thought; rather, "the original protector of the woman is her being (a piece of) property to be enslaved, but this lapsed because of the apostasy" (*innamā ᶜāṣimuhā fī al-aṣl annahā mālun yustaraqqu wa qad baṭala dhālika bi-'l-ridda*). This apparently means that since a woman apostate can no longer serve her Muslim husband or master (as a wife or a concubine?), and therefore is no longer so valuable as property, she loses the protection that she had enjoyed before.[110]

The Ḥanbalī jurist Ibn Qudāma gives a very different explanation of the female apostate's liability to capital punishment: she is a legally responsible *persona* (*shakhṣun mukallaf*) who changed her true religion for a false one and should be punished exactly in the same way as her male counterpart. As for Abū Bakr's treatment of the Banū Ḥanīfa, it has not been proved that the woman whom he enslaved and presented to ᶜAlī had been Muslim before the *ridda*. Ibn Qudāma maintains – without giving any explanation or basis for this view – that not all the Banū Ḥanīfa embraced Islam and those who did were men.[111]

IV

Another question is whether the nature of the religion to which an apostate converted has any bearing on his status in Islamic law. As is well known, Islam does not treat all religions alike: religions whose adherents are eligible for *dhimmī* status are viewed in a distinct way. And, indeed, some jurists differentiate between apostates who converted to Judaism, Christianity or Zoroastrianism on the one

[108] Saḥnūn b. Saᶜīd, *al-Mudawwana al-kubrā*, vol. 2, p. 478 infra; Abū Yūsuf, *Ikhtilāf Abī Ḥanīfa wa Ibn Abī Laylā*, p. 200; Shaybānī, *Kitāb al-siyar al-kabīr*, p. 207; Ibn Ḥanbal, *Masāʾil*, vol. 3, p. 46 (no. 1308); Khallāl, *Ahl al-milal*, pp. 495–498 (1222–1235, 1237), p. 503 (no. 1256; the above quotation is found here), pp. 511–512 (no. 1283); Ibn Rushd, *Bidāyat al-mujtahid*, vol. 2, pp. 383–384; Dimashqī, *Raḥmat al-umma*, p. 491; Ibn Qudāma, *al-Kāfī*, vol. 4, p. 60; Ibn Taymiyya, *al-Ṣārim al-maslūl*, p. 253. Among the early jurists who supported this view, the following names are mentioned: al-Ḥasan (al-Baṣrī), al-Zuhrī, Ibrāhīm al-Nakhaᶜī, Makḥūl, Ḥammād (b. Abī Sulaymān), al-Layth, Mālik b. Anas, al-Awzāᶜī, and Isḥāq. However, there are also reports according to which al-Ḥasan and Ibrāhīm held the opposite view. See Ibn Qudāma, *al-Mughnī*, vol. 8, p. 123; Nawawī, *al-Majmūᶜ sharḥ al-Muhadhdhab*, vol. 18, p. 10; ᶜAsqalānī, *Fatḥ al-bārī*, vol. 15, p. 293 infra; ᶜAynī, *ᶜUmdat al-qāriʾ*, vol. 24, p. 77.

[109] ᶜAsqalānī, *Fatḥ al-bārī*, vol. 15, p. 293.

[110] Ibn al-ᶜArabī, *Kitāb al-qabas*, vol. 3, p. 909. The editor of the book observes that these words (it is not clear which ones exactly) are missing in two of the manuscripts that he used. One hopes that a parallel passage will further clarify the meaning of Ibn al-ᶜArabī's statement.

[111] Ibn Qudāma, *al-Mughnī*, vol. 8, pp. 123–124, 136–137.

hand, and those who converted to *zandaqa* – probably Manichaeism – on the other. The relevant difference between the first three groups and the Manichaeans is that adherents of the former three faiths were awarded *dhimmī* status and therefore could practice their religion openly, while the Manichaeans were not eligible for it and therefore professed Islam outwardly while practicing their real faith in a clandestine fashion.[112] When a person abandons Islam for a religion practiced openly, repents and returns to Islam, the change in his religious lifestyle is immediately apparent and the sincerity of his repentance can easily be assessed. The situation is essentially different in the case of an apostate who poses as a Muslim while secretly practicing another religion. When such a person is exposed, repents and makes a profession of Islam, his lifestyle does not change, the credibility of his repentance is open to doubt and there is therefore room for divergent interpretations of his legal status.

Mālik b. Anas attributed a great deal of importance to this distinction and reached the conclusion that repentance of apostates who converted to a religion practiced secretly cannot be accepted. Since these apostates outwardly behaved like Muslims even before their repentance, their credibility is low and they are to be killed without being asked to repent.[113] The repentance option is granted only to those who practice openly the religion to which they converted (*man irtadda sirran qutila wa lam yustatab kamā tuqtalu al-zanādiqa. wa innamā yustatābu man aẓhara dīnahu alladhī irtadda ilayhi*).[114] According to a more lenient formulation, the repentance of a *zindīq* can be accepted only if he came forward on his own initiative and repented before he was exposed and taken into custody (*lā tuqbalu al-tawba min al-zindīq illā an yatūba qabl al-ᶜilm bihi wa al-qudra ᶜalayhi*).[115] The Ḥanbalī *qāḍī* Abū Yaᶜlā is reported to have held a similar opinion, though his argumentation is different: the characteristic of a *zindīq* is his clandestine belief; once he comes forward and makes an open confession of it, he is no longer a *zindīq*. His repentance can then be accepted.[116]

[112] Chokr maintains that the Manichaeans were involved in intense missionary activity in the Umayyad period. In his view, this was the reason for their exclusion from the *dhimmī* category and for their persecution during the reign of the ᶜAbbāsī caliph al-Mahdī; see *Zandaqa et zindīqs*, pp. 55, 62.

[113] Mālik b. Anas, *al-Muwaṭṭa*ʾ, vol. 2, p. 736 (*Kitāb al-aqḍiya* 18) (ed. Turki, Beirut: Dār al-gharb al-islāmī, 1994, p. 245; translated in Goldziher, *Muslim Studies*, London: George Allen and Unwin, 1971, vol. 2, pp. 200–201); Khallāl, *Ahl al-milal*, pp. 524–525 (no. 1332); Jaṣṣāṣ, *Mukhtaṣar ikhtilāf al-ᶜulamā*ʾ, vol. 3, p. 502 supra (no. 1651); Bayhaqī, *Sunan*, vol. 8, p. 201 infra; Ibn ᶜAbd al-Barr al-Namarī, *al-Tamhīd*, vol. 10, p. 155. The same view is ascribed to Ibn Wahb and Rabīᶜa (b. Abī ᶜAbd al-Raḥmān b. Farrūkh, Rabīᶜat al-Raʾy; see for him Sezgin, *GAS*, vol. 1, pp. 406–407 and index).

Griffel maintains (*Apostasie und Toleranz*, p. 93) that the *zanādiqa* mentioned by Mālik b. Anas in the passage quoted above are the so-called hypocrites (*munāfiqūn*) among the contemporaries of the Prophet. This interpretation is in my view very unlikely. The classical jurists maintained that all inhabitants of the Arabian peninsula became Muslims while the Prophet was still alive (see above, at the end of Chapter Two and elsewhere). Whether this is historically true or not, it is very unlikely that Mālik b. Anas would refer to the *munāfiqūn* as a group existing in his own lifetime and would stipulate special laws for their treatment. On the other hand, the persecution of the Manichaeans was a living issue during the lifetime of Mālik and it is more than plausible that when he refers to the *zanādiqa* he means the Manichaeans rather than any other group.

[114] Ibn ᶜAbd al-Barr al-Namarī, *Tamhīd*, vol. 5, p. 309.

[115] Māwardī, *al-Ḥawī al-kabīr*, vol. 13, p. 152; Cf. Kraemer, "Apostates, …" p. 40.

[116] Ibn Taymiyya, *al-Ṣārim al-maslūl*, p. 361.

The views of the Ḥanafī *madhhab* are described as diverse. According to al-Māwardī, two opposite views were attributed to Abū Ḥanīfa: one was identical with the view of Mālik b. Anas (who refused to grant the repentance option to apostates who became *zindīqs*), while the other treated all apostates alike. Al-Māwardī maintains that Abū Ḥanīfa supported the former view by reference to Qurʾān 3:90.[117] Furthermore, he argued, the lifestyle of the *zindīq* after repentance is the same as it had been before; therefore his action has no effect on his standing in law. And there is an additional reason for the severity of Abū Ḥanīfa's former stance. According to his understanding, *zandaqa* spreads even more corruption in the land than brigandage (*ḥirāba*); it corrupts religion and the affairs of this world alike. Therefore, in the same way as repentance of rebels is not accepted after they are taken into custody, repentance of *zindīqs* should not be accepted either.[118]

Al-Jaṣṣāṣ also refers to the two views of Abū Ḥanīfa and mentions that according to one of them he made no distinction between an apostate to *zandaqa* and any other apostate: he gave the repentance option to all. As for Abū Yūsuf, he is said to have adhered to this latter view for a time, but when he saw that the *zanādiqa* tend to revert to their clandestine faith, he decided to kill a *zindīq* brought before him without asking him to repent; nevertheless, if the *zindīq* repented before being killed, he would be left alone (... *illā anna Abā Yūsuf lammā raʾā mā yaṣnaᶜu al-zanādiqa wa annahum yaᶜūdūna baᶜda al-istitāba, qāla: arā idhā utītu bi-zindīq amartu bi-ḍarbi ᶜunuqihi wa lā astatībuhu fa-in tāba qabla an aqtulahu lam aqtulhu wa khallaytuhu*).[119] Perhaps the clearest formulation of this view appears in a tradition about ᶜAlī b. Abī Ṭālib, reported by the Ḥanbalī *faqīh* al-Zarkashī:

> ... An Arab man who had embraced Christianity was brought before ᶜAlī. ᶜAlī asked him to repent, but the man refused to comply and ᶜAlī killed him. Then a group of people who performed their (Muslim) prayers while being *zanādiqa* was brought before him. Trustworthy witnesses testified against them to this effect. They denied the charge and said: "We have no religion except the religion of Islam." ᶜAlī killed them without asking for their repentance. Then he said: "Do you know why I asked the Christian to repent? I asked him to repent because he practiced his religion openly. As for the *zanādiqa*, I killed them because they denied the charge after a proof had been brought against them" (*wa qad rawā al-Athram bi-isnādihi ᶜan ᶜAlī ... annahu utiya bi-rajulin ᶜarabī qad tanaṣṣara fa-'statābahu fa-abā an yatūba fa-qatalahu. wa utiya bi-rahṭin yuṣallūna wa hum zanādiqa qad qāmat ᶜalayhim bi-dhālika al-shuhūd al-ᶜudūl fa-jaḥadū wa qālū: laysa lanā dīnun illā dīn al-islām. fa-qatalahum wa-lam yastatibhum. thumma qāla:*

117 "Surely those who disbelieve after they have believed and then increase in unbelief – their repentance shall not be accepted; those are the ones who stray."

118 ᶜAbd Allah b. Wahb, *al-Muwaṭṭaʾ, kitāb al-muḥāraba*, pp. 38–39; Ibn ᶜAbd al-Barr al-Namarī, *Tamhīd*, vol. 5, pp. 310–311; vol. 10, p. 156; Māwardī, *Kitāb al-Ḥāwī al-kabīr*, vol. 13, p. 152; for a Ḥanbalī discussion of these issues, see Zarkashī, *Sharḥ*, vol. 6, p. 238 (no. 3071). Māwardī, Ibn ᶜAbd al-Barr and al-Jaṣṣāṣ (*Mukhtaṣar ikhtilāf al-ᶜulamāʾ*, vol. 3, p. 501, no. 1651) mention both views of Abū Ḥanīfa. See also Dimashqī, *Raḥmat al-umma*, p. 491. Al-Khallāl (*Ahl al-milal*, pp. 524–527) and Ibn Qudāma report (*al-Mughnī*, vol. 8, p. 126) that both views on the issue were also attributed to Aḥmad b. Ḥanbal, but in his *al-Kāfī* (vol. 4, p. 61 infra) Ibn Qudāma says only that Ibn Ḥanbal was not willing to accept the repentance of a *zindīq*.

119 Ibn ᶜAbd al-Barr al-Namarī, *Tamhīd*, vol. 5, p. 311; Ibn Taymiyya, *al-Ṣārim al-maslūl*, p. 344; Jaṣṣāṣ, *Mukhtaṣar ikhtilāf al-ᶜulamāʾ*, vol. 3, p. 501 (no. 1651).

tadrūna limā 'statabtu al-naṣrānī? istatabtuhu li-annahu aẓhara dīnahu. fa-ammā al-zanādiqa alladhīna qāmat ᶜalayhim al-bayyina fa-innamā qataltuhum li-annahum jaḥadū wa qad qāmat ᶜalayhim al-bayyina).[120]

The views of Aḥmad b. Ḥanbal are said to have moved away from an uncompromising attitude to the *zanādiqa*. Initially, he is reported to have denied the repentance option to clandestine apostates, but he changed his view because he found no evidence in the *ḥadīth* to support distinctive treatment for different types of apostates.[121] But pride of place in the uniform treatment of all apostates belongs to al-Shāfiᶜī. As we have seen, al-Shāfiᶜī makes no distinction among apostates along the lines of gender. He is similarly willing to accept the repentance of an apostate to *zandaqa* in the same way as he accepts the repentance of persons who abandoned Islam for Judaism, Christianity or Zoroastrianism. His point of view is in line with a principle frequently broached in the early collections of *ḥadīth*: a declaration of faith should be taken at face value, even if its credibility is open to grave doubt because of the circumstances in which it was made. There is no way to test the sincerity of what people say, because their inner thoughts are known to Allah alone. Legal decisions in this world must therefore be based on the apparent situation. Al-Shāfiᶜī argues that the Prophet implemented this principle even if it was quite clear to him that the outward behavior of some of his contemporaries had nothing in common with their real beliefs. His treatment of the *munāfiqūn* is a case in point: though they were outwardly Muslims and inwardly infidels (*innamā aẓharū al-islām wa asarrū al-kufr*), the Prophet treated them as Muslims. They intermarried with Muslims, inherited from them, received their share of spoils if they participated in battle and were allowed to enter the mosques. And, in any case, even an apostate to an openly practiced religion such as Christianity who repented and became seemingly a Muslim may inwardly preserve his non-Muslim beliefs: such an apostate may believe that it is legitimate for him to adhere to Christianity without mixing with the Christians socially or frequenting their churches.[122] Al-Māwardī supported this Shāfiᶜī view by referring to Qurᵓān 4:94 and to a tradition according to which the Prophet said: "I make my ruling only on the basis of the apparent: God takes care of the inner thoughts" (*innamā aḥkumu bi-'l-ẓāhir wa*

[120] Zarkashī, *Sharḥ*, vol. 6, p. 264, no. 3099; Khallāl, *Ahl al-milal*, pp. 526–527 (no. 1339); Ibn Qudāma, *al-Mughnī*, vol. 8, p. 141; Ibn Taymiyya, *al-Ṣārim al-maslūl*, p. 360. The tradition about ᶜAlī's punishment of the *zanādiqa* is repeatedly reported in the *ḥadīth* literature in a different form: a group of *zanādiqa* who had renounced Islam were brought before ᶜAlī. He ordered a fire to be kindled and threw them into the fire, together with their books. When this came to the attention of Ibn ᶜAbbās, he said that he would have killed them because of the *man baddala* … *ḥadīth*, but would not have burned them because "the Prophet forbade the Muslims to torture with the torture of God" (*lā tuᶜadhdhibū bi-ᶜadhāb Allāh*). In this version, ᶜAlī also does not ask for the repentance of the *zanādiqa*, but this is not the point of the story. This version is used to oppose execution by fire. See, for instance, Ṭaḥāwī, *Mushkil al-āthār*, vol. 4, p. 63.

[121] Khallāl, *Ahl al-milal*, pp. 524–526 (nos. 1332–1333, 1335–1338); Ibn Ḥanbal, *Masāᵓil*, vol. 3, p. 131 (no. 1499). For inconclusive traditions about Aḥmad b. Ḥanbal's views on this issue, see Ibn ᶜAbd al-Barr al-Namarī, *al-Tamhīd*, vol. 10, p. 157 and Muranyi, *Beiträge*, p. 145.

[122] Shāfiᶜī, *Kitāb al-umm*, vol. 1, pp. 432–433, vol. 6, pp. 222 supra, 229–233; Jaṣṣāṣ, *Mukhtaṣar ikhtilāf al-ᶜulamāᵓ*, vol. 3, p. 502 (no. 1651); Ibn ᶜAbd al-Barr al-Namarī, *Tamhīd*, vol. 5, p. 310.

Allāh yatawallā al-sarāʾir).[123] He also rejects Abū Ḥanīfa's comparison between the apostate and the rebel: the punishment inflicted on the rebel is for actions which cannot be undone by repentance, while the punishment imposed on the apostate is for his beliefs which he can renounce.[124]

The thirteenth-century jurist and traditionist al-Nawawī[125] describes the views of the Shāfiʿī school on this matter as more diverse. While accepting the relatively lenient view of al-Shāfiʿī as the most correct one, he mentions four other views which can be found among the Shāfiʿīs. The first of these is that the repentance of a *zindīq* is not accepted and he is to be killed; however, if the repentance was sincere, it will help him in the Hereafter and he will be admitted into Paradise. The second group maintains that the repentance of a *zindīq* can be accepted only once. The third group thinks that repentance can be accepted from the *zindīq* only if he came forward and embraced Islam on his own initiative, before he was apprehended and exposed. According to the fourth group, repentance is not accepted from a *zindīq* who was actively preaching his false religion, but may be accepted from a passive *zindīq*.[126]

V

Special attention is devoted to an apostate who moves through the cycle of apostasy and repentance time and again. The question is whether a person who behaves in such a frivolous manner and repeatedly takes advantage of the repentance option can be allowed to do this endlessly. The basic traditions which gave rise to the repentance option do not deal with this issue, and the jurists have therefore considerable leeway in making their ruling. Ibrāhīm al-Nakhaʿī maintains that there is no limit to the number of times the apostate can abandon Islam and repent. The recurrent cases of repentance must be evaluated in the same way as the first one: in all cases, the ruling must be made on the basis of the apparent situation, because there is no possibility to assess the sincerity of the repentance, or to gauge what is really in the apostate's heart (*li-annahu lā yumkinu al-wuqūf ʿalā ḍamīrihi*).[127] This stance is a natural corollary of al-Nakhaʿī's willingness to extend the duration of the repentance option for apostates indefinitely.[128] Abū Ḥanīfa and al-Shāfiʿī agree

[123] Māwardī, *al-Ḥāwī al-kabīr*, vol. 13, p. 153. For another Shāfiʿī jurist supporting this view, see Shīrāzī, *Muhadhdhab*, vol. 3, pp. 257–258.

[124] Māwardī, *al-Ḥāwī al-kabīr*, vol. 13, p. 155.

[125] See on him *EI²*, s.v. (W. Heffening).

[126] The passage in Nawawī, *Sharḥ Ṣaḥīḥ Muslim*, ed. Khalīl al-Mays, Beirut, 1987, vol. 1, p. 321, is corrupt. The correct version of this passage is found in the Cairo: Dār al-Rayyān li-'l-turāth edition, 1987, vol. 1, p. 207. In view of this material, Chokr's statement according to which the Shāfiʿīs in general were willing to accept the *zindīq*'s repentance needs to be modified. See his *Zandaqa et zindīqs*, p. 22, note 16.

[127] Sarakhsī, *Sharḥ Kitāb al-siyar al-kabīr*, vol. 5, p. 1939 (no. 3883); Ibn Abī Shayba, *Muṣannaf*, vol. 12, p. 272 (no. 12798); Nazwī, *Muṣannaf*, vol. 11, p. 191.

[128] See above at note 44.

in principle that cases of recurrent apostasy and repentance are not to be punished by death, but they stipulate that apostates engaged in such a practice should be subjected to severe beating as a discretionary punishment (*taᶜzīr*).

Abū Yūsuf views the issue of repeated apostasy and repentance in a substantially different way. In his opinion, apostates of this kind are to be killed without warning: since another apostasy can be anticipated from them, they may be placed under surveillance and killed immediately upon declaring their infidelity again, without being accorded a further opportunity to repent (*idhā faᶜala dhālika mirāran yuqtal ghīlatan wa huwa an yuntaẓara fa-idhā aẓhara kalimat al-shirk qutila qabla an yustatāba*). Such a summary execution is justified by the mockery and contempt toward Islam which is manifest in the apostate's behavior. This stance can be supported by traditions about ᶜAlī b. Abī Ṭālib and ᶜUmar b. al-Khaṭṭāb who thought that a person who apostatizes and repents more than three times should be killed without being asked to repent, on the basis of Qurʾān 4:137.[129] This apostate is comparable to an infidel whom the Muslim *daᶜwa* has reached and who has chosen to ignore it; such a person may be killed without further ado.[130] Contradictory traditions are reported about Aḥmad b. Ḥanbal. According to one, the repentance of an apostate is accepted as long as he is willing to repent. According to another, recurrent apostasy is tantamount to mockery of Islam and the culprit is to be put to death.[131]

VI

The laws of apostasy take into consideration the prohibition of forcible conversions: according to most jurists, these are not valid and a person so converted who reverts to his former faith is not deemed an apostate. According to this general principle, the apostasy of a person who acted under duress is not considered valid. The general condition in which apostasy took place is taken into account. There is, for instance, the presumption that a prisoner is not acting out of his own free will. His apostasy is therefore not considered valid unless it is proven that he committed it while safe and free from compulsion; on the other hand, the apostasy of a free person is considered valid unless compulsion is proved. Even if a free person pronounced the words of infidelity in the Abode of War, this is not, in itself, proof that he was under compulsion and he is deemed an apostate.[132]

According to the same principle, a *dhimmī* or a *mustaʾmin* whom it is not permissible to coerce into embracing Islam and who is nevertheless compelled to

[129] "Those who believe, and then disbelieve, and then believe, and then disbelieve, and then increase in unbelief – God is not likely to forgive them, neither to guide them on any way."

[130] Sarakhsī, *Mabsūṭ*, vol. 10, pp. 99 infra – 100.

[131] Khallāl, *Ahl al-milal*, p. 492 (1212–1213).

[132] Ibn Qudāma, *al-Kāfī*, vol. 4, p. 60; Shīrāzī, *Muhadhdhab*, vol. 3, p. 256; Nawawī, *al-Majmūᶜ sharḥ al-Muhadhdhab*, vol. 18, p. 7.

do so is not considered a Muslim unless he retained his new faith after the compelling force was no longer applied to him. If he dies while still under compulsion, his conversion is not valid and he is considered an infidel. This being so, it is not legitimate to kill him or to force him into Islam if he reverts to his former faith.[133] This is the view of Abū Ḥanīfa and al-Shāfiᶜī. Supporting this opinion, Ibn Qudāma invokes Qur'ān 2:256 and compares the forcibly converted *dhimmī* or *musta'min* to a Muslim who was compelled to renounce Islam. Both types of compulsion are illegal and so are their results. This is the ruling with regard to Muslims, *dhimmīs* or *musta'mins*; on the other hand, if a *ḥarbī* or an apostate is compelled to embrace Islam, this compulsion is legal and if they succumb to it, they are considered Muslims. Such compulsion is similar to compelling a Muslim to pray: this is permissible and therefore does not invalidate the prayer which was performed as a result of it.[134]

Muḥammad b. al-Ḥasan al-Shaybānī views these cases in a different light. In his view, a *dhimmī* or a *musta'min* who was forced to embrace Islam becomes outwardly a Muslim. If he later renounces Islam, he is to be killed because of the all-encompassing validity of the tradition according to which the Prophet was commanded "to fight the people until they say *lā ilāha illā Allāhu*."[135] Similar is the status of a Muslim who was forced to renounce his religion: outwardly he is an infidel, his marriage must be dissolved, Muslims do not inherit from him if he dies, and Muslim rituals are not performed at his burial. He is a Muslim only in the eyes of God.[136] Ibn Ḥanbal seems to have held a similar opinion. Discussing the case of a Muslim who fell captive and embraced Christianity, he maintains that his wife must be separated from him after her "waiting period" (*ᶜidda*) comes to an end. While Ibn Ḥanbal does not say so explicitly, his ruling implies that the apostasy is considered valid despite the fact that it took place in captivity, and, perhaps, under duress.[137]

133 Goldziher has drawn attention to al-Qifṭī's biography of Maimonides which is relevant to the issue discussed above. According to al-Qifṭī, Maimonides accepted Islam under pressure before his emigration from Spain. When he eventually reached Egypt, he reverted to the Jewish faith. He was consequently denounced as an apostate, but the judge ruled that Maimonides converted under duress, the conversion was therefore invalid and so was also the charge of apostasy. See Goldziher, *Introduction*, p. 33, note 5. In addition to al-Qifṭī (*Ta'rīkh al-ḥukamā'*, ed. Lippert, Leipzig: Dieterich'sche Verlagsbuchhandlung, 1903, pp. 317–319), the story is included also in Ibn al-ᶜIbrī, *Ta'rīkh mukhtaṣar al-duwal*, p. 239. For the controversy in Jewish scholarship regarding the historicity or otherwise of Maimonides' conversion, see "Maimonides, Moses", in *Encyclopaedia Judaica*, vol. 11, pp. 780 infra – 781. See also Goitein, *A mediterranean society*, vol. 2, p. 300 for relevant events in the period of the Fāṭimī caliph al-Ḥākim, and Goldziher, *loc. cit.*, for a similar episode from the Ottoman period. Other cases of comparable import are recounted in Arnold, *The preaching of Islam*, pp. 421–422. For a judicious discussion of the tradition concerning Maimonides' conversion to Islam, see now M. A. Friedman, Ha-Rambam, ha-mashi'aḥ be-Teman ve ha-shemad ("Maimonides, the messiah in the Yemen and apostasy"). Jerusalem: The Ben Zvi Institute, 2002, pp. 31–37.

134 Ibn Qudāma, *al-Mughnī*, vol. 8, pp. 144–145.

135 For an exhaustive discussion of this tradition, see M. J. Kister, "... *illā bi-ḥaqqihi* ...".

136 Ibn Qudāma, *al-Mughnī*, vol. 8, pp. 144–145; Nawawī, *al-Majmūᶜ sharḥ al-Muhadhdhab*, vol. 18, p. 7; Sarakhsī, *al-Mabsūṭ*, vol. 10, p. 123, lines 9–12.

137 Khallāl, *Ahl al-milal*, pp. 501 (no. 1248), 503 (no. 1259).

VII

Let us return now to the *man baddala … ḥadīth*, the tradition which serves as the basis for the discussions about the illegality of changing a person's religion. The tradition sounds all-inclusive and does not explicitly specify the religious changes for which the death penalty is mandatory. Some commentators deem it necessary to spell out the self-evident: the tradition imposes the death penalty only for abandonment of Islam, and not for conversion to it. It is clear, however, that these two cases are not the only ones in which our tradition may be applicable. There may be incidents of religious change in which Islam is not involved at all, though no large scale conversions from one non-Muslim religion to another seem to have occurred in the classical period of Islam.[138] Nevertheless, the issue is debated, and there are two views of it in Muslim jurisprudence. One is attributed to the fourth caliph ᶜAlī b. Abī Ṭālib, who ruled that it was permissible to change one non-Muslim religion for another, or, in other words, one infidelity for another. When a Christian or a Jew became Manichaean (*zindīq*), he said: "Let him move from one religion to another" (*daᶜūhu yataḥawwal min dīnin ilā dīnin*), or: "… from one infidelity to another" (*min kufrin ilā kufrin*).[139] This view is said to have been supported by Abū Ḥanīfa and Mālik b. Anas. Al-Sarakhsī sees no problem if a Christian wife of a Muslim converts to Judaism, or if the Christian wife of a Christian becomes a Zoroastrian. This approach draws its inspiration from the general perception that "all unbelief is one community" (*al-kufr milla wāḥida*), and from the Muslim vantage point it is therefore immaterial whether a person belongs to one infidel religion or to another.[140]

Al-Shāfiᶜī does not agree with this interpretation. He concedes that if a Jew converts to Christianity or to Zoroastrianism – or if any person changes his religion from one infidelity to another – he is not to be killed because the *man baddala …*

[138] In the modern period, the conversion of some Zoroastrians to the Bahāʾī faith should be mentioned. See Susan Stiles, "Early Zoroastrian conversions to the Bahāʾī faith in Yazd, Iran", in J. R. Cole and M. Momen, eds., *From Iran east and west* (*Studies in Bābī and Bahāʾī history*, vol. 2), Los Angeles: Kalimat Press, 1984, pp. 67–93. This article deals mainly with the Zoroastrian leadership's opposition to these conversions, but on p. 80, in a description of a mob attack on Zoroastrian Bahāʾīs, it is mentioned that the *ᶜulamāʾ* turned the mob back, saying that the Zoroastrians were a protected minority (and their status does not change if they convert to the Bahāʾī faith?). The author is quoting ᶜAzīz Allāh Sulaymānī Ardakānī, *Maṣābīḥ-i hidāyat*, vol. 4. pp. 407–408, which was not available to me.

See also Denis MacEoin, *A people apart*, p. 4: "… the Bahāʾīs … are *murtaddūn*, apostates from Islam (the position of Bahāʾī converts from Zoroastrian and Jewish backgrounds or of individuals born into Bahāʾī families has not, to my knowledge, ever been clarified in terms of Islamic law)."

[139] Ṣanᶜānī, *Muṣannaf*, vol. 6, p. 48 (no. 9970); vol. 10, pp. 318–319 (nos. 19228–19229).

[140] *Pace* A. K. S. Lambton, who disregards this opinion when she states categorically that "no *dhimmī* was permitted to change his faith except for Islam" (*State and government in medieval Islam*, Oxford: Oxford University Press, 1981, p. 206). See Ṣanᶜānī, *Muṣannaf*, vol. 10, pp. 318–319 (nos. 19228–19229); Ṭaḥāwī, *Mukhtaṣar*, p. 261; Jaṣṣāṣ, *Mukhtaṣar ikhtilāf al-ᶜulamāʾ*, vol. 3, p. 502 (no. 1651), p. 508 (no. 1656); Ibn Ḥazm, *Muḥallā*, vol. 11, p. 191; Sarakhsī, *Mabsūṭ*, vol. 5, p. 48, lines 6–7; p. 50, l. 7. See Ibn Shās, *ᶜIqd al-jawāhir*, vol. 2, p. 54 where the view is attributed to the early Mālikī scholars Aṣbagh, Muṭrif and Ibn ᶜAbd al-Ḥakam. Another early Mālikī, Ibn al-Mājishūn, maintains that a Jew or a Christian who converted to the Manichaean faith should be killed, because he moved to a religion which no one is allowed to retain (*lā yuqarru ᶜalayhi aḥad*). Nazwī, *Muṣannaf*, vol. 11, p. 197. Fattal, *Le statut légal*, pp. 130, 165.

tradition envisaged capital punishment only for those who abandon Islam. This does not mean, however, that such a shift in religious affiliation can be allowed to pass without repercussions. The legal reaction to it should be based on the principle that the right of non-Muslims to retain their religion is restricted to the one which they held when Islam emerged and contracted the *dhimma* treaty with them. Allah made it permissible to take *jizya* from the infidels and accord them protection as long as they clung to their original faith. If they do not abide by this condition and abandon it, they should be given the opportunity to return.[141] If they insist, nevertheless, on converting to another religion – barring, of course, Islam – their rights as *dhimmī*s lapse and they should be expelled from the land of Islam.[142] According to one version of al-Shāfiᶜī's formulation, such a person may even face execution if the Muslims take him into custody, apparently as a *ḥarbī* infidel, sometime in the future. According to the same principle, it would be wrong to grant *dhimmī* status to an idolater who converted in the Islamic period to Christianity, Judaism or Zoroastrianism. This would imply the cessation of *jihād* against the infidels until they embrace Islam, and al-Shāfiᶜī is not willing to countenance such an eventuality. Similarly, if a Jewish woman converts to Christianity, or a Christian woman to Judaism, she is no longer eligible for marriage to a Muslim.[143] All these rules are designed to discourage any religious change other than conversion to Islam. The rules are less stringent if a Jewish or Christian woman converted to

[141] In Sarakhsī's *Mabsūṭ* (vol. 5, p. 48, lines 10–13) we find vehement opposition to this idea. In Sarakhsī's view, it is inconceivable that Muslims would encourage someone to return to his former infidel religion. In particular, it would be absurd to encourage a Christian who converted to Judaism to believe again in the trinity after he had become, outwardly at least, a monotheist (*wa al-naṣrānī idhā tahawwada fa-qad iᶜtaqada al-tawḥīd ẓāhiran fa-kayfa yujbaru ᶜalā al-ᶜawd ilā al-tathlīth baᶜda mā iᶜtaqada al-tawḥīd*).

[142] According to one tradition, Shāfiᶜī would accept the return of the person in question to any religion from whose believers *jizya* is taken. See Shāfiᶜī, *Kitāb al-umm*, vol. 5, p. 13, lines 10–12; Jaṣṣāṣ, *Mukhtaṣar ikhtilāf al-ᶜulamā*ᵓ, vol. 3, p. 508 (no. 1656).

[143] Shāfiᶜī, *Kitāb al-umm*, vol. 2, p. 367, ll. 5–7; vol. 4, p. 260, ll. 6–15; *Mukhtaṣar al-Muzanī ᶜalā al-Umm*, in Shāfiᶜī, *Kitāb al-umm*, vol. 9, pp. 295, l. 28 – 296, l. 1; Jaṣṣāṣ, *Mukhtaṣar ikhtilāf al-ᶜulamā*ᵓ, vol. 3, p. 508 (no. 1656); Fattal, *Le statut légal*, p. 130. Muzanī prefers a more lenient view: if the woman's conversion is to Judaism or Christianity, a Muslim is allowed to marry her. For the case of a Christian or Jewish woman married to a Muslim husband who reneges on her religion, see Shāfiᶜī, *Kitāb al-umm*, vol. 6, p. 224, lines 17–19, and Māwardī, *al-Ḥāwī al-kabīr*, vol. 9, pp. 231–232 (the Dār al-kutub al-ᶜilmiyya edition is corrupt in several places; a better text can be found in the Dār al-fikr 1994 edition, vol. 11, pp. 317–319).

In his article "Apostasy (Muhammadan)" in the *Encyclopaedia of Religion and Ethics* (New York 1908, s.v.), Th.W. Juynboll writes that according to the Shāfiᶜīs even a change from one non-Muslim religion to another is punishable by death. We have seen that in his *Kitāb al-umm* Shāfiᶜī does not accept this opinion. However, the Mālikī jurist Ibn al-ᶜArabī attributes this view to Shāfiᶜī in his *Nūr al-qabas*, vol. 3, pp. 909–910, and Sarakhsī maintains that this was one of three views attributed to Shāfiᶜī; see Sarakhsī, *Mabsūṭ*, vol. 5, p. 48, lines 8–9. See also Ibn ᶜAbd al-Barr al-Namarī, *al-Tamhīd*, vol. 5, p. 312, where the same view is also attributed to Shāfiᶜī: "If a *dhimmī* moves from one religion to another, the *imām* may put him to death according to the plain meaning of the tradition" (... *al-dhimmī idhā kharaja min dīnin ilā dīn kāna li-'l-imām qatluhu bi-ẓāhir al-ḥadīth*). The same view is said to have been supported by the *qāḍī* Abū Bakr (Ibn al-ᶜArabī al-Mālikī?) who maintained that a Jew who embraces Christianity or a Christian who converts to Judaism should be killed (unless he subsequently embraces Islam) because he changed the status in which he was given the *dhimma*. See Ibn Shās, *ᶜIqd al-jawāhir*, vol. 2, p. 54.

Zoroastrianism or another religion other than that of the People of the Book while she was married to a Muslim: in that case she can keep her marriage intact if she returns to Judaism or Christianity within the *ᶜidda* period, or, of course, if she converts to Islam.[144]

Aḥmad b. Ḥanbal views the issue of religious change between religions other than Islam from a different perspective. Rather than discussing the effects of such a change on the religious struggle between Islam and infidelity in the manner of al-Shāfiᶜī, he ponders whether the change is detrimental to the social and economic interests of the Muslim community. From this vantage point, not all changes included in this category have the same significance. If a Jew or a Christian abandons his religion and becomes a Manichaean (*aẓhara al-zandaqa*), such a shift in religious affiliation is harmful to the Muslim community because the person in question stops paying the *jizya*;[145] furthermore, the Muslims are not allowed to eat from what a Manichaean slaughters or to wed Manichaean women. Such a convert must therefore either return to his original faith, or be induced to embrace Islam; according to some formulations, this demand is coupled with the threat of execution. Conversion of Christians (or Jews) to Zoroastrianism is viewed in a similar light; though Zoroastrians are required to pay *jizya* (and the conversion will therefore not have any effect on the economic interests of the Muslim community), the Muslims may not consume meat slaughtered by them or wed their women. Hence, conversion to Zoroastrianism reduces the number of people whose daughters Muslims may marry and who may slaughter for Muslim consumption; such a reduction is therefore perceived as inflicting weakness on Islam (*fa-hādhā wahnun fī al-islām*) and must be prevented.[146] On the other hand, conversion of Jews to Christianity, of Christians to Judaism, or of Zoroastrians to either of these two faiths has no effect on the economic or social welfare of the Muslim community. In view of this consideration, Ibn Ḥanbal seems to have ruled that the *man baddala … ḥadīth* does not apply to such religious changes; these are inconsequential for the Muslims and the converts should therefore be left alone.[147]

[144] Shāfiᶜī, *Kitāb al-umm*, vol. 5, p. 13, ll. 7–9; p. 76, ll. 15–17; Māwardī, *al-Ḥāwī al-kabīr*, vol. 9, p. 231. The passage in the Dār al-Kutub al-ᶜilmiyya edition of *al-Ḥāwī* is corrupt in some places; a better text can be found in the Dār al-fikr edition (1994), vol. 11, pp. 317–319.

[145] Apparently because the Manichaeans, who could not practice their religion openly, posed as Muslims. See above, section IV.

[146] Khallāl, *Ahl al-milal*, pp. 352–356 (nos. 778–786). This perception of conversion of *kitābī*s to the Zoroastrian faith may clarify an otherwise obscure passage in Saḥnūn's *Mudawwana* (vol. 2, p. 307, ll. 16–18). The passage speaks about the permissibility of marriage between a Zoroastrian man and a Christian woman. The question is whether "Mālik b. Anas disliked such an alliance in view of the status of the children, because God … allowed us to wed *kitābī* women" (*a-kāna Mālik yakrahu hādhā li-makān al-awlād li-anna Allāh … aḥalla lanā nikāḥa nisāʾi ahl al-kitāb*). Though the ruling of Ibn al-Qāsim in the *Mudawwana* is that such a marriage is not to be prevented, the problem implied in the question seems to be the same as that envisaged by al-Khallāl: the children of this marriage may be considered Zoroastrians, and this would diminish the number of women eligible to be taken in marriage by the Muslims.

See also Chapter Three, end of section VII, for a ruling on a *kitābī* woman married to a Muslim who wants to convert to a non-*kitābī* religion.

[147] Khallāl, *Ahl al-milal*, pp. 354–356 (no. 786), 524 (no. 1330); see also Ibn Qudāma, *al-Mughnī*, vol. 6, pp. 593–594, who attributes to Ibn Ḥanbal other views as well.

VIII

Among the various manners of apostasy mentioned in Ibn Qudāma's passage,[148] vilifying the Prophet (*sabb al-rasūl, shatm al-rasūl*) received extensive attention in the books of law.[149] The issue is of central importance in rules concerning the *dhimmīs*: there the question is whether a *dhimmī* who vilifies the Prophet thereby loses the protection of the Muslim community.[150] It goes without saying that a *dhimmī* cannot be accused of apostasy, and these discussions are therefore outside the scope of this chapter. However, the sources discuss also the legal standing of Muslims guilty of the same transgression. In these discussions, the jurists consider the question whether vilifying the Prophet amounts to apostasy, and what are the consequences of such a perception on the punishment of the culprit. They also provide us with some insight into their own understanding of what vilification means.

Numerous episodes relevant to the legal question at hand can be found in sources purporting to describe the early period of Islam. At the time of his takeover of Mecca, the Prophet ordered the execution of two singing girls belonging to ᶜAbd Allah b. Khaṭal who ridiculed him in their songs, as well as of a female *mawlā* of the Banū ᶜAbd al-Muṭṭalib who seems to have been guilty of a similar transgression.[151] A woman who vilified the Prophet was killed by Khālid b. al-Walīd.[152] Another tradition relates the same story about a man and emphasizes that the culprit was killed without having been given the opportunity to repent.[153] A certain blind man is said to have killed a slave-girl who bore him children (*umm walad*) because she repeatedly vilified the Prophet and refused to desist. When the man's action was brought to the Prophet's attention, he approved of it and made

[148] See above, section I of the present chapter.

[149] Wiederhold ("Blasphemy against the Prophet Muḥammad ...", p. 44) says that blasphemy against the Prophet or his companions is not mentioned in the "formative texts of the *madhhabs*" among the acts that constitute apostasy. Among the "formative texts", he mentions Mālik's *al-Muwaṭṭa*ᵓ, Saḥnūn's *Mudawwana*, Shāfiᶜī's *Kitāb al-umm* and Shaybānī's *Kitāb al-aṣl*. It should be noted, however, that in Abū Yūsuf's *Kitāb al-kharāj* (p. 182) we read that "any Muslim who vilifies the Prophet, declares him a liar, finds fault with him or degrades him becomes an infidel. His wife is separated from him. If he repents, (all is well); if not, he is to be killed" (*ayyumā rajulin muslimin sabba rasūl Allāh ... aw kadhdhabahu aw ᶜābahu aw tanaqqaṣṣahu fa-qad kafara bi-'llāh wa bānat minhu zawjatuhu fa-in tāba wa illā qutila*). See also Abū ᶜUbayd, *Kitāb al-amwāl*, p. 179 (no. 482). In early Ḥanbalī literature, the issue is mentioned in al-Khallāl's *Ahl al-milal* (pp. 339–342). The issue also appears in the canonical collections of *ḥadīth*; see, for instance, Abū Dāwūd, *Sunan*, *Kitāb al-ḥudūd* 2 (vol. 4, pp. 183–184, no. 4361).

[150] See, for instance, Bukhārī, *Ṣaḥīḥ*, *Kitāb istitābat al-murtaddīn* 4 (vol. 4, p. 330); Jaṣṣāṣ, *Mukhtaṣar ikhtilāf al-ᶜulamā*ᵓ, vol. 3, p. 504–506 (no. 1652); Jaṣṣāṣ, *Aḥkām al-Qur*ᵓ*ān*, vol. 3, pp. 105–107; Ibn Qayyim al-Jawziyya, *Aḥkām ahl al-dhimma*, pp. 810, 870, 830–831. See also Fattal, *Le statut légal*, pp. 122–124; A. Turki, "Situation du tributaire qui insulte l'Islam, ...", *Studia Islamica* 30 (1969), pp. 39–72; M. Fierro, "Andalusian *fatāwā* on blasphemy", *Annales Islamologiques* 25 (1991), pp. 103–117. For further references to research on this issue in al-Andalus, see J. Safran, "Identity and differentiation ...", at p. 590, note 66. I am indebted to Prof. David Wasserstein for this reference.

[151] Ibn Taymiyya, *al-Ṣārim al-maslūl*, p. 404.

[152] Bayhaqī, *Sunan*, vol. 8, p. 203, ll. 1–2.

[153] Ibn Taymiyya, *al-Ṣārim al-maslūl*, pp. 5, 300.

the offending woman's blood licit.[154] Many traditions convey the idea that denouncing Islam and vilifying the Prophet is as harmful as an attack with the force of arms. This can be learned in an indirect manner from the way in which the Prophet viewed verbal attacks against non-Muslims. While Ḥassān b. Thābit was denouncing and satirizing the polytheists in his poems, the Prophet spurred him on by saying: "Fight them!" (*ughzuhum wa ghāzihim*). He also said that "the best *jihād* is to pronounce the word of truth in the presence of an oppressive ruler" (*afḍalu 'l-jihād kalimatu ḥaqqin ᶜinda sulṭānin jāʾir*). If verbal *jihād* against the polytheists is seen in this light, the same holds true for non-Muslims' denunciations of Islam and its Prophet: they are also to be considered as real war.[155]

According to numerous traditions, vilifying the Prophet places the perpetrator beyond the pale of Islam. It is inconceivable that a Muslim would vilify the Prophet;[156] if he does engage in such an activity, he ceases to be a Muslim and is, consequently, liable to the death penalty. It is interesting to note that the Muslim tradition uses this idea as an additional way to enhance the standing and prestige of the Prophet by pointing out that it is only vilification of the Prophet that carries this sanction. No other person has this deterrent punishment at his disposal.[157] Abū Bakr is said to have formulated the principle that after the death of the Prophet, nobody has the right to order the execution of his vilifiers. In a manner of speaking, this was the prerogative of the Prophet alone.[158]

What is the nature of the vilification which transforms it into such a serious crime against religion? In the episodes surveyed so far, most transgressors were guilty of writing satirical poems against the Prophet.[159] Yet in the eyes of the Muslim tradition, the vilifier *par excellence* seems to have been ᶜAbd Allah b. Saᶜd b. Abī Sarḥ. As is well known, Ibn Abī Sarḥ was for some time one of the "scribes of revelation" (*kuttāb al-waḥy*), but later abandoned Islam and rejoined the infidels of Quraysh. He is seen as the perpetrator of a most serious transgression: he called into question the reliability and accuracy of the Qurʾān as transmitted by the Prophet to the community of believers. He used to say that when the Prophet instructed him to write something down as revelation, he would suggest modifications of the revealed words and the Prophet would approve of anything he suggested. According to some versions of the tradition, this seemingly casual attitude of the Prophet to the revealed text caused Ibn Abī Sarḥ to lose confidence in the genuineness of the revelation, to abandon Islam and to return to Mecca.[160] Naturally enough, such reports about the Prophet's conduct were an anathema to the faithful. They were seen as attempts to undermine the very basis of the nascent religion of Islam: Ibn Abī Sarḥ ridiculed the Prophet, claimed that he was

[154] Abū Dāwūd, *Sunan*, vol. 4, pp. 183–184 (no. 4361); Ibn Taymiyya, *al-Ṣārim al-maslūl*, pp. 67–68.

[155] Ibn Taymiyya, *al-Ṣārim al-maslūl*, pp. 206–207.

[156] ᶜUmar b. ᶜAbd al-ᶜAzīz is reported to have said that "a Muslim does not vilify the Prophet …" (*lā yashtumu muslimun al-nabiyya ṣallā 'llāhu ᶜalayhi wa sallama*). See Ibn Taymiyya, *al-Ṣārim al-maslūl*, p. 5; cf. ᶜAbd Allāh b. Wahb, *al-Muwaṭṭaʾ, kitāb al-muḥāraba*, p. 40 (Arabic pagination).

[157] ᶜAbd Allah b. Wahb, *Kitāb al-muḥāraba*, pp. 39–40.

[158] Ibn Taymiyya, *al-Ṣārim al-maslūl*, pp. 92–94.

[159] Ibn Taymiyya, *al-Ṣārim al-maslūl*, pp. 85, 95.

[160] Ibn Taymiyya, *al-Ṣārim al-maslūl*, pp. 111–114.

recording as revelation whatever he wanted, that he used to change words in the revelation which the Prophet was commanded to transmit and that the Prophet let his contrived version stand. All this was designed to create doubts about Muḥammad's prophethood and went beyond infidelity and apostasy. It is vilification (*wa huwa min anwāᶜ al-sabb*).[161] ᶜAbd Allah b. Saᶜd b. Abī Sarḥ returned to Islam before the conquest of Mecca, but, nonetheless, the Prophet made his blood licit. Though he was eventually not executed – probably because of the intervention of his suckling brother (*akh min al-riḍāᶜa*) ᶜUthmān b. ᶜAffān – some jurists draw from his story the conclusion that the crime of the Prophet's vilifier is more heinous than that of an apostate, and that he should suffer the capital punishment even if he repents and returns to Islam.[162]

Having surveyed the relevant traditions, we should now turn our attention to the analysis of the issue in the books of law. The unanimous opinion of the jurisprudents is that vilification of the Prophet is a capital offense. There is, however, no unanimity on the question whether the culprit should be given the opportunity to repent, and whether the capital punishment is imposed because of the implied apostasy, or because of the vilification itself. Furthermore, opposite and incompatible views are ascribed to some schools of law and to their putative founders. Mālik b. Anas, Aḥmad b. Ḥanbal and al-Layth held that the vilifier of the Prophet, whether Muslim or not, is to be punished by death.[163] According to one tradition, Aḥmad b. Ḥanbal and Mālik b. Anas maintained that his repentance cannot be accepted,[164] but according to another they held the opposite view.[165] Since Mālik b. Anas considered the vilification of the Prophet as apostasy, some Mālikīs concluded that the vilifier should be treated like any other apostate and should be given the opportunity to repent. If he repents, he is chastised; only if he refuses to do so, must he face execution (*fa-in tāba nukkila wa-in abā qutila wa yuḥkamu lahu bi-ḥukm al-murtadd*).[166] The Shāfiᶜī school is also reported to have held two views. According to the first, the vilifier is like any other apostate and is spared the death penalty if he repents. According to the other view, the punishment for vilifying the Prophet is a *ḥadd* and as such cannot be set aside by repentance.[167]

Abū Ḥanīfa and his associates maintained that the repentance of the vilifier is acceptable.[168] Abū Yūsuf held the same opinion. He contended that a Muslim who vilified the Prophet, called him a liar or found fault with him becomes an infidel and is liable for the death penalty – unless he repents.[169]

The most comprehensive treatment of the transgression discussed here can be found in Ibn Taymiyya's *al-Ṣārim al-maslūl ᶜalā shātim al-rasūl*. In his treatment of the subject, Ibn Taymiyya had to contend with a complex situation. One the one

[161] Ibn Taymiyya, *al-Ṣārim al-maslūl*, p. 115 infra.
[162] See *EI*², s.v. ᶜAbd Allah b. Saᶜd (C. H. Becker); Ibn Saᶜd, *Kitāb al-ṭabaqāt al-kabīr*, vol. 7, part 2, pp. 190–191; Ibn Taymiyya, *al-Ṣārim al-maslūl*, pp. 117–118.
[163] Khallāl, *Ahl al-milal*, p. 339–342 (no. 729–739); Ibn Taymiyya, *al-Ṣārim al-maslūl*, p. 254.
[164] Jaṣṣāṣ, *Mukhtaṣar ikhtilāf al-ᶜulamāʾ*, vol. 3, p. 504 (no. 1652); Ibn Taymiyya, *al-Ṣārim al-maslūl*, pp. 301, 311.
[165] Ibn Taymiyya, *al-Ṣārim al-maslūl*, p. 313 infra; Jubūrī, *Fiqh al-imām al-Awzāᶜī*, vol. 2, p. 344.
[166] Ibn Taymiyya, *al-Ṣārim al-maslūl*, p. 311.
[167] Ibn Taymiyya, *al-Ṣārim al-maslūl*, pp. 312, 313.
[168] Ibn Taymiyya, *al-Ṣārim al-maslūl*, p. 313.
[169] Abū Yūsuf, *Kitāb al-kharāj*, p. 182.

hand, he knew of traditions according to which some *ṣaḥāba* killed those who vilified the Prophet without allowing them to repent, and he thought that such persons deserved to be treated in this harsh manner. On the other hand, numerous traditions maintain that vilifying the Prophet is a kind of apostasy, and apostates are allowed the repentance option according to most schools of law. In order to solve this contradiction, Ibn Taymiyya created new conceptual tools and classified apostasy into two distinct types: "common apostasy" (*ridda mujarrada* or *maḥḍa*), and "aggravated apostasy" (*ridda mughallaẓa*). He perceived major differences between these two transgressions as far as the motives and the mind set of the culprit are concerned. *Ridda mujarrada* is falling away from the faith, replacing Islam with another religion. It is caused only by "a doubt corrupting the heart, or a desire suppressing the mind" (*shubha qādiḥa fī al-qalb aw shahwa qāmiʿa li-'l-ʿaql*).[170] The purpose of such apostasy is achieved only if the apostate is allowed to make his new religious affiliation permanent. Hence, allowing the apostates to repent cannot be seen as encouraging people to fall away from the faith: they know that they will be forced to repent or face execution, and the purpose of their transgression – namely the permanent change of their religious affiliation – will not be attained. The purpose of the vilifier, who is guilty of "aggravated apostasy", is substantially different: he sets out to impugn the Prophet's honor and his transgression is therefore far worse than "common apostasy". His purpose is accomplished by the very act of vilification, which cannot be undone by repentance. Therefore, if vilifiers are allowed to repent and evade punishment, it would encourage them to engage repeatedly, and with impunity, in their outrageous activities. Vilifying the Prophet is akin to transgressions such as illicit intercourse, robbery, theft or wine drinking and these can not be forgiven even if the culprit repents. Hence, vilifiers of the Prophet are apostates who cannot be forgiven because of the severity of their crime. Their case is similar to that of apostates whose transgression is coupled with crimes such as murder or rebellion; these must also be denied the repentance option.[171] Neither is it permissible to enslave them, give them quarter or hold them for ransom.[172]

IX

When classical Muslim tradition and law came into being, few Muslims lived under infidel rule. Cases of Muslims being forced to change their faith were therefore few and far between, and Muslim law normally views apostasy as a voluntary renunciation of Islam. There is, however, one significant period in which the

[170] Muslim traditionists frequently express the opinion that people of sound intelligence naturally choose Islam as their religion because of its clarity and self-evident truth. This idea can be found, for instance, in the interpretations of Qurʾān 2:256: *lā ikrāha fī al-dīn qad tabayyana al-rushd min al-ghayy*. See Ṭabarī, *Jāmiʿ al-bayān*, vol. 3, p. 18.

[171] Ibn Taymiyya, *al-Ṣārim al-maslūl*, pp. 363–367 (the terms *ridda mujarrada* and *ridda mughallaẓa* appear on p. 366, l. 16); cf. also ibid., pp. 337–343.

[172] Ibn Taymiyya, *al-Ṣārim al-maslūl*, p. 253.

situation was different: the twelve years (610–622 A.D.) during which the Prophet and his early coreligionists lived in Mecca before the *hijra*. In the course of that period, some of them are said to have been subjected to pressure and even torture, designed to compel them to renege on their newly adopted faith. There were also cases of Muslim prisoners of war whom the Meccans or the Byzantines tried to convert forcibly to their respective faiths. These cases of religious coercion practiced against the Muslims gave rise to an important question: how is the believer to behave in such conditions? Is he to yield to his tormentors and outwardly disavow Islam in order to save his life, or must he stand firm regardless of the consequences? What would his religious status be if he succumbed? Would he be deemed an apostate?[173]

Islamic tradition describes the Meccan period of the Prophet's life as a time when the fledgling Muslim community experienced religious persecution by the unbelievers and faced the danger of extinction. A group of Qur'ānic verses includes critical references to religious restrictions and compulsion as practiced in Mecca before its takeover by the Muslims. In Qur'ān 22:39–40, the polytheists are accused of expelling the Muslims from the city simply because they considered Allah as their Lord. Qur'ān 2:114 speaks of the iniquity suffered by those Muslims whom the infidels barred from mentioning Allah in the mosques. In both verses the unbelievers are berated for denying Muslims freedom of worship and belief. These conditions are characterized as *fitna*; in our context the word denotes attempts to induce the Muslim believer, by torture or other means, to abandon his faith. This interpretation is indicated in a number of Qur'ānic verses[174] and is compatible with the usage of the word in some early documents attributed to the Prophet.[175] The historical tradition speaks of two *fitna*s, or waves of persecution, in Mecca: the first resulted in the escape of some Muslims to Abyssinia; the second brought about the *hijra* of the Prophet and of his followers to Medina.[176]

This is the historical context in which some early Muslims of weak social standing (*al-mustaḍ*ᶜ*afūn*)[177] faced pressure to abandon their faith and "experienced

[173] For a basic survey of similar dilemmas in Judaism and Christianity, see "Kiddush ha-shem and Ḥillul ha-shem", in *Encyclopaedia Judaica*, Jerusalem: Keter Publishing House, 1971, s.v. (Norman Lamm and Haim Hillel Ben-Sasson); "Persecution" ("Jewish Experience" by Robert Chazan, "Christian Experience" by W. H. C. Frend), in *The Encyclopaedia of Religion*, s.v.

[174] See Qur'ān 5:49 ("... and beware of them lest they tempt you [*wa-'ḥdharhum an yaftinūka*] away from any of what God has sent down ...") and 17:73 ("Indeed they were near to seducing you from [*wa-in kādū la-yaftinūnaka* ...] what We revealed to you ...").

[175] In the instructions said to have been issued by the Prophet with regard to the religious and fiscal policy to be followed in the Yemen, we read: "A Jew will not be induced to abandon his Judaism" (*lā yuftanu yahūdiyyun* ᶜ*an yahūdiyyatihi*). See Abū ᶜUbayd, *Kitāb al-amwāl*, p. 27, no. 65, and a similar tradition in the following section (no. 66). See also Ṭabarī, *Jāmi*ᶜ *al-bayān*, vol. 9, p. 249: *i'tamarat ru'ūsuhum an yaftinū man ittaba*ᶜ*ahu* ᶜ*an dīn Allāh min abnā'ihim* ... On the same page we read the phrase *ḥattā lā yaftura mu'minun* ᶜ*an dīnihi*; this is read in the Cairo 1327 edition (reprint Beirut, vol. 9, p. 162): *ḥattā lā yuftana mu'minun* ᶜ*an dīnihi*. See also Suyūṭī, *al-Durr al-manthūr*, vol. 1, p. 206: *kāna al-islām qalīlan wa kāna al-mu'min yuftanu fī dīnihi*; and Ibn Qayyim al-Jawziyya, *Aḥkām ahl al-dhimma*, vol. 2, p. 698.

[176] Ṭabarī, *Ta'rīkh*, series I, pp. 1181, 1224, 1228; cf. Khaṭṭābī, *A*ᶜ*lām al-ḥadīth*, vol. 2, p. 1354.

[177] They are described as being defenseless because they had no tribal connections in Mecca (*al-mustaḍ*ᶜ*afūn qawmun lā* ᶜ*ashā'ira lahum bi-Makka wa laysat lahum man*ᶜ*a wa lā quwwa*). See Ibn Saᶜd, *Ṭabaqāt*, vol. 3, part 1, p. 177, ll. 12–13.

torture for the sake of Allah" (*kānū yuᶜadhdhabūna fī Allāh*).[178] This group included some prominent personalities of early Islam, such as Bilāl b. Rabāḥ and ᶜAmmār b. Yāsir. Bilāl was a black slave, and is considered the first Muslim of Abyssinian origin (*sābiq al-ḥabasha*). His tormentors used to expose him to the sun, with heavy stones placed on his chest; they demanded that he believe in al-Lāt and al-ᶜUzzā and disbelieve in the Lord of Muḥammad (*ukfur bi-rabbi Muḥammadin*). Eventually the Prophet found a way to purchase his freedom; Bilāl became a *mawlā* of Abū Bakr and gained fame as the first *muʾadhdhin* in Islam.[179] ᶜAmmār b. Yāsir was a *mawlā* of Makhzūm and the son of a slave-girl; he was tortured so severely that "he became unconscious of what he said" (*kāna ... yuᶜadhdhabu ḥattā lā yadrī mā yaqūlu*).[180] Ṣuhayb b. Sinān,[181] ᶜĀmir b. Fuhayra[182], Abū Fukayha, Khabbāb b. al-Aratt and ᶜAmmār's parents (Yāsir and Sumayya) were tormented in a similar manner.[183] Not all of them acquitted themselves in the same way. ᶜAmmār is said to have uttered words of infidelity demanded by his tormentors. Bilāl, on the other hand, was steadfast in his belief; his response to torture is said to have been a constant restatement of his monotheism by repeating the words "One, One" (*aḥad aḥad*). Khabbāb[184], Abū Fukayha,[185] Yāsir[186] and Sumayya[187] also remained firm and the Meccans were not able to extract from them any recantation of Islam. Khabbāb and Abū Fukayha survived the ordeal, but Yāsir and Sumayya were done to death. The fate of Khubayb b. ᶜAdī was similar. When he was captured by the Meccans in 625, they demanded that he vilify the Prophet and mention their idols favorably. When he refused to comply, he was killed.[188]

We can conclude this brief survey by saying that the early *ḥadīth* presents more than one model of a believer's behavior under duress. Most examples show the

[178] See, for instance, Ibn Saᶜd, *Ṭabaqāt*, vol. 3, part 1, p. 162, l. 19.

[179] Ibn Saᶜd, *Kitāb al-ṭabaqāt al-kabīr*, vol. 3, part 1, pp. 165–179; Ibn al-Athīr, *Usd al-ghāba*, vol. 1, pp. 206–209; ᶜAsqalānī, *Iṣāba*, vol. 1, pp. 326 (no. 736).

[180] Ibn Saᶜd, *Kitāb al-ṭabaqāt al-kabīr*, vol. 3, part 1, p. 177; Bayhaqī, *Sunan*, vol. 8, pp. 208–209; Ibn al-Athīr, *Iṣāba*, vol. 4, pp. 43–47.

[181] Ibn al-Athīr, *Usd al-ghāba*, vol. 3, pp. 30–33; ᶜAsqalānī, *Iṣāba*, vol. 3, pp. 449–452 (4108).

[182] Ibn al-Athīr, *Usd al-ghāba*, vol. 3, pp. 90–91; ᶜAsqalānī, *Iṣāba*, vol. 3, pp. 594–595 (no. 4418).

[183] Ibn Saᶜd, *Ṭabaqāt*, vol. 3, part 1, pp. 116, 117, 162, 164, 177–178; Zamakhsharī, *Kashshāf*, vol. 2, p. 430.

[184] See Ibn al-Athīr, *Usd al-ghāba*, vol. 2, p. 106: "Khabbāb was steadfast and did not give the infidels what they wanted" (*inna Khabbāban ṣabara wa lam yuᶜṭi al-kuffār mā saʾalūhu*); ᶜAsqalānī, *Iṣāba*, vol. 2, pp. 258–259 (no. 2212).

[185] Ibn al-Athīr, *Usd al-ghāba*, vol. 5, p. 273; ᶜAsqalānī, *Iṣāba*, vol. 7, pp. 322–323 (no. 10391).

[186] Ibn al-Athīr, *Usd al-ghāba*, vol. 5, p. 99 (no reference to his death under torture); ᶜAsqalānī, *Iṣāba*, vol. 6, p. 639 (no. 9214).

[187] Ibn al-Athīr, *Usd al-ghāba*, vol. 5, p. 481; ᶜAsqalānī, *Iṣāba*, vol. 7, pp. 712–713 (no. 11236).

[188] Sarakhsī, *Mabsūṭ*, vol. 24, p. 44. It is noteworthy that in the standard biographical literature the killing of Khubayb is presented as an act of revenge rather than as a case of religious coercion. See Ibn Saᶜd, *Ṭabaqāt*, vol. I, ii, pp. 39–40; ᶜAsqalānī, *Iṣāba*, vol. 2, pp. 262–264 (no. 2224); Ibn al-Athīr, *Usd al-ghāba*, vol. 2, pp. 103–105. Yet, even in the biographies, Khubayb's death is given religious significance: he instituted the *sunna* of praying two *rakᶜa*s before being killed; and after the execution his head miraculously turned toward the *qibla*. According to Sarakhsī (*Mabsūṭ*, vol. 24, p. 44, lines 12–13), he wanted to be killed while lying on the ground prostrating to Allah, but the executioners denied his request. The story of Khubayb as it appears in the *sīra* and in classical poetry was analyzed in W. ᶜArafāt, "The development of a dramatic theme in the story of Khubaib b. ᶜAdī and the related poems", *BSOAS* 21(1958), pp. 15–30.

believers as unyielding exemplars of fortitude, sometimes to the point of dying for the faith; but ᶜAmmār's collapse under torture is presented in a favorable light as well.[189]

This issue is discussed in the *ḥadīth* literature and in commentaries on Qurʾān 16:106. This is a verse denouncing apostasy, but it makes an exception for a person who reneged on Islam "under coercion while his heart remained firm in belief" (... *illā man ukriha wa qalbuhu muṭmaʾinnun bi-'l-īmān*). According to this verse, persons who were coerced into renouncing Islam verbally while truly clinging to their faith will not be visited with divine wrath. The verse is said to have been revealed in connection with ᶜAmmār b. Yāsir who felt dejected because he had vilified the Prophet and uttered words of unbelief while under torture. The *ḥadīth* reflects diverse approaches to the issue. One prophetic tradition is in keeping with the spirit of the verse: the Prophet approved of ᶜAmmār's action and instructed him to behave likewise should he face similar circumstances in the future (*fa-in ᶜādū fa-ᶜud*).[190] In a similar vein, the Prophet is reported to have said that "whenever ᶜAmmār was given a choice between two options, he chose the superior one" (*mā khuyyira ᶜAmmār bayna amrayn illā 'khtāra arshadahumā*).[191]

In other traditions, the Prophet seems to be more demanding. When Khabbāb b. al-Aratt came to him to complain and ask for help in his predicament, the Prophet told him about people in the past who suffered unspeakable tortures, but were not deflected from their faith. The Prophet seems to imply that fortitude in face of adversity was the only legitimate course of action for Khabbāb. He has little sympathy for Khabbāb, and there is certainly no suggestion here that Khabbāb could have followed ᶜAmmār's example in order to alleviate his suffering.[192] Elsewhere the Prophet was asked to compare the behavior of two Muslims taken prisoner by Musaylima. One acknowledged Musaylima's prophethood in addition to that of Muḥammad and was set free; the other[193] evaded the question concerning Musaylima's status and was put to death. Comparing the actions of his two contemporaries, the Prophet said: "The first acted according to God's concession[194]; the second declared the truth loud and clear. Good for him!" (*ammā al-awwal fa-qad akhadha bi-rukhṣat Allāh wa ammā al-thānī fa-qad ṣadaᶜa bi-'l-ḥaqqi fa-hanīʾan lahu*). In his commentary on Qurʾān 16:106, Zamakhsharī compares

[189] Kohlberg refers to some of these episodes in his analysis of the concept of martyrdom in early Islam. See his "Medieval Muslim views on martyrdom", pp. 21–22.

[190] Ṭabarī, *Jāmiᶜ al-bayān*, vol. 14, pp. 181–182; Tabrisī, *Majmaᶜ al-bayān*, vol. 14, pp. 128–129; Rāzī, *al-Tafsīr al-kabīr*, vol. 20, p. 97. Sarakhsī (*Mabsūṭ*, vol. 24, p. 44, ll. 2–7) has a different explanation of the Prophet's words. In his view, it is unthinkable that the Prophet would encourage ᶜAmmār to vilify him again and speak once more favorably about the idols; the phrase should rather be understood as instructing ᶜAmmār to return to his unshaken belief should he face the idolaters' coercion again (*fa-in ᶜādū ilā al-ikrāh fa-ᶜud ilā ṭumaʾnīnat al-qalb bi-'l-īmān*).

[191] Qurṭubī, *al-Jāmiᶜ li-aḥkām al-Qurʾān*, vol. 10, p. 164 infra.

[192] Bukhārī, *Ṣaḥīḥ, kitāb al-ikrāh, bāb 1* (ed. Krehl, vol. 4, p. 336); Ibn Qudāma, *al-Mughnī*, vol. 8, p. 146; Ibn al-Athīr, *Usd al-ghāba*, vol. 2, p. 98.

[193] Identified in some sources as Ḥabīb b. Zayd al-Anṣārī. See ᶜAsqalānī, *Iṣāba*, vol. 2, pp. 19–20 (no. 1586); Ibn Kathīr, *Tafsīr*, vol. 4. p. 228 (on Qurʾān 16:106).

[194] On the concept of concession (*rukhṣa*) in early Islam, see M. J. Kister, "On 'concessions' and conduct".

the steadfastness of Yāsir and Sumayya with the behavior of their son and comes to the conclusion that the behavior of the former is preferable because "abandonment of precautionary dissimulation and willingness to suffer violent death increase the honor of Islam" (*li-anna fī tark al-taqiyya wa al-ṣabr ᶜalā al-qatl iᶜzāzan li-'l-islām*).[195] Ibn Kathīr reaches similar conclusions after relating the story of ᶜAbd Allāh b. Ḥudhāfa al-Sahmī. ᶜAbd Allah was taken prisoner by the Byzantines. Their king attempted to compel him to embrace Christianity, both by tempting promises and by vivid threats of torture; but ᶜAbd Allah stood firm and was eventually released together with other Muslim prisoners. Ibn Kathīr concludes that "it is more meritorious and better for a Muslim to cling firmly to his religion, even if this causes his death" (*wa al-afḍal wa al-awlā an yathbuta ᶜalā dīnihi wa law afḍā ilā qatlihi*).[196] The thrust of Fakhr al-Dīn al-Rāzī's commentary is the same. Uttering words of infidelity is permissible only under extreme conditions: death threats, violent beating and unbearable torture. Even then, when the tortured Muslim pronounces the words of infidelity, he must simultaneously clear his heart from any acquiescence with what he is saying. He should also try to use ambiguous expressions: if he says that "Muḥammad is a liar" – another Muḥammad should be intended; the sentence could also be taken as a rhetorical question (*al-istifhām bi-maᶜnā al-inkār*). Only if he is constrained to clarify all the ambiguities and declare his infidelity in unequivocal terms may he utter the words, but it is more meritorious if he refuses and exposes himself to danger of death. He is certainly not obliged to declare his infidelity in order to save his life, as would be the case if he was coerced to drink wine or consume pork or carrion.[197] Al-Qurṭubī takes a similar view. If a person is coerced to utter a declaration of infidelity, he must do it in an ambiguous fashion (*idhā talaffaẓa al-mukrahu bi-'l-kufr fa-lā yajūzu lahu an yujriyahu ᶜalā lisānihi illā majrā al-maᶜārīḍ*); otherwise he really becomes an infidel. Qurṭubī suggests various ways to accomplish this goal: one would be to mean "I disbelieve in the heedless" (*akfuru bi-'l-lāhī*) when asked to say "I disbelieve in God" (*akfuru bi-'llāhi*).[198]

In books of law and *ḥadīth*, there is extensive discussion concerning the validity and legal consequences pertaining to acts performed under coercion. The coercion (*ikrāh*) discussed in these sources is not only religious: questions such as the validity of coerced marriage, divorce, manumission or sale are also subject to detailed scrutiny.[199] The thrust of the legal opinion expressed in these sources is not substantially different from that evident in the exegetical literature, but certain specific features can be discerned.

There is, first of all, high praise for persons who preferred death to apostasy. The prevalent principle is that standing firm under pressure is better than acting upon the *rukhṣa*. A person who chose to be killed rather than renounce Islam is

[195] Zamakhsharī, *al-Kashshāf*, vol. 2, p. 430; Rāzī, *al-Tafsīr al-kabīr*, vol. 20, pp. 97–98.
[196] See Ibn Kathīr, *Tafsīr*, vol. 4, p. 229 (on Qurᵓān 16:106), and ᶜAsqalānī, *Iṣāba*, vol. 4, pp. 57–59 (4625).
[197] Rāzī, *al-Tafsīr al-kabīr*, vol. 20, pp. 97–98.
[198] Qurṭubī, *al-Jāmiᶜ li-aḥkām al-Qurᵓān*, vol. 10, pp. 170 infra – 171.
[199] Bukhārī, *Ṣaḥīḥ, Kitāb al-ikrāh*; Sarakhsī, *Mabsūṭ*, vol. 24, pp. 38ff.

lodged in Paradise with the prophets, the righteous, the martyrs and the just rulers (*fī al-janna dārun lā yanziluhā illā nabī aw ṣiddīq aw shahīd aw imām ᶜadl aw mukhayyar bayna al-qatl wa al-kufr yakhtār al-qatl ᶜalā al-kufr*).[200] In a similar vein, al-Māwardī relates a prophetic tradition according to which a person who preferred death to embracing infidelity (*muḥkam fī nafsihi*) will be given a special palace in Paradise.[201]

Nevertheless, most jurists allow the person facing coercion to give in to his tormentors' demands. Al-Māwardī recommends this option especially for a person who is likely to inflict damage on the enemy or contribute to the implementation of the *sharīᶜa* in the future;[202] should he be killed, the Muslim community would not be able to benefit from such activities. The coercion that is sufficient to justify acting according to the *rukhṣa* is precisely defined. Mere imprisonment or shackling do not belong to this category. Even beating that does not exceed the thirty-nine lashes allowed in *taᶜzīr* punishments and is therefore presumed non-fatal is excluded, because it does not amount to constraint (*iljāʾ*). Only actions which endanger life or limb can be defined as coercion. According to some jurists, since people differ in their endurance of beating and other kinds of pressure, the decision whether such a danger exists or not rests with the coerced person himself. If all these conditions are met, the person who uttered the words of infidelity – while his heart was firm in belief – is not considered apostate: his wife is not separated from him and his rights of inheritance are not affected.[203]

X

It is now in order to make a number of general observations on the material surveyed in this chapter. It would be valuable if the legal views of the various jurists on the question of apostasy could be subsumed under some general categories, and if a few general principles characterizing their legal thought would emerge from our analysis.

Abū Ḥanīfa – and possibly the whole Ḥanafī *madhhab* – held that it was not mandatory but only recommended to ask the male apostates to repent. Only Ḥasan

[200] Ṣanᶜānī, *Muṣannaf*, vol. 5, p. 265 (no. 9560).

[201] Māwardī, *al-Ḥāwī al-kabīr*, vol. 13, p. 180. This interpretation of *muḥkam fī nafsihi* is given by al-Māwardī himself.

[202] Māwardī, *al-Ḥāwī al-kabīr*, vol. 13, p. 180.

[203] Saḥnūn b. Saᶜīd, *al-Mudawwana al-kubrā*, vol. 3, p. 388 infra; Shaybānī, *Sharḥ al-siyar al-kabīr*, vol. 4, pp. 1427–1428; Shāfiᶜī, *Kitāb al-umm*, vol. 4, p. 407, ll. 11–19 (the one thing which the coerced person is not allowed to do even under duress is to kill a Muslim); vol. 6, p. 226; Ṭabarī, *Ikhtilāf al-fuqahāʾ*, pp. 197–198; Sarakhsī, *Mabsūṭ*, vol. 24, p. 49; Marghinānī, *Hidāya*, vol. 3, p. 277; Shīrāzi, *al-Muhadhdhab*, vol. 3, p. 256; Zarkashī, *Sharḥ al-Zarkashī*, vol. 5, pp. 392–393; Jubūrī, *Fiqh al-imām al-Awzāᶜī*, vol. 2, p. 345. Muḥammad b. al-Ḥasan (al-Shaybānī) is also credited with the opposite opinion: such a person is, outwardly at least, an apostate: his wife must be separated from him, Muslims no longer inherit from him and Muslim rituals are not performed at his funeral, though "he is a Muslim in his relationship with God" (*huwa kāfir fī al-ẓāhir tabīnu minhu 'mraʾatuhu wa lā yarithuhu al-muslimūn in māta wa lā yughsalu wa lā yuṣallā ᶜalayhi wa huwa muslimun fīmā baynahu wa bayna Allāh li-annahu naṭaqa bi-kalimat al-kufr fa-ashbaha al-mukhtār*). See Ibn Qudāma, *al-Mughnī*, vol. 8, p. 145; Nawawī, *al-Majmūᶜ sharḥ al-muhadhdhab*, vol. 18, p. 7.

al-Baṣrī, Ṭāwūs and the *ahl al-ẓāhir* took a more ruthless view and explicitly demanded the instantaneous execution of apostates. On the question of apostates who join the Manichaean creed, our sources ascribe to Abū Ḥanīfa two views: according to one, he refused to grant the repentance option to apostates who became *zanādiqa*, while according to the other, he treated all apostates alike. The sources do not indicate whether Abū Ḥanīfa changed his view at a certain point in time, and do not give us any clue regarding the nature of this discrepancy. We know more about the development of the views of Abū Yūsuf, who was Abū Ḥanīfa's student and the *qāḍī al-quḍāt* of the ᶜAbbāsīs. He is said to have treated all apostates alike for a time, but later adopted the view that the *zanādiqa* are not eligible for the repentance option. This means that on the question of male apostates' punishment, the Ḥanafīs are near the farther end of the severity scale. As for the treatment of female apostates, Abū Ḥanīfa's views are substantially different and at variance with the views of most early jurists.[204] A free woman who abandoned Islam should not be executed; she should rather be forced to return to the fold by imprisonment or other forms of brutal punishment. As for a slave-girl guilty of apostasy, her punishment may be dispensed with completely. Her master should attempt to force her to return to Islam, but he is allowed to continue using her services regardless of his success or failure in this endeavor. The religious duty to return the apostate slave-girl to the fold, or to punish her, is secondary to her earthly usefulness. In Abū Ḥanīfa's perception, apostasy of male Muslims is primarily a political crime, entailing a danger of rebellion. The severe punishment it carries is a matter of public policy, designed to protect the wellbeing of the Muslim state. Apostasy of females who have no fighting ability and do not endanger the Muslim polity is different. It is primarily a religious transgression, a transgression between the apostate and her Maker. Its punishment may therefore be postponed to the hereafter.

If we compare the notions of Abū Ḥanīfa and of Abū Yūsuf on these matters with those of al-Shāfiᶜī, we shall find that the latter offers a much less nuanced perception. Al-Shāfiᶜī held that apostates – regardless of gender – should be asked to repent and should be put to death in case of refusal. The nature of the religion to which they apostatized is of no consequence. Apostasy is a religious transgression, to be punished in accordance with the prophetic *ḥadīth* and the prophetic *sunna*. No other considerations are taken into account.

It would be tempting to interpret the differences between Abū Ḥanīfa and Abū Yūsuf on the one hand and al-Shāfiᶜī on the other by taking into account the Ḥanafī involvement with the early ᶜAbbāsīs. The harsh policies of that dynasty with regard to the Manichaeans are well known. Abū Ḥanīfa had died before the persecution of the Manichaeans reached its peak under the ᶜAbbāsī caliph al-Mahdī (r. 775–785 A.D.) and the stringent view ascribed to him may be only a late attribution, designed to justify the stance of later Ḥanafī scholars. The case of Abū

[204] See above, section III, after note 104 for a list of jurists who disagreed with Abū Ḥanīfa on this issue.

Yūsuf, who served as the chief *qāḍī* under the ᶜAbbāsīs, is different. His adoption of the stern anti-Manichaean policies is significant especially when contrasted with his attitudes to another group of non-Muslims, namely non-Arab (especially Indian) polytheists. Despite the apparently idolatrous nature of their worship, despite the fact that in the Muslim perception the Indians had no revealed book in their possession, and despite the uncompromising stance on idolatry adopted by the Qurᵓān – both Abū Ḥanīfa and Abū Yūsuf were willing to incorporate these people into the category of *ahl al-dhimma* and in this way provide Islamic legitimacy for their continued existence as Hindūs under Muslim rule. Their ruling on the status of non-Arab polytheists was congruent with the policies of the Muslim rulers from their first significant encounter with the Indian subcontinent at the beginning of the eighth century.[205] While there seems to be an inconsistency between Abū Yūsuf's harshness towards the Manichaeans and his leniency towards the Indian polytheists, there is, in fact, a common denominator between the two: both provide legal justification and support for the policies of the powers that be. Abū Ḥanīfa's real or attributed perception of apostasy as primarily a political crime points in the same direction. The high regard he displays for the well being of slave-girl owners – whose rights take precedence even over the rights of Allah – indicates that he has the interests of the affluent also at heart.

It goes without saying that this analysis falls short of interpreting all the differences between the *madhāhib* on the issues under discussion. Nevertheless, the explanation of the seeming contradiction between the leniency of the Ḥanafīs toward the non-Arab polytheists and their stringency toward the Manichaeans seems to be of some value.

[205] See Friedmann, "The temple of Multān", pp. 176–182, and above, Chapter Two, section V.

CHAPTER FIVE

Interfaith marriages

> Do not marry idolatresses until they believe; a believing slave-girl is better than an idolatress, though you may admire her. And do not marry idolaters, until they believe. A believing slave is better than an idolater, though you may admire him …
>
> (Qur'ān 2:221)

> O believers, when believing women come to you as emigrants, test them … Then, if you know them to be believers, return them not to the unbelievers. They are not permitted to the unbelievers, nor are the unbelievers permitted to them … Do not hold fast to the ties of unbelieving women …
>
> (Qur'ān 60:10)

> Today the good things are permitted to you, and the food of those who were given the Book is permitted to you, and permitted to them is your food. Likewise believing women in wedlock, and in wedlock women of them who were given the Book before you if you give them their wages, in wedlock and not in license, or as taking lovers.
>
> (Qur'ān 5:5)

I

In its attitude to the question of interfaith marriages, Islam is substantially different from Judaism and Christianity. In the religious laws of these two traditions, the attitude to all religiously mixed marriages is negative. Both the Old Testament and the Talmud contain explicit injunctions forbidding matrimony between Jews and non-Jews.[1] While Christian canon law allowed for the continuation of religiously mixed marriages contracted before the conversion of one of the spouses to Christianity, numerous councils of the church urged Christians of both genders not

[1] A brief survey of the relevant material in Jewish sources can be found in *Encyclopaedia Judaica*, s.v. "Mixed marriage, Intermarriage". For a detailed discussion, see L. M. Epstein, *Marriage laws in the Bible and the Talmud*, Cambridge, Mass.: Harvard University Press, 1942, pp. 145–219.

to enter into wedlock with any non-Christian and some of them imposed stiff penalties for the contravention of this rule.[2]

In Islam, the situation is different. Since the very beginning of its development, Islam made distinctions between marriages with various types of unbelievers and established different rules for interfaith marriages of Muslim males and Muslim females. Muslim sources abound with discussions of the laws governing interfaith marriages. Nevertheless, research on this facet of Islamic law is still in its infancy and deserves our attention.

The Qur'ān deals with the question of mixed marriages in three verses which have become the basis for the development of the pertinent Muslim law.[3] The first verse clearly prohibits Muslims from wedding polytheist women (*mushrikāt*), as well as giving Muslim women in marriage to polytheists. The second, though using the term *kawāfir* rather than *mushrikāt*, is understood in the same manner.[4] The third verse allows Muslims to marry "virtuous" or free (*muḥṣanāt*) women of the People of the Book. The verse does not refer to the possibility of giving Muslim women in marriage to scriptuary men, but this possibility is firmly and unanimously rejected in the books of tradition and law. Several Muslims of the first century A.H. are credited with unequivocal statements to this effect.[5] A marriage of a Muslim woman to a non-Muslim man would result in an unacceptable incongruity between the superiority which the woman should enjoy by virtue of being Muslim, and her unavoidable wifely subservience to her infidel husband. In terms of Islamic law, such a marriage would involve an extreme lack of *kafā'a*, that is, of the compatibility between husband and wife, which requires that a woman not

2 *Encyclopaedia of Religion and Ethics*, s.v. Marriage (Christian); Moy de Sons, *Das Eherecht der Christen in der morgenländischen und abendländischen Kirche bis zu der Zeit Karls des Grossen*, Regensburg, 1883 (reprint Aalen: Scientia Verlag, 1970), pp. 76–80, 195–204, 344–348; J. Dauvillier, *Le mariage dans le droit classique de l'église depuis le décret de Gratien (1140) jusqu'à la mort de Clément V (1314)*, Paris 1933, pp. 183–184; J. Freisen, *Geschichte des kanonischen Eherechts bis zum Verfall der Glossenliteratur*, Paderborn, 1893 (reprint Aalen: Scientia Verlag, 1963), pp. 635–643; James A Brundage, "Intermarriage between Christians and Jews in medieval canon law", in *Jewish History* 3 (1988), pp. 25–40 (with extensive documentation and bibliography); A. Linder, *The Jews in Roman imperial legislation*, Detroit: Wayne State University Press and The Israel Academy of Sciences and Humanities, 1987, pp. 178–182; Linder, *The Jews in the legal sources of the early Middle Ages*, index, s.v. "Marriage and sexual relations", especially p. 211; D. Nirenberg, *Communities of violence. Persecutions of minorities in the Middle Ages*, Princeton: Princeton University Press, 1996, pp. 127–165.

3 The arrangement of the three verses at the head of this chapter follows the traditional chronology of their revelation.

4 See, for instance, Ṭabarī, *Jāmi' al-bayān*, vol. 28, pp. 69–73; Ibn Qayyim al-Jawziyya, *Aḥkām ahl al-dhimma*, p. 422.

5 A partial list includes 'Umar b. al-Khaṭṭāb, 'Alī b. Abī Ṭālib, Sulaymān b. Yasār (d. 103 A.H.; Ibn Sa'd, *Ṭabaqāt*, vol. 5, p. 130), al-Qāsim b. Muḥammad (d. 108 A.H.; Ibn Sa'd, *Ṭabaqāt*, vol. 5, pp. 139–143); Abū Salama b. 'Abd al-Raḥmān (d. 104 A.H.; see Ibn Sa'd, *Ṭabaqāt*, vol. 5, pp. 115–117. See Ṣan'ānī, *Muṣannaf*, vol. 6, pp. 78–79 (no. 10058); vol. 7, p. 175 (no. 12663); Saḥnūn b. Sa'īd, *Mudawwana*, vol. 2, p. 298.

It may be noted here that in Saḥnūn b. Sa'īd, *Mudawwana*, Beirut 1994, vol. 2, p. 212 and Cairo 1324, vol. 2, p. 211 we read: … *inna al-muslim yankiḥu al-naṣrāniyya wa yankiḥu al-naṣrānī al-muslima*. This is evidently a misprint; see the Cairo 1323 edition, vol. 4, p. 148 which correctly reads: … *inna al-muslima yankiḥu al-naṣrāniyya wa lā yankiḥu al-naṣrānī al-muslima*.

marry a man lower in status than herself.[6] This principle is applied not only in matters of religion; the husband should be higher also in his social standing. A tradition related on the authority of ᶜUmar b. al-Khaṭṭāb, reads after ordaining in the usual manner that a Muslim may marry a Christian woman but that a Christian man may not marry a Muslim woman:

> An emigrant may marry a Bedouin woman, but a Bedouin man may not marry an emigrant woman so as to make her leave the place to which she migrated (*yatazawwaju 'l-muhājir al-aᶜrābiyya wa lā yatazawwaju 'l-aᶜrābiyyu 'l-muhājira li-yukhrijahā min dāri hijratihā*).[7]

The emigrant mentioned in this tradition is an urban Muslim. He is higher in status than a Bedouin and therefore may marry a Bedouin woman, but the reverse situation is unacceptable. As some traditionists have put it, marriage is a sort of enslavement (*al-nikāḥ nawᶜu riqqin*), the husband is considered master with regard to his wife, and if it is not permissible for an infidel to own a Muslim slave, it is not permissible for him to have a Muslim wife either. It is therefore legitimate for a Muslim to enslave an infidel woman by marrying her, but it is not legitimate for an infidel to enslave a Muslim woman in the same manner because Islam is exalted and nothing is exalted above it (*fa-juwwiza li-'l-muslim an yastariqqa hādhihi al-kāfira wa lam yujawwaz li-'l-kāfir an yastariqqa hādhihi al-muslima li-anna al-islām yaᶜlū wa lā yuᶜlā ᶜalayhi*).[8] Aḥmad b. Ḥanbal supports his refusal to allow the continuation of a marriage between two *kitābī*s in which the woman embraced Islam by saying that "we can possess them, but they cannot possess us" (*namlikuhum wa lā yamlikūnanā*).[9] The affinity between marriage and slavery is exemplified in the work of Ibn Ḥazm. As is well known, Islam forbids non-Muslims

[6] See "Kafāʾa", *EI*², s.v. (Y. Linant de Bellefonds); B. Lewis, *Race and slavery*, pp. 85–91 (with extensive documentation). A modern Egyptian scholar explains that "a noble woman and her next of kin are disparaged (*tuᶜayyaru*) if her husband – who is in charge of her and to whom her children are related – is lowly, but a noble man is not disparaged if his wife is lowly. Many a king and a caliph had wives who were slave-girls." See ᶜAbd al-Wahhāb Khallāf, *Aḥkām al-aḥwāl al-shakhṣiyya fī al-sharīᶜa al-islāmiyya*, Cairo: Maṭbaᶜat Dār al-kutub, 1938, p, 74. For the author, see Kaḥḥāla, *Muᶜjam al-muʾallifīn*, Beirut: Muʾassasat al-risāla, 1993, vol. 2, p. 341. Khallāf speaks of social rather than religious considerations in the determination of marital compatibility, but the principle is the same. See also [Muḥammad Qadrī], *Kitāb al-aḥkām al-sharᶜiyya ᶜalā madhhab Abī Ḥanīfa*, Cairo: al-Maktaba al-ᶜuthmāniyya, 1347 A.H., p. 10. The author's name does not appear on the title page; for his identification, see Sarkīs, *Muᶜjam al-maṭbūᶜāt al-ᶜarabiyya wa al-muᶜarraba*, Cairo: Maṭbaᶜat Sarkīs, 1928, p. 1495 and (as Qadrī al-Miṣrī) Kaḥḥāla, *Muᶜjam al-muʾallifīn*, vol. 2, p. 658.

[7] Ṣanᶜānī, *Muṣannaf*, vol. 7, pp. 176–177 (nos. 12664, 12671).

[8] Ibn Taymiyya, *Majmūᶜ fatāwā*, vol. 32, pp. 184–185. The idea that for the woman marriage is tantamount to enslavement is sometimes attributed to the Prophet himself, even when no difference in religion between the spouses is involved; see Sarakhsī, *al-Mabsūṭ*, vol. 5, p. 23, l. 21: "Marriage is enslavement; let every one of you weigh carefully where (i.e., with whom) he places his daughter" (*al-nikāḥu riqqun fa-'l-yanẓur aḥadukum ayna yaḍaᶜu karīmatahu*). In another tradition the Prophet is reported to have said: "Show fear of God in your relations with women, for they suffer in your homes" (*ittaqū Allāha fī al-nisāʾ fa-innahunna ᶜawānin ᶜindakum*). See Ibn Taymiyya, *Majmūᶜ fatāwā*, vol. 32, pp. 184, line 18. Veiled criticism of the social inferiority of women can be discerned in these traditions.

[9] Khallāl, *Ahl al-milal*, p. 269 (no. 540).

to own Muslim slaves and Ibn Ḥazm links this prohibition to the prohibition on giving Muslim women in marriage to unbelievers.[10]

Severe punishment is ordained for a *dhimmī* who weds a Muslim woman and consummates the marriage; according to a view attributed to Mālik b. Anas, the culprit is even liable to be executed since he broke the conditions of his *dhimma* treaty. Such is the enormity perceived in this type of wedlock that the offending *dhimmī* is said to resemble one "who transformed himself into the vanguard of a polytheist army" (*fa-huwa naẓīr al-dhimmī idhā jaᶜala nafsahu ṭalīᶜatan li-'l-mushrikīn*).[11] According to the view of the Ḥanafīs as expressed by al-Sarakhsī, the offending *dhimmī* is not to be killed; rather, he should suffer corporal punishment (*yūjaᶜu ᶜuqūbatan*) and the person who facilitated the marriage (*alladhī saᶜā baynahumā*) should suffer discretionary punishment (*taᶜzīr*). Even if the *dhimmī* later embraces Islam, the marriage will not be valid "because the marriage was invalid originally and it does not become valid by means of conversion" (... *li-anna aṣl al-nikāḥ kāna bāṭilan fa bi-'l-islām lā yanqalibu ṣaḥīḥan*). The view of al-Shāfiᶜī is similar, though he speaks about an apostate rather than about an "original" unbeliever.[12] In the *Mudawwana* there is a question concerning the view of Mālik b. Anas on a *dhimmī* who marries a Muslim woman with the consent of her guardian and consummates the marriage: are the *dhimmī* and the woman liable to the *ḥadd* punishment, and is the guardian to be painfully chastised? Mālik b. Anas did not give an explicit ruling on this question, but he did say that if a *dhimmī* buys a Muslim (slave) woman and engages in sexual relations with her, a collective punishment should be inflicted on the *dhimmī*s: they should be severely reprimanded, punished and beaten (*qāla: arā an yutaqaddama ilā ahl al-dhimma fī dhālika bi-ashadd al-taqaddum wa yuᶜāqabū ᶜalā dhālika wa yuḍrabū baᶜda al-taqaddum*).[13] And a *dhimmī* who rapes a Muslim woman, or has consensual sexual relations with her, is liable to the death penalty.[14]

A marriage between a Muslim woman and a non-Muslim man may result not only from a Muslim woman having been given to a non-Muslim man (which, as we have seen, is illegal), but also from the conversion to Islam of the wife in an existing marriage between two non-Muslims. Classical Muslim jurisprudents devote considerable attention to this problem and stipulate what should be done if such a conversion takes place. Once a wife in a non-Muslim marriage embraces

[10] Ibn Ḥazm, *Muḥallā*, vol. 9, p. 449 (no. 1818).

[11] Sarakhksī, *Mabsūṭ*, vol. 5, p. 45, ll. 9–11.

[12] Sarakhsī, *Mabsūṭ*, vol. 5, p. 45, ll. 11–15; Shāfiᶜī, *Kitāb al-umm*, vol. 5, pp. 85 infra – 86. Shāfiᶜī discussed the legal ramifications of the case. If the marriage was consummated, the woman deserves to retain the dowry; if a child is born, it is legitimate. The woman does not become a *muḥṣan*. If she is a divorcee, she does not become licit to the husband who had divorced her; in other words, the apostate cannot be her *muḥallil*. If the marriage was not consummated, the woman does not deserve any part of the dowry.

[13] Saḥnūn, *al-Mudawwana*, vol. 2, p. 297 infra.

[14] Abū ᶜUbayd, *Kitāb al-amwāl*, pp. 181–182 (no. 485); Ibn Ḥanbal, *Aḥkām al-nisāʾ*, pp. 60–62 (nos. 198–204); Khallāl, *Ahl al-milal*, pp. 347–350 (nos. 763–771), p. 351 (no. 776); Ibn Qayyim al-Jawziyya, *Aḥkām ahl al-dhimma*, pp. 790–792.

Islam, a separation between her and her infidel husband comes into effect. If the husband converts to Islam within the wife's *ᶜidda* period, the marriage is restored. Such were the cases of Ṣafwān b. Umayya[15] and ᶜIkrima b. Abī Jahl[16] whose wives converted to Islam at the time of the Prophet. Having fled from Islam in the beginning, both husbands eventually followed their wives and embraced Islam. These marriages remained therefore valid and are considered as legal precedents for the disposition of comparable cases.[17] If, however, the husband does not convert within the *ᶜidda*, the marital relationship (*al-ᶜiṣma*) between the spouses is (irrevocably) severed. According to the Ḥanbalī jurist al-Khallāl, even if the husband does convert during the *ᶜidda*, a new marriage contract is necessary before conjugal relations are resumed.[18] If the conversion of the wife took place before the consummation of the marriage, the (irrevocable) separation takes immediate effect because there is no *ᶜidda* requirement in such a situation.[19]

According to Mālik b. Anas, if a Christian woman embraces Islam while her Christian husband is away on a journey, she is to be ordered (!) to marry (a Muslim, presumably) when her *ᶜidda* is over. Even if her husband converts to Islam before

[15] Ṣafwān b. Umayya belonged to a prominent Meccan family. His father, a leader of the clan of Jumaḥ, is said to have been entrusted with the divination arrows in the Jāhiliyya and to have died fighting the Muslims in the battle of Badr. Ṣafwān himself fled Mecca after the Muslim takeover, but was promised safety by the Prophet and returned. He was present at the battle of Ḥunayn before his conversion. Eventually he embraced Islam as a result of the Prophet's generosity toward him; he is considered one of the *muʾallafa qulūbuhum*. The Prophet is said to have reunited him with his wife, who had converted earlier, after 4 months (of separation?). Ṣafwān died in 656 A.D. or slightly later. See Ibn Ḥabīb, *Kitāb al-Munammaq*, Ḥaydarābād (Deccan): Dāʾirat al-maᶜārif al-ᶜuthmāniyya, 1964, p. 412; Ibn al-Athīr, *Usd al-ghāba*, vol. 3, pp. 22–23; ᶜAsqalānī, *Iṣāba*, vol. 3, pp. 432–434 (no. 4077).

[16] ᶜIkrima was the son of Abū Jahl, a staunch opponent of the Prophet. He was one of six persons whom the Prophet ordered to be killed after the takeover of Mecca. ᶜIkrima escaped to the Yemen, but was brought back by his Muslim wife after the Prophet gave him a guarantee of safety. Eventually he embraced Islam and fought in the *ridda* wars on the side of the Muslims. He was killed in battle during the conquest of Syria. See Ibn al-Athīr, *Usd al-ghāba*, vol. 4, pp. 4–6; ᶜAsqalānī, *Iṣāba*, vol. 4, pp. 538–539 (no. 5642).

[17] Several other cases of similar nature are mentioned. See Wāqidī, *Maghāzī*, vol. 2, p. 855; Ṣanᶜānī, *Muṣannaf*, vol. 7, pp. 169–171 (no. 12646–12647); Mālik b. Anas, *Muwaṭṭaʾ, Kitāb al-nikāḥ* 20 (pp. 543–545, nos. 44–46); Saḥnūn, *Mudawwana*, vol. 2, pp. 298–300; Ibn ᶜAbd al-Barr al-Namarī, *Tamhīd*, vol. 12, pp. 17–19, p. 33, ll. 1–10; Shāfiᶜī, *Kitāb al-umm*, vol. 4, p. 385, l. 14 – 386, l. 3; vol. 5, p. 71, ll. 19–21; Khallāl, *Ahl al-milal*, pp. 269 (nos. 541–543); Ibn Qayyim al-Jawziyya, *Aḥkām ahl al-dhimma*, pp. 323, ll. 16ff.

[18] Khallāl, *Ahl al-milal*, p. 272 (no. 545), ll. 4–5.

[19] Ṣanᶜānī, *Muṣannaf*, vol. 6, pp. 81 (nos. 10070–10073), 83–84 (nos. 10080–10082); vol. 7, pp. 172–174 (nos. 12650–12651, 12654, 12657–12658), p. 183 (nos. 12700–12704); Qudūrī, *Mukhtaṣar*, p. 150, ll. 10–11; Saḥnūn, *Mudawwana*, vol. 2, p. 301, ll. 5–16; p. 303, ll. 3–8; Ibn ᶜAbd al-Barr al-Namarī, *Tamhīd*, vol. 12, p. 26, ll. 1–8, p. 30, ll. 1–6; Shāfiᶜī, *Kitāb al-umm*, vol. 5, p. 76, ll. 12–15; Māwardī, *al-Ḥāwī al-kabīr*, vol. 9, p. 258 infra – 259; Ibn Ḥanbal, *Aḥkām al-nisāʾ*, pp. 26–27 (nos. 62–66); Khiraqī, *Mukhtaṣar*, p. 141 infra; Ibn Qayyim al-Jawziyya, *Aḥkām ahl al-dhimma*, p. 319, ll. 13–15; p. 320, ll. 7–10; Ibn Ḥazm, *Muḥallā*, vol. 7, pp. 364–369 (no. 939). For a case in which a 14 years old Jewish girl converted to Islam and was, consequently, separated from her Jewish husband by the *sharᶜī* court in Jerusalem in 1131 A.H. / 1719 A.D., see Amnon Cohen, Elisheva Simon-Pikali and Ovadia Salama, *Jews in Moslem religious court. Society, economy and communal organization in the XVIII century: documents from Ottoman Jerusalem*, Jerusalem: Yad Izhak Ben Zvi, 1996, pp. 265–266 (in Hebrew translation).

his return but after the expiry of the ᶜidda, the marriage remains dissolved. Only if the husband's conversion takes place within the ᶜidda period and the husband returns before the woman had remarried, the marital relationship continues uninterrupted.[20]

An apparently rare view was held by Ibn Ḥazm, some other Ẓāhirīs, and is attributed also to a number of first century scholars. They held that the conversion of both spouses must be absolutely simultaneous. If one spouse embraces Islam even a twinkling of an eye before the other, the marriage is irrevocably annulled. Ibn Ḥazm insists that traditions indicating a different ruling are unreliable or irrelevant.[21]

Muslim jurists are willing to go to extreme lengths in order to preclude any possibility of a marital relationship between a Muslim woman and a non-Muslim man. In order to achieve this objective to the fullest extent possible, they are willing to impose the prohibition on wedding a non-Muslim even on women whose affiliation with the Muslim community is, to say the least, in doubt. The following ruling may shed additional light on the jurists' total commitment to this principle. Thus, if Christian parents give their minor daughter in marriage to a Christian and subsequently embrace Islam, while the girl is still a minor, the marriage is dissolved because the conversion of the parents transforms a minor daughter into a Muslim. Similarly, if a minor Zoroastrian boy marries a Zoroastrian girl and his parents then convert to Islam while he is still a minor, Islam is offered to the girl and the marriage is dissolved if she refuses to embrace it.[22] In a similar vein, al-Shāfiᶜī maintains that if one parent of a girl embraces Islam while she is a minor, she will be forbidden to any polytheist or idolater;[23] furthermore, even if both her parents remain polytheists, but she is able to describe what Islam is and understands it, she becomes forbidden to any polytheist, and, presumably, also to any other non-Muslim. Al-Shāfiᶜī would have preferred to forbid her marriage to polytheists even if she describes Islam without understanding it, but he did not make up his mind on this issue in an unequivocal manner.[24] It would appear that al-Shāfiᶜī tends to treat the girl in all these cases as if she were a Muslim.

Cases in which an unbeliever uses deceit in order to obtain a Muslim woman are treated with exceptional severity. If a Christian poses as a Muslim, is given a Muslim woman in marriage and then embraces Islam for fear of being exposed, the spouses are still to be separated because the marriage was invalid when it had been contracted. The offending Christian also suffers economic loss: the woman is

[20] Ibn ᶜAbd al-Barr al-Namarī, *Tamhīd*, vol. 12, p. 29, ll. 1–9. It is not clearly stated who is supposed to issue the order. The guardian (*walī*) is the most likely person to do this. This rule is to be seen as reflecting a notion widespread among the classical jurisprudents: they do not envisage a situation in which a woman remains single or a divorcee does not remarry.

[21] Ibn Ḥazm, *Muḥallā*, vol. 7, pp. 364–369 (no. 939); for a rejection of this view, see Ibn Qayyim al-Jawziyya, *Aḥkām ahl al-dhimma*, pp. 317–318; 322, ll. 4ff; 327–328.

[22] Saḥnūn, *Mudawwana*, vol. 2, p. 308, ll. 13–17.

[23] According to some views, a child is deemed to adhere to his parents' non-Muslim religion only if both parents are non-Muslims. For discussion, see above, Chapter Three, at notes 122 and 123.

[24] Shāfiᶜī, *Kitāb al-umm*, vol. 5, p. 9, ll. 10–13.

allowed to retain her dowry. And if he reneges on Islam after his scheme had been foiled in this manner – the assumption being that he converted only in an attempt to preserve his marriage – he is to be executed as an apostate.[25]

II

The rule stipulating the annulment of a marriage between two unbelievers in which the wife embraces Islam and the husband refuses to follow suit became the established law. Nevertheless, careful perusal of the relevant sources suggests that in the earliest period of Islam there was a considerable variety of views on the matter; some of these have been preserved in relatively late literature. When a Christian by the name of Hāniʾ b. Hāniʾ b. Qabīṣa al-Shaybānī,[26] whose four wives embraced Islam,[27] came to Medina, ʿUmar allowed their marriage to stand (*aqarrahunna ʿUmar ʿindahu*). This ruling contradicts the opinion attributed to ʿUmar elsewhere.[28] Al-Ḥakam b. ʿUtayba,[29] the transmitter of the story of Hāniʾ, explains that "this is a well-known (or customary) thing" (*hādhā shayʾun maʿrūf*).[30] ʿAlī b. Abī Ṭālib is reported to have expressed the same opinion and not to have demanded the separation of the spouses in such a case (*lā yufarraqu baynahumā*).[31] He maintained that the non-Muslim's right to preserve his marriage if the wife embraced Islam is guaranteed by the *dhimma* treaty (*idhā aslamat imraʾatu al-yahūdī aw al-naṣrānī kāna aḥaqqa bi-buḍʿihā li-anna lahu ʿahdan*).[32] Al-Zuhrī is said to be among numerous (unnamed) traditionists who reported that according to the Prophet's view, such a marriage remains in force even if twenty years elapse between the conversion of the two spouses (… *wa in kāna baynahumā*

[25] Saḥnūn, *Mudawwana*, vol. 2, p. 298, ll. 9–11.

[26] I was not able to locate this person in the biographical dictionaries.

[27] A tradition about a Christian having four wives is, of course, odd.

[28] See above, note 5 to the present chapter.

[29] The biographical literature knows two persons bearing this name. The first was a *mawlā* of the tribe of Kinda, a Kūfan *faqīh* and transmitter of *ḥadīth*. He died in 113, 114 or 115 A.D. See Ibn Saʿd, *Ṭabaqāt*, vol. 6, p. 231; ʿAsqalānī, *Tahdīb al-tahdhīb*, vol. 2, pp. 432–434 (no. 756). The other al-Ḥakam b. ʿUtayba (b. al-Naḥḥās; or al-Nahhās) was *qāḍī* in Kūfa. See ʿAsqalānī, *Lisān al-mīzān*, Beirut: Muʾassasat al-Aʿlamī, 1971, vol. 2, p. 336 (no. 1370); idem, *Tahdhīb al-tahdhīb*, vol. 2, pp. 434–435 (no. 757). Bukhārī seems to have thought that there was only one person bearing this name; see his *al-Taʾrīkh al-kabīr*, vol. 2, pp. 332–333 and the editor's discussion of the problem.

[30] Ibn Ḥazm, *Muḥallā*, vol. 7, p. 365, ll. 8–11 (no. 939). Cf. Ibn Abī Shayba, *Muṣannaf*, Riyāḍ 1409 (CD ROM edition, *Maktabat al-fiqh wa uṣūlihi*, ʿAmmān: Turāth Company, 1999), vol 4, p. 106 (no. 18312). Bayhaqī (*Sunan*, vol. 7, p. 190, ll. 1–4) has a substantially different version of this story. According to his version, it was the husband who embraced Islam and ʿUmar allowed him to keep his four Christian wives. Evidently, this version reflects the established law. In the *Muḥallā*, the tradition is adduced in the context of other reports according to which marriages between Muslim women and unbelievers are allowed to stand. It therefore stands to reason that Ibn Ḥazm had in front of him the version in which the women embraced Islam and the man remained Christian. The transmission and development of this tradition remain to be investigated.

[31] Khallāl, *Ahl al-milal*, pp. 270 (no. 544), l. 19 – 271, l.1.

[32] Ibn Ḥazm, *Muḥallā*, vol. 7, p. 365 (no. 939), ll. 5–7. Cf. Ibn Abī Shayba, *Muṣannaf*, Riyāḍ 1409 (CD ROM edition, ʿAmmān), vol 4, p. 106 (nos. 18307–18311).

[sic] *ʿishrūna sana kāna* [sic] *ʿalā nikāḥihimā*).[33] Aḥmad b. Ḥanbal characterized ʿAlī's view as reflecting "the well established precedent" (*aʿlamu anna ʿAliyyan ittabaʿa bi-hādhā al-sunna al-māḍiya*).[34] He himself vacillated on the issue because of the existence of contradictory *aḥādīth*; he seems eventually, to have concluded that if the husband does not embrace Islam, the marriage remains valid only for the duration of the *ʿidda*.[35] Even then he refused to characterize ʿAlī's view as "reprehensible" (*munkar*) (*lā yuʿjibunī an yuʿmala bihi lākin lā aqūlu munkaran*).[36] An explicit reference to this early opinion is found in al-Sarakhsī's *Mabsūṭ*:

> ... it is well settled in the law is that a Muslim woman is not licit for an infidel – though this was permissible in the beginning. They should be separated ... (... *fa-'staqarra al-ḥukm fī al-sharʿ ʿalā anna al-muslima lā taḥillu li-'l-kāfir wa in kāna dhālika ḥalālan fī al-ibtidāʾ fa-yufarraqu baynahumā* ...)[37]

Interpreting Qurʾān 10:78, where Lūṭ seems to be offering his daughters in marriage to unbelievers, Fakhr al-Dīn al-Rāzī indicates that "it was permissible in his (scil. Lūṭ's) law to give a believing woman to an unbeliever in marriage, as was the case in early Islam" (*annahu kāna yajūzu tazwīj al-muʾmina min al-kāfir fī sharīʿatihi wa hākadhā kāna fī awwal al-islām*). He mentions Zaynab's marriage to Abū al-ʿĀṣ in substantiation of this view.[38] Ibn Qayyim al-Jawziyya also speaks of a stage in the development of Muslim law when marriages in which the woman embraced Islam and the man clung to infidelity were not annulled; interestingly enough, he maintains that this had been the rule before the commandment of *jihād* was promulgated.[39] This seems to have been a period in which the idea of Islam as a religion exalted above all others had not yet gained its crucial importance in the Muslim world-view.

Ibn Qayyim al-Jawziyya includes in his *Aḥkām ahl al-dhimma* an impressive array of views, and some of them are rather remarkable when compared with the established law. ʿUmar b. al-Khaṭṭāb had to decide a case in which a Christian woman embraced Islam while married to a Christian. He is said to have given her the option either of leaving her husband, or of staying with him. Ibn Qayyim al-Jawziyya comments that the latter option does not mean that:

> she would stay under him while he is a Christian, but that she waits and bides her time; when he embraces Islam, she will be his wife (again), even if she stays (in this condition) for years on end ... This is the most correct way in this matter ... and it is the choice of *shaykh al-islām* (Ibn Taymiyya) (*wa laysa maʿnāhu annnahā tuqīmu taḥtahu wa huwa*

[33] Khallāl, *Ahl al-milal*, p. 270 (no. 544, lines 5–7).
[34] Khallāl, *Ahl al-milal*, p. 271 (no. 544), ll. 7–8. For this term and its significance, see Schacht, *Introduction*, pp. 29–31.
[35] Khallāl, *Ahl al-milal*, pp. 259–266 (nos. 516–529). Ibn Ḥanbal's final opinion is expressed at the end of no. 527.
[36] Khallāl, *Ahl al-milal*, p. 275 (no. 551), l. 1.
[37] Sarakhsī, *Mabsūṭ*, vol. 5, p. 45, ll. 4–5.
[38] Rāzī, *al-Tafsīr al-kabīr*, vol. 18, p. 27, ll. 25–27.
[39] Ibn Qayyim al-Jawziyya, *Aḥkām ahl al-dhimma*, vol. 1, p. 69, ll. 1–3.

naṣrānī bal tantaẓiru wa tatarabbaṣu fa-matā aslama fa-hiya 'mraʾatuhu wa law makathat sinīna ... wa huwa aṣaḥḥu 'l-madhāhib fī hādhihi 'l-masʾala ... wa huwa ikhtiyār shaykh al-islām).[40]

This seems to mean that the woman may choose to stay in her matrimonial home, but should refuse conjugal relations; at the same time, she will not suffer the possible economic hardship of a divorcee and her support will be assured (*tajibu lahā al-nafaqa wa al-suknā*).[41] Ibrāhīm al-Nakhaᶜī[42] and Ḥammād b. Abī Sulaymān[43] maintained that the now Muslim woman will be left in her husband's house (*tuqarru ᶜindahu*), while Dāwūd b. ᶜAlī (al-Ẓāhirī) agreed, but stipulated that the husband will have no conjugal rights (*yumnaᶜu min waṭʾihā*). And al-Zuhrī thought that such a marriage remains valid unless the ruler separates between the spouses.[44]

Traditionists who endorse the idea that a marriage of two unbelievers is not immediately annulled if the woman embraces Islam find support in the traditions concerning Zaynab, the eldest daughter of the Prophet. She had married a prominent Qurashī named Abū al-ᶜĀṣ b. al-Rabīᶜ b. ᶜAbd al-ᶜUzzā in the Jāhiliyya, before her father received the call. When Muḥammad proclaimed his prophethood, Zaynab embraced Islam. Traditions differ regarding the question of whether she migrated to Medina together with the Prophet, or stayed behind and joined her father only later. In any case, Abū al-ᶜĀṣ initially refused to follow his wife into Islam, fought on the side of the polytheists in Badr, fell into captivity and was released as a result of Zaynab's intervention. According to a report in Ibn al-Athīr's *Usd al-ghāba*, he was nevertheless friendly to the Prophet and refused to divorce the Prophet's daughter when the Meccans pressed him to do so. For this he earned the Prophet's gratitude. Abū al-ᶜĀṣ converted only in the year 7 A.H. / 628 A.D. Depending on which tradition one chooses, one year, or two years or six years

40 Ibn Qayyim al-Jawziyya, *Aḥkām ahl al-dhimma*, pp. 320 infra – 321; p. 323, ll. 4–6; 326, ll. 1ff. Cf. Ṣanᶜānī, *Muṣannaf*, vol. 6, p. 84 (no. 10083); vol. 7, p. 175 (no. 12660); Ibn Ḥazm, *Muḥallā*, vol. 7, p. 365, ll. 16–18.

41 Ibn Qayyim al-Jawziyya, *Aḥkām ahl al-dhimma*, pp. 320, ll. 10 – 321, ll. 1; pp. 321, ll. 11 – 322, l. 1. Cf. Ibn Taymiyya, *Majmūᶜ fatāwā*, vol. 32, pp. 337–338. According to a note by Ṣubḥī al-Ṣāliḥ, the editor of *Aḥkām ahl al-dhimma* (p. 321, note 1), this was also the view of Mālik b. Anas; however, his reference to the *Mudawwana* seems to be faulty (there is no p. 236 in vol. 4 of the Maṭbaᶜat al-Saᶜāda 1323 edition), and on p. 153 of the same volume (reprint Dār Ṣādir, Beirut, vol. 2, p. 303) Mālik b. Anas seems to be expressing a different view.

42 See on him "al-Nakhaᶜī, Ibrāhīm", *EI*², s.v. (G. Lecomte).

43 Ḥammād b. Abī Sulaymān was a student of Ibrāhīm al-Nakhaᶜī. He was a Kūfan *faqīh*, considered knowledgeable about "the permissible and the prohibited" (*al-ḥalāl wa al-ḥarām*). He is described as a supporter of the Murjiʾa. He died in 119 or 120 A.H. See Ibn Saᶜd, *Ṭabaqāt*, vol. 6, pp. 231–232; ᶜAsqalānī, *Tahdhīb al-tahdhīb*, vol. 3, pp. 16–18.

44 Ibn Qayyim al-Jawziyya, *Aḥkām ahl al-dhimma*, p. 321, ll. 6–10. According to a report of Ibn ᶜAbd al-Barr al-Namarī (*Tamhīd*, vol. 12, p. 23), Ibrāhīm al-Nakhaᶜī stated that "most of our associates do not annul the marriage because the wife had embraced Islam earlier; only after a certain period lapses, all agree upon the nullification. This is because the marriage was originally valid and there is a difference of opinion concerning it" (*aktharu aṣḥābinā lā yafsakhu 'l-nikāḥa li-taqaddumi islāmi 'l-zawja illā bi-muḍiyyi muddatin yattafiqu 'l-jamīᶜ ᶜalā faskhihi li-ṣiḥḥati wuqūᶜihi fī aṣlihi wa wujūd al-tanāzuᶜ fīhi*).

elapsed between the conversion of Zaynab and that of her husband; even the shortest of these time spans is, of course, much longer than the "waiting period" (*ᶜidda*). Despite this lengthy interval, the Prophet did not annul Zaynab's marriage to Abū al-ᶜĀṣ, though according to some reports, the purpose of which is to lessen the contradiction between this episode and the established law, he instructed Zaynab to refuse conjugal relations with her husband as long as he remained a polytheist. According to a tradition attributed to ᶜĀᵓisha,

> Islam separated Abū al-ᶜĀṣ from Zaynab when she converted, but the Prophet could not bring about their separation because of his weakness in Mecca. (There) he was unable to declare things permissible or forbidden (*wa kāna al-islām qad farraqa bayna Zaynab wa bayna Abī al-ᶜĀṣ ḥīna aslamat illā anna rasūl Allāh ... kāna lā yaqdiru ᶜalā an yufarriqa baynahumā wa kāna rasūl Allāh ... maghlūban bi-Makka lā yuḥillu wa lā yuḥarrimu ...*).[45]

This would mean that the continuation of Zaynab's marriage to Abū al-ᶜĀṣ was allowed not because it accorded with the law that was in force at that time, but only because the Prophet's political position was too weak to allow him to annul it. It is also argued that the conversion of Abū al-ᶜĀṣ took place before the revelation of Qurᵓān 60:10, which prohibits the marriage of Muslim women to polytheists;[46] this argument is designed to eliminate the contradiction between this episode and the law according to which such a marriage must be nullified by the end of the *ᶜidda* period (which is to be "counted" from the wife's conversion).[47] It should be pointed out, however, that this does not tally with the traditional chronology of the Qurᵓān, which dates Sūrat al-Baqara (where the prohibition had appeared earlier, in verse 221) to the early Medinan period. According to another attempt at interpretation, Abū al-ᶜĀṣ converted a short while after the revelation of Qurᵓān 60:10; at that time Zaynab was still within the *ᶜidda* period, which should begin, according to this line of reasoning, only when Qurᵓān 60:10 was revealed.[48] As to what happened when Abū al-ᶜĀṣ finally embraced Islam, there are again two traditions: according to one, which makes the marriage compatible with what became the established law, the Prophet returned Zaynab to her husband by means of a new marriage and hence a new dowry. According to the other and more frequently quoted version, he returned her on the basis of the original marriage contract. The latter tradition evidently implies that the Prophet considered his daughter's marriage to the polytheist to have remained in force. Since this implication stands in

[45] Ibn al-Athīr, *Usd al-ghāba*, vol. 5, p. 467, ll. 24–27.
[46] Ibn Ḥazm, *Muḥallā*, vol. 7, p. 368, ll. 4–6; for a similar argument, see Ibn ᶜAbd al-Barr al-Namarī, *Tamhīd*, vol. 12, pp. 20–21. According to the traditional chronology, Qurᵓān 60:10 was revealed after the Ḥudaybiyya treaty of 6 A.H. / 628 A.D; see below, section V.
[47] See above, at note 16 to the present chapter.
[48] Bayhaqī, *Sunan*, vol. 7, p. 188, ll. 1–5.

glaring contradiction to what became the well settled rule, some scholars, such as Ibn ᶜAbd al-Barr al-Namarī, unequivocally reject the tradition or explain it away.[49]

Diverse views have been expressed on the question whether Islam should be offered to the husband after his wife embraced Islam. Mālik b. Anas thought that this should not be done;[50] it seems that according to his view, the husband must convert on his own initiative if he wants his marriage to be restored. According to a report in al-Sarakhsī's *al-Mabsūṭ*, al-Shāfiᶜī also supported this position. He maintained that Islam should not be offered to the husband because such an offer would be contrary to the obligation of the Muslims not to coerce *dhimmī*s into Islam (*wa lā yuᶜraḍu al-islām ᶜalā al-ākhar wa 'stadalla fī dhālika fa-qāla: qad ḍaminnā bi-ᶜaqd al-dhimma an lā nataᶜarraḍa lahum fī al-ijbār ᶜalā al-islām*). Linguistically speaking, this is a rather unwarranted intepretation of *yuᶜraḍu ᶜalayhi al-islām*; al-Sarakhsī does not accept it and thinks that conversion (and the resulting preservation of his marriage) should, indeed, be offered to the husband.[51] In support of this stance, he quotes a number of relevant precedents from the period of the *rāshidūn*, explains that the offer of conversion to Islam is not to be made in a coercive manner (*ᶜarḍ al-islām ᶜalā al-kāfir minhumā lā bi-ṭarīq al-ijbār ᶜalayhi*) and that the failure to accept such an offer by the unconverted spouse is indispensable for the dissolution of the marriage.[52]

III

Marriage of a Muslim woman to a non-Muslim man can also result from the man's apostasy. Though the early jurists differ on some details concerning the ensuing situation, they all agree that the marriage of an apostate to a Muslim woman cannot be allowed to stand.[53] Some provide legal substantiation for this principle. Since

[49] The traditions concerning Zaynab and their implications for the development of marriage laws in early Islam need further scrutiny. See Wāqidī, *Kitāb al-maghāzī*, vol. 1, pp. 130–131; Ibn Saᶜd, *Kitāb al-ṭabaqāt al-kabīr*, ed. Sachau, vol. 8, pp. 20–24; Ibn Ḥabīb, *Kitāb al-muḥabbar*, p. 53; Ṭabarī, *Ta'rīkh al-rusul wa al-mulūk*, series I, pp. 1346–1351; Ibn al-Athīr, *Usd al-ghāba*, vol. 5, pp. 236–238, especially p. 237, ll. 6–9; ᶜAsqalānī, *Iṣāba*, vol. 7, pp. 665–666 (no. 11217); Ṣanᶜānī, *Muṣannaf*, vol. 7, p. 168 (nos. 12643–12644), pp. 171–172 (nos. 12648–12649); Bayhaqī, *al-Sunan al-kubrā*, vol. 7, pp. 185–188; Ibn ᶜAbd al-Barr al-Namarī, *Tamhīd*, vol. 12, pp. 23–25; Māwardī, *al-Ḥāwī al-kabīr*, vol. 9, p. 259 infra; Khallāl, *Ahl al-milal*, pp. 500 (no. 1242); pp. 504–505 (no. 1264); Ibn Qayyim al-Jawziyya, *Aḥkām ahl al-dhimma*, pp. 323–338; see also "Zainab bint Muḥammad", EI[1], s.v. (V. Vacca), though the article is too brief to be relevant for the issue at hand.

[50] Saḥnūn, *Mudawwana*, vol. 2, p. 303, ll. 14–15.

[51] Sarakhsī, *Mabsūṭ*, vol. 5, p. 45, ll. 18–23; Ibn ᶜAbd al-Barr al-Namarī, *Tamhīd*, vol. 12, p. 28, ll. 4–8, 14–15.

[52] Sarakhsī, *Mabsūṭ*, vol. 5, pp. 46, l. 2 – 47, l. 14.

[53] The dissolution of an apostate's marriage is still an issue when Muslims are declared apostates for one reason or another. The last famous case of this kind is that of Professor Naṣr Ḥāmid Abū Zayd. For details, see "The case of Abu Zaid", *Index on censorship* 25 iv (1996), pp. 30–39; C. Hirschkind, "Heresy and hermeneutics: the case of Naṣr Ḥāmid Abū Zayd", *American Journal of Islamic Social Sciences* 12 (1995), pp. 465–477. For the case of Ḥusayn ᶜAlī Qanbar, a Kuwaytī Shīᶜī who in 1994 abandoned Islam for the Evangelical Church and was consequently separated from his wife, see Anh Nga Longva, "Apostasy and the liberal predicament", in *ISIM Newsletter* 8 (September 2001), p. 14.

the apostate committed a capital crime, he is, legally speaking, "lifeless" (*ka-annahu lā ḥayāta lahu ḥukman*).[54] Marriage is designed for the preservation of the human species; it is therefore not lawful for someone who is liable to the death penalty and whose execution is postponed only in order to enable him to reflect on what he had done and to repent. Marriage would distract his attention from the only purpose for which he is (still) alive.[55]

If the husband apostatizes after consummation, the marriage is annulled and the woman is entitled to retain the whole dowry. If he reneges before consummation, she is entitled to half the dowry.[56] There is some discussion of the question as to when exactly the separation of the spouses comes into effect. Abū Ḥanīfa thought that the marriage is annulled at once; it is immaterial whether the husband's apostasy took place before consummation or after it.[57] Al-Sarakhsī supports this stance because of the basic incompatibility of marriage with the apostate's status.[58] On the other hand, Ibn Abī Laylā and al-Shāfiᶜī maintained that the annulment of the consummated marriage comes into effect only at the end of the *ᶜidda* period, provided that the husband does not repent and revert to Islam by then.[59] Ibn Ḥanbal was hesitant when he faced this question. When Muhannā[60] asked him about a Muslim who reneges on Islam and goes to *dār al-ḥarb*, Ibn Ḥanbal said that the apostate's property is to be sequestered (*yūqafu māluhu*)[61] until it becomes clear whether he will return to Islam or not. When Muhannā asked further whether the

[54] The same attitude toward the apostate can be found in Jewish tradition. See Menahem Kister, "Leave the dead to bury their own dead", in James L. Kugel, *Studies in ancient Midrash*, Boston: Harvard University Press, 2001, p. 55, note 44. For the Jewish custom of mourning an apostate as if he had died, see A. Grossman, *Ḥakhmey Ashkenaz ha-rishonim: qoroteyhem, darkam be-hanhagat ha-tsibbur, yetsiratam ha-ruḥanit.* ("The early sages of Ashkenaz: their lives, leadership and works (900–1096)"), Jerusalem: The Magnes Press, 1988, p. 112. For a general survey of Jewish attitudes to the apostate (*meshummad*), see Jacob Katz, "Af ᶜal pi she ḥaṭa, Yisrael hu" ("Though he sinned, he is Israel"), in idem, *Halakha and Kabbalah: studies in the history of Jewish religion, its various faces and social relevance.* Jerusalem: The Magnes Press, 1984, pp. 255–269. I am grateful to my colleague Professor A. Grossman for the last two references. See also above, Introduction, at notes 16 and 17; and Morony, "Madjūs", *EI*², vol. 5, p. 1111a for the Zoroastrians considering the apostates as legally dead.

[55] Sarakhsī, *Mabsūṭ*, vol. 5, p. 48, l. 21 – p. 49, l. 3, and cf. vol. 10, p. 100, ll. 23–25.

[56] Qudūrī, *Mukhtaṣar*, pp. 150 infra – 151; Sarakhsī, *Mabsūṭ*, vol. 5, p. 49, ll. 16–17 (instead of full dowry Sarakhsī mentions maintenance during the *ᶜidda* period); Shāfiᶜī, *Kitāb al-umm*, vol. 6, p. 224, l. 15; Māwardī, *al-Ḥawī al-kabīr*, vol. 9, p. 295; Khiraqī, *Mukhtaṣar*, p. 142 (without mentioning the payment of full dowry in case of the husband's apostasy after consummation).

[57] Māwardī, *al-Ḥawī al-kabīr*, vol. 9, p. 295, ll. 20–23.

[58] Sarakhsī, *Mabsūṭ*, vol. 5, p. 49, ll. 12–13.

[59] Sarakhsī, *Mabsūṭ*, vol. 5, p. 49, ll. 10–12; Shāfiᶜī, *al-Umm*, vol. 6, p. 223, l. 21–25; Māwardī, *al-Ḥawī al-kabīr*, vol. 9, pp. 295 infra – 296, l. 5.

[60] Muhannā b. Yaḥyā al-Shāmī al-Sulamī was a close and life-long associate of Aḥmad b. Ḥanbal. A few biographical details as well as extensive material related by Muhannā from Aḥmad b. Ḥanbal can be found in Ibn Abī Yaᶜlā, *Ṭabaqāt al-Ḥanābila*, vol. 2, pp. 345–381 (no. 496).

[61] Shāfiᶜī (*Kitāb al-umm*, vol. 6, p. 225) has a detailed account of this practice. The apostate's property, apart from his female slaves, is placed under the control of a trustworthy male administrator (*ᶜadl*). The female slaves are placed under the control of a trustworthy female administrator (*ᶜadla*). If the apostate returns to Islam, the control of the property is restored to him. If he dies as an apostate or is executed for his transgression, the property is treated as spoils: one fifth goes to the *aṣḥāb al-khums*, while the rest becomes the property of the Muslim community. The whole issue deserves separate treatment.

apostate's wife should also keep herself for him (and refuse to marry any one else) because "she resembles his property" (*a-laysa 'mraʾatuhu mithla mālihi yanbaghī lahā an taḥbisa nafsahā ʿalayhi*), he refused to answer directly. Muhannā gained the impression that Ibn Ḥanbal disliked the idea,[62] but according to another tradition Ibn Ḥanbal maintained that the marriage remained in force until the end of the *ʿidda* period.[63]

Ibn Ḥanbal also held that even if the man's apostasy was a result of his falling into captivity – and hence presumably occurred under duress – the rules are still the same: the marriage can be restored only if the husband returns, repents and becomes again a Muslim within the *ʿidda*.[64] During his apostasy, he may not have conjugal relations with his Muslim wife; but if he repents and returns to Islam, he can renew his marriage on the basis of the original contract. Ibn Ḥanbal's view has not been unanimously accepted. According to al-Khallāl, it is well settled (*istaqarra amruhum*) that a marriage in which a spouse reneged on Islam can be restored only by a new marriage contract, and, presumably, a new dowry.[65]

It is noteworthy that an apostate's marriage is annulled even if his wife is Jewish or Christian.[66]

IV

We have seen in section II that in the earliest period of Islam there was a current of opinion willing to countenance the preservation of a Muslim woman's marriage to an unbeliever. This possibility was not destined to last and it was excluded from the law as established in the major compendia. Eventually, few legal issues in Islam came to be addressed with such unanimity of opinion as the prohibition imposed on giving a Muslim woman in marriage to an infidel. An interfaith marriage in the Islamic context is therefore a marriage between a Muslim man and a scriptuary woman. This is a general principle of Muslim law of personal status and it now seems appropriate to expound and interpret the reasons underlying it in the sources of classical Islam.

The rule according to which Muslims may take non-Muslim women in matrimony (but a Muslim woman cannot be married outside her faith) is intimately related to the idea that Islam is exalted above other religions and that men are the superior and dominant part of the household. The idea of Islamic superiority is repeatedly expressed in the Qurʾān. The prophetic tradition has also taken up the idea and used it in many different contexts, and we have already had the opportunity to highlight its importance.[67] That Muslims are entitled to take women of

[62] Khallāl, *Ahl al-milal*, vol. 2, p. 499 (no. 1238).
[63] Khallāl, *Ahl al-milal*, vol. 2, p. 500 (no. 1243).
[64] Khallāl, *Ahl al-milal*, pp. 501–502 (nos. 1248–1253), 503–504 (nos. 1260–1261).
[65] Khallāl, *Ahl al-milal*, pp. 506 (no. 1266), p. 508 (no. 1272).
[66] Sarakhsī, *Mabsūṭ*, vol. 5, p. 49, l. 6; cf. Shāfiʿī, *al-Umm*, vol. 6, p. 224, ll. 16–17;
[67] See above, Chapter One, section IV.

others while others are not entitled to wed Muslim women is seen as a reflection of Islamic exaltedness.[68] The assertion according to which "Islam is exalted and nothing is exalted above it" (*al-islām yaᶜlū wa lā yuᶜlā ᶜalayhi*) expresses the principle according to which Muslims are allowed to marry *kitābī* women, but no unbeliever is accorded the privilege of having a Muslim wife.[69] Placing a non-Muslim woman in a Muslim's conjugal bed is seen as honor for Islam (... *wa fī 'stifrāshihā ᶜizzatun li-'l-islām*),[70] while the reverse situation is deemed demeaning to it.[71] Perhaps the most striking expression of this idea can be found in a tradition related on the authority of Ibn ᶜAbbās:

> God sent Muḥammad with the truth to make it prevail over all religion(s). Our religion is the best of religions and our faith stands above (all other) faiths. Our men are above their women, but their men are not to be above our women (*inna Allāh ... baᶜatha Muḥammadan ... bi-'l-ḥaqq li-yuẓhirahu ᶜalā al-dīn kullihi fa-dīnunā khayr al-adyān wa millatunā fawqa al-milal wa rijālunā fawqa nisāʾihim wa lā yakūnu rijāluhum fawqa nisāʾinā*).[72]

68 See Ṣanᶜānī, *Muṣannaf*, vol. 7, p. 174 (no. 12656); p. 176 (no. 12665): p. 179 (no. 12677–12678): *nisāʾ ahl al-kitāb lanā ḥillun wa nisāʾunā ᶜalayhim ḥarām*; *Sharḥ al-Zarkashī ᶜalā Mukhtaṣar al-Khiraqī*, vol. 6, p. 257, note 1 infra; Zaylaᶜī, *Naṣb al-rāya*, vol. 3, p. 213.

69 For the *ḥadīth* itself, see Bukhārī, *Ṣaḥīḥ*, *Kitāb al-Janāʾiz*, 80. For the use of this *ḥadīth* to justify the laws of interfaith marriages in Islam, see Sarakhsī, *al-Mabsūṭ*, vol. 5, p. 45, ll. 3–4; Ṭaḥāwī, *Sharḥ maᶜānī al-āthār*, vol. 3, p. 257 (no. 5227): *yufarraqu baynahumā; al-islām yaᶜlū wa lā yuᶜlā ᶜalayhi;* Khallāl, *Ahl al-milal*, p. 269 (no. 540); Ibn Taymiyya, *Majmūᶜ fatāwā*, vol. 32, pp. 184–185; Ibn Ḥazm, *Muḥallā*, vol. 7, p. 397, ll. 2–3.

70 Ibn al-ᶜArabī al-Mālikī, *Kitāb al-qabas*, vol. 2, p. 711. But see below, section VII, where another Mālikī scholar, Ibn ᶜAbd al-Barr al-Namarī (d. 463 A.H. / 1070 A.D.), articulates a very different perception of this issue.

71 Qurṭubī, *al-Jāmiᶜ li-aḥkām al-Qurʾān*, vol. 3, p. 67: *ajmaᶜat al-umma ᶜalā anna al-mushrik lā yaṭaʾu al-muʾmina bi-wajhin li-mā fī dhālika min al-ghaḍāḍa ᶜalā al-islām.* Qurṭubī's observation is quoted verbatim by the nineteenth-century Indian author, Ṣiddīq Ḥasan Khān, *Ḥusn al-uswa*, p. 23.

72 Bayhaqī, *Sunan*, vol. 7, p. 172, ll. 26–31. See also Ṣanᶜānī, *Muṣannaf*, vol. 7, p. 174 (no. 12654): *lā yaᶜlū al-naṣrāniyyu al-muslima*, and Ibn ᶜAbd al-Barr al-Namarī, *al-Tamhīd*, vol. 12, p. 22: *rawā Saᶜīd b. Jubayr wa ᶜIkrima ᶜan Ibn ᶜAbbās: lā yaᶜlū muslimatan mushrikun fa-inna al-islām yaẓharu wa lā yuẓharu ᶜalayhi.*

Explanations of modern Muslim authors are a far cry from the classical point of view. Permission to wed a *kitābī* woman reflects, in their view, Islamic tolerance: it is evident that a religion which allows its men to wed women of other faiths does not harbor any enmity to these faiths. When asked why, on the other hand, Muslim women are forbidden to marry non-Muslim men, the answer is that this would create a wholly different situation. Muslims believe in the prophethood of Moses and Jesus and are commanded not to impose their religion by force. They are therefore unlikely to embarrass or inconvenience their non-Muslim wives because of their religion. Conversely, a Muslim wife wedded to a *kitābī* husband (who does not believe in the prophethood of Muḥammad and is not prohibited from spreading his religion by force) would not be able to stand in his way; she and her children would be in danger of changing their religion. See ᶜAbd al-Raḥmān al-Jazīrī, *al-Fiqh ᶜalā al-madhāhib al-arbaᶜa*, Cairo, n.d., fifth edition, vol. 4, pp. 76–77); Ahmed Shukri, *Muhammedan law of marriage and divorce*, New York: Columbia University Press, 1917, p. 30; A. T. Khoury, *Der Koran. Arabisch–Deutsch. Übersetzung und wissenschaftlicher Komentar*, Gütersloh: Gütersloher Verlagshaus Gerd Mohn, 1992, vol. 3, pp. 61–68; al-Ḥūfī, *Samāḥat al-islām*, pp. 78–79. See also Muḥammad Asad, *The road to Mecca*, New York, 1954, pp. 200–201, where an Egyptian *ᶜumda* is quoted as offering the same explanation of the asymmetrical nature of the law concerning interfaith marriages in Islam. Cf. Ghassan Ascha, *Mariage, polygamie et répudiation en Islam. Justifications des auteurs musulmans contemporains.* Paris and Montréal: L'Harmattan, 1998, pp. 67–83; Manfred J. Backhausen and Inayat K. Gill, *Die Opfer sind schuld. Machtmissbrauch in Pakistan. Eine Dokumentation unter Mitarbeit von Shaikh Raheal Ahmad.* n.p.: Akropolis Verlag, 1994, pp. 115–116.

Rules concerning marriages between members of non-Muslim religions are also influenced by a perception of hierarchical relationship between these religions. As we have seen above,[73] this descending hierarchy consists of Christianity, Judaism, Zoroastrianism and polytheism. Ibn Ḥanbal maintained that the ruler or the imām should dissolve the marriage between a Zoroastrian man and a Christian woman, saying in a rather cryptic manner that such a union is tantamount to "corruption" (*li-anna hādhā fī fasād*).[74] Ibn Qayyim al-Jawziyya is much more lucid in the explanation of this rule. Faithful to the idea that a husband must be of equal or higher religion than his wife, he maintains that a Zoroastrian or a polytheist is not allowed to wed a Christian woman because her religion is higher than his, but, according to the same principle, a Christian may marry a Zoroastrian woman. And if a Zoroastrian acquires a Christian slave-girl, she must be separated from him: her religion is "higher" and she must not be placed in a position of subordination to an adherent of a "lower" religion (*majūsī malaka amatan naṣrāniyyatan yuḥālu baynahumā innamā dhālika li-anna dīnahā aʿlā min dīnihi*).[75]

The principle that the husband must be of higher standing than his wife is applied also when the difference between the spouses is of ethnic rather than religious nature. In the context of anti-Shuʿūbī controversy, Salmān al-Fārisī is made to say: "O Arabs, we shall give you precedence (*nufaḍḍilukum*) because the Prophet ... gave you precedence: we shall not wed your women and shall not lead you in prayer" (... *lā nankiḥu nisāʾakum wa lā naʾummukum fī al-ṣalāt*).[76] Leading people in prayer, which is clearly a reflection of the leader's superiority, is placed on a par with marrying women belonging to a different (and subordinate) social group.

The hierarchical relationship between the parents' respective religions also determines the religion of children, though the consequences of this principle are not always agreed upon. According to most views, the children follow the parent whose religion is "better" (*yatbaʿu khayra abawayhi dīnan*). Allah placed Islam above all other religions and the superior deserves a ruling in his favor (... *li-anna Allāh aʿlā al-islām ʿalā al-adyān wa al-aʿlā awlā an yakūna al-ḥukmu lahu*).[77] A

[73] See Chapter One, at the end of section V.

[74] Khallāl, *Ahl al-milal*, vol. 2, p. 475 (nos. 1161–1162). The expression quoted above is not quite clear and the text may be corrupt.

[75] Ibn Qayyim al-Jawziyya, *Aḥkām ahl al-dhimma*, pp. 394, 396. On p. 396 we have also a different view on a *dhimmī*'s alliance with a Zoroastrian or polytheist woman: since a Muslim is not allowed to enter in such matrimony, the *dhimmī* is not allowed to do it either. Cf. Ṣanʿānī, *Muṣannaf*, vol. 6, p. 80–81 (nos. 10067–10069); vol. 7, pp. 182–183 (nos. 12697–12698).

[76] Ibn Taymiyya, *Iqtidāʾ al-ṣirāṭ*, vol. 1, pp. 397–398. Another version reads: "O Arabs, you are superior to us in two [respects]: we shall not lead you in prayer and we shall not wed your women" (*faḍaltumūnā yā maʿāshir al-ʿarab bi-'thnatayni: lā naʾummukum fī al-ṣalāt wa lā nankiḥu nisāʾakum*). See also Bayhaqī, *Sunan*, vol. 7, p. 134, ll. 13–14 and Ṭaḥāwī, *Mukhtaṣar ikhtilāf al-ʿulamāʾ*, vol. 2, p. 253 (no. 717) where the text is corrupt. For further references and a discussion of this tradition in a different context, see Bashear, *Arabs and others*, p. 37.

[77] Shaybānī, *Sharḥ Kitāb al-siyar al-kabīr*, vol. 5, p. 2268 (no. 4523); *Mukhtaṣar al-Muzanī ʿalā al-Umm*, in Shāfiʿī, *Kitāb al-umm*, vol. 9, p. 334, lines 18–19; see also ibid., vol. 4, p. 381, ll. 8–12.

child of a *kitābī* and a non-*kitābī* is a *kitābī* according to al-Sarakhsī.[78] In a family in which one parent is Muslim, the children are Muslim. Therefore, if someone kills a child after one of his parents embraced Islam, he is liable for retaliation because the child is deemed Muslim.[79] If a *kitābī* man marries a Zoroastrian woman, the child is *kitābī*; if a Zoroastrian man weds a *kitābī* woman (in contravention of the law mentioned above), the child is Zoroastrian according to Mālik b. Anas,[80] but *kitābī* according to Ibn Qayyim al-Jawziyya. In a marriage between a Jew and a Christian, the child is Christian regardless of the question whether Christianity is the religion of the father or of the mother.[81] Kāsānī adduces an additional reason for considering children of a mixed marriage as belonging to the "higher" religion: that religion is closer to Islam and there are better chances that the child in question will eventually become a Muslim.[82]

The Mālikī scholar Ashhab b. ᶜAbd al-ᶜAzīz (d. 204 A.H. / 819 A.D.)[83] gives a different ruling in the case of a Christian woman who embraced Islam while pregnant by her Christian husband. In this case, "the child follows his father and becomes a Christian because of the Christianity of his father (*yatbaᶜu abāhu wa yakūnu naṣrāniyyan li-naṣrāniyyati abīhi*).[84] Mālik b. Anas gave an identical ruling, but specified that the children will be left in the custody of their mother as long as they are minors.[85] According to a view quoted by al-Shāfiᶜī, children born as polytheists, whose fathers subsequently embraced Islam, will retain their religion until they grow up and make a decision concerning their religious affiliation. Al-Shāfiᶜī unequivocally rejects this view without identifying its supporters.[86] We have seen above, however, that Mālik b. Anas seems to have been among them.[87]

V

At the beginning of the present chapter we have briefly mentioned the basic principles of Muslim law on interfaith marriages. We shall now discuss this law in greater detail.

Qurʾān 2:221 prohibits marriages with polytheistic women in an unequivocal manner. Qurʾān 60:10 is traditionally interpreted in a similar sense. It is understood

[78] Sarakhsī, *Mabsūṭ*, vol. 5, p. 44, l. 6; cf. Qudūrī, *Mukhtaṣar*, p. 151, 4–6.

[79] Shāfiᶜī, *Kitāb al-umm*, vol. 6, p. 58, ll. 1–3. [80] Saḥnūn, *Mudawwana*, vol. 2, p. 307, ll. 18–20.

[81] Khallāl, *Ahl al-milal*, p. 92 (no. 64). Ibn Qayyim al-Jawziyya, *Aḥkām ahl al-dhimma*, p. 397; cf. Ibn Ḥazm, *Muḥallā*, vol. 7, p. 377 infra.

[82] Kāsānī, *Badāʾiᶜ al-ṣanāʾiᶜ*, vol. 7, pp. 104 lines 4–26; Shāfiᶜī, *Kitāb al-umm*, vol. 6, p. 58, ll. 1–2. The same view is attributed to both Shāfiᶜī and Aḥmad b. Ḥanbal in al-Mundhirī, *Kitāb al-ishrāf ᶜalā madhāhib ahl al-ᶜilm*, Ms. Dār al-kutub, Fiqh Shāfiᶜī 20, fol. 154 verso. I am grateful to Dr. M. Muranyi for this reference.

[83] See *EI*², vol. 6, col. 279a and Muranyi, *Beiträge ...*, index.

[84] *Majālis Ashhab b. ᶜAbd al-ᶜAzīz, al-juzʾ al-awwal*, p. 11, Qayrawān manuscript. The passage continues with the view of Ibn Wahb in whose view the child in the case would be Muslim. I am grateful to Dr. M. Muranyi for this reference.

[85] Saḥnūn, *Mudawwana*, vol. 2, pp. 307, ll. 21 – 308, l. 3.

[86] Shāfiᶜī, *Kitāb al-umm*, vol. 4, p. 381, ll. 12–16.

[87] See above, Chapter Three, section VIII.

to address a stipulation of the Ḥudaybiyya accord according to which the Muslims were obliged to return to the unbelievers any Meccan who migrated to Medina in order to join the Muslim community.[88] The verse is said to have revoked this agreement as far as women converts were concerned.[89] Its declared intention was to preclude a situation in which a Muslim woman would be forced to maintain, or resume, a marital relationship with a polytheist husband. Furthermore, it instructed the Muslims to sever marital relationships with any idolatrous women whom they may have left in Mecca when they embraced Islam and migrated to Medina. It is in response to this verse that ᶜUmar b. al-Khaṭṭāb is said to have divorced two wives whom he had in Mecca.[90] Prohibition of matrimony with idolaters became an important and undisputed element in the Muslim laws of personal status. The Meccan traditionist ᶜAṭāʾ b. Abī Rabāḥ said that there is nothing wrong with wedding scriptuary women, but that "Muslims do not wed Bedouin women" (*lā baʾsa bi-nikāḥi nisāʾi ahli 'l-kitāb wa lā yankiḥu 'l-muslimūn nisāʾa 'l-ᶜarab*).[91] Al-Shāfiᶜī's formulation, the like of which can easily be found in other sources, reads: "… the ruling concerning idolaters is: a Muslim is not to wed a woman of theirs, nor is one of their men to wed a Muslim woman" (… *al-ḥukm fī ahl al-awthān an lā yankiḥa muslimun minhum imraʾatan kamā lā yankiḥu rajulun minhum muslimatan*).[92] Al-Shāfiᶜī maintains that this rule applies also to polytheist or Zoroastrian women who have fallen into captivity; according to him, none of the Prophet's companions had sexual relations with captured Bedouin women until they embraced Islam.[93] A man who acquired a slave-girl who is an idolater or Zoroastrian may not engage in sexual relations with her until she performs ablution, performs a Muslim prayer, and has her menses once while in his house.[94] Marital relationships with idolaters of either sex are forbidden even if they result from the conversion to Islam of one partner in an idolatrous – or Zoroastrian – marriage. If one spouse in a marriage between idolaters, Zoroastrians or – in al-Shāfiᶜī's view alone – Jews or Christians who are ethnically not related to Banū Isrāʾīl embraces Islam and the other does not follow suit within the *ᶜidda*, the marriage is nullified.[95] We have also seen[96] that according to the prevalent view of

88 See Ṭabarī, *Taʾrīkh al-rusul wa al-mulūk*, series I, vol. 3, p. 1546.

89 See Wāqidī, *Kitāb al-maghāzī*, vol. 2, p. 631: *qāla rasūl Allāh … : inna Allāh naqaḍa al-ᶜahd fī al-nisāʾ wa anzala Allāh fīhinna (Sūrat) al-Mumtaḥana.*

90 Ṭabarī, *Jāmiᶜ al-bayān*, vol. 28, pp. 65–73; Bayhaqī, *al-Sunan al-kubrā*, vol. 7, p. 171, ll. 3–14; Ibn ᶜAbd al-Barr al-Namarī, *Tamhīd*, vol. 12, p. 27, ll. 3–9.

91 Ṣanᶜānī, *Muṣannaf*, vol. 7, p. 176 (no. 12666). "Bedouin" (*al-ᶜarab*, or *al-aᶜrāb*), in the parlance of the early sources, means those Arabs who have not embraced Islam. But see below, at notes 99 and 100 for traditions representing an opposite trend.

92 Shāfiᶜī, *Kitāb al-umm*, vol. 5, p. 234, ll. 11–12; Bayhaqī, *al-Sunan al-kubrā*, vol. 7, p. 171, ll. 15–22; Ibn Qudāma, *al-Mughnī*, vol. 6, p. 592.

93 Shāfiᶜī, *Kitāb al-umm*, vol. 5, p. 244, ll. 3–7; Ibn Ḥazm, *Muḥallā*, vol. 9, p. 545, ll. 17–23.

94 Ṣanᶜānī, *Muṣannaf*, vol. 7, p. 195–197 (nos. 12751–12757).

95 Shāfiᶜī, *Kitāb al-umm*, vol. 5, p. 72, ll. 1–15; pp. 73, ll. 22 – 74, l. 2; p. 81, ll. 10 – 16 and passim in *Kitāb al-nikāḥ*; Māwardī, *al-Ḥāwī al-kabīr*, vol. 9, p. 303 infra. *Pace* Shatzmiller, "Marriage, family and the faith …", p. 243 who says that only the husband can save the marriage by converting within the *ᶜidda* period, while "a delayed conversion of the pagan wife … did not count."

96 Chapter Three, section VII.

the traditionists, a female polytheist must be converted to Islam, by coercive measures if necessary, before any sexual relationship with her can take place.

Female apostates fall into the same category as polytheists: Muslims are not allowed to marry them or to preserve the marriage if the apostate in question is a woman married to a Muslim. This is so even if the woman apostatized to Judaism or Christianity:[97] the fact that Muslims are allowed to marry Jewish or Christian women who are not apostates from Islam has no bearing on the case. According to Sufyān al-Thawrī, if a Muslim wife reneges on Islam, but repents within the *ᶜidda* period, the husband is entitled to restore the marriage by means of a new marriage contract and a new dowry.[98] This seems to mean that the marriage is deemed null and void immediately after the wife's apostasy. It is noteworthy that Sufyān al-Thawrī is willing to impose a considerable financial burden on the husband – who is clearly not to be blamed for what happened in this case – in order to highlight the enormity of the renegade wife's crime. The ruling of Ibn Ḥanbal is different: the husband is forbidden intimacy with his apostate wife, but if she repents before the *ᶜidda* has elapsed, the marriage is resumed without the necessity of a new contract or a new dowry.[99] Surprisingly enough, Sufyān al-Thawrī, Mālik b. Anas and Ibn Ḥanbal ruled that if the wife apostatized after the consummation of the marriage, she is entitled to her full dowry.[100] Dealing with such a case, al-Shāfiᶜī and al-Sarakhsī do not mention the dowry, but rule that the woman apostate is not entitled to maintenance during the *ᶜidda* period. If the apostasy occurrs before consummation, she is not entitled to dowry at all.[101]

All this notwithstanding, some traditions ascribe to the Prophet actions that appear to be incompatible with the opinion prevalent in later sources. Al-Shāfiᶜī himself, who indicated in a passage quoted above[102] that the Prophet's companions did not engage Arab captives sexually before they embraced Islam, says elsewhere that the Prophet only ruled that sexual relations are not permitted with captives who were pregnant when captured, and that one menstrual period must elapse before sexual relations with those who are not (*istibrāʾ*). Conversion to Islam is not mentioned here as a necessary condition for sexual relations.[103] In the opinion of Mujāhid, the captive girl should shave her pubic hair, trim her hair and pare her nails. Then she should perform ablution, wash her clothes, pronounce the *shahāda* and perform a Muslim prayer. But even if she refuses to do these things, her master is still allowed to have sexual relations with her once she has had one menstrual period in his house. And Saᶜīd b. al-Musayyab simply says that "there is nothing

97 Shāfiᶜī, *Kitāb al-umm*, vol. 6, p. 224, ll. 11–12.
98 Khallāl, *Ahl al-milal*, p. 504 (no. 1262).
99 Khallāl, *Ahl al-milal*, pp. 504 (no. 1263), p. 508 (no. 1272).
100 Khallāl, *Ahl al-milal*, p. 506 (no. 1267); Saḥnūn, *Mudawwana*, vol. 2, p. 235, ll. 14–18.
101 Shāfiᶜī, *al-Umm*, vol. 6, p. 224, ll. 10–12; Sarakhsī, *Mabsūṭ*, vol. 5, p. 49, ll. 17–18.
102 See above, notes 92, 93, to this chapter.
103 Shāfiᶜī, *Kitāb al-umm*, vol. 4, p. 384, ll. 12–14; vol. 5, p. 224, ll. 11–12. In vol. 4, p. 384, l. 13 there is an erroneous reading: the text should read: ... *fa-'llāʾī subīna wa 'stuʾmīna* ..., "the women who were captured and made into slave-girls ..." and not ... *fa-'llāʾī subīna wa 'stuʾminna* ..., "the women who were captured and given guarantee of safety ..." which is meaningless in the context of the passage.

wrong in a man having sexual relations with his Zoroastrian slave-girl" (*lā baʾsa an yaṭaʾa al-rajulu jāriyatahu al-majūsiyya*).[104]

The question of marrying polytheistic women or of using them as concubines is raised in connection with several battles of the Prophet. Responding to questions about the battle against the tribe of Hawāzin, Aḥmad b. Ḥanbal tentatively suggests that the female captives with whom Muslims had sexual relations may have embraced Islam.[105] Describing the aftermath of the battle against Banū al-Muṣṭaliq, Ibn Qayyim al-Jawziyya devotes some attention to the case of Juwayriya bint al-Ḥārith who was taken prisoner. The Prophet decided to manumit her and married her (*qaḍā rasūl Allāh kitābatahā wa tazawwajahā*). The tradition is not of one mind concerning Juwayriya's religion when she married the Prophet. According to Wāqidī, Juwayriya declared herself a Muslim and pronounced the *shahāda* at the time of her manumission and marriage.[106] Ibn Qayyim al-Jawziyya observes, on the other hand, that:

> they (i.e., the Prophet's companions) did not make sexual relations with Arab captives contingent on their conversion; rather they had sexual relations with them after one menstrual period. God allowed them to do this and did not make it conditional on conversion (*wa lam yakūnū yatawaqqafūna fī waṭʾi sabāyā al-ʿarab ʿalā al-islām bal kānū yaṭaʾūnahunna baʿda al-istibrāʾ wa abāḥa Allāh lahum dhālika wa lam yashtariṭ al-islām*).

Summing up, Ibn Qayyim al-Jawziyya says that there is not a single tradition which makes sexual relations with female captives contingent on their conversion.[107]

Let us now return to Qurʾān 2:221. Despite the view of Ibn Qayyim al-Jawziyya mentioned above, the verse sounds like a general and unequivocal prohibition on marrying polytheist women, though the preference given in it to believing slave-girls may create the impression that the prohibition is directed primarily against wedding polytheistic slave-girls. Nevertheless, the commentators do not raise this latter exegetical possibility: they maintain that the verse was intended to criticize those Muslims who preferred to marry highly placed polytheist women rather than lowly Muslim slave-girls. The commentators also discuss the meaning of the term *mushrikāt*. Some of them maintain that the term relates only to Arab polytheists.

[104] Ṣanʿānī, *Muṣannaf*, vol. 7, p. 197 (nos. 12758, 12760).

[105] Khallāl, *Ahl al-milal*, p. 246 (no. 477).

[106] Wāqidī, *Maghāzī*, vol. 1, pp. 408, 411.

[107] Ibn Qayyim al-Jawziyya, *Zād al-maʿād*, vol. 3, p. 113–114, 258. Ibn Qayyim al-Jawziyya's account of the episode indicates that Juwayriya did not embrace Islam before her marriage to the Prophet. Other sources mentioning her marriage to the Prophet also do not mention her conversion explicitly (see, e.g., Bayhaqī, *al-Sunan al-kubrā*, vol. 7, p. 72, ll. 13–14; Zarkashī, *Sharḥ* ..., vol. 6, p. 467), but Ibn Saʿd reports that when Juwayriya died in the year 50 or 56 A.H. (670 or 675 A.D.), Marwān b. al-Ḥakam, then the governor of Medina, prayed at her funeral; this would indicate that she died as a Muslim. See Ibn Saʿd, *Ṭabaqāt*, ed. Sachau, vol. 8, p. 85. There is no reference to the conversion of the female captives of Banū al-Muṣṭaliq prior to their use as concubines in Ibn Saʿd, *Ṭabaqāt*, vol. 2, part 1, p. 46, in Saḥnūn, *Mudawwana*, vol. 2, p. 305, ll. 20–23; cf. ibid., vol. 2, p. 314, ll. 3–5, and in Wāqidī, *Kitāb al-maghāzī*, vol. 1, p. 411, l. 18. Ibn al-Athīr (*Usd al-ghāba*, vol. 5, pp. 419–421) also does not say anything about Juwayriya's conversion, though he relates that the Prophet saw her "in her mosque" for a substantial part of a day (p. 421, ll. 1–3).

If this interpretation is correct, the verse can be considered as legally valid: since a prohibition on marriage to polytheist women later became part of the *sharīʿa*, this view of the verse interprets it in a way consistent with the *sharīʿa* in its developed form. This is, however, not the only interpretation of the term. As we have seen above,[108] it frequently happens that all non-Muslims are included in the category of polytheists. Commentators who support this interpretation of *mushrikāt* must consider Qurʾān 2:221 as abrogated by Qurʾān 5:5, which allowed Muslim males to marry "virtuous" scriptuary women.[109] The meaning of this last term, *muḥṣanāt* in the original, is another problem of interpretation: are the *muḥṣanāt* free Jewish or Christian women (in contradistinction to slave-girls), or are they women who can be described as chaste? Furthermore, does the verse apply to all scriptuaries, or, perhaps, is a specific ethnic affiliation essential for being included in this category?

We have discussed some of these issues in Chapter Two, and we can now concentrate on the question of interfaith marriage and disregard the general problem of classifying the unbelievers. Among the early traditionists, Qatāda b. Diʿāma, Saʿīd b. Jubayr, al-Ḥasan (al-Baṣrī), Ibrāhīm (al-Nakhaʿī) and (ʿĀmir) al-Shaʿbī are mentioned as understanding the *mushrikāt* in Qurʾān 2:221 as referring only to Arab polytheist women. Muqātil's commentary is also compatible with this understanding,[110] and it became indeed the prevalent interpretation of the verse.[111] A good case can be constructed in its favor: Qurʾānic usage, which clearly considers the People of the Book as a distinct category, seems to favor understanding *mushrikāt* as referring only to Arab polytheist women. But even without interpreting Qurʾān 2:221 in this restrictive way, the permissibility of wedding Jewish and Christian women would have gained the upper hand by virtue of Qurʾān 5:5 and of a prophetic *ḥadīth*, saying: "We marry scriptuary women, but they do not marry ours" (*natazawwaju nisāʾa ahl al-kitāb wa lā yatazawwajūna nisāʾanā*).[112]

Qurʾān 5:5 also had its share of interpretative difficulties, connected mainly with the precise meaning of *muḥṣanāt*.[113] According to one view, the *muḥṣanāt* mentioned in this verse are free scriptuary women, both chaste and promiscuous. This understanding of the verse would prohibit marriage with *kitābī* slave-girls.

[108] See Chapter Two, section III.

[109] See, for instance, Zuhrī, *al-Nāsikh wa al-mansūkh*, p. 21. Some commentators consider this *takhṣīṣ* rather than *naskh*, but their legal conclusion is still the same. See Ibn al-Jawzī, *al-Muṣaffā*, p. 19.

[110] Muqātil b. Sulaymān, *Tafsīr*, vol. 1, pp. 190–191; Khallāl, *Ahl al-milal*, pp. 245–246 (nos. 474–476); Jaṣṣāṣ, *Aḥkām al-Qurʾān* vol. 2, p. 398; Shāfiʿī, *Aḥkām al-Qurʾān*, vol. 1, pp. 186–189; Bayhaqī, *al-Sunan al-kubrā*, vol. 7, p. 171, ll. 17–35; Ibn Qudāma, *al-Mughnī*, vol. 6, p. 590.

[111] Naḥḥās, *al-Nāsikh wa al-mansūkh*, vol. 2, p. 5 (no. 195); Qurṭubī, *al-Jāmiʿ li-aḥkām al-Qurʾān*, vol. 3, p. 64.

[112] Ṭabarī, *Jāmiʿ al-bayān*, vol. 2, p. 378, ll. 15–16; Ṣanʿānī, *Muṣannaf*, vol. 6, pp. 78–79 (nos. 10056, 10058, 10061); vol 7, p. 174 (no. 12656); p. 176 (no. 12665): *nisāʾu ahl al-kitāb lanā ḥillun wa nisāʾunā ʿalayhim harām.* Numerous other traditions express the same idea. See also Māwardī, *al-Ḥāwī al-kabīr*, vol. 9, p. 255 infra; Ibn Ḥazm, *Muḥallā*, vol. 9, p. 543–548 (no. 1817).

[113] In his "The meaning of *iḥṣān*" (*Journal of Semitic Studies* 19 (1974), pp. 47–75), John Burton does not deal extensively with the meaning of *muḥṣanāt* in Qurʾān 5:5, but see his brief remark on pp. 61–62.

According to another view, chaste scriptuary women are intended, both free and slave. Muqātil opts for a harmonizing interpretation: in his view free and chaste *kitābī* women are intended in the verse.[114] The commentators define chastity as observance of ritual purity and abstaining from illicit sex (*iḥṣān al-yahūdiyya wa al-naṣrāniyya allā tazniya wa an taghtasila min al-janāba*).[115]

In this way, matrimony with free *kitābī* women became permissible according to all Sunnī schools of law. The Samaritans are usually also included in the *kitābī* category, while the inclusion of the Ṣābiʾa is disputed. Ibn Qudāma al-Maqdisī, who lived in Jerusalem and Damascus during the Crusades, mentions the Armenians and the Franks.[116] Consequently, a marriage between two Christians (or Jews) in which the husband embraced Islam was allowed to stand.[117]

The rules governing such an interfaith marriage are the same as those pertaining to marriages with Muslim women. Al-Shāfiʿī and Ibn Ḥanbal maintained that it is permissible for a Muslim husband to marry a *kitābī* woman even if he already has one or more Muslim wives. It is permissible for a Muslim to wed four *kitābī* women. It is essential that two Muslims witness the ceremony, and the woman is given away by a guardian (*walī*) who is her coreligionist. Except the wife herself, the guardian is the only person involved in the marriage who may be a non-Muslim; the permissibility of this seems unavoidable because a non-Muslim woman would not normally have a Muslim father or brother who could give her away. Impediments to marrying a *kitābī* woman are the same as those of a Muslim one. The rules of divorce are also the same. A Christian may also serve as a *muḥallil*. Everything must be done according to Islamic law: the rules of the woman's religion are not to be taken into account.[118]

A rarely mentioned view is attributed to Ibn ʿAbbās. He is said to have held that a Muslim may not wed a scriptuary woman if he already has a Muslim wife.[119] This view may have emerged because of concerns about possible quarrels between the Muslim wives and their *kitābī* counterparts, but the more important reason seems

114 Muqātil b. Sulaymān, *Tafsīr*, vol. 1, p. 455; Jaṣṣāṣ, *Aḥkām al-Qurʾān*, vol. 2, p. 397.

115 Ṭabarī, *Jāmiʿ al-bayān*, vol. 6, p. 105 infra.

116 Qudūrī, *Mukhtaṣar*, p. 145, infra; Ibn Qayyim al-Jawziyya, *Aḥkām ahl al-dhimma*, pp. 431–432; Ibn Qudāma, *al-Mughnī*, vol. 6, pp. 590 infra – 591. The inclusion of the Franks had little significance for the relationship between the Muslim population and the Crusaders, whose own laws forbad conjugal unions with Muslims. See James A. Brundage, "Marriage law in the Latin kingdom of Jerusalem", in B. Z. Kedar, H. E. Mayer and R. C. Small, eds., *Outremer. Studies in the history of the crusading kingdom of Jerusalem*, Jerusalem: Yad Izhaq Ben-Zvi Institute, 1982, pp. 262–263. I am indebted to Daniella Talmon-Heller for this reference. See also above, Chapter Two, at note 22.

117 Khallāl, *Ahl al-milal*, pp. 257–259 (nos. 509–514). In no. 514, Ibn Ḥanbal refers to the possibility that the woman would refuse in such a case to maintain the marriage. If this happens, the husband should, in Ibn Ḥanbal's view, "beat her over the head" (*yaḍribu raʾsahā*). See also Saḥnūn, *Mudawwana*, vol. 2, p. 301, ll. 2–3, 15–17; Qudūrī, *Mukhtaṣar*, p. 150, ll. 16–17; Bayhaqī, *al-Sunan al-kubrā*, vol. 7, p. 190, ll. 1–4; Māwardī, *al-Ḥāwī al-kabīr*, vol. 9, p. 258 infra.

118 Ṣanʿānī, *Muṣannaf*, vol. 6, p. 79–80 (nos. 10062–10066); vol. 7, p. 181 (no. 12690); Ibn Abī Shayba, *Muṣannaf*, vol. 4, p. 159; Ibn Ḥanbal, *Aḥkām al-nisāʾ*, pp. 25–26; Khallāl, *Ahl al-milal*, pp. 247–251 (nos. 479–491); Shāfiʿī, *Kitāb al-umm*, vol. 5, p. 11, ll. 7–13; Ibn Qayyim al-Jawziyya, *Aḥkām ahl al-dhimma*, pp. 433–434.

119 Ibn Abī Shayba, *Muṣannaf*, vol. 4, p. 149 infra. Because of considerations of a similar nature, some traditionists have ruled that a man is not to wed a slave-girl if he is already married to a free woman.

to be different: the general rule which stipulates that all wives, regardless of religion, are to be treated equally by their husband may be seen by some as contradicting the inherent superiority of Muslim women over the *kitābī* ones. Alternatively, this view may be a remnant of the trend which forbade marrying scriptuary women under any circumstances.[120]

Al-Shāfiᶜī allows interfaith marriages only with Jewish and Christian women ethnically related to the Banū Isrāᵓīl and does not allow it with Jewish and Christian women of Arab extraction. He explains this restriction by stating that the original religion of the Arabs was the *ḥanīfiyya* which degenerated into idolatry. Only later did these Arabs join the religion of the People of the Book; hence they were not among those who were originally given the Tawrāt and the Injīl and believed in it.[121] This is, according to Shāfiᶜī's close reading of the text, the reason why Qurᵓān 5:5 is not applicable to them.

Another restriction applies to a *kitābī* woman one of whose parents was not a *kitābī*, but rather an idolater, a Zoroastrian or an apostate. Such a woman is not eligible for marriage to a Muslim according to the Ḥanbalīs; al-Shāfiᶜī agrees with the Ḥanbalī ruling if the non-*kitābī* in this marriage is the father because in such a case "the woman is not pure *kitābiyya*" (*li-annahā ghayru kitābiyya khāliṣa*). If it is the mother, both views have been reported from him.[122]

VI

Important figures from the early Islamic period availed themselves of the possibility to seek matrimony outside the Muslim community: ᶜUthmān b. ᶜAffān and Ṭalḥa b. ᶜUbayd Allah married Christian women, while Ḥudhayfa b. al-Yamān married a Jewess.[123] Nevertheless, echoes of negative attitudes to this practice can be found in the literature of *ḥadīth* and *fiqh*. In a repeatedly quoted tradition, Jābir b. ᶜAbd Allah reports that Muslims who participated in the conquest of Iraq with Saᶜd b. Abī Waqqāṣ married Jewish and Christian women only because few Muslim women were available; when the Muslims returned from the military expedition, they divorced their non-Muslim wives. When Shāfiᶜī states that marriages with scriptuary women are allowed, he adds that he would prefer it if no

120 See below, at notes 128–133 to the present chapter. It is noteworthy that the tradition adopting this stance is also related on the authority of Ibn ᶜAbbās. The rules concerning the composition of a polygamous Muslim household and the relationship between the husband, the wives and the slave-girls deserve a separate study.

121 Shāfiᶜī, *Kitāb al-umm*, vol. 5, p. 10, ll. 10–14, p. 76, ll. 17–18. For this distinction in Shāfiᶜī's thinking, see above, Chapter Two, section II.

122 Shāfiᶜī, *Kitāb al-umm*, vol. 5, p. 85, ll. 7–8; Māwardī, *al-Ḥāwī al-kabīr*, vol. 9, p. 304, ll. 11–14; Ibn Qudāma, *al-Mughnī*, vol. 6, pp. 592–593.

123 Shāfiᶜī, *Kitāb al-umm*, vol. 4, p. 389, ll. 12–17; vol. 5, p. 11, ll. 7–13; Ṣanᶜānī, *Muṣannaf*, vol. 7, pp. 176–179; Bayhaqī, *al-Sunan al-kubrā*, vol. 7, p. 172, ll. 11–25; p. 173, ll. 1–11; Ibn Qudāma, *al-Mughnī*, vol. 6, p. 589 infra; Ibn Qayyim al-Jawziyya, *Aḥkām ahl al-dhimma*, p. 419; cf. Lecker, "Ḥudhayfa b. al-Yamān…", p. 151.

Muslim were to avail himself of this possibility.[124] Mālik b. Anas is reported to have disliked such marriages intensely and considered them as "burdensome and reprehensible" (*mustathqal madhmūm*).[125] He did not prohibit them, but disliked them because the *dhimmī* woman

> eats pork and drinks wine; he copulates with her and kisses her while (all) this is in her mouth; she bears him children, feeds them according to her religion, gives them forbidden food to eat and wine to drink (*qāla Mālik: akrahu nikāḥa nisā'i ahl al-dhimma al-yahūdiyya wa al-naṣrāniyya ... wa mā uḥarrimuhu wa dhālika annahā ta'kulu al-khinzīr wa tashrabu al-khamr wa yuḍājiʿuhā wa yuqabbiluhā wa dhālika fī fīhā wa talidu minhu awlādan fa-tughadhdhī waladahā ʿalā dīnihā wa tuṭʿimuhu al-ḥarām wa tasqīhi al-khamr*).[126]

Aḥmad b. Ḥanbal also expressed his disapproval of such marriages, though he admitted their permissibility.[127]

In the earliest period of Islam, there were also more categorical views on this issue. In a rarely quoted but highly interesting tradition transmitted by Ibn ʿAbbās, the Prophet himself prohibited marriage except with "believing emigrant women, and forbade women of all religions, except Islam" (*nahā rasūl Allāh ... ʿan aṣnāf al-nisā' illā mā kāna min al-mu'mināt al-muhājirāt wa ḥarrama kulla dhāti dīnin ghayri 'l-islām*).[128] When read in conjunction with Qur'ān 5:5, this tradition is quite remarkable. Following the idea expressed in it, ʿUmar b. al-Khaṭṭāb prevailed upon Ṭalḥa b. ʿUbayd Allah and Ḥudhayfa b. al-Yamān, who married a Jewish and a Christian woman respectively, to sever their relationship with them in a humiliating fashion, without formal divorce: divorce proceedings would be called for only if the marriage had been valid in the first place. In another version of the same tradition, which does assume the legality of wedding Jewish or Christian women, ʿUmar admits that the marriages of Ṭalḥa and Ḥudhayfa were not illegal, and demands their dissolution only for fear that the Muslims would forge relationships with *kitābī* whores (*lā azʿumu annahā ḥarām wa lākin akhāfu an taʿāṭaw al-mūmisāt minhunna*). The basis of ʿUmar's fear is not clear; there is no indication that the two women in question were engaged in prostitution.[129] The most

[124] Shāfiʿī, *Kitāb al-umm*, vol. 5, p. 10; p. 235, ll. 3–4; Bayhaqī, *Sunan*, vol. 7, p. 172, ll. 6–10; see also Saḥnūn, *Mudawwana*, vol. 2, p. 308, ll. 4–6.

[125] Saḥnūn, *Mudawwana*, vol. 2, p. 307, ll. 4–5; Qurṭubī, *al-Jāmiʿ li-aḥkām al-Qur'ān*, vol. 3, p. 63, infra.

[126] Saḥnūn, *Mudawwana*, vol. 2, p. 306, ll. 7–11; p. 307, ll. 4–5.

[127] Aḥmad b. Ḥanbal, *Aḥkām al-nisā'*, pp. 24–25 (nos. 51–54); Khallāl, *Ahl al-milal*, p. 240 (no. 454); Ibn Qayyim al-Jawziyya, *Aḥkām ahl al-dhimma*, p. 421. For similar views entertained by a modern scholar, see Khallāf, *Aḥkām al-aḥwāl al-shakhṣiyya*, p. 124.

[128] Ṭabarī, *Jāmiʿ al-bayān*, vol. 2, p. 377, ll. 14–15; Ibn Kathīr, *Tafsīr*, vol. 1, p. 456 (on Qur'ān 2:221). The tradition is not unanimous regarding the views of Ibn ʿAbbās; see the opposite view attributed to him in Bayhaqī, *Sunan*, vol. 7, p. 172 (quoted above at note 72).

[129] Ṭabarī, *Jāmiʿ al-bayān*, vol. 2, pp. 376–379; Saḥnūn, *Mudawwana*, vol. 2, p. 308, ll. 7–11; Jaṣṣāṣ, *Aḥkām al-Qur'ān* vol. 2, p. 397; Qurṭubī, *al-Jāmiʿ li-aḥkām al-Qur'ān*, vol. 3, p. 64; Zamakhsharī, *al-Kashshāf*, vol. 1, p. 360. In a third version, ʿUmar demands that Ṭalḥa divorce his Jewish wife because of her bad character (*ṭalliqhā fa-innahā jamra*). See Ṣanʿānī, *Muṣannaf*, vol. 6, p. 78 (no. 10057); vol. 7, pp. 176–177 (no. 12667); Aḥmad b. Ḥanbal, *Masā'il*, vol. 2, pp. 320–322 (nos. 949–951). According to a completely different version, Ṭalḥa's wife embraced Islam (*ḥanafat*) when she reached Medina. The same is reported about the Christian wife of ʿUthmān b. ʿAffān. See Bayhaqī, *Sunan*, vol. 7, p. 172, ll. 11–25.

outspoken opponent of marriages with *kitābī* women seems to have been ᶜAbd Allah b. ᶜUmar.[130] He maintained that marrying *kitābī* women was forbidden because they were polytheists covered by the prohibition in Qurʾān 2:221: in his view, no *shirk* is more reprehensible than when a woman says that "her Lord is ᶜĪsā while he is (merely) a slave of God" (*wa lā aᶜlamu min al-ishrāk shayʾan akbara min an taqūla al-marʾa rabbuhā ᶜĪsā wa huwa ᶜabd min ᶜibād Allāh*).[131] In his view, the permission included in Qurʾān 5:5 is valid only with regard to Jewish and Christian women who converted to Islam.[132] An identical view was held by a group of scholars (*qawm*) who maintained – contrary to the prevalent opinion – that Qurʾān 2:221 abrogated Qurʾān 5:5 and, consequently, marriage with any non-Muslim woman is forbidden.[133] According to another tradition, ᶜAbd Allah b. ᶜUmar was less outspoken: when asked about the permissibility of marrying *dhimmī* women, he recited Qurʾān 2:221 and 5:5, but refused to interpret the verses or draw conclusions from them.[134]

The traditions concerning the Prophet's relationship with women of Jewish origin are of some interest in this context. Two such women were in his household. The first one was Ṣafiyya bint Ḥuyayy, a young Jewish captive from Khaybar, barely seventeen years old when the city was conquered in 7 A.H. / 628 A.D. The Prophet appropriated her as his *ṣafī*, the booty portion which the expedition commander chooses for himself before the division of the spoils.[135] The beginning of the Prophet's relationship with her is described in two ways. According to the first tradition, he offered to manumit her if she "chose Allah and His Prophet" (*ᶜaraḍa ᶜalayhā al-nabī … an yuᶜtiqahā in ikhtārat Allāh wa rasūlahu*). She embraced Islam, whereupon the Prophet manumitted her and married her. The manumission was considered her dowry.[136] Another tradition describes the initial conversation between the Prophet and Ṣafiyya in a significantly different manner. The Prophet started by referring to Ḥuyayy's intense hostility to him. With surprising knowledge of Islam, Ṣafiyya disclaimed responsibility for this by quoting Qurʾān 6:164: "… No bearer of burdens can bear the burden of another … (*lā taziru wāziratun wizra ukhrā*). Then the Prophet gave her the following options: if she chose Islam, he would keep her for himself; and if she chose

[130] See *EI²*, s.v. (L. Vaccia Vaglieri). The article has nothing to say about ᶜAbd Allāh b. ᶜUmar' legal views, though these abound in the literature of *ḥadīth* and *fiqh*.

[131] Bukhārī, *Ṣaḥīḥ, kitāb al-ṭalāq* 18 (ed. Krehl, vol. 3, pp. 467–468). This tradition is found in a corrupted version in Jaṣṣāṣ, *Aḥkām al-Qurʾān*, vol. 2, p. 397, ll. 26–27 and elsewhere.

[132] Sarakhsī, *Mabsūṭ*, vol. 4, p. 210, ll. 16–18; Aḥmad b. Ḥanbal, *Masāʾil*, vol. 3, p. 59 (no. 1337); Naḥḥās, *al-Nāsikh wa al-mansūkh*, vol. 1, p. 52; vol. 2, pp. 5–6; Jaṣṣāṣ, *Aḥkām al-Qurʾān*, vol. 2, p. 397 infra. Both Sarakhsī and al-Jaṣṣāṣ reject Ibn ᶜUmar's ruling; see Jaṣṣāṣ, *Aḥkām al-Qurʾān* vol. 2, pp. 398 infra – 399 supra; Sarakhsī, *Mabsūṭ*, vol. 4, p. 210, lines 18ff; Ibn Ḥazm, *Muḥallā*, vol. 9, p. 543, ll. 16.

[133] Naḥḥās, *al-Nāsikh wa al-mansūkh*, vol. 2, p. 5 (no. 195); Qurṭubī, *al-Jāmiᶜ li-aḥkām al-Qurʾān*, vol. 3, p. 64.

[134] Jaṣṣāṣ, *Aḥkām al-Qurʾān* vol. 2, p. 398 supra.

[135] See Ibn Manẓūr, *Lisān al-ᶜarab*, s.v. *ṣ-f-y: al-ṣafī min al-ghanīma mā 'khtārahu al-raʾīs min al-maghnam wa 'ṣṭafāhu li-nasfsihi qabla al-qisma.* See also Ṭabarī, *Ikhtilāf al-fuqahāʾ*, pp. 140–141; *EI²*, s.v. *fayʾ* (F. Løkkegard); s.v. *ṣafī* (Ann K. S. Lambton).

[136] Ibn Saᶜd, *Ṭabaqāt*, vol. 8, p. 86, ll. 10–15.

Judaism, he would manumit her and enable her to rejoin her people. Ṣafiyya responded by saying that she no longer had family members among the Jews (her father, husband and brother had all been killed by the Muslims), and had no desire for Judaism; Allah and His Prophet are more desirable to her than manumission or return to her people. As a result of this decision, the Prophet kept her for himself (*amsakahā li-nafsihi*).[137] The traditional accounts abound with references to the Prophet defending Ṣafiyya when she was taunted by his other wives – especially by ᶜĀᵓisha – because of her Jewish origins.[138]

The other woman of Jewish descent was Rayḥāna bint Shamᶜūn bint Zayd whose case is more complex. She was captured by the Muslims after the massacre of Banū Qurayẓa. According to one version, her story is similar to that of Ṣafiyya: she was also the Prophet's *ṣafī*, was offered the option of converting to Islam and accepted it. Consequently, the Prophet manumitted her, married her, and treated her like his other wives.[139] According to another version, Rayḥāna initially refused to embrace Islam and preferred to be the Prophet's slave-girl. When she eventually converted, she declined the Prophet's offer of manumission, remained his slave-girl and had a sexual relationship with him until her death.[140]

VII

Zoroastrian women constitute a special category. As we have seen above,[141] the Zoroastrians were given *dhimmī* status, though most schools of law do not consider them People of the Book, and so Qurᵓān 5:5 is not applicable to them: Muslims may not marry Zoroastrian women and may not consume meat slaughtered by Zoroastrians. According to the Mālikī scholar Ibn ᶜAbd al-Barr al-Namarī, the permissibility of marriage to a *kitābī* woman is an honor done to the People of the Book; those who have no book, cannot share in this honor (*... dhālika makrumatun bi-'l-kitābiyyīn li-mawḍiᶜi kitābihim wa 'ttibāᶜihim al-rusul fa-lam yajuz an*

[137] Ibn Saᶜd, *Ṭabaqāt*, vol. 8, p. 88, ll. 1–10. Ibn Hishām (*Sīrat rasūl Allāh*, pp. 354, 758, 763, 1001) and Ibn al-Athīr (*Usd al-ghāba*, vol. 5, pp. 490–491) say nothing about Ṣafiyya being Jewish or about her conversion. ᶜAsqalānī (*Iṣāba*, vol. 7, pp. 738–742, no. 11401) mentions Ṣafiyya's Jewish origins, but does not reproduce the conversation in which the Prophet asked her to convert.

[138] Ṣanᶜānī, *Muṣannaf*, vol. 11, pp. 430–431 (no. 20921); Ibn Saᶜd, *Ṭabaqāt*, vol. 8, p. 87, ll. 23–27; pp. 90–91; Wāqidī, *Kitāb al-maghāzī*, vol. 2, p. 675. Ṣafiyya was derided for her Jewish origins for a long time. Apparently after the Prophet's death, ᶜUmar was informed that she still observed the Sabbath and maintained family ties with the Jews (*tuḥibbu al-sabt wa taṣilu al-yahūd*). She denied the observance of the Sabbath, which God replaced for her with Friday, but admitted maintaining ties with her Jewish relatives. See ᶜAsqalānī, *Iṣāba*, vol. 7, p. 741.

[139] Ibn Saᶜd, *Ṭabaqāt*, vol. 8, pp. 92–93.

[140] Ibn Saᶜd, *Ṭabaqāt*, vol. 8, pp. 93 l. 27 – 94 l. 12; Wāqidī, *Kitāb al-maghāzī*, vol. 2, pp. 520–521. Ibn al-Athīr (*Usd al-ghāba*, vol. 5, pp. 460–461) has only this version of Rayḥāna's story. Both versions of the story are reproduced in ᶜAsqalānī, *Iṣāba*, vol. 7, pp. 658–660 (no. 11197). Bayhaqī (*al-Sunan al-kubrā*, vol. 7, p. 72, ll. 2 9–31) describes her as "a slave-girl of the People of the Book" *walīda ... min ahl al-kitāb*). Cf. Māwardī, *al-Ḥāwī al-kabīr*, vol. 9, pp. 23–24.

[141] Chapter Two, section IV.

yalḥaqa bihim man lā kitāba lahu fī hādhihi al-makruma).[142] Several scholars of the first century A.H. are mentioned as supporters of this view. ᶜUmar b. al-Khaṭṭāb took great care to preclude any possibility of marriage with Zoroastrian women. His circumspection is said to have been one of the reasons why he instructed Ḥudhayfa b. al-Yamān to divorce his scriptuary wife in Kūfa. He argued that since the place was at that time inhabited mainly by Zoroastrians, some Muslims might draw from Ḥudhayfa's marriage to a Jewess the conclusion that marriage with Zoroastrians was also permissible, ignoring the fact that the concession (*rukhṣa*) which God gave the Muslims was restricted to scriptuaries alone.[143] Mālik b. Anas is reported to have prohibited both concubinage with Zoroastrian slave-girls and marriage with free Zoroastrian women. Aḥmad b. Ḥanbal held a similar opinion.[144] Similarly, if the husband in a Zoroastrian marriage converts to Islam, the marriage is dissolved if the wife, having been given a reasonable time to follow her husband's example, nonetheless resolves to retain her ancestral religion.[145] If this takes place before the consummation of the marriage, the dissolution is considered *faskh* rather than *ṭalāq*, and the husband incurs no financial obligation.[146] And it goes without saying that a when a Zoroastrian who was married to his own daughter or sister embraces Islam, the marriage is dissolved.[147]

Shāfiᶜī prohibited concubinage with Zoroastrian women, unless it was possible to claim that they should be considered Muslims because they were captured without their parents, or because one of their parents embraced Islam.[148] Aḥmad b. Ḥanbal explained that Zoroastrian women are forbidden to the Muslims because they have "neither book nor (ritual) purity" (*li-annahum laysa lahum lā kitāb wa lā ṭahāra*) and vehemently rejected any other pertinent view.[149]

Only Abū Thawr[150] and Ibn Ḥazm allow Muslims to wed Zoroastrian women. Abū Thawr supports this view on the basis of the famous *ḥadīth* enjoining the Muslims to treat the Zoroastrians in the same way as they treat the People of the

142 Ibn ᶜAbd al-Barr al-Namarī, *Tamhīd*, vol. 2, p. 117. We have seen above (in section II of the present chapter) that many traditionists consider the permissibility of taking *kitābī* women in marriage (while denying the *kitābī*s reciprocity in this matter) as a reflection of Islamic superiority; Ibn ᶜAbd al-Barr al-Namarī sees the issue in a very different light.

143 Ṣanᶜānī, *Muṣannaf*, vol. 7, p. 178 (no. 12676). The text of the tradition seems to be partly corrupt, but the meaning is clear enough. See also Ibn ᶜAbd al-Barr al-Namarī, *Tamhīd*, vol. 2, p. 128, ll. 7–12.

144 Saḥnūn, *Mudawwana*, vol. 2, p. 307, ll. 11–13; Ibn Qudāma, *al-Mughnī*, vol. 6, pp. 591 – 592; Ibn Taymiyya, *Majmūᶜ fatāwā*, vol. 32, pp. 186–189. See also Qudūrī, *Mukhtaṣar*, p. 145, infra.

145 Qudūrī, *Mukhtaṣar*, p. 150, ll. 12–14; Saḥnūn, *Mudawwana*, vol. 2, p. 298, ll. 12–16; Ibn ᶜAbd al-Barr al-Namarī, *Tamhīd*, vol. 12, pp. 26, ll. 8 – 27, l. 2; p. 28, ll. 10–13; Khallāl, *Ahl al-milal*, pp. 473–474 (nos. 1154–1159); Ibn Qayyim al-Jawziyya, *Aḥkām ahl al-dhimma*, p. 319, ll. 15–16. Cf. Saḥnūn, *Mudawwana*, vol. 2, p. 301, ll. 4–11 for a similar ruling when the husband of the Zoroastrian woman was originally Christian and embraced Islam.

146 Saḥnūn b. Saᶜīd, *Mudawwana*, vol. 2, pp. 301, l. 22 – 302, l. 1.

147 Khallāl, *Ahl al-milal*, vol. 2, p. 367 (no. 816), p. 368 (no. 817).

148 Shāfiᶜī, *Kitāb al-umm*, vol. 4, p. 389, ll. 7–11.

149 Khallāl, *Ahl al-milal*, p. 240 (nos. 454–456); Ibn Qayyim al-Jawziyya, *Aḥkām ahl al-dhimma*, pp. 434–436. Cf. Patricia Crone and Fritz Zimmermann, *The epistle of Sālim b. Dhakwān*, Oxford: Oxford University Press, 2001, pp. 68–71.

150 See on him "Abū Thawr", in *EI*², s.v. (J. Schacht) and Jabr, *Fiqh al-imām Abī Thawr*. Abū Thawr also held a distinct view on the consumption of meat slaughtered by the Zoroastrians which he considered licit. See Khallāl, *Ahl al-milal*, pp. 447–448 (no. 1053), pp. 469–470 (no. 1139).

Book, and, also on the basis of the (rather disputed) tradition according to which Ḥudhayfa b. al-Yamān married a Zoroastrian woman.[151] As for Ibn Ḥazm, he considers the Zoroastrians to be People of the Book;[152] hence the permissibility of wedding Zoroastrian women is for him only natural.

VIII

In the preceding section we have discussed the permissibility or otherwise of wedding *dhimmī* women. As we have seen above, these may belong to the Jewish or Christian faiths. Furthermore, they are assumed to be living in *dār al-islām*, under the protection of the Muslim state and community.[153] The question of wedding non-Muslim women whose domicile is in *dār al-ḥarb* is a disputed matter. Ibn ᶜAbbās thought that Muslims are not allowed to wed *ḥarbī* women of Jewish or Christian faith.[154] According to another view, the permission to marry free *kitābī* women applies both to *dhimmiyyāt* and to *ḥarbiyyāt*. The most prevalent view, attributed to Mālik b. Anas and others, is that marriage with *ḥarbī* women is legal, but reprehensible (*yajūzu li-'l-muslim an yatazawwaja kitābiyya fī dār al-ḥarb wa lākinnahu yukrahu*).[155] The early jurists enumerate several reasons for this. One is the possibility that the woman might trade in wine or pork and thereby offend her husband's religious sensibilities. More important is the apprehension that the husband, in contravention of an explicit prophetic injunction,[156] may choose to live among the unbelievers in *dār al-ḥarb*. Consequently, he may be induced by the *ḥarbī*s to abandon his religion, and his wife may impart infidel values to her children (*takhluqu al-wuld bi-akhlāq al-kuffār*). The children may also be enslaved or forced into unbelief. That this is the main reason for the opposition to matrimony with scriptuaries outside the realm of Islam is made clear by numerous scholars: even if a Muslim marries a Muslim woman in *dār al-ḥarb*, he must practice *coitus interruptus* (*ᶜazl*) so that she does not conceive; and if a Muslim buys a slave-girl in *dār al-ḥarb*, he must not engage in vaginal intercourse with her (*lam yaṭaʾhā fī al-farj*) as long as he resides there.[157]

Naturally enough, all these considerations are not valid if the marriage is contracted in *dār al-islām*. Thus, if a *ḥarbī* scriptuary woman migrates to the

[151] Khallāl, *Ahl al-milal*, pp. 240–241 (no. 457); Ibn Qudāma, *al-Mughnī*, vol. 6, p. 591; Ibn Qayyim al-Jawziyya, *Aḥkām ahl al-dhimma*, vol. 2, p. 435; Jabr, *Fiqh al-imām Abī Thawr*, pp. 468–469.

[152] Ibn Ḥazm, *Muḥallā*, vol. 7, pp. 404–405 (no. 958); vol. 9, pp. 543, 547–548.

[153] See Chapter Two, section I.

[154] Ṭabarī, *Jāmiᶜ al-bayān*, vol. 6, p. 107, ll. 16–20; Ibn Abī Shayba, *Muṣannaf*, vol. 4, p. 159; Qurṭubī, *al-Jāmiᶜ li-aḥkām al-Qurʾān*, vol. 3, p. 65.

[155] Sarakhsī, *Mabsūṭ*, vol. 5, p. 50, ll. 17–18.

[156] "I renounce all ties with any Muslim living among the polytheists" (*anā barīʾun min kulli muslimin yuqīmu bayna aẓhur al-mushrikīn*). See Abū Dāwūd, *Sunan, Kitāb al-jihād* 105 (vol. 3, p. 62); for the usage of this *ḥadīth* in our context, see Sarakhsī, *Mabsūṭ*, vol. 5, p. 50, ll. 18–19.

[157] Khiraqī, *Mukhtaṣar*, p. 204; Ibn Qudāma, *al-Mughnī*, vol. 8, pp. 455–456; see also *Sharḥ al-Zarkashī*, vol. 6, p. 531; Ibn al-Bannāʾ, *Kitāb al-muqniᶜ*, vol. 3, pp. 117–118; Ibn Qayyim al-Jawziyya, *Aḥkām ahl al-dhimma*, p. 430–431; cf. Sarakhsī, *Mabsūṭ*, vol. 5, p. 50, ll. 16ff; vol. 10, p. 96, ll. 14–17; Saḥnūn, *Mudawwana*, vol. 2, p. 300, ll. 17–20; p. 304, ll. 16–19; p. 306, ll. 2–7; Qurṭubī, *al-Jāmiᶜ li-aḥkām al-qurʾān*, vol. 3, p. 65; Shāfiᶜī, *Kitāb al-umm*, vol. 4, p. 379, ll. 5–12.

Muslim territory and marries a Muslim or a *dhimmī*, the marriage is valid and the woman acquires the status of *dhimmiyya*, in view of her dependency on her husband.[158] Marriage with a *ḥarbī* scriptuary woman is not reprehensible if contracted in a place where the offspring are not in danger of being forced into infidelity. Al-Shāfiʿī also explains that marriage with a *ḥarbī* woman is not, in itself, forbidden; it is reprehensible only if there is danger that the child will be enslaved or forced into infidelity because born in *dār al-ḥarb*. It seems that this is also the meaning of an apparently early, but rarely quoted, tradition according to which "a *kitābī* woman is not to be wedded unless she is under (a *dhimma*) agreement" (*lā tunkaḥu al-marʾatu min ahl al-kitāb illā fī ʿahd*).[159] Al-Shāfiʿī explains that the basic factor determining a woman's eligibility for marriage to a Muslim is her religion, not her domicile (*dār*); the domicile is important only if it places the offspring of the religiously mixed family in danger of infidelity or enslavement. If the woman's domicile were a material impediment to marriage, a Muslim man would be forbidden to marry even a Muslim woman residing in *dār al-ḥarb*.[160]

IX

Once the interfaith marriage is concluded, the non-Muslim wife is to be treated equally with the other wives. Some of the rules pertaining to her may sound specific to a non-Muslim, but they are, according to most interpretations, a consequence of the husband's right to regulate the lives of his wives to suit his convenience. In general, the obligations of the spouses toward each other are the same as in a marriage between Muslims. The husband is obliged to spend with his non-Muslim wife the same amount of time as he spends with her Muslim counterparts. He should also provide her with the same living allowances (*nafaqa*). The non-Muslim wife is not treated like a slave-girl, who is entitled only to one half (or one third) of the time devoted by the husband to each of his free wives. The rules pertaining to divorce and to the waiting period are also the same for all wives. There are, however, certain differences. According to the rule that prevents cross-religious inheritance, the non-Muslim wife does not inherit any of her deceased husband's property.[161] And if the husband falsely accuses his *kitābī* wife of

[158] Sarakhsī, *Mabsūṭ*, vol. 5, p. 53, ll. 14–16.

[159] Ṣanʿānī, *Muṣannaf*, vol. 6, pp. 84–85 (nos. 10086–10089); vol. 7, p. 188 (nos. 12722–12724).

[160] Ṭabarī, *Jāmiʿ al-bayān*, vol. 6, pp. 107–108; Shāfiʿī, *Kitāb al-umm*, vol. 5, pp. 76, ll. 21–26, 85, ll. 25–26; Aḥmad b. Ḥanbal, *Masāʾil*, vol. 1, p. 395 (no. 374). For the distinction between *kitābī* women ethnically related to Banū Isrāʾīl and those who belong to other ethnic groups, see Chapter Two, section II.

[161] Ṣanʿānī, *Muṣannaf*, vol. 7, pp. 181–182 (nos. 12691–12693); Ibn Abī Shayba, *Muṣannaf*, vol. 4, p. 151; Sarakhsī, *Mabsūṭ*, vol. 4, p. 210, l. 23 – p. 211, l. 1; vol. 5, pp. 218–219; Saḥnūn, *Mudawwana*, vol. 2, p. 424, ll. 18–20; Shāfiʿī, *Kitāb al-umm*, vol. 5, pp. 11–12; 18, ll. 3–4; 235, l. 4; 280, ll. 8–9; 312, ll. 2–3; 351, ll. 12–13; Māwardī, *al-Ḥāwī al-kabīr*, vol. 9, pp. 226–227; Khallāl, *Ahl al-milal*, pp. 248–249 (nos. 484–486), p. 274 (no. 550), p. 284 (no. 580): *al-yahūdiyya wa al-naṣrāniyya fī al-ʿidda wa al-ṭalāq mithl al-muslima illā fī al-irth*; pp. 362–365 (nos. 805, 808–809); Aḥmad b. Ḥanbal, *Aḥkām al-nisāʾ*, p. 25–26 (nos. 58–61).

adultery (*qadhf*), he is not punished by *ḥadd* but only by *taᶜzīr*.[162] The husband may force her to perform ablution after her menses – since otherwise it would not be legal for him to engage her sexually. He may demand that she purify herself from other impurities, but cannot force her to comply with this demand. According to Ibn Qudāma, he may order her to refrain from drinking wine, but cannot force her to do so. Shāfiᶜī does not refer to the possibility of non-compliance: he maintains that the husband may prevent his wife from drinking wine because it effects her mind adversely. However, according to a view adduced by al-Māwardī, he cannot prevent her from drinking a small amount of wine in the framework of a religious ritual of hers. According to al-Shāfiᶜī, he is entitled to prevent her from eating pork since it pollutes him; from eating garlic or onion since they are malodorous, though licit; or from donning a garment which has a foul smell or which was prepared from a carcass.[163]

Some of these strictures relate to matters which are permitted to the *kitābī* woman, but not to the Muslim; however, the dominant reason for their prohibition seems to be to prevent the husband's discomfort and the diminution of his enjoyment. Ibn Qayyim al-Jawziyya adduces two views on such issues. According to the first, the husband may force his wife to perform ablution after her menses and purify herself from other impurities as well. According to the other, the husband may force his *dhimmī* wife to purify herself after the menses because her failure to do so would make conjugal relations illegal; he cannot, however, force her to purify herself after actions (e.g., excretion) which bring about a state of pollution, or after drinking wine. The reason why he must tolerate such things is that they do not in law preclude him from having sexual relations with the woman, even though they may diminish his enjoyment (*li-annahu yamnaᶜu min kamāl al-waṭʾi wa lā yamnaᶜu min aṣlihi*). The husband's right to force his wife to pare her nails and trim her hair is discussed in a similar fashion.[164]

Rules which seem most specifically related to a non-Muslim wife pertain to her freedom to practice her religion. Material about non-Muslim religious observance inside the matrimonial home is not abundant. Aḥmad b. Ḥanbal states that the Muslim husband should forbid his wife to bring a cross into his home, but cannot effectively prevent her from doing it.[165] According to Ibn Qayyim al-Jawziyya, he cannot prevent her from observing a fast prescribed in her religion, even if as a result of her fasting he cannot enjoy her on that day. He cannot prevent her from praying towards the east, cannot force her to violate the Sabbath (*kasr al-sabt*), and cannot force her to eat meat or use fat of a kind forbidden by her religion. He also

[162] This is a result of a general rule against applying *ḥadd* for defaming a non-Muslim rather than a specific rule concerning interfaith marriages.

[163] Shāfiᶜī, *Kitāb al-umm*, vol. 4, pp. 381, l. 25 – 382, l. 5; vol. 5, p. 12, l. 11 – 13, l. 7; Māwardī, *al-Ḥāwī al-kabīr*, vol. 9, p. 230 l. 1; Khallāl, *Ahl al-milal*, pp. 114–115 (nos. 117–120); Ibn Qudāma, *Mughnī*, vol. 8, pp. 537–538.

[164] Ibn Qayyim al-Jawziyya, *Aḥkām ahl al-dhimma*, pp. 436–438 (the transliterated sentence speaks about wine drinking); Saḥnūn, *al-Mudawwana al-kubrā*, vol. 1, pp. 32–33; Ibn Qudāma, *Mughnī*, vol. 8, p. 538, supra; Māwardī, *al-Ḥāwī al-kabīr*, vol. 9, pp. 227–228.

[165] Khallāl, *Ahl al-milal*, p. 430 (nos. 997–998); cf. Ibn Qayyim al-Jawziyya, *Aḥkām ahl al-dhimma*, p. 440.

cannot prevent her from reading her holy Book, provided that she does not raise her voice excessively. He should not buy a *zunnār* for her, but he cannot prevent her from buying one herself.[166]

More copious is the material about a non-Muslim wife's participation in religious ceremonies in a synagogue or a church. While discussing this issue we must keep in mind that a woman's participation in public worship is debated with respect to Muslim women as well. In order to place the rules concerning the non-Muslim wife in proper perspective, it is necessary to survey the rules applicable to her Muslim counterpart.

The classical collections of *ḥadīth* contain a statement in which the Prophet enjoined his followers not to prevent women from going to the mosques (*lā tamnaᶜū imāʾa 'llāh masājida 'llāh* ...); it is clear, however, that this view was not easily accepted and other prophetic traditions give preference to women praying in the privacy of their homes (*mā ṣallat imraʾatun fī mawḍiᶜin khayrin lahā min qaᶜri baytihā illā an yakūna 'l-masjida 'l-ḥarām aw masjida rasūl Allāh*). According to one trend of thought, which seems to have been supported by ᶜUmar b. al-Khaṭṭāb, women should be prevented from frequenting the mosque and certainly should not participate in public worship without their husbands' permission.[167]

In view of these divergent views concerning Muslim women, it is not surprising that the attitude to a non-Muslim wife's participation in worship is also in dispute. Mālik b. Anas maintains that a Muslim husband

> may not prevent his Christian wife from eating pork, drinking wine or going to her church (*qāla Mālik: laysa li-'l-rajul an yamnaᶜa 'mraʾatahu al-naṣrāniyya min akl al-khinzīr wa shurb al-khamr wa al-dhahāb ilā kanīsatihā idhā kānat naṣrāniyya*).[168]

Al-Awzāᶜī seems to have considered this issue as devoid of any importance: he is reported to have said that he sees no harm in allowing a Christian slave-girl from going to the church, but also sees no harm in preventing her (*lā arā baʾsan an yaʾdhana lahā fī al-kanīsa wa lā arā baʾsan an yamnaᶜahā*).[169] On the other hand, al-Shāfiᶜī is also on traditionally safe ground when he asserts that a husband may

166 Ibn Qayyim al-Jawziyya, *Aḥkām ahl al-dhimma*, vol. 2, pp. 440–441; Khallāl, *Ahl al-milal*, pp. 115–116 (no. 121). Al-Khallāl's passage includes a curious statement according to which the Muslim husband cannot force his non-Muslim wife to break her fast and engage her sexually "until she purifies herself from that fast of hers" (... *ḥattā taghtasila min ṣawmihā dhālika*). Cf. Ibn Qudāma, *Mughnī*, vol. 8, p. 538, supra.

167 ᶜAbd al-Malik b. Ḥabīb, *Adab al-nisāʾ*, pp. 239–243 (nos. 164–170); Bukhārī, *Ṣaḥīḥ, Kitāb al-jumᶜa 13* (ed. Krehl, vol. 1, p. 228) and elsewhere; see Wensinck, *Concordance* ..., vol. 1, p. 123 supra (s.v. *ama*). See also Bukhārī, *Kitāb al-adhān 162: khurūj al-nisāʾ ilā al-masājid* (ed. Krehl, vol. 1, pp. 221–222); Aḥmad b. Ḥanbal, *Aḥkām al-nisāʾ*, pp. 45–46 (nos. 142–145). Excellent examples of the controversial nature of this issue can be found in Ibn Māja, *Sunan*, vol. 1, p. 8 (*Muqaddima*, no. 16) and in Muslim b. al-Ḥajjāj, *Ṣaḥīḥ*, vol. 1, pp. 326–329 (*Kitāb al-ṣalāt*, nos. 134–144) where Bilāl b. ᶜAbd Allah b. ᶜUmar dares to resist the prophetic injunction allowing women to go to the mosque. Cf. Mālik b. Anas, *Muwaṭṭaʾ, Kitāb al-qibla* 6 (pp. 197–198, nos. 12–15).

168 Saḥnūn, *Mudawwana*, vol. 2, p. 307, ll. 2–4.

169 Khallāl, *Ahl al-milal*, p. 431 (no. 1001). The editor of this text maintains that al-Awzāᶜī sees no harm in preventing the girl from visits (to her relatives, or perhaps to the tombs of saints?). The meaning of the passage is obscure; the text says once *yamnaᶜuhā min al-ziyārāt* and another time *yamnaᶜuhā min ahl al-ziyārāt*.

prevent his Muslim wife from going to a mosque where the true religion is being practiced; this being so, his right to prevent her non-Muslim counterpart from frequenting her false place of worship or from participating in processions during her religious holidays is not in any doubt (*idhā kāna lahu manᶜu l-muslima ityāna 'l-masjid wa huwa ḥaqq, kāna lahu fī al-naṣrāniyya manᶜu ityāni 'l-kanīsa li-annahu bāṭil*).[170] Ibn Ḥanbal held the same view.[171] Ibn Qayyim al-Jawziyya maintains that the prohibition stems from the principle that a Muslim should not assist others in the performance of infidel rituals. Therefore a Muslim wife may not be prevented from going to the mosque, but a non-Muslim one should be prevented from attending the church or the synagogue.[172] Other scholars maintained that these prohibitions stem from the desire to keep all women, regardless of their faith, confined to their homes, rather than to impose restrictions on the religious freedom of the *kitābī* woman. The Ḥanbalī *qāḍī* Abū Yaᶜlā maintained that a Muslim husband's refusal to let his *kitābī* wife visit a church or a synagogue derives from his right to enjoy her company at all times rather than from a desire to restrict her right to observe the commandments of her faith. It is therefore not surprising that the husband's right to prevent his *dhimmī* wife from leaving his house is mentioned not only in connection with her desire to go to the church or the synagogue.[173] Commenting on al-Shāfiᶜī's statement, al-Māwardī explains that the husband's right to prevent his wife from leaving home is designed to avert the possibility that he will not be able to enjoy her while she is away. The prophetic injunction to allow women to go to the mosques is restricted, in his view, to the mosque of Mecca during the pilgrimage season.[174]

X

It is now appropriate to make a number of final observations on interfaith marriages in Sunnī Muslim tradition and law. We have seen that the major compendia of the ninth century A.D. and onward are unanimous on a number of principles regarding the issue under discussion. The first principle is that matrimony between Muslim males and free (and chaste) scriptuary women is licit; according to the second, a Muslim woman may not be given in marriage to any non-Muslim, be he a scriptuary, a Zoroastrian or a polytheist; the third is that any marriage between a Muslim, male or female, and a polytheist or a Zoroastrian is illicit.

It is evident, however, that these principles were far from agreed upon when Muslim tradition began to develop; it is difficult if not impossible to discern *ijmāᶜ* on these matters in the first two centuries of Islam. Goldziher's classic formulation

[170] Shāfiᶜī, *Kitāb al-umm*, vol. 5, p. 13, ll. 2–3; Muzanī, *Mukhtaṣar* (in *Kitāb al-umm*, vol. 9, p. 182, l. 16); Māwardī, *al-Ḥāwī al-kabīr*, vol. 9, p. 228–229.
[171] Khallāl, *Ahl al-milal*, pp. 430–431 (nos. 998–1001); Ibn Qudāma, *Mughnī*, vol. 8, p. 537, infra.
[172] Ibn Qayyim al-Jawziyya, *Aḥkām ahl al-dhimma*, vol. 1, pp. 438–439.
[173] Ibn Qayyim al-Jawziyya, *Aḥkām ahl al-dhimma*, pp. 437, ll. 2–3; 438–439.
[174] Māwardī, *al-Ḥāwī al-kabīr*, vol. 9, p. 229.

according to which the *ḥadīth* "contains invaluable evidence for the evolution of Islam ... from powerful mutually opposed forces"[175] is a germane characterization of the material analyzed in the present chapter. In order to understand this evolutionary process as evidenced in our treatment of interfaith marriages, it may be instructive to subject the three principles outlined above to further scrutiny. Let us commence with the right of the Muslims to wed free (and chaste) scriptuary women. Qurʾān 5:5, the verse in which this right was bestowed upon the Muslims, is included in a very late, if not the latest, part of the revelation. According to some traditions, it was revealed during the Prophet's last pilgrimage (*ḥajjat al-wadāᶜ*) in the year 10 A.H. / 632 A.D.[176] If this traditional dating is accepted, permission to wed Jewish and Christian women was granted after the "break with the Jews", that is, after the Prophet decreed their expulsion from Medina and after the conquest of Khaybar. This timing may seem surprising if we follow the very rare view expressed by Ibn ᶜAbd al-Barr al-Namarī, who suggested that permission to wed *kitābī* women was a gesture honoring the People of the Book;[177] were this the case, we would expect the permission to have been given during the first two years of the Prophet's sojourn in Medina. During that period, the gesture would have accorded with the mood of the times and would have coincided with the Prophet's desire to conciliate the People of the Book by adopting certain rituals associated with the Jewish (and Christian) tradition.[178] However, Ibn ᶜAbd al-Barr al-Namarī's perception of the permissibility of marriages with Jewish and Christian women is not the prevalent one. If we attempt to interpret Qurʾān 5:5 according to the predominant view, in which the permission to wed *kitābī* women is a symbol of Islamic superiority, the timing of the permission becomes understandable: once the great victory of Islam over its adversaries had been assured, the time was ripe to symbolize this victory by permitting the Muslims to take women of the vanquished in matrimony. Our sources say nothing to explain Qurʾān 5:5 in this way and our explanation is therefore a mere conjecture; however, if it is correct, it provides a revealing explanation of the promulgation of Qurʾān 5:5 at a time when the dominance of Islam in the peninsula was assured and the relations with the Jews of Arabia were at their lowest possible point.[179]

This is, however, not the only issue to be discussed in this context. We also need to explain the persistent appearance of traditions which frown upon marrying

[175] I. Goldziher, *Muslim Studies*, translated by C. R. Barber and S. M. Stern, London: George Allen and Unwin Ltd., 1971, vol. 2, p. 19.

[176] Wāḥidī, *Asbāb al-nuzūl*, pp. 126–127; Suyūṭī, *Itqān*, vol. 1, p. 27, ll. 27–29: *ākhiru sūratin nazalat al-māʾida fa-mā wajadtum fīhā min ḥalāl fa-'staḥillūhu*; Naḥḥās, *al-Nāsikh wa al-mansūkh*, vol. 2, p. 8; Nöldeke–Schwally, *Geschichte des Qorāns*, vol. 1, p. 227.

[177] See above, the beginning of section VII of the present chapter.

[178] See Chapter One, section IV, at notes 83–87.

[179] Qurʾān 5:5 includes also the permission to consume meat slaughtered by the People of the Book. Though this cannot be explained as a symbol of Muslim superiority, it is noteworthy that some Muslim traditions perceive the permission as favorable to Muslims. This is the reason Aḥmad b. Ḥanbal opposed the conversion of scriptuaries to Zoroastrianism: such conversion would reduce the number of people from whose slaughter the Muslims may eat and whose daughters they may marry. See Chapter Four, at the end of section VII.

kitābī women, seemingly disregarding the permission included in the Qurʾān. Those who opposed interfaith marriages were willing to say that the prohibition in Qurʾān 2:221 (which in their view applies not only to the polytheists but also to the scriptuaries) abrogated the permission in Qurʾān 5:5, despite the fact that such an argument entailed a total disregard for the traditional chronology of the Qurʾān, according to which Sūra 5 was revealed long after Sūra 2 and, consequently, could not be abrogated by it. Views which consider marrying *kitābī* women reprehensible but permitted may be seen as compatible with the Qurʾānic ruling, according to which Muslims were allowed to marry scriptuary women but were certainly not obliged to follow this path. It is more difficult to explain the significance of traditions which prohibit such marriages altogether. Especially the *ḥadīth* according to which the Prophet himself prohibited marriages with *kitābī* women calls for comment. As I have indicated earlier, this utterance is rarely quoted and I do not remember having seen it discussed or commented upon in the sources used in the preparation of this inquiry. Traditional scholars of *ḥadīth*, who accept the authenticity of this pronouncement, would probably say that the Prophet must have promulgated the prohibition before the revelation of *Sūrat al-Māʾida*; thus, according to traditional criteria, we have here a *ḥadīth* which precedes the relevant Qurʾānic verse and reflects an earlier legal situation. Naturally enough, from the historical point of view we cannot easily substantiate the notion that marriage with *kitābī* women was forbidden until the revelation of Qurʾān 5:5. Yet we can say with reasonable certainty that marriage to Jewish and Christian women confronted widespread opposition during the first two centuries of Muslim history and continued to be viewed as reprehensible even after the law came firmly down on the side of permissibility. It is noteworthy that licitness of wedding *kitābī* women is based on the existence of the Qurʾānic verse and is supported by its symbolic value as a reflection of Islamic superiority. At times, the opposition to this type of matrimony draws its inspiration also from matters of principle, such as the perception of Jews and Christians as polytheists. In most cases, however, the opposition to interfaith marriage is based on practical considerations, such as the difficulty of raising the children according to Islamic values, and the revulsion which the Muslim husband is bound to feel toward a wife who consumes pork or drinks wine.

Let us now review the prohibition on engaging in marital relationships of any kind with non-*kitābī* unbelievers. The Qurʾānic prohibition is unequivocal on this issue. Its dating is not certain, but it seems to have been promulgated for the first time in the early Medinese period (Qurʾān 2:221) and again after the Ḥudaybiyya treaty in 6 A.H. / 628 A.D. (Qurʾān 60:10).[180] In the books of law, this principle deals mainly with the prohibition to wed Zoroastrian women. Yet in the earliest period of Islam, the non-*kitābī*s were mainly Arab polytheists, and the tradition has

[180] Qurʾān 2:221 is not precisely dated in the *asbāb al-nuzūl*. The tradition describes the verse as a negative response to the desire of Marthad b. Abī Marthad to wed his *jāhilī* beloved ʿAnāq who was still a polytheist, but does not specify the date of this event. See Nöldeke–Schwally, *Geschichte des Qorāns*, vol. 1, pp. 173, 183; Wāḥidī, *Asbāb al-nuzūl*, pp. 45–46; Naḥḥās, *al-Nāsikh wa al-mansūkh*, vol. 2, p. 8: *al-Baqara min awwali mā nazala bi-'l-Madīna wa al-Māʾida min ākhiri mā nazala.*

faithfully preserved both historical episodes and legal pronouncements indicating that marital relationships with polytheist women were not always avoided during the earliest period of Islam. The traditions concerning the aftermath of the battle against the Banū al-Muṣṭaliq are a case in point. In the major compendia of law, however, the prohibition is unequivocal. It seems that the tone of legal pronouncements on this matter becomes more and more strident in inverse relationship to the magnitude of the problem; it becomes absolutely uncompromising when the problem disappears as a result of the complete Islamization of the Arabian peninsula.

Finally, let us turn to the prohibition to give Muslim women in matrimony to unbelievers. We have seen that this is one of the strictest and least disputed prohibitions in Muslim law of personal status. Nevertheless, even on this matter we encounter traditions that are incompatible with the law as it crystallized in the major compendia. The rulings attributed to ᶜUmar b. al-Khaṭṭāb and to ᶜAlī b. Abī Ṭālib who did not intervene in marriages in which only the wife embraced Islam seem to reflect an ancient *sunna* which was eventually rejected and did not find its way into the major compendia. This must be the "*sunna* of the past", or the "the well-established precedent" (*al-sunna al-māḍiya*), the term by which Ibn Ḥanbal characterized ᶜAlī's refusal to annul interfaith marriages resulting from the wife's conversion to Islam.

The traditions concerning the marriage of the Prophet's daughter Zaynab to the polytheist Abū al-ᶜĀṣ are particularly significant in this context. On the one hand, they include tortuous explanations by which the jurists try to resolve the seeming contradictions between their laws and the traditions describing an episode from the first decade of Islam, an episode in which the Prophet was personally involved. On the other hand, these traditions provide us with valuable insights into the problems created in Mecca by the emergence of the new religion. Abū al-ᶜĀṣ suddenly finds himself wedded to the newly proclaimed Prophet's daughter who lost no time in converting to her father's religion. The polytheistic milieu of Abū al-ᶜĀṣ tries to induce him to divorce the daughter of the man who now became their arch enemy, but Abū al-ᶜĀṣ stands firm, clings to his marriage and treats his father-in-law with friendliness; at the same time, he refuses to join his religion for years on end. From the vantage point of crystallized Islam, Zaynab's story is embarrassing and replete with religious difficulties. Yet it is precisely these difficulties which endow the story with a unique ring of authenticity and trustworthiness.

We may conclude by saying that on the question of interfaith marriages, the Muslim sources do not attempt to paint a monolithic picture. Like in other cases, they do not eliminate traditions that seem to contradict the law as it crystallized in the second and third centuries. Traditions that apparently disregard explicit Qurʾānic precepts are preserved in the books of *ḥadīth*. The traditionists employ much ingenuity to make these traditions compatible with the law as it developed later, but they do not render their work easy by expunging the problematic material. The enormous corpus of *ḥadīth* provides us with precious indications concerning the variety of views and the early development of the law on the subject of this inquiry.

CHAPTER SIX

Concluding observations

The themes treated in this enquiry bear upon a number of issues relevant to interfaith relations as explored by early Muslim traditionists and jurisprudents. The great variety of pertinent views and the nature of the arguments marshalled by their protagonists testify to the vibrant intellectual life of Islam in the early period of its history. The mere existence of this variety is not in any doubt in view of previous research and in view of the material surveyed in the preceding five chapters. It is much more difficult to interpret its significance. Students of Islamic tradition are aware of the extensive literature that has been devoted to this issue. Does it reflect regional variations the existence of which is again being debated recently?[1] Is it related to differences between the emerging *madhāhib*? Is it possible to discern features common to a certain school of law? Or does the variety represent perhaps a development in time? In other words, is it possible to identify Schacht's "well established precedent" or "ancient practice"[2] in the topics which we have studied and suggest that it had certain characteristics – later to be marginalized or relegated to the recesses of "forged" traditions (*mawḍūʿāt*) and superseded rulings?

It was not the primary goal of this work to attempt a comprehensive answer to these much debated questions. We have rather devoted our attention to the survey and analysis of material related to a limited number of concrete topics and it seems that certain tentative conclusions concerning the development of Muslim thinking on these can be suggested. It seems that an ancient layer of tradition, a layer that was in general more considerate toward the People of the Book than that which eventually became the established law, can be discerned in the literature of *ḥadīth* and *fiqh*. Clearly, this does not mean that the stringent views which achieved primacy in the established law did not exist simultaneously with the more lenient ones. Unfortunately, the nature of our sources does not allow us to date the emergence and the subsequent partial demise of these lenient views with any precision, but on certain topics our findings seem to reflect the general tendency "toward

[1] See Christopher Melchert, *The formation of the Sunnī schools of law, 9th–10th centuries C. E.*, Leiden: Brill, 1997, and the critique of Wael B. Hallaq, "From regional to personal schools of law? A reevaluation", *Islamic law and society* 8 (2001), pp. 1–26.

[2] Schacht, *Introduction*, pp. 29–31.

strictness and rigorism", discerned by Schacht.[3] The lenient views have not been preserved in the same manner in all the fields scrutinized in this inquiry. In some cases, the ancient layer became the accepted ruling of a certain *madhhab*, while in others it did not preserve its validity at all. Sometimes we are told that the Prophet made certain rulings in the early years of his career and changed them subsequently as a result of later revelation or a change of heart. It is probable, however, that the relevant developments lasted much longer, though the tradition had to compress them, of necessity, into the lifetime of the Prophet. By adopting this approach, the jurisprudents could argue that it was the Prophet himself who changed the rulings included in the ancient layer and could employ the principle of abrogation (*naskh*) in order to reach the desired conclusions. They could give legitimacy to views that became part of the mainstream and delegitimize the others by showing that the Prophet himself had discarded the latter. Any other approach would increase the legitimacy of laws and opinions that the lawyers preferred to reject in the compendia written from the early ninth century onwards.

It stands to reason that these legal developments were part and parcel of a more general picture of the evolving relationship between Islam and the religions which it encountered in the Arabian peninsula and in the territories occupied by the Muslims during the first century of their history. In Chapter One we have discussed the transformation which effected the relationship between Islam and the two older monotheistic faiths. We have dealt with a rarely quoted tradition suggesting that at a certain stage the Jews and the Christians belonged to the community of Muḥammad. In other words, the tradition has preserved a barely discernible, but highly significant, vestige of a period when the boundaries of the Muslim community had not been precisely delineated. Such a tradition is clearly an anathema to crystallized Islam and it is only natural that it would be assailed in later literature with unusual vehemence.[4] Qur'ān 2:62 may be mentioned here as well: its plain meaning promises divine reward for the Jews, the Christians and the Ṣābi'a, but its significance was later restricted to those of them who believed in Muḥammad and embraced Islam.[5] We have also seen how certain Muslim religious customs, in the beginning identical with Jewish tenets, were gradually abandoned. Islam describes itself as having disengaged from Judaism and Christianity and having adopted characteristically Muslim modes of ritual. According to the tradition, this process was brief and culminated in less than two years after the *hijra* – with the establishment of the *qibla* to Mecca, the fast of Ramaḍān and the adoption of *adhān* by human voice.[6] Historically speaking, there is nothing certain about this chronology; but the present inquiry has not unearthed material which would enable us to challenge this traditional time span and to argue that the process of disengagement took longer: the tradition insists on an intimate connection between the change in

[3] Schacht, *Introduction*, p. 35.
[4] See Chapter One, section IV, at notes 93–96.
[5] Ṭabarī, *Jāmi' al-bayān*, vol. 1, p. 320 infra; Zamakhsharī, *Kashshāf*, vol. 1, p. 285 l.1 from bottom. This verse is pivotal for Sachedina's theology; see above, Introduction, note 21.
[6] See Chapter One, section IV.

Muslim ritual and the political developments in Medina during the first two to three years of the Prophet's sojourn in the city. No material on which a different view of this development could be based seems to exist. The absence of an alternative version is of course not a guarantee of the existing version's veracity. However, the traditional description has a significance of its own, even if its historicity is ultimately unverifiable.

In other matters, however, the situation is even more difficult and the sources do not provide us with any indication concerning the chronology of the change in ideas or in doctrinal emphases. Muslim traditions concerning the relative worth of the prophets and the relationship between the Prophet Muḥammad and his predecessors in the prophetic office are a case in point. The Qur'ān includes various views on this issue. Some verses deny any distinction of rank between the prophets;[7] others assert the existence of such distinctions[8] and were later interpreted as implying the Prophet Muḥammad's superiority,[9] but no Qur'ānic verse includes an explicit statement to this effect. The situation is different in the *ḥadīth*. There we find, first of all, the egalitarian approach according to which the Prophet Muḥammad refused to be preferred even to a minor prophet such as Jonah, refused to be addressed as the "best of creation" (*khayr al-bariyya*), refused to be preferred to Moses and enjoined his followers, in more general terms, not to make any distinctions of rank between prophets. Tor Andrae rightly observed that these traditions must reflect very early attitudes and date from a period in which the self-consciousness of Muslims as a separate community had not yet become fully developed.[10] All Biblical prophets are integrated into the Islamic tradition and are deemed Muslims in a certain sense. Therefore, treating them as equals does not necessarily mean that the two Biblical religions are equal to Islam, but it is evident that the egalitarian approach is more considerate to Judaism and Christianity and is more respectful of them than any other prophetological stance.

The egalitarian approach in prophetology was, however, not destined to last. The chronology of this development is unverifiable, but Islamic tradition soon began to assert that Muḥammad was the best of creation and consequently worthier than any other prophet. It insisted that the change in attitude occurred while the Prophet was still alive, and that he had uttered the egalitarian statements before he became aware that he indeed was the best prophet and even the "Lord of the sons of Adam" (*sayyid wuld Ādam*). As in other cases, this explanation seems to ascribe

[7] See Qur'ān 2:136 ("Say you: 'We believe in God, an in that which has been sent down on us and sent down on Abraham, Ishmael, Isaac and Jacob, and the Tribes, and that which was given to Moses and Jesus and the Prophets, of their Lord; we make no division between any of them, and to Him we surrender'"), 2:285, 3:84, 4:152.

[8] Qur'ān 2:253 ("And those Messengers, some We have preferred above others; some there are to whom God spoke, and some He raised in rank ..."), 17:55.

[9] See, for instance, Rāzī, *Mafātīḥ al-ghayb*, vol. 6, p. 165, ll. 18–20.

[10] Tor Andrae, *Die Person Muhammeds in Lehre und Glauben seiner Gemeinde*, Stockholm: P. A. Norstedt & Söner, 1917, p. 245. Cf. Rubin, *The eye of the beholder*, pp. 256–257 where the author explains that the Satanic verses episode may have been put into circulation "when its provocative aspects were not yet noticed, since the dogma of the *iṣma* had not yet reached its extreme and most vivid state of development."

to the Prophet a development of Muslim consciousness, which probably occurred only sometime after his death, but it does reflect the actual process by which the Muslim community gradually acquired the self-confidence and conviction of superiority which was to become a leading feature of the Islamic world-view.[11] The available material does not enable us to date the stages of this evolution with any precision. There is, however, little doubt that the egalitarian approach preceded the assertion of Muḥammad's superiority, which became an important element in the crystallized world-view of Islam.

Another field in which an egalitarian approach can be discerned and related to the earliest period of Islam is the idea of equality before the law. Three of the four schools of law reject this notion and maintain that the lives of *dhimmīs* or other non-Muslims are not protected by the *lex talionis* in the same way as Muslim lives: a Muslim who intentionally killed an unbeliever is not to be killed in retaliation. Similarly, the amount of blood-money payable when an unbeliever is unintentionally killed by a Muslim is substantially lower than that payable when the victim is a Muslim. This is the view of the Mālikīs, the Shāfiᶜīs and the Ḥanbalīs. The Ḥanafī *madhhab* adopted the opposite, egalitarian approach on this issue. In contradistinction to the egalitarian approach in prophetology, which we deemed to belong to the earliest period of Islam by conjecture alone, here we stand on a substantially safer ground. The *Muṣannaf* of ᶜAbd al-Razzāq al-Ṣanᶜānī (d. 211 A.H. / 827 A.H.), justifiedly described by Motzki as a source of authentic *aḥādīth* from the first century A.H., contains explicit traditions which date the egalitarian approach on this matter to the period of the Prophet and his companions.[12] Some traditions credit Ibrāhīm al-Nakhaᶜī and ᶜĀmir al-Shaᶜbī, two scholars who died at the turn of the second century A.H., with supporting this stance. Other sources show how Abū Yūsuf (d. 192 A.H. / 807 A.D.), the Ḥanafī *qāḍī al-quḍāt* in Baghdad, had to succumb to the pressures of the dominant Muslim community when he tried to apply the full rigor of the law to a Muslim who killed a *dhimmī*.[13] It is, nevertheless, significant that on this matter the ancient egalitarian principle was preserved in a major school of law, though some of the supporting traditions were systematically delegitimized and declared unreliable in the *rijāl* literature and in the books of the Ḥanafī scholars. One wonders to what extent the *dhimmīs*' equality before the law was actually put into practice in the vast areas in which the Ḥanafī *madhhab* has been the dominant school of law for centuries on end.

There are credible indications that an ancient layer of legal opinion existed also in matters related to interfaith marriages. As is well known, established Muslim law allows Muslims to wed Jewish and Christian women. We have seen, however, that a considerable number of traditions frown upon this kind of matrimony and would prefer a situation in which no Muslim avails himself of it. There is even a

[11] For a fuller discussion of this process and references to primary sources, see Friedmann, *Prophecy continuous*, pp. 51–53.

[12] See Chapter One, sections VI, VII, and VIII.

[13] See Chapter One, section VI, at note 159.

rarely quoted tradition in which the Prophet himself is reported to have prohibited interfaith marriages as a matter of principle.[14] This is rather remarkable in view of Qur'ān 5:5, which explicitly allows marriages with scriptuary women. The full understanding of the issue is further complicated by the fact that according to the prevalent opinion among Muslim traditionists, the permission to wed scriptuary women is a symbol of Muslim exaltedness rather than an indication of a favorable attitude to the scriptuary communities. Nevertheless, a considerable segment of legal opinion in the earliest period of Islam looked at interfaith marriages with disfavor, despite an unequivocal Qur'ānic verse asserting their permissibility. On the other hand, we have evidence to support the idea that in this period the leaders of the Muslim community did not always implement the absolute prohibition of matrimony between a Muslim woman and an unbeliever. The relevant traditions attempt to smooth out the contradiction between the various cases in which such alliances were allowed to stand and the total ban on marriages between Muslim women and unbelievers; yet these attempts cannot obliterate the impression that in the earliest period such marriages were not always annulled. The two issues discussed in the present paragraph point in different directions regarding interfaith relations, but both indicate that the general acceptance and implementation of the Qur'ānic rulings pertinent to interfaith marriages were not immediate.

If attitudes to the People of the Book gradually moved in the direction of increased rigor, the Muslim stance toward Zoroastrianism and idolatry took, in a certain sense, an opposite course. We have seen the rarely quoted report according to which the Prophet demanded the conversion of the Zoroastrians on the pain of death[15] as well as some other traditions which opposed their inclusion in the *dhimmī* category.[16] It stands to reason that the Zoroastrian tradition with its fire-worship, dualistic beliefs and marital laws – some of which seem incestuous when contrasted with those of the three monotheistic faiths – would be an anathema to the fiercely monotheistic Islam. It is therefore plausible that the uncompromising ideas concerning the Zoroastrians seem to represent, again, the ancient layer of tradition which equated Zoroastrianism with idolatry and was superseded after the establishment of Muslim rule over Zoroastrian Iran: it then became clear that the inclusion of the Zoroastrians among the *dhimmī*s was the only feasible way of governing their newly occupied country.

The development regarding the polytheists is more complex and is not identical in all the *madhāhib*. While the Shāfiʿīs and some Ḥanbalīs seem to have preserved the stern Qur'ānic attitudes and maintained that Islam can nowhere forge a compromise with idolatry of any kind, the Ḥanafīs, the Mālikīs and other Ḥanbalīs were willing to include all idolaters and polytheists – except the Arabs – among the *dhimmī*s.[17] It seems that the uncompromising attitude to idolatry reflects the

[14] See Chapter Five, section VI, at note 128.
[15] See Chapter Two, section IV, at note 93.
[16] See Chapter Two, section IV, at notes 94–97.
[17] For details, see Chapter Two, section V.

conditions in the Arabian peninsula in which Islam aspired to absolute hegemony and would brook no compromise with any other religion – Judaism and Christianity included. The more lenient approach appears to have been the result of conditions prevailing in the vast expanses of the Muslim empire in which a Muslim minority initially ruled over a religiously heterogeneous population which included Jews, Christians, Zoroastrians, Hindūs, Buddhists and various other groups of idolaters.[18]

An ancient layer of tradition is discernible also in the attitude to the apostate, but in this case it is not uniform as far as its contents are concerned. We have seen that the Qurʾān relegates the punishment of the apostates to the hereafter, though the tradition, true to its consistent methodology, makes an attempt to show that this stance was abandoned while the Prophet was still alive. ʿUmar b. al-Khaṭṭāb is reported to have determined imprisonment (for an unspecified period) as the punishment of choice for apostasy. Other scholars maintain that the apostate – even a recidivist one – should be asked to repent forever, or "as long as there is hope for his repentance." The inevitable conclusion from the formulations of these scholars – the pride of place among whom belongs again to Ibrāhīm al-Nakhaʿī – is that the capital punishment for apostasy is practically abandoned. These views are comparable with the layer that we have labeled as "more considerate" toward the religious "other" and thus accords with the general development that we have tried to describe at the beginning of the present essay. However, on the question of apostasy we have also another ancient view which denies the opportunity of repentance altogether and demands the instant execution of the apostate.[19] We may conclude that in this case – as well as in the cases of interfaith marriages and the attitude to Zoroastrians and polytheists – the ancient layer is not more lenient than the established law, which gives the apostate the opportunity to repent and inflicts the capital punishment only in case of refusal. In the field of interfaith relations, it is therefore not possible to suggest a consistent evolution from leniency to rigor, which Schacht posited for the development of Muslim law in general. Paradoxically enough, it is the attitude to the Zoroastrians and idolaters which moved from rigor to leniency, while the attitude to the People of the Book, who are religiously much closer to Islam than the two former groups, seems to have evolved in the opposite direction.

[18] See Chapter Two, section VII.
[19] See Chapter Four, section I.

Selected Bibliography

ᶜAbd Allah b. Wahb. *al-Muwaṭṭaʾ: Kitāb al-muḥāraba*. Ed. M. Muranyi. Quellenstudien zur Ḥadīth und Rechtsliteratur in Nordafrika. Wiesbaden: Otto Harrasowitz, 1992.

ᶜAbd al-Malik b. Ḥabīb. *Kitāb Adab al-nisāʾ al-mawsūm bi-kitāb al-ghāya wa al-nihāya*. Ed. ᶜAbd al-Majīd Turkī. Beirut: Dār al-gharb al-islāmī, 1992.

Abou el-Fadl, Khaled. "Islamic law and Muslim minorities: The juristic discourse on Muslim minorities from the second/eighth to the eleventh/seventeenth centuries," *Islamic Law and Society* 1 (1994), pp. 141–187.

Abū ᶜAwāna, Yaᶜqūb b. Isḥāq al-Isfarāʾīnī. *Musnad*. Ḥaydarābād (Deccan): Dāʾirat al-maᶜārif al-ᶜUthmāniyya, 1362 A.H.

Abū Dāwūd, Sulaymān b. Ashᶜath al-Sijistānī. *al-Marāsīl*. Ed. Shuᶜayb al-Arnāwūṭ. Beirut: Muʾassasat al-risāla, 1988.

——. *Sunan*. Ed. Muḥammad Muḥyi al-Dīn ᶜAbd al-Ḥamīd. Cairo: Maṭbaᶜat Muṣṭafā Muḥammad, 1950.

Abū ʾl-Fidāʾ, ᶜImād al-Dīn Ismāᶜīl. *al-Mukhtaṣar min taʾrīkh al-bashar*. Cairo: Al-Maṭbaᶜa al-Ḥusayniyya al-Miṣriyya, 1325 A.H.

Abū Ḥayyān. *al-Baḥr al-muḥīṭ*. Cairo: Maṭbaᶜat al-saᶜāda, 1328 A.H.

Abu Sahlieh, Sami A. Aldeeb. "Le délit d'apostasie aujourd'hui et ses conséquences en droit arabe et musulman." *Islamochristiana* 20 (1994), pp. 93–116. Pontificio Istituto di Studi Arabi e d'Islamistica.

Abū Shuhba, Muḥammad b. Muḥammad. *al-Ḥudūd fī al-islām wa muqāranatuhā bi-'l-qawānīn al-waḍᶜiyya*. al-Hayʾah al-ᶜāmma li-shuʾūn al-maṭābiᶜ al-amīriyya. Cairo, 1974.

Abū Suᶜūd, Muḥammad b. al-ᶜImādī al-Ḥanafī. *Tafsīr Abī Suᶜūd, aw Irshād al-ᶜaql al-salīm ilā mazāyā al-kitāb al-karīm*. Ed. ᶜAbd al-Qādir Aḥmad ᶜAṭāʾ. Riyāḍ: Maktabat al-Riyāḍ al-ḥadītha, n.d.

Abū ᶜUbayd al-Qāsim b. Sallām al-Harawī. *Kitāb al-amwāl*. Ed. Muḥammad Ḥāmid al-Fiqqī. Cairo: al-Maktaba al-tijāriyya al-kubrā, 1353 A.H.

——. *Kitāb al-nāsikh wa al-mansūkh*. Ed. J. Burton. E. J. W. Gibb Memorial Trust. Cambridge: St Edmundsbury Press, 1987.

——. *al-Nāsikh wa al-mansūkh fī al-Qurʾān al-ᶜazīz wa mā fīhi min al-farāʾiḍ wa al-sunan*. Ed. Muḥammad Ṣāliḥ al-Mudayfir. Riyāḍ: Maktabat al-rushd, 1990.

Abū Yūsuf, Yaᶜqūb b. Ibrāhīm. *Ikhtilāf Abī Ḥanīfa wa Ibn Abī Laylā*. Ed. Abū al-Wafāʾ al-Afghānī. Cairo: Maṭbaᶜat al-wafāʾ, 1357 A.H.

——. *Kitāb al-āthār*. Ed. Abū al-Wafāʾ. Ḥaydarābād (Deccan): Dāʾirat al-maᶜārif al-ᶜUthmāniyya, 1355 A.H.

——. *Kitāb al-kharāj*. Cairo: al-Maktaba al-salafiyya wa maktabatuhā, 1352 A.H.

Adang, Camilla. "Islam as the inborn religion of mankind: the concept of fiṭra in the works of Ibn Ḥazm." *al-Qanṭara* 21 (2000), pp. 391–410.

Ahmad, Syed Barakat. "Conversion from Islam." In *The Islamic world from classical to modern times: essays in honor of Bernard Lewis*, ed. C. E. Bosworth et alii, pp. 3–25. Princeton: The Darwin Press, 1988.

——. *Muhammad and the Jews: a re-examination*. Indian Institute of Islamic Studies. New Delhi: Vikas Publishing House, 1979.

Ahmed, Shihab. "Ibn Taymiyya and the Satanic Verses." *Studia Islamica* 87 (1988), pp. 67–124.

ᶜAlī, Jawād. *Taʾrīkh al-ᶜarab qabl al-islām*. Baghdad: al-Majmaᶜ al-ᶜilmī al-ᶜIrāqī, 1956.

Alūsī, Abū al-Faḍl Shihāb al-Dīn Maḥmūd. *Rūḥ al-maᶜānī fī tafsīr al-Qurʾān al-karīm wa al-sabᶜ al-mathānī*. Cairo: Dār al-qawmiyya al-ᶜarabiyya li-'l-ṭibāᶜa, n.d.

Amanat, Abbas. *Resurrection and renewal: the making of the Bābī movement in Iran, 1844–1850*. Ithaca and London: Cornell University Press, 1988.

Āmidī, Sayf al-Dīn Abū al-Ḥasan ᶜAlī b. Abī ᶜAlī b. Muḥammad. *al-Iḥkām fī uṣūl al-aḥkām*. Cairo: Muʾassasat al-Ḥalabī wa shurakāʾihi li-'l-nashr wa al-tawzīᶜ, 1967.

Arnold, T. W. *The preaching of Islam. A history of the propagation of the Muslim faith*. London: Constable and Company, 1913.

Asnawī, Jamāl al-Dīn ᶜAbd al-Raḥīm. *Ṭabaqāt al-Shāfiᶜiyya*. Ed. ᶜAbd Allāh al-Jabbūrī. Bagdad: Maṭbaᶜat al-irshād 1390 A.H.

ᶜAsqalānī, Ibn Ḥajar Ṣhihāb al-Dīn Abū al-Faḍl. *Fatḥ al-bārī bi-sharḥ Ṣaḥīḥ al-Bukhārī*. Cairo: Maktabat Muṣṭafā al-Bābī al-Ḥalabī, 1959.

——. *al-Iṣāba fī tamyīz al-ṣaḥāba*. Ed. ᶜAlī Muḥammad al-Bijāwī. Cairo: Dār nahḍat Miṣr li-'l-ṭabᶜ wa al-nashr, 1970.

ᶜAynī, Badr al-Dīn Abū Muḥammad Maḥmūd b. Aḥmad. *al-Bināya fī sharḥ al-Hidāya*. Ed. Muḥammad ᶜUmar Nāṣir al-Islām Rāmpūrī. Beirut: Dār al-fikr, 1990.

——. *ᶜUmdat al-qāriʾ sharḥ Ṣaḥīḥ al-Bukhārī*. Beirut: Dār iḥyāʾ al-turāth al-ᶜarabī, 1348 A.H. (reprint Beirut).

Ayoub, Mahmoud. "Religious freedom and the law of apostasy in Islam." *Islamochristiana* 20 (1994), pp. 75–91. Pontificio Istituto di Studi Arabi e d'Islamistica.

——. "The Islamic context of Muslim – Christian relations." In *Indigenous Christian communitites in Islamic lands: eighth to eighteenth centuries*, ed. R. J. Bikhazi and M. Gervers, Toronto: Pontifical Institute of Mediaeval Studies, 1990, pp. 461–477.

Azemmouri, Thami. "Les *Nawāzil* d'Ibn Sahl. Section relative a l'*iḥtisāb*." *Hespéris Tamuda* 14 (1973), pp. 7–107.

Azharī, Abū Manṣūr Muḥammad b. Aḥmad b. al-Azhar. *al-Zāhir fī gharīb alfāẓ al-Shāfiᶜī*. Beirut, 1994. Printed in the introductory volume of al-Māwardī's *al-Ḥāwī al-kabīr*, pp. 195–400.

ᶜAẓīmābādī, Abū al-Ṭayyib Muḥammad Shams al-Ḥaqq. *ᶜAwn al-maᶜbūd sharḥ Sunan Abī Dāwūd, maᶜa Sharḥ al-ḥāfiẓ Ibn Qayyim al-Jawziyya*. Ed. ᶜAbd al-Raḥmān Muḥammad ᶜUthmān. Medina: al-Maktaba al-Salafiyya, 1968.

Baghawī, Abū Muḥammad al-Ḥusayn b. Masᶜūd al-Farrāʾ. *Maᶜālim al-tanzīl*. Beirut: Dār al-fikr, 1979.

——. *Sharḥ al-sunna*. Ed. Saᶜīd Muḥammad al-Laḥḥām. Beirut: Dār al-fikr, 1994.

Bājī, Abū al-Walīd Sulaymān b. Khalaf b. Saᶜd b. Ayyūb b. Wārith. *Iḥkām al-fuṣūl fī aḥkām al-uṣūl*. Ed. ᶜAbd al-Majīd Turkī. Beirut: Dār al-gharb al-Islāmī, 1986.

——. *al-Muntaqā Sharḥ Muwaṭṭaʾ Mālik b. Anas*. Cairo: Maṭbaᶜat al-saᶜāda, 1331 A.H.

Balādhurī, Abū al-ʿAbbās Aḥmad b. Yaḥyā b. Jābir. *Futūḥ al-buldān*. Ed. M. J. de Goeje. Leiden: E. J. Brill, 1866.

Bashear, Suliman. *Arabs and others in early Islam*. Studies in late antiquity and early Islam. Princeton: The Darwin Press, 1997.

Bayḍāwī, Nāṣir al-Dīn Abū Saʿīd ʿAbd Allah b. ʿUmar b. Muḥammad al-Shīrāzī. *Anwār al-tanzīl wa asrār al-taʾwīl*. Ed. H. O. Fleischer. Leipzig, 1846.

Bayhaqī, Abū Bakr Aḥmad b. al-Ḥusayn b. ʿAlī. *Maʿrifat al-sunan wa al-āthār ʿan al-imām Abī ʿAbd Allāh Muḥammad b. Idrīs al-Shāfiʿī mukhraj ʿalā tartīb Mukhtaṣar Abī Ibrāhīm Ismāʿīl b. Yaḥyā al-Muzanī*. Ed. Sayyid Kisrawī Ḥasan. Beirut: Dār al-kutub al-ʿilmiyya, 1991.

——. *al-Sunan al-kubrā*. Ḥaydarābād (Deccan): Dāʾirat al-maʿārif al-ʿUthmāniyya, 1356 A.H.

Ben Shammai, H. "Raʿyon ha-beḥira ba-Islam ha-qadum [The idea of chosenness in early Islam]." In *Raʿyon ha-beḥira be-Yisrael uva-ʿammim* [The idea of chosenness in Israel and the nations]; English title: *Chosen People, Elect Nation and Universal Mission*, ed. S. Almog and M. Heyd, pp. 147–177. Jerusalem: The Zalman Shazar Center for Jewish History, 1991.

Benzakour, Abdelaziz and Bouab, Taibi. *L'Islam et la liberté de culte*. Casablanca: Editions Al-Ofok, 1992.

Binswanger, K. *Untersuchungen zum Status der Nichtmuslime im osmanischen Reich des 16. Jahrhunderts. Mit einer neuen Definition des Begriffes "Ḏimma"*. Beiträge zur Kenntnis Südost Europas und des Nahen Orients. München: R. Trofenik, 1977.

Biqāʿī, Burhān al-Dīn Abū al-Ḥasan Ibrāhīm b. ʿUmar. *Naẓm al-durar fī tanāsub al-āyāt wa al-ṣuwar*. Ed. Muḥammad ʿAbd al-Muʿīn Khān. Ḥaydarābād (Deccan): Dāʾirat al-maʿārif al-ʿUthmāniyya, 1972.

Birujirdī, Sayyid Ibrāhīm. *Tafsīr-i jāmiʿ*. Tehran, 1375 A.H.

Bosworth, C. E. "The concept of *dhimma* in early Islam." In *Christians and Jews in the Ottoman empire: the functioning of a plural society*, ed. B. Lewis and B. Braude, New York: Holmes and Meier, 1982.

Budhūrī, Abū al-Qāsim Jamāl al-Dīn b. ʿAbd al-Raḥmān. *Qabḍat al-bayān fī nāsikh wa mansūkh al-Qurʾān, riwāyat Abī 'l-Faraj ʿAbd al-Raḥmān b. ʿAlī b. al-Jawzī*. Ed. Zuhayr al-Shāwīsh and Muḥammad Kanʿān. n.p.: al-Maktab al-Islāmī, n.d.

Bukhārī, Muḥammad b. Ismāʿīl. *Ṣaḥīḥ*. Ed. L. Krehl. Leiden: E. J. Brill, 1864.

Bulliet, Richard W. "Conversion stories in early Islam." In *Indigenous Christian communities in Islamic lands: eighth to eighteenth centuries*, ed. R. J. Bikhazi and M. Gervers, Toronto: Pontifical Institute of Mediaeval Studies, 1990, pp. 123–133.

Burjulānī, Muḥammad b. al-Ḥusayn. *Kitāb al-karam wa al-jūd wa sakhāʾ al-nufūs wa maʿahu min ḥadīth Abī ʿAbd Allah al-Ḥusayn b. Muḥammad b. al-ʿAskarī ʿan shuyūkhihi*. Ed. ʿĀmir Ḥasan Ṣabrī. Beirut: Dār Ibn Ḥazm li-'l-ṭibāʿa wa al-nashr wa al-tawzīʿ, 1991.

Chokr, Melhem. *Zandaqa et zindīqs en Islam au second siècle de l'hégire*. Damascus: Institut Français de Damas, 1993.

Dāghir, Yūsuf Asʿad. *Maṣādir al-dirāsa al-adabiyya*. Beirut: al-Maktaba al-sharqiyya, 1972.

Daiber, Hans. "Abū Ḥātim Ar-Rāzī (10th century A.D.) on the unity and diversity of religions." In *Dialogue and syncretism. An interdisciplinary approach,* Jerald D. Gort et alii, Amsterdam: Editions Rodopi, 1989, pp. 87–104.

Daniel, Elton L. "(Conversion) of Iranians to Islam." *Encyclopaedia Iranica*, vol. 5, pp. 229–232.

Dāraquṭnī, ʿAlī b. ʿUmar. *Sunan*. Ed. ʿAbd Allah Hāshim Yamānī al-Madanī. Medina: Sharikat al-ṭibāʿa al-fanniyya al-muttaḥida, 1966.

Dārimī, Abū Muḥammad ᶜAbd Allāh b. ᶜAbd al-Raḥmān. *Sunan*. Silsilat maṭbūᶜāt al-sunna al-nabawiyya. Medina: Sharikat al-ṭibāᶜa al-fanniyya al-muttaḥida, 1966.

Dhahabī, Shams al-Dīn Abū ᶜAbd Allah Muḥammad b. Aḥmad b. ᶜUthmān b. Qāymāz. *Dīwān al-ḍuᶜafāʾ wa-'l-matrūkīn*. Ed. Khalīl al-Mays. Beirut: Dār al-qalam, 1988.

——. *Kitāb al-kabāʾir*. Cairo: al-Maktaba al-tijāriyya al-kubrā, 1352 A.H.

Dimashqī, Abū ᶜAbd Allah Muḥammad b. ᶜAbd al-Raḥmān al-ᶜUthmānī al-Shāfiᶜī. *Raḥmat al-umma fī ikhtilāf al-aʾimma*. Ed. ᶜAlī al-Shurbajī and Qāsim al-Nūrī. Beirut: Muʾassasat al-risāla, 1994.

Douglas, Elmer H. "The theological position of Islam concerning religious liberty." *The Ecumenical Review* 13 (1960–1961), pp. 450–462.

Eraqi-Klorman, Bat-Zion. "The forced conversion of Jewish orphans in Yemen." *International Journal of Middle Eastern Studies* 33 (2001), pp. 23–47.

——. *The Jews of Yemen in the nineteenth century. A portrait of a messianic community*. Brill's Series in Jewish Studies. Leiden, New York and Köln: E.J. Brill 1993.

Fākihī, Abū ᶜAbd Allāh Muḥammad b. Isḥāq b. al-ᶜAbbās. *Akhbār Makka fī qadīm al-dahr wa ḥadīthihi*. Ed. ᶜAbd al-Malik b. ᶜAbd Allāh b. Duhaysh. Mecca: Maṭbaᶜat al-Nahḍa al-Ḥadītha, 1986.

Farrāʾ, Abū Zakariyā Yaḥyā b. Ziyād. *Maᶜānī al-Qurʾān*. Cairo, 1980.

Fattal, A. *Le statut légal des non-musulmanes en pays d'Islam*. Beirut: Institut de Lettres Orientales de Beyrouth, 1958.

Forte, David F. "Religious toleration in classical Islam." In *International perspectives on church and state*. ed. Menahem Mor, Omaha: Creighton University Press, 1993. pp. 209–218.

Frantz-Murphy, Gladys. "Conversion in early Islamic Egypt: the economic factor." In *Documents de l'Islam médiéval. Nouvelles perspectives de recherche*. ed. Y. Rāghib, Cairo: Institut français d'archéologie orientale, 1991. pp. 11–17.

Franz, Erhard. *Minderheiten im vorderen Orient: Auswahlbibliographie*. Hamburg: Deutsches Orient-Institut, 1978.

Friedmann, Yohanan. "Classification of unbelievers in Sunnī Muslim law and tradition." *Jerusalem Studies in Arabic and Islam* 22 (1998), pp. 163–195.

——. *Prophecy continuous. Aspects of Aḥmadī religious thought and its medieval background*. Berkeley and Los Angeles: University California Press, 1989.

——. "The temple of Multān. A note on early Muslim attitudes to idolatry." *Israel Oriental Studies* 2 (1972), pp. 176–182.

Ghazālī, Abū Ḥāmid Muḥammad b. Muḥammad. *Iḥyāʾ ᶜulūm al-dīn*. Cairo: al-Maktaba al-tijāriyya al-kubrā, n.d.

——. *al-Mustaṣfā min ᶜilm al-uṣūl*. Cairo: al-Maṭbaᶜa al-amīriyya, 1322 A.H.

Goitein, S. D. *Jews and Arabs. Their contacts through the ages*. New York: Schoken Books, 1964.

——, S. D., ed. *Religion in a religious age*. Cambridge, Mass. 1974.

Griffel, F. *Apostasie und Toleranz im Islam: Die Entwicklung zu al-Ġazālīs Urteil gegen die Philosophie und die Reaktionen der Philosophen*. Islamic Philosophy, Theology and Science. Leiden: E. J. Brill, 2000.

Hallaq, Wael B. *A history of Islamic legal theories. An introduction to Sunnī Uṣūl al-fiqh*. Cambridge: Cambridge University Press, 1997.

Ḥamāwī, Muḥammad Rushdī. *al-Mūjaz fī tafsīr al-Qurʾān al-karīm*. Cairo: Maṭbaᶜat ᶜĪsā al-Bābī al-Ḥalabī, n.d.

Ḥanbalī, Abū al-Faraj ᶜAbd al-Raḥmān b. Aḥmad Ibn Rajab. *Kalimat al-ikhlāṣ wa taḥqīq maᶜnāhā*. Ed. Zuhayr al-Shāwīsh. Beirut: al-Maktab al-Islāmī, 1397 A.H.

Ḥaqqī, Ismāʿīl al-Bursawī. *Tafsīr rūḥ al-bayān*. Istanbul: Maṭbaʿa ʿUthmāniyya, 1330 A.H.
Hawting, G. R., *The idea of idolatry and the emergence of Islam. From polemics to history*. Cambridge: Cambridge University Press, 1999.
Haykal, Muḥammad Khayr. *al-Jihād wa al-qitāl fī al-siyāsa al-sharʿiyya*. Beirut: Dār al-bayāriq, 1993.
Haythamī, Nūr al-Dīn ʿAlī b. Abī Bakr. *Majmaʿ al-zawāʾid wa manbaʿ al-fawāʾid*. Cairo: Maktabat al-Qudsī, 1353 A.H.
Ḥūfī, Aḥmad Muḥammad. *Samāḥat al-islām*. Cairo: Dār nahḍat Miṣr li-'l-ṭabʿ wa al-nashr, 1979.
Heffening, W. "Murtadd", *EI²*, s.v.
Hindī, ʿAlāʾ al-Dīn al-Muttaqī b. Ḥusām al-Dīn. *Kanz al-ʿummāl fī sunan al-aqwāl wa al-afʿāl*. Ed. Bakrī Ḥayyānī and Ṣafwat al-Saqqāʾ. Beirut: Muʾassasat al-risāla, 1979.
Ibn ʿAbd al-Barr al-Namarī, Abū ʿUmar Yūsuf b. ʿAbd Allah b. Muḥammad. *al-Tamhīd li-mā fī al-Muwaṭṭaʾ min al-maʿānī wa al-asānīd*. Ed. Muṣṭafā b. Aḥmad al-ʿAlawī and Muḥammad ʿAbd al-Kabīr al-Bakrī. Rabāṭ: al-Maṭbaʿa al-malakiyya, vol. 1 – 1967; vols. 2ff. 1988.
Ibn Abī Ḥātim al-Rāzī. *Kitāb al-jarḥ wa al-taʿdīl*. Ḥaydarābād (Deccan): Dāʾirat al-maʿārif al-ʿUthmāniyya, 1953.
Ibn Abī Shayba, ʿAbd al-Raḥmān b. Muḥammad b. Abī Shayba Ibrāhīm b. ʿUthmān Abū Bakr al-Kūfī al-ʿAbsī. *Kitāb al-muṣannaf fī al-aḥādīth wa al-āthār*. n.p., n.d.
Ibn Abī Zayd al-Qayrawānī. *Kitāb al-jihād min kitāb al-nawādir wa al-ziyādāt*. Ed. Mathias von Bredow. Beirut and Stuttgart: Franz Steiner Verlag, 1994.
Ibn al-ʿArabī al-Mālikī. *Aḥkām al-Qurʾān*. Beirut: Dār al-maʿrifa, n.d.
——. *al-Nāsikh wa al-mansūkh fī al-Qurān al-karīm*. Ed. ʿAbd al-Kabīr al-ʿAlawī al-Madghirī. Cairo: Maktabat al-thaqāfa al-dīniyya, 1992.
——. *Kitāb al-qabas fī sharḥ Muwaṭṭaʾ Mālik b. Anas*. Ed. Muḥammad ʿAbd Allah Ould Krim. Beirut: Dār al-gharb al-islāmī, 1992.
Ibn al-ʿArabī, Muḥyi al-Dīn. *Tafsīr al-Qurʾān al-karīm*. Beirut: Dār al-yaqẓa al-ʿarabiyya, 1968.
Ibn ʿĀshūr, Muḥammad al-Ṭāhir. *Tafsīr al-taḥrīr wa al-tanwīr*. Tunis: al-Dār al-Tūnisiyya li-'l-nashr, 1973.
Ibn al-Athīr, ʿIzz al-Dīn. *al-Kāmil fī al-taʾrīkh*. Beirut: Dār Ṣādir and Dār Bayrūt, 1965.
Ibn al-Bannāʾ, Abū ʿAlī al-Ḥasan b. Aḥmad b. ʿAbd Allāh. *Kitāb al-muqniʿ fī sharḥ Mukhtaṣar al-Khiraqī*. Ed. ʿAbd al-ʿAzīz b. Sulaymān b. Ibrāhīm al-Buʿaymī. Riyāḍ: Maktabat al-rushd, 1993.
Ibn al-Bārizī. *Nāsikh al-Qurʾān al-ʿazīz wa mansūkhuhu*. Ed. Ḥātim Ṣāliḥ al-Ḍāmin.
Ibn al-Farrāʾ, Abū Yaʿlā Muḥammad b. al-Ḥusayn al-Baghdādī al-Ḥanbalī. *al-Aḥkām al-sulṭāniyya*. Ed. Muḥammad Ḥāmid al-Fiqqī. Cairo: Maṭbaʿat Muṣṭafā al-Bābī al-Ḥalabī, 1938.
——. *al-ʿUdda fī uṣūl al-fiqh*. Ed. Aḥmad b. ʿAli Sīr Mubārakī. Beirut: Muʾassasat al-risāla, 1980.
Ibn al-Ḥājj al-ʿAbdarī. *al-Mudkhal*. Alexandria (?): al-Maṭbaʿa al-waṭaniyya, 1293 A.H.
Ibn Ḥanbal, Aḥmad. *Aḥkām al-nisāʾ*. Ed. ʿAbd al-Qādir Aḥmad ʿAṭāʾ. Beirut: Dār al-kutub al-ʿilmiyya, 1986.
——. *Masāʾil*. Ed. Faḍl al-Raḥmān Dīn Muḥammad. Delhi: al-Dār al-ʿilmiyya, 1988.
——. *Musnad*. Beirut: al-Maktab al-islāmī li-'l-ṭibāʿa wa al-nashr (rep.), 1978.
Ibn Ḥazm, Abū Muḥammad ʿAlī. *al-Iḥkām fī uṣūl al-aḥkām*. Ed. Muḥammad Aḥmad ʿAbd al-ʿAzīz. Cairo: Maktabat ʿĀṭif, 1978.

——. *al-Muḥallā*. Ed. Muḥammad Khalīl Harās Cairo: Maktabat al-imām, 1964.

Ibn Hishām. *Sīrat Rasūl Allāh*. Ed. F. Wüstenfeld. Göttingen: Dieterich'sche Universitäts-Buchhandlung, 1858–1860.

Ibn Humām, Kamāl al-Dīn Muḥammad b. ᶜAbd al-Wāḥid al-Siwāsī. *Fatḥ al-qadīr ᶜalā al-Hidāya*. Cairo: Maṭbaᶜat Muṣṭafā al-Bābī al-Ḥalabī, 1970.

Ibn al -ᶜIbrī. *Taʾrīkh Mukhtaṣar al-duwal*. Beirut: Catholic Press, 1958.

Ibn al-Jawzī, Jamāl al-Dīn Abū ʾl-Faraj ᶜAbd al-Raḥmān. *Kitāb al-mawḍūᶜāt*. Ed. ᶜAbd al-Raḥmān Muḥammad ᶜUthmān. Medina: al-Maktaba al-salafiyya, 1966–1968.

——. *al-Muṣaffā bi-akuff ahl al-rusūkh min ᶜilm al-nāsikh wa al-mansūkh*. Ed. Ḥātim Ṣāliḥ al-Ḍāmin. Beirut: Muʾassasat al-risāla, 1984.

——. *Zād al-masīr fī ᶜilm al-tafsīr*. Damascus and Beirut: al-Maktab al-islāmī li-'l-ṭibāᶜa wa al-nashr, 1965.

Ibn Kathīr, ᶜImād al-Dīn Abū al-Fidāʾ Ismāᶜīl. *al-Masāʾil al-fiqhiyya allatī infarada bihā al-imām al-Shāfiᶜī min dūni ikhwānihi min al-aʾimma*. Ed. Ibrāhīm b. ᶜAlī Ṣanduqjī. Medina: Maktabat al-ᶜulūm wa al-ḥikam, 1986.

——. *Tafsīr al-Qurʾān al-ᶜaẓīm*. Beirut: Dār al-fikr, 1970.

Ibn Māja. *Sunan*. Ed. Muḥammad Fuʾād ᶜAbd al-Bāqī. Cairo: ᶜĪsā al-Bābī al-Ḥalabī, 1952.

Ibn al-Murajjā b. Ibrāhīm al-Maqdisī. *Faḍāʾil Bayt al-Maqdis wa al-Khalīl wa faḍāʾil al-Shām*. Ed. O. Livne-Kafri. Shfaram (Israel): al-Mashriq, 1995.

Ibn al-Murtaḍā, Aḥmad b. Yaḥyā. *Kitāb al-baḥr al-zakhkhār al-jāmiᶜ li-madhāhib ᶜulamāʾ al-amṣār*. Eds. ᶜAbd Allah Muḥammad al-Ṣiddīq and ᶜAbd al-Ḥafīẓ Saᶜd ᶜAṭiyya. Beirut: Muʾassasat al-risāla, 1975.

Ibn Qayyim al-Jawziyya. *Aḥkām ahl al-dhimma*. Ed. Ṣubḥī al-Ṣāliḥ. Damascus, 1961.

——. *Hidāyat al-ḥayārā fī al-radd ᶜalā al-yahūd wa al-naṣārā*. Ed. Sayf al-Dīn al-Kātib. Beirut: Dār Maktabat al-ḥayāt, 1980.

——. *Ighāthat al-lahfān min maṣāʾid al-shayṭān*. Ed. Ḥassān ᶜAbd al-Mannān and ᶜIṣām Fāris al-Ḥirastiyānī. Beirut: Muʾassasat al-risāla, 1994.

——. *Kitāb al-ṣalāt wa aḥkām tārikihā*. Cairo: al-Maṭbaᶜa al-ᶜāmira al-sharafiyya, 1323 A.H.

——. *al-Manār al-munīf fī al-ṣaḥīḥ wa al-ḍaᶜīf*. Ed. ᶜAbd al-Raḥmān al-Muᶜallimī. Riyāḍ: Dār al-ᶜĀṣima, 1996.

——. *Zād al-maᶜād fī hady khayr al-ᶜibād*. Ed. Shuᶜayb al-Arnaʾūṭ and ᶜAbd al-Qādir al-Arnaʾūṭ. Beirut: Muʾassasat al-risāla, 1987.

Ibn Qudāma, ᶜAbd Allah b. Aḥmad b. Muḥammad. *al-Kāfī fī fiqh al-imām Aḥmad b. Hanbal*. Ed. Muḥammad Fāris and Masᶜad ᶜAbd al-Ḥamīd al-Saᶜdanī. Beirut: Dār al-kutub al-ᶜilmiyya, 1994.

——. *al-Mughnī*. Cairo: Dār al-manār, 1367 A.H.

——. *Rawḍat al-nāẓir wa junnat al-munāẓir fī uṣūl al-fiqh*. Ed. Abd al-Karīm b. ᶜAlī b. Muḥammad al-Namla. Riyāḍ: Maktabat al-rushd, 1993.

Ibn Qutayba, Abū Muḥammad ᶜAbd Allah b. Muslim. *Kitāb al-maᶜārif*. Ed. Tharwat ᶜUkkāsha. Cairo: Maṭbaᶜat Dār al-kutub, 1960.

Ibn Rushd, Abū al-Walīd Muḥammad b. Aḥmad. *Bidāyat al-mujtahid wa nihāyat al-muqtaṣid*. n.p.: Dār al-fikr, Maktabat al-Khānjī, n.d.

Ibn Saᶜd, Muḥammad. *Kitāb al-ṭabaqāt al-kabīr*. Ed. E. Sachau et alii. Leiden: E. J. Brill, 1905–1921.

Ibn Shās, Jalāl al-Dīn ᶜAbd Allāh b. Najm. *ᶜIqd al-jawāhir al-thamīna fī madhhab ᶜālim al-Madīna*. Ed. Muḥammad Abū al-Ajfān and ᶜAbd al-Ḥafīẓ Manṣūr. Beirut: Dār al-gharb al-islāmī, 1995.

Ibn Taymiyya, Abū al-ᶜAbbās Taqī al-Dīn Aḥmad b. ᶜAbd al-Ḥalīm. *al-Fatāwā al-kubrā*. Cairo: Dār al-kutub al-ḥadītha, 1966.

——. *Majmūᶜ fatāwā*. Ed. ᶜAbd al-Raḥmān b. Muḥammad b. Qāsim al-ᶜĀṣimī al-Najdī al-Ḥanbalī. Riyāḍ: Maṭābiᶜ al Riyād, 1381 A.H.

——. *Iqtiḍāʾ al-ṣirāṭ al-mustaqīm li-mukhālafat aṣḥāb al-jaḥīm*. Ed. Nāṣir b. ᶜAbd al-Karīm al-ᶜAql. Riyāḍ: Maktabat al-rushd, 1991.

——. *al-Ṣārim al-maslūl ᶜalā shātim al-rasūl*. Ed. Muḥammad Muḥyi al-Dīn ᶜAbd al-Ḥamīd. Ṭanṭā: Maktabat al-Tāj, 1960.

——. *Majmūᶜat tafsīr Shaykh al-Islām Ibn Taymiyya*. Ed. ᶜAbd al-Ṣamad Sharaf al-Dīn. Bombay: al-Dār al-Qayyima, 1954.

Ibn al-Turkmānī, ᶜAlāʾ al-Dīn ᶜAlī b. ᶜUthmān al-Mārdīnī. *al-Jawhar al-naqī*. Ḥaydarābād (Deccan): Dāʾirat al-maᶜārif al-ᶜUthmāniyya, 1356 A.H. (on the margin of Bayhaqī, *al-Sunan al-kubrā*).

Ibn ᶜUmar, ᶜAbd Allāh. *Musnad ᶜAbd Allāh b. ᶜUmar, takhrīj Abī Umayya Muḥammad b. Ibrāhīm al-Ṭarsūsī*. Ed. Aḥmad Rātib ᶜUrmūsh. Beirut: Dār al-nafāʾis, 1987.

Ibn Zanjawayhi, Ḥumayd. *Kitāb al-amwāl*. Ed. Shākir Dhīb Fayyāḍ. Riyāḍ: Markaz al-malik Fayṣal li-'l-buḥūth wa al-dirāsāt al-islāmiyya, 1986.

Idris, H. R. "Les tributaires en occident musulman médiéval d'après le *Miᶜyār* d'al-Wansharīsī." In *Mélanges d'islamologie. Volume dédié à la memoire de Armand Abel par ses collègues, ses élèves et ses amis*, ed. Pierre Salmon, pp. 172–200. Leiden: E. J. Brill, 1974.

Iskandarī, Nāṣir al-Dīn Aḥmad b. Muḥammad b. al-Munīr al-Mālikī. *al-Inṣāf fīmā taḍammanahu al-Kashshāf min al-iᶜtizāl*. Cairo: Maṭbaᶜat Muṣṭafā al-Bābī al-Ḥalabī, n.d.

Jabr, Saᶜdī Ḥusayn ᶜAlī. *Fiqh al-imām Abī Thawr*. Beirut: Muʾassasat al-risāla, 1983.

Jaṣṣāṣ, Abū Bakr Aḥmad b. ᶜAlī al-Rāzī. *Aḥkām al-Qurʾān*. Cairo: al-Maṭbaᶜa al-bahiyya al-Miṣriyya, 1347 A.H.

——. *Mukhtaṣar ikhtilāf al-ᶜulamāʾ taṣnīf Abī Jaᶜfar Aḥmad b. Muḥammad b. Salāma al-Ṭaḥāwī*. Ed. ᶜAbd Allāh Nadhīr Aḥmad. Beirut: Dār al-bashāʾir al-islāmiyya, 1995.

Jubūrī, ᶜAbd Allah Muḥammad. *Fiqh al-imām al-Awzāᶜī*. Baghdad: Maṭbaᶜat al-irshād, 1977.

Kalwadhānī, Abū al-Khaṭṭāb Maḥfūẓ b. Aḥmad b. al-Ḥusayn al-Ḥanbalī. *al-Tamhīd fī uṣūl al-fiqh*. Ed. Mufīd Muḥammad Abū ᶜAmsha. Mecca: Markaz al-baḥth al-ᶜilmī wa Iḥyāʾ al-turāth al-islāmī, 1985.

Kamali, M. H. *Principles of Islamic Jurisprudence*. Cambridge: The Islamic Texts Society, 1997.

Karabélias, Evangelos. "Apostasie et dissidence religieuse à Byzance de Justinien Ier jusqu'à l'invasion arabe (variations Byzantines sur l'intolérance)." *Islamochristiana* 20 (1994), pp. 41–74.

Kardarī, Ḥāfiẓ al-Dīn b. Muḥammad. *Manāqib Abī Ḥanīfa*. Beirut: Dār al-kitāb al-ᶜarabī, 1981.

Kāsānī, ᶜAlāʾ al-Dīn Abū Bakr Masᶜūd. *Badāʾiᶜ al-ṣanāʾiᶜ fī tartīb al-sharāʾiᶜ*. Cairo: Maṭbaᶜat sharikat al-maṭbūᶜāt al-ᶜilmiyya, 1327 A.H.

Kerber, Walter, ed., *Wie tolerant ist der Islam?* München: Kindt Verlag, 1991.

Khadduri, Majid. *The Islamic law of nations: Shaybānī's Siyar*. Baltimore: The Johns Hopkins Press, 1966.

Khallāl, Abū Bakr Muḥammad b. Hārūn b. Yazīd al-Baghdādī al-Ḥanbalī. *Ahl al-milal wa al-ridda wa al-zanādiqa wa tārik al-ṣalāt wa al-farāʾiḍ min Kitāb al-Jāmiᶜ*. Ed. Ibrāhīm b. Ḥamad b. Sulṭān. Riyāḍ: Maktabat al-maᶜārif li-'l-nashr wa al-tawzīᶜ, 1996.

——. *al-Sunna*. Ed. ᶜAṭiyya b. ᶜAtīq al-Zahrānī. Riyāḍ: Dār al-rāya li-'l-nashr wa al-tawzīᶜ, 1994.

Kharbuṭlī, Alī Ḥusnī. *al-Islām wa ahl al-dhimma*. Cairo: al-Majlis al-aᶜlā li-'l-shuʾūn al-islāmiyya, 1969.

Khaṭīb al-Baghdādī. *Taʾrīkh Baghdād*. Beirut: Dār al-kitāb al-ᶜarabī, 1966 (?).

Khaṭṭāb, Muḥammad Maḥmūd. *Fatḥ al-malik al-maᶜbūd, takmilat al-manhal al-ᶜadhb al-mawrūd Sharḥ Sunan al-imām Abī Dawūd*. Cairo: Maṭbaᶜat al-istiqāma, 1959.

Khaṭṭābī, Abū Sulaymān Aḥmad b. Muḥammad. Aᶜlām al-*ḥadīth fī sharḥ Ṣaḥīḥ al-Bukhārī*. Ed. Muḥammad b. Saᶜīd b. ᶜAbd al-Raḥmān Āl Saᶜūd. Mecca: Markaz iḥyāʾ al-turāth al-islāmī, 1988.

Khāzin, ᶜAlāʾ al-Dīn b. Muḥammad b. Ibrāhīm al-Baghdādī. *Lubāb al-taʾwīl fī maᶜānī al-tanzīl*. Beirut: Dār al-fikr, 1979.

Khiraqī, Abū al-Qāsim ᶜUmar b. al-Ḥusayn. *Mukhtaṣar al-Khiraqī ᶜalā al-imām al-mubajjal Aḥmad b. Hanbal*. Ed. Muḥammad Zuhayr al-Shāwīsh. Damascus: Muʾassasat dār al-salām, 1379 A.H.

Khuḍayrī, Muḥammad b. ᶜAbd Allāh b. ᶜAlī. *Tafsīr al-tābiᶜīn: ᶜarḍ wa dirāsa muqārina*. Riyāḍ: Dār al-waṭan li-'l-nashr, 1999.

Khusruwānī, ᶜAlī Riźā. *Tafsīr-i Khusrawī*. Tehran: Kitāb furūshī Islāmiyya, 1390 A.H.

Khwārizmī, Abū al-Muʾayyad Muḥammad b. Maḥmūd b. Muḥammad. *Jāmiᶜ Masānīd al-imām al-aᶜẓam Abī Ḥanīfa*. Ḥaydarābād (Deccan), 1332 A.H.

Kister, M. J. "Ādam: A study of some legends in tafsīr and ḥadīth literature." *Israel Oriental Studies* 13 (1993), pp. 113–174.

——. "*... illā bi-ḥaqqihi...* A study of an early *ḥadīth*." *Jerusalem Studies in Arabic and Islam* 5 (1984), pp. 33–52 (= *Society and Religion from Jāhiliyya to Islam*, IX)

——. "Land property and *jihād*. A discussion of some early traditions." *Journal of the Economic and Social History of the Orient* 34 (1991), pp. 270–311.

——. "'O God, tighten Thy grip on Muḍar...'. Some socio-economic and religious aspects of an early *ḥadith*." *Journal of the Economic and Social History of the Orient* 24 (1981), pp. 242–273.

Kohlberg, Etan. "The development of the Imāmī Shīᶜī doctrine of jihād." *Zeitschrift der deutschen morgenländischen Gesellschaft* 126 (1976), pp. 64–86.

——. "Medieval Muslim views on martyrdom." Amsterdam: Mededelingen der Koninklijke Nederlandse Akademie an Wetenschappen, 1997, pp. 281–307.

——. "Some Shīᶜī views of the antediluvian world." *Studia Islamica* 52 (1980), pp. 41–66.

Kraemer, Joel L. "Apostates, rebels and brigands" *Israel Oriental Studies* 10 (1980), pp. 34–73.

Krcsmárik, J. "Beiträge zur Beleuchtung des islamitischen Strafrechts, mit Rücksicht auf Theorie und Praxis in der Türkei." *Zeitschrift der deutschen morgenländischen Gesellschaft* 58 (1904), pp. 69–113, 316–360, 539–581.

Küng, H., van Ess, J., and Bechert, H. *Christianity and world religions: paths to dialogue*. Translated by P. Heinegg. Maryknoll: Orbis Books, 1993.

Lāhijī, Bahāʾ al-Dīn Muḥammad b. Shaykh ᶜAlī. *Tafsīr-i sharīf-i Lāhijī*. Ed. Mīr Jalāl al-Dīn Ḥusaynī Armawī. Tehran (?): Muʾassasa-yi maṭbūᶜāt-i ᶜilmī, 1381 A.H.

Lecker, M. "ᶜAmr b. Ḥazm al-Anṣārī and Qurʾān 2:256: 'No compulsion is there in religion'." *Oriens* 35 (1996), pp. 57–64.

——. "The conversion of Ḥimyar to Judaism and the Jewish Banū Hadl of Medina." *Die Welt des Orients* 26 (1995), pp. 129–136.

——. "Ḥudhayfa b. al-Yamān and ᶜAmmār b. Yāsir, Jewish converts to Islam." *Quaderni di Studi Arabi* 11 (1993), pp. 149–162.

——. *Muslims, Jews and Pagans: Studies on Early Islamic Medina*. Islamic History and Civilization: Studies and Texts 13. Leiden: E. J. Brill, 1995.

Lewis, Bernard. "L'Islam et les non-musulmans." *Annales: économies, sociétés, civilisations* 35 (1980), pp. 784–800.

——. *The Muslim discovery of Europe*. London: Weidenfeld and Nicholson, 1982.

——. *Race and slavery in the Middle East. An historical inquiry*. New York and Oxford: Oxford University Press, 1990.

Linder, A. *The Jews in the legal sources of the early Middle Ages*. Detroit: Wayne State University Press, Jerusalem: Israel Academy of Sciences and Humanities, 1997.

Little, D. P. "Coptic converts to Islam during the Baḥrī Mamlūk Period." In *Indigenous Christian communities in Islamic lands: eighth to eighteenth centuries*, ed. R. J. Bikhazi and M. Gervers, Toronto: Pontifical Institute of Mediaeval Studies, 1990, pp. 263–288.

Little, David, Kelsay, John and Sachedina, Abdulaziz A. *Human rights and the conflict of cultures: Western and Islamic perspectives on religious liberty*. Columbia: University of South Carolina Press, 1988.

McAuliffe, Jane Dammen. "Exegetical Identification of the Ṣābiʾūn." *The Muslim World* 72 (1982), pp. 95–106.

——. "Fakhr al-Dīn al-Rāzī on *āyat al-jizya* and *āyat al-sayf*." In *Conversion and continuity: indigenous Christian communities in Islamic lands, eighth to eighteenth centuries,* ed. M. Gervers, and R. J. Bikhazi, Papers in Medieval Studies 9. Toronto: Pontifical Institute of Mediaeval Studies, 1990, pp. 103–19.

Madkhalī, Rabīᶜ b. Hādī ᶜUmayr. *al-Taᶜṣṣub al-dhamīm wa āthāruhu*. Riyāḍ: Maktabat al-salaf, 1995.

Mālik b. Anas. *al-Muwaṭṭaʾ*. Ed. Muḥammad Fuʾād ᶜAbd al-Bāqī. Cairo: ᶜĪsā al-Bābī al-Ḥalabī, 1951.

Marghīnānī, Burhān al-Dīn Abū al-Ḥasan ᶜAlī b. Abī Bakr b. ᶜAbd al-Jalīl. *al-Hidāya, sharḥ Bidāyat al-mubtadiʾ*. Ed. Muḥammad Muḥammad Qāmir and Ḥāfiẓ ᶜĀshūr Ḥāfiẓ. Cairo: Dār al-salām, 2000.

Marin, Manuela and El-Hour, Rachid. "Captives, children and conversion: a case from late Naṣrid Granada." *Journal of the Economic and Social History of the Orient* 41 (1998), pp. 453–473.

Masᶜūdī, ᶜAlī b. al-Ḥusayn. *Murūj al-dhahab wa maᶜādin al-jawhar*. Ed. Ch. Pellat. Beirut: Catholic Press, 1966.

Māwardī, Abū al-Ḥasan ᶜAlī b. Muḥammad b. Ḥabīb. *al-Ḥāwī al-kabīr fī fiqh madhhab al-imām al-Shāfiᶜī ... wa huwa sharḥ Mukhtaṣar al-Muzanī*. Ed. ᶜAlī Muḥammad Muᶜawwaḍ and ᶜĀdil Aḥmad ᶜAbd al-Mawjūd. Beirut: Dār al-kutub al-ᶜilmiyya, 1994.

——. *Kitāb al-aḥkām al-sulṭāniyya wa al-wilāyāt al-dīniyya*. Ed. Aḥmad Mubārak al-Baghdādī. Kuwayt: Maktabat Dār Ibn Qutayba, 1989.

——. *al-Nukat wa al-ᶜuyūn: Tafsīr al-Māwardī*. Ed. al-Sayyid b. ᶜAbd al-Manṣūr b. ᶜAbd al-Raḥīm. Beirut: Dār al-kutub al-ᶜilmiyya wa Muʾassasat al-kutub al-thaqāfiyya, 1992.

——. *Les statuts gouvernementaux ou règles de droit public et administratif*. Traduit et annnotés par E. Fagnan. Alger: Libraire de l'Université, 1915.

Mayer, Ann Elisabeth. *Islam and human rights*. Bolder: Westview Press, 1991.

Mensching, G. *Tolerance and truth in religion*. Translated into English by H. J. Klimkeit. Alabama: The University of Alabama Press, 1971.

Mizzī, Jamāl al-Dīn Abū al-Ḥajjāj Yūsuf al-Mizzī. *Tahdhīb al-kamāl fī asmā᾽ al-rijāl*. Ed. Bashshār ᶜAwwād Maᶜrūf. Beirut: Mu᾽assasat al-risāla, 1985–1992.

Mohamed, Y. "The Interpretations of fiṭra." *Islamic Studies* 34 (1995), pp. 129–151.

Monnot, Guy. *Islam et religions. Islam d'hier et d'aujourd'hui*. Paris: Éditions Maisonneuve et Larose, 1986.

Motzki, Harald. Anfänge der islamischen Jurisprudenz. Ihre Entwicklung in Mekka bis zur Mitte des 2./8. Jahrhunderts. Stuttgart: Komission Verlag Franz Steiner, 1991.

——. "The Muṣannaf of ᶜAbd al-Razzāq al-Ṣanᶜānī as a source of authentic aḥādīth of the first century A.H." *Journal of Near Eastern Studies* 50 (1991), pp. 1–21.

Muḥāsibī, al-Ḥārith b. Asad. *al-ᶜAql wa fahm al-Qur᾽ān*. Ed. Ḥusayn al-Quwwatlī. Beirut (?): Dār al-Kindī, Dār al-fikr, 1978.

Müller, Lorenz. *Islam und Menschenrechte. Sunnitische Muslime zwischen Islamismus, Säkularismus und Modernismus*. Hamburg: Deutsches Orient-Institut, 1996.

Muqātil b. Sulaymān. *al-Ashbāh wa al-naẓā᾽ir fī al-Qur᾽ān al-karīm*. Ed. ᶜAbd Allāh Maḥmūd Shaḥḥāta. Cairo: Markaz taḥqīq al-turāth, 1994.

——. *Tafsīr*. Ed. ᶜAbd Allah Maḥmūd Shaḥḥāta. Cairo: al-Hay᾽a al-Miṣriyya al-ᶜāmma li-'l-kitāb, 1978.

Muqri᾽, Hibat Allah b. Salāma b. Naṣr. *al-Nāsikh wa al-mansūkh min kitāb Allah taᶜālā*. Ed. Zuhayr al-Shāwīsh and Muḥammad Kanᶜān. n.p., n.d.

Muranyi, Miklos. *Beiträge zur Geschichte der Ḥadīṯ- und Rechtsgelehrsamkeit der Mālikiyya in Nordafrika bis zum 5. JH. D.H. Bio-bibliographische Notizen aus der Moscheebibliothek von Qairawān*. Quellenstudien zur Ḥadīṯ- und Rechtsliteratur in Nordafrika. Wiesbaden: Otto Harrasowitz, 1997.

——. *Die Rechtsbücher des Qairawāners Saḥnūn b. Saᶜīd. Entstehungsgeschichte und Werküberlieferung*. Deutsche morgenländische Gesellschaft, Abhandlungen für die Kunde des Morgenlandes, Band LII, 3. Stuttgart: Franz Steiner, 1999.

Mūsā b. ᶜUqba. *al-Maghāzī*. Ed. Muḥammad Bā Qashsīsh Abū Mālik. Akādīr: Jāmiᶜat Ibn Zahr, kulliyyat al-ādāb wa al-ᶜulūm al-insāniyya, 1994.

Muslim b. al-Ḥajjāj. *Ṣaḥīḥ Muslim*. Ed. Muḥammad Fu᾽ād ᶜAbd al-Bāqī. Cairo: Maṭbaᶜat ᶜĪsā al-Bābī al-Ḥalabī, 1955.

Naḥḥās, Abū Jaᶜfar Ahmad b. Muḥammad b. Ismāᶜīl. *al-Nāsikh wa al-mansūkh fī kitāb Allah taᶜālā wa-'khtilāf al-ᶜulamā᾽ fī dhālika*. Ed. Sulaymān b. Ibrāhīm b. ᶜAbd Allah al-Lāḥim. Beirut: Mu᾽assasat al-risāla, 1991.

Nasā᾽ī, Aḥmad b. ᶜAlī. *Sunan, bi-sharḥ Jalāl al-Dīn al-Suyūṭī wa-ḥāshiyat al-Suddī*. Ed. Ḥasan Muḥammad al-Masᶜūdī. Cairo: al-Maṭbaᶜa al-Miṣriyya bi-'l-Azhar, n.d.

Nawawī, Muḥyi al-Dīn Abū Zakariyā Yaḥyā b. Sharaf. *al-Majmūᶜ sharḥ al-Muhadhdhab*. Cairo: Maṭbaᶜat al-imām, 1966 (?).

——. *Sharḥ Ṣaḥīḥ Muslim*. Ed. Khalīl al-Mays. Beirut: Dār al-qalam, 1987.

Nazir-Ali, Michael. *The roots of Islamic tolerance: origin and development*. Oxford project for peace studies. Oxford, 1990.

Nazwī, Abū Bakr Aḥmad b. ᶜAbd Allāh b. Musā al-Kindī al-Samadī. *al-Muṣannaf*. Ed. ᶜAbd al-Munᶜim ᶜĀmir and Jār Allāh Aḥmad. ᶜUmān: Wizārat al-turāth al-qawmī wa al-thaqāfa, 1979-1989.

Nederman, C. J. and Laursen, J. C. eds. *Difference and dissent: theories of toleration in medieval and early modern Europe*. Lanham (MD): Rowman and Littlefield, 1997.

Nöldeke, Th. and Schwally, F. *Geschichte des Qorāns*. Leipzig: Dieterich'sche Verlagsbuchhandlung, 1909.

Noth, A. "Abgrenzungsprobleme zwischen Muslimen and nicht-Muslimen. Die 'Bedingungen ᶜUmars *(aš-š-urūṭ al-ᶜumariyya)*' unter einem anderen Aspekt gelesen."*Jerusalem Studies in Arabic and Islam* 9 (1987), pp. 290–315.

——. "Möglichkeiten und Grenzen islamischer Toleranz." *Saeculum* 29 (1993), pp. 190–204.

Paige, Glenn D., Satha-Anand, Chaiwat and Gilliatt, Sarah, eds. *Islam and non-violence*. Honolulu: Matsunaga Institute for Peace, University of Hawai, 1993.

Pānipatī, Muḥammad Thanāᵓ Allāh ᶜUthmānī Mujaddidī. *Tafsīr-i Maẓharī*. Delhi: Nadwat al-muṣannifīn, n.d.

Paret, R. "Innerislamischer Pluralismus." In *Die Islamische Welt zwischen Mittelalter und Neuzeit*, ed. P. Bachmann, and U. Haarmann, Beirut: Beiruter Texte und Studien, 1979, pp. 523–529.

——. "Sure 2,256: Lā ikrāha fī d-dīni. Toleranz oder Resignation?" *Der Islam* 45 (1969), pp. 299–300.

——. "Toleranz und Intoleranz im Islam." *Saeculum* 21 (1970), pp. 344–365.

Peters, R. and de Vries, G. J. J. "Apostasy in Islam." *Die Welt des Islams* 17 (1976–1977), pp. 1–25.

Qaffāl, Sayf al-Dīn Abū Bakr Muḥammad b. Aḥmad al-Shāshī. *Ḥilyat al-ᶜulamāᵓ fī maᶜrifat madhāhib al-fuqahāᵓ*. Ed. Darādika, Yāsīn Aḥmad Ibrāhīm. ᶜAmmān: Maktabat al-risāla al-ḥadītha, 1988.

Qalᶜajī, Muḥammad Rawwās. *Mawsūᶜat fiqh Sufyān al-Thawrī*. Silsilat mawsūᶜāt fiqh al-salaf. Beirut: Dār al-nafāᵓis, 1990.

Qāsimī, Jamāl al-Dīn. *Maḥāsin al-taᵓwīl*. Cairo: Dār iḥyāᵓ al-kutub al-ᶜarabiyya, 1957–1960.

Qasṭallānī, Aḥmad b. Muḥammad b. al-Ḥusayn b. ᶜAlī. *Irshād al-sārī sharḥ Ṣaḥīḥ al-Bukhārī*. Cairo: al-Maṭbaᶜa al-kubrā al-amīriyya, 1304 A.H.

Qatāda b. Diᶜāma al-Sadūsī. *Kitāb al-nāsikh wa al-mansūkh fī kitāb Allāh taᶜālā*. Ed. Ḥātim Ṣāliḥ al-Ḍāmin. Beirut: Muᵓassasat al-risāla, 1984.

Qudūrī, Aḥmad b. Muḥammad b. Aḥmad b. Jaᶜfar. *Mukhtaṣar al-Qudūrī fī al-fiqh al-ḥanafī*. Ed. Kāmil Muḥammad Muḥammad ᶜUwayḍa. Beirut: Dār al-kutub al-ᶜilmiyya, 1997.

Qummī, Abū al-Ḥasan ᶜAlī b. Ibrāhīm. *Tafsīr*. Najaf: Maktabat al-hudā, 1386 A.H.

Qurṭubī, Abū ᶜAbd Allah Muḥammad b. Aḥmad al-Anṣārī. *al-Jāmiᶜ li-aḥkām al-Qurᵓān*. Beirut: Dār al-fikr, 1993–1995

Qurṭubī, Abū al-ᶜAbbās Aḥmad b. ᶜUmar b. Ibrāhīm. *al-Mufhim li-mā ashkala min talkhīṣ Kitāb Muslim*. Ed. Aḥmad Muḥammad al-Sayyid et alii. Damascus: Dār al-kalim al-ṭayyib, 1996.

Ramlī, Shams al-Dīn Muḥammad b. Abī al-ᶜAbbās Aḥmad b. Ḥamza b. Shihāb al-Dīn. *Nihāyat al-muḥtāj ilā sharḥ al-Minhāj fī al-fiqh ᶜalā madhhab al-imām al-Shāfiᶜī*. Cairo: Muṣṭafā al-Bābī al-Ḥalabī, 1967.

Rāzī, Fakhr al-Dīn Muḥammad b. ᶜUmar b. al-Ḥusayn. *al-Tafsīr al-kabīr aw Mafātīḥ al-ghayb*. Beirut: Dār al-kutub al-ᶜilmiyya, 1990.

Ratzaby, Yehuda. "The Mawzaᶜ Exile." *Sefunot* 5 (1961), pp. 339–375.

——. "New Sources to the Mawzaᶜ Exile." *Zion* 37 (1972), pp. 197–215.

Ritter, H. "Studien zur Geschichte der islamischen Frömmigkeit." *Der Islam* 21 (1933), pp. 1–83.

Rosenthal, Franz. *The Muslim concept of freedom prior to the nineteenth century*. Leiden: E. J. Brill, 1960.

Roux, J. P. "La tolerance religieuse dans les empires Turco-mongols." *Revue d'histoire des religions* 203 (1986), pp. 131–168.

Rūyānī, Abū Bakr Muḥammad b. Hārūn. *Musnad al-Rūyānī*. Cairo: Muʾassasat Qurṭuba, 1995.

Sāʿātī, Aḥmad ʿAbd al-Raḥmān al-Bannā. *Badāʾiʿ al-minan fī jamʿ wa tartīb Musnad al-Shāfiʿī wa al-sunan*. Cairo: Dār al-anwār li-'l-ṭibāʿa wa al-nashr, 1369 A.H.

Saʿīd b. Manṣūr. *Sunan*. Ed. Saʿd b. ʿAbd Allah b. ʿAbd al-ʿAzīz Āl Ḥumayyid. Riyāḍ: Dār al-Ṣamīʿī li-'l-nashr wa al-tawzīʿ, 1993.

Saʿīd b. al-Musayyab. *Fiqh al-imām Saʿīd b. al-Musayyab*. Ed. Hāshim Jamīl ʿAbd Allah. Baghdād: Maktabat al-irshād, 1974.

Sachedina, Abdulaziz. "Freedom of conscience and religion in the Qurʾān.", In *Human rights and the conflict of cultures*. ed. D. Little, J. Kelsay and A. A. Sachedina, Columbia: University of South Carolina Press, 1988.

——. *The Islamic roots of democratic pluralism*. New York: Oxford University Press, 2001.

——. "Political implications of the Islamic notion of 'supersession' as reflected in Islamic jurisprudence." *Islam and Christian Muslim relations* 7 (1996), pp. 159–168.

Sadan, Joseph. "The 'Latrines Decree' in the Yemen versus the *dhimma* principles." In *Pluralism and identity*, ed. J. Platvoet and K. Van der Toorn, pp.167–185. Leiden: E. J. Brill, 1995.

Ṣaffār, Ḥasan. *al-Taʿaddudiyya wa al-ḥurriyya fī al-islām*. Beirut: Dār al-bayān al-ʿarabī, 1990.

Sahāranpūrī, Khalīl Aḥmad. *Badhl al-majhūd fī ḥall Abī Dāwūd*. Beirut: Dār al-kutub al-ʿilmiyya, n.d.

Saḥnūn b. Saʿīd. *al-Mudawwana al-kubrā*. Beirut and Baghdad: Maṭbaʿat al-saʿāda, (reprint) 1323 A.H.

Ṣaʿīdī, ʿAbd al-Mutaʿāl. *al-Ḥurriyya al-dīniyya fī al-islām*. Cairo: Dār al-fikr al-ʿarabī, n.d.

——. *Ḥurriyyat al-fikr fī al-islām*. Cairo (?): Muʾassasat al-maṭbūʿāt al-ḥadītha, n.d. (ca. 1960).

Samarqandī, Abū al-Layth Naṣr b. Aḥmad b. Ibrāhīm. *Tafsīr al-Samarqandī al-musammā Baḥr al-ʿulūm*. Ed. ʿAlī Muḥammad Mufawwaḍ and ʿĀdil Aḥmad ʿAbd al-Mawjūd. Beirut: Dār al-kutub al-ʿilmiyya, 1993.

Samarqandī, ʿAlāʾ al-Dīn. *Tuḥfat al-fuqahāʾ*. Beirut: Dār al-kutub al-ʿilmiyya, 1984.

Ṣanʿānī, ʿAbd al-Razzāq b. Humām. *al-Muṣannaf*. Ed. Ḥabīb al-Raḥmān al-Aʿẓamī. Beirut: Dār al-qalam, 1970–1972.

Sarakhsī, Abū Bakr Muḥammad b. Aḥmad b. Abī Sahl. *al-Mabsūṭ*. Cairo: Maṭbaʿat al-saʿāda, 1324–1331 A.H.

——. *Sharḥ Kitāb al-siyar al-kabīr li-Muḥammad b. al-Ḥasan al-Shaybānī*. Ed. Ṣalāḥ al-Dīn al-Munajjid. Cairo, 1971.

——. *al-Muḥarrar fī uṣūl al-fiqh*. Ed. Abū ʿAbd al-Raḥmān Ṣalāḥ b. Muḥammad b. ʿArīḍa. Dār al-kutub al-ʿilmiyya, 1996.

——. *Uṣūl*. Ed. Abū al-Wafāʾ al-Afghānī. Beirut: Dār al-maʿrifa li-'l-ṭibāʿa wa al-nashr, 1973.

Ṣāwī, Ṣalāḥ D. *al-Taṭarruf al-dīnī: al-raʾy al-ākhar*. Al-Āfāq al-dawliyya li-'l-iʿlām. Cairo, 1993.

Shāfiʿī, Muḥammad b. Idrīs. *Aḥkām al-Qurʾān*. Ed. ʿIzzat al-ʿAṭṭār al-Ḥusaynī, Cairo: Maktab nashr al-thaqāfa al-islāmiyya, 1951–1952.

——. *Ikhtilāf al-ḥadīth*. Cairo, 1325 A.H., on the margin of *Kitāb al-umm*, vol. 7.

——. *Kitāb al-umm*. Ed. Maḥmūd Maṭrajī. Beirut: Dār al-kutub al-ʿilmiyya, 1993.

Shāshī, Abū Sa^cd al-Haytham b. Kulayb. *al-Musnad*. Medina: Maktabat al-ʿulūm wa al-ḥikam, 1989.

Shatzmiller, M. "Marriage, family and the faith: women's conversion to Islam." *Journal of Family History* 21 (1996), pp. 235–266.

Shaybānī, Abū ʿAbd Allah Muḥammad b. al-Ḥasan. *al-Jāmiʿ al-ṣaghīr maʿa sharḥihi al-Nāfiʿ al-kabīr li-Abī al-Ḥasanāt ʿAbd al-Ḥayy al-Lakhnawī*. Karachi: Idārat al-Qurʾān, 1987.

——. *Kitāb al-aṣl*. Ed. Abū al-Wafāʾ al-Afghānī. Ḥaydarābād (Deccan): Dāʾirat al-maʿārif al-ʿUthmāniyya, 1973.

——.*Kitāb al-ḥujja ʿalā ahl al-madīna*. Ed. Mahdī Ḥasan al-Kīlānī al-Qādirī. Beirut: ʿĀlam al-kutub, 1983.

——. *Kitāb al-siyar al-kabīr*. Ed. Majīd Khaddūrī. Beirut: al-Dār al-muttaḥida li-'l-nashr, 1975.

Shaybānī, Muḥammad b. al-Ḥasan. *Nahj al-bayān ʿan kashf maʿānī al-Qurʾān*. Ed. Ḥusayn Dargāhī. Tehran: Muʾassasat Dāʾirat al-maʿārif al-islāmiyya, 1992.

Shaykh, al-Ḥusaynī Yūsuf. *al-Tasāmuḥ fī al-islām*. Kharṭūm: Jāmiʿat Umm Durmān al-Islāmiyya. Kharṭūm, 1968(?).

Shepard, William. "Conversations in Cairo: some contemporary Muslim views of other religions." *The Muslim World* 70(1980), pp. 171–195.

Shīrāzī, Abū Isḥāq Ibrāhīm. *Sharḥ al-Lumaʿ*. Ed. ʿAbd al-Majīd Turkī. Beirut: Dār al-gharb al-Islāmī, 1988.

Shīrāzī, Abū Isḥāq Ibrāhīm b. ʿAlī b. Yūsuf al-Fīrūzābādī. *al-Muhadhdhab fī fiqh al-imām al-Shāfiʿī*. Ed. Zakariyā ʿUmayrāt. Beirut: Dār al-kutub al-ʿilmiyya, 1995.

Shoufani, E. *Al-ridda and the Muslim conquest of Arabia*. Toronto: University of Toronto Press and The Arab Institute for Research and Publishing, 1973.

Ṣiddīq Ḥasan Khān. *Ḥusn al-uswa bimā thabata min Allāh wa rasūlihi fī al-niswa*. Ed. Muṣṭafā al-Ḥann and Muḥyī al-Dīn Mastū. Beirut: Muʾassasat al-risāla, 1976.

Sonn, T. *Islam and the question of minorities*. Atlanta: Scholars' Press, 1996.

Sourdel, D. "Peut-on parler de liberté dans la société de l'Islam mediéval?" In *La notion de liberté au moyen âge: Islam, Byzance, Occident*, ed. G. Makdisi et alii, Paris: Les Belles Lettres, 1985, pp. 119–33.

Speight, R. M. "Attitudes toward Christians as revealed in the *Musnad* of al-Ṭayālisī." *The Muslim World* 53 (1973), pp. 49–68.

Stroumsa, S. and Stroumsa, G.G. "Aspects of anti-Manichaean polemics in late antiquity and early Islam." *Harvard Theological Review* 81 (1988), pp. 37–58.

Subkī, Abū al-Ḥasan Taqī al-Dīn ʿAlī b. ʿAbd al-Kāfī. *Fatāwā al-Subkī*. Cairo: Maktabat al-Qudsī, 1355 A.H.

Suyūṭī, Jalāl al-Dīn. *al-Laʾāliʾ al-maṣnūʿa fī al-aḥādīth al-mawḍūʿa*. Cairo: al-Maktaba al-Ḥusayniyya al-Miṣriyya bi-'l- Azhar, n.d.

——. *al-Durr al-manthūr fī al-tafsīr bi-'l-maʾthūr*. Cairo: al-Maṭbaʿa al-Maymaniyya, 1314 A.H.

——. *al-Wasāʾil ilā maʿrifat al-awāʾil*. Ed. ʿAbd al-Qādir Aḥmad ʿAbd al-Qādir. Kuwayt: Maktabat Dār Ibn Qutayba, 1990.

Swidler, L. *Muslims in dialogue: the evolution of a dialogue*. Religions in Dialogue, 3. Lewiston, NY: The Edwin Meller Press, 1992.

Ṭabarī, Muḥammad b. Jarīr. *Jāmiʿ al-bayān ʿan taʾwīl āy al-Qurʾān*. Cairo, 1954.

——. *Das Konstantinopler Fragment des Kitāb Ikhtilāf al-fuqahāʾ*. Ed. Joseph Schacht. Leiden: E. J. Brill, 1933.

——. *Taʾrīkh al-rusul wa al-mulūk*. Ed. de Goeje. Leiden: E.J Brill, 1879.

Ṭabrisī, Aḥmad b. ᶜAlī. *Majmaᶜ al-bayān fī tafsīr al-Qurʾān*. Beirut: Dār al-fikr wa Dār al-kitāb al-Lubnānī, 1954–1957.

Ṭaḥāwī, Abū Jaᶜfar Aḥmad b. Muḥammad b. Salāma. *Mukhtaṣar al-Ṭaḥāwī*. Ed. Abū al-Wafāʾ al-Afghānī. Cairo: Maṭbaᶜat Dār al-kitāb al-ᶜarabī, 1370 A.H.

——. *Mushkil al-āthār*. Ḥaydarābād (Deccan): Dāʾirat al-maᶜārif, 1333 A.H.

——. *Sharḥ Maᶜānī al-āthār*. Eds. Muḥammad Zuhrī al-Najjār and Muḥammad Sayyid Jādd al-Ḥaqq. Beirut: ᶜĀlam al-kutub, 1994.

Ṭahṭāwī, Muḥammad ᶜIzzat. *al-Mīzān fī muqāranat al-adyān*. Damascus, 1993.

Ṭawīl, Tawfīq. *Qiṣṣat al-idṭihād al-dīnī fī al-masīḥiyya wa al-islām*. Alexandria: Dār al-fikr al-ᶜarabī, 1947.

Tirmidhī, Muḥammad b. ᶜĪsā. *Ṣaḥīḥ*. Cairo: Maṭbaᶜat al-Ṣāwī, 1934.

Tobi, Y. "Conversion to Islam among Yemenite Jews under Zaidi rule – the position of Zaidi law, the Imām and Muslim Society." *Peᶜamim* 42 (1990), pp. 105–126 (in Hebrew).

Tolan, J. V., ed. *Medieval Christian perceptions of Islam. A book of essays*. Garland Reference Library of the Humanities, vol. 1768. New York and London: Garland Publishing, 1996.

Ṭurayqī, ᶜAbd Allah b. Ibrāhīm b. ᶜAlī. *al-Istiᶜāna bi-ghayr al-muslimīn fī al-fiqh al-islāmī*. Riyāḍ, 1414 A.H.

Ṭūsī, Abū Jaᶜfar Muḥammad b. al-Ḥasan. *al-Tibyān fī tafsīr al-Qurʾān*. Najaf: al-Maṭbaᶜa al-ᶜilmiyya, 1957.

Tsafrir, Nurit. "Semi-Ḥanafīs and Ḥanafī Biographical Sources." *Studia Islamica* 84 (1996), pp. 67–85.

Waardenburg, J. "Jugements musulmans sur les religions non-islamiques à l'époque mediévale." In *La signification du bas moyen âge*. ed. I. ᶜAbbās, and J. Baljon, pp. 323–341, Aix-en-Provence: Union européenne des arabisants et islamisants, 1978.

Wāḥidī, Abū al-Ḥasan ᶜAlī b. Aḥmad. *Asbāb al-nuzūl*. Cairo: Muʾassasat al-Ḥalabī wa shurakāʾihi li-'l-nashr wa al-ṭibāᶜa, 1968.

Wakīᶜ, Muḥammad b. Khalaf b. Ḥayyān. *Akhbār al-quḍāt*. Ed. ᶜAbd al-ᶜAzīz Muṣṭafā al-Marāghī. Cairo: Maṭbaᶜat al-istiqāma, 1950.

Wāqidī, Muḥammad b. ᶜUmar. *Kitāb al-maghāzī*. Ed. Marsden Jones. London: Oxford University Press, 1966.

Wāqidī, Muḥammad b. ᶜUmar b. Wāqid. *Kitāb al-ridda*. Ed. Yaḥyā al-Jubūrī. Beirut: Dār al-gharb al-islāmī, 1990.

Ward, Seth. "A Fragment from an Unknown Work by al-Ṭabarī on the Tradition 'Expel the Jews and Christians from the Arabian Peninsula (and the Lands of Islam)'." *Bulletin of the School of Oriental and African Studies* 53 (1990), pp. 407–420.

Wasserstein, David J. "A *fatwā* on conversion in Islamic Spain." In Studies in Muslim-Jewish Relations 1 (1993), ed. Ronald E. Nettler, pp. 177–188.

Watt, W. Montgomery. "Conditions of membership of the Islamic community." *Studia Islamica* 21 (1964), pp. 5–12.

——. "Conversion in Islam at the time of the Prophet." in *Early Islam. Collected Articles*, pp. 34–42. Edinburgh: Edinburgh University Press, 1990.

Wiederhold, Lutz. "Blasphemy against the Prophet Muḥammad and his Companions (*sabb al-rasūl, sabb al-ṣaḥāba*): The introduction of the topic into Shāfiᶜī legal literature and its relevance for legal practice under Mamlūk rule." *Journal of Semitic Studies* 52 (1997), pp. 39–70.

Wismar, Adolph L. *A study in tolerance as practiced by Muḥammad and his immediate successors*. New York: Columbia University Press, 1927.

Yaḥyā b. Ādam. *Kitāb al-kharāj*. Ed. Ḥusayn Muʾnis. Cairo: Dār al-shurūq, 1987.

Yaḥyā b. Maʿīn. *Taʾrīkh*. Ed. Aḥmad Muḥammad Nūr Yūsuf. Mecca: Markaz al-baḥth al-ʿilmī wa iḥyāʾ al-turāth al-islāmī, 1979.

Yaʿqūbī, Aḥmad b. Abī Yaʿqūb b. Jaʿfar b. Wahb b. Wāḍiḥ. *Taʾrīkh*. Ed. M. Th. Houtsma. Leiden: E. J. Brill, (reprint) 1969.

Zamakhsharī, Abū al-Qāsim Jār Allah Maḥmūd b. ʿUmar. *al-Kashshāf ʿan ḥaqāʾiq al-tanzīl wa ʿuyūn al-aqāwīl fī wujūh al-taʾwīl*. Ed. Muḥammad al-Ṣādiq Qumārī. Cairo: Maṭbaʿat Muṣṭafā al-Bābī al-Ḥalabī, 1972.

——. *Ruʾūs al-masāʾil*. Ed. ʿAbd Allāh Nadhīr Aḥmad. Beirut: Dār al-bashāʾir al-islāmiyya, 1987.

Zarkashī, Badr al-Dīn Muḥammad b. Bahādur b. ʿAbd Allāh al-Shāfiʿī. *al-Baḥr al-muḥīṭ fī uṣūl al-fiqh*. Ed. ʿAbd al-Qādir ʿAbd Allāh al-ʿĀnī. Ghardaqa: Dār al-Ṣafwa, 1992.

——. *al-Ijāba li-īrād mā istadrakathu ʿĀʾisha ʿalā al-ṣaḥāba*. Ed. Saʿīd al-Afghānī. Damascus: al-Maṭbaʿa al-Hāshimiyya, 1939.

——. *Sharḥ al-Zarkashī ʿalā Mukhtaṣar al-Khiraqī fī al-fiqh ʿalā madhhab al-imām Aḥmad b. Ḥanbal*. Ed. ʿAbd Allah b. ʿAbd al-Raḥmān b. ʿAbd Allah al-Jibrīn. Riyāḍ: Maktabat al-ʿUbaykān, 1993.

Zaydān, ʿAbd al-Karīm. *Aḥkām al-dhimmiyyīn wa al-mustaʾminīn fī dār al-islām*. Baghdād: Maṭbaʿat al-burhān, 1963.

——. *al-Qiṣāṣ wa al-diyāt fī al-sharīʿa al-islāmiyya*. Beirut: Muʾassasat al-risāla, 1998.

Ziāuddin Aḥmad. "Abū Bakr al-Khallāl – the compiler of the teachings of Imām Aḥmad b. Ḥanbal." *Islamic Studies* 9 (1970), pp. 245–254.

Zuhrī, Muḥammad b. Shihāb. *al-Nāsikh wa al-mansūkh*. Ed. Ḥātim Ṣāliḥ al-Ḍāmin. n.p., n.d.

Zwemer, Samuel M. *The law of apostasy in Islam*. London, Edinburgh and New York: Marshall Brothers Ltd., 1924

General Index

Index of Qur᾽ānic verses

2:61 34
2:62 30, 82, 195
2:85 116
2:109 124 n. 20
2:114 153
2:135 22 n. 51
2:136 22 n. 49, 196 n. 7
2:142 31 n. 91
2:144 31
2:151 43 n. 159
2:178 39, 44
2:179 41
2:185 32
2:193 97 n. 57, 98, 105
2:213 14, 15
2:217 124 n. 21, 128 n. 41
2:221 70, 71 106, 160, 169, 175, 178, 179, 183, 192
2:251 43 n. 159
2:253 196 n. 8
2:256 68, 78 n. 127, 87, 94, 100, 101, 102, 103, 104, 105, 106, 107, 120, 121, 145, 152 n. 170
2:282 35
2:285 22 n. 49, 196 n. 7
3:3–4 23 n. 55
3:19 34 n. 106
3:84 22 n. 49, 196 n. 7
3:85–90 33, 95, 124 n. 21, 128 n. 41, 141
3:95 22 n. 51
3:97 32
3:100 128 n. 41
3:110 34
3:112 34 n. 114
3:139 34
3:163 54 n. 3
4:92 48, 49
4:94 142
4:124 22 n. 51
4:125 20 n. 38
4:137 124 n. 21, 128 n. 41, 144
4:152 196 n. 7
4:162 54 n. 3
5:3 34 n. 106
5:5 62, 66, 70, 76, 160, 179, 181, 182, 183, 184, 191, 192, 198
5:45 27, 39, 44, 46
5:47 20 n. 39, 24
5:48 20, 22
5:49 98 n. 58, 153
5:54 124 n. 21, 128 n. 41
5:69 30 n. 83, 82
5:106 36
6:90 20 n. 39, 24
6:91 23 n. 55
6:106 89 n. 7
6:156 75
6:164 183
7:172 15 n. 10
8:38 128
8:39 97, 98, 105 n. 93
8:67 116, 117, 119
8:68 118
8:69 118

Index of prophetic traditions

Other titles in the series

Popular Culture in Medieval Cairo
BOAZ SHOSHAN 0 521 43209 X

Early Philosophical Shiism *The Ismaili Neoplatonism of Abū Yaʿqūb al-Sijistāni*
PAUL E. WALKER 0 521 44129 3

Indian Merchants and Eurasian Trade, 1600–1750
STEPHEN FREDERIC DALE 0 521 45460 3

Palestinian Peasants and Ottoman Officials *Rural Administration around Sixteenth-century Jerusalem*
AMY SINGER 0 521 45238 4 hardback 0 521 47679 8 paperback

Arabic Historical Thought in the Classical Period
TARIF KHALIDI 0 521 46554 0 hardback 0 521 58938 X paperback

Mongols and Mamluks *The Mamluk-Īlkhānid War, 1260–1281*
REUVEN AMITAI-PREISS 0 521 46226 6

Hierarchy and Egalitarianism in Islamic Thought
LOUISE MARLOW 0 521 56430 1

The Politics of Households in Ottoman Egypt *The Rise of the Qazdağlis*
JANE HATHAWAY 0 521 57110 3

Commodity and Exchange in the Mongol Empire *A Cultural History of Islamic Textiles*
THOMAS T. ALLSEN 0 521 58301 2

State and Provincial Society in the Ottoman Empire *Mosul, 1540–1834*
DINA RIZK KHOURY 0 521 59060 4

The Mamluks in Egyptian Politics and Society
THOMAS PHILIPP AND ULRICH HAARMANN (eds) 0 521 59115 5

The Delhi Sultanate *A Political and Military History*
PETER JACKSON 0 521 40477 0

European and Islamic Trade in the Early Ottoman State *The Merchants of Genoa and Turkey*
KATE FLEET 0 521 64221 3

Reinterpreting Islamic Historiography *Harun al-Rashid and the Narrative of the ʿAbbāsid Caliphate*
TAYEB EL-HIBRI 0 521 65023 2

The Ottoman City between East and West *Aleppo, Izmir, and Istanbul*
EDHEM ELDEM, DANIEL GOFFMAN AND BRUCE MASTERS 0 521 64304 X

A Monetary History of the Ottoman Empire
SEVKET PAMUK 0 521 44197 8

The Politics of Trade in Safavid Iran: *Silk for Silver, 1600–1730*
RUDOLPH P. MATTHEE 0 521 64131 4

The Idea of Idolatry and the Emergence of Islam: *From Polemic to History*
G.R. HAWTING 0 521 65165 4

Classical Arabic Biography: *The Heirs of the Prophets in the Age of al-Ma'mūn*
MICHAEL COOPERSON 0 521 66199 4

Empire and Elites after the Muslim Conquest: *The Transformation of Northern Mesopotamia*
CHASE F. ROBINSON 0 521 78115 9

Poverty and Charity in Medieval Islam: *Mamluk Egypt, 1250–1517*
ADAM SABRA 0 521 772915

Christians and Jews in the Ottoman Arab World: *The Roots of Sectarianism*
BRUCE MASTERS 0 521 803330

Culture and Conquest in Mongol Eurasia
THOMAS T. ALLSEN 0 521 803357

Law, Society, and Culture in the Maghrib, 1300–1500
DAVID S. POWERS 0 521 816912

Arabic Administration in Norman Sicily: *The Royal Dīwān*
JEREMY JOHNS 0 521 816920

Revival and Reform in Islam: *The Legacy of Muhammad al-Shawkani*
BERNARD HAYKEL 0 521 816289 hardback 0 521 528909 paperback

CPSIA information can be obtained
at www.ICGtesting.com
Printed in the USA
LVHW091301281220
675133LV00002BA/104

9 780521 026994